D0907205

MILITARY REALISM

MILITARY REALISM

The Logic and Limits of Force and Innovation in the US Army

PETER CAMPBELL

UNIVERSITY OF MISSOURI PRESS
Columbia

Copyright © 2019 by

The Curators of the University of Missouri

University of Missouri Press, Columbia, Missouri 65211

Printed and bound in the United States of America

All rights reserved. First printing, 2019.

Library of Congress Cataloging-in-Publication Data

Names: Campbell, Peter P., author.
Title: Military realism : the logic and limits of force and innovation in the
   U.S. Army / by Peter Campbell.
Description: Columbia, Missouri : University of Missouri, [2019] | Series:
   American military experience | Includes bibliographical references and
   index. |
Identifiers: LCCN 2018054040 (print) | LCCN 2018055464 (ebook) | ISBN
   9780826274267 (e-book) | ISBN 9780826221841 (hardback)
Subjects: LCSH: United States--Military policy. | Military doctrine--United
   States--History--20th century. | Military doctrine--United
   States--History--21st century. | BISAC: HISTORY / Military / Strategy. |
   HISTORY / Military / United States.
Classification: LCC UA23 (ebook) | LCC UA23 .C234 2019 (print) | DDC
   355/.03357309045--dc23
LC record available at https://lccn.loc.gov/2018054040

Typefaces: Frutiger and Minion

CONTENTS

ACKNOWLEDGMENTS

THIS BOOK WOULD not have made it into print without the patience and un-wavering support of Michael Desch. Deciding on a topic could not have been easier. At our first meeting, Mike swiveled around in his chair and said: "Have you thought about why the U.S. Army got back into counterinsurgency?" That settled it. In attempting to answer that question, I was drawn into a much wider debate on the causes of military innovation. This book is the result of the struggle to make sense of this fascinating process. Thanks also to Sebastian Rosato and Dan Lindley, whose timely advice saved me from innumerable diversionary wars during the research and writing process.

The germ of this book began much earlier, however, when James Muir in-troduced me to the study of philosophy, politics, and strategy at the University of Winnipeg in Canada. Through Jamie, I encountered Carl von Clausewitz for the first time. Together they led me into the systematic study of the nex-us between politics, strategy, and military affairs. To further my studies, Ja-mie recommended I attend King's College London and read for a master in war studies. I did so, and there Jan Willem Honig, John Mackinlay, and the other incredible war studies faculty ably guided my study of strategy, war, and Clausewitz. While at King's I immersed myself especially in the study of counterinsurgency. This was in 2005 and 2006, after all, as things were falling apart in Iraq. I wrote my thesis on the U.S. Marine Corps' Combined Action Platoons in Vietnam.

While studying in Winnipeg I met Rob and Beth L'Arrivee, two other lov-ers of learning. We would all three go on to receive our doctorates in political science at Notre Dame. A special thanks to Rob, who dedicated so much time to helping me prepare for presenting the ideas that fill the pages of this book. His sense of humor made sure that we never took ourselves too seriously.

After completing my PhD, I was truly blessed to become part of the faculty of political science at Baylor University. David Clinton was a stalwart and kind supporter of this project from my earliest days at Baylor. He has been an incredible mentor. He was always there with kind words of encouragement when my spirits flagged in the course of the writing process. David read countless drafts of early chapters and helped shepherd this project. I also benefited greatly from the advice of Carey Newman, director of Baylor University Press, who helped me navigate the world of academic book publishing. I would be remiss if I did not also thank Jenice Langston, our office manager at Baylor political science, for helping me adjust to a new job and a new campus and with innumerable day-to-day tasks.

Although we have never met, I would like to acknowledge Robert Boice, author of *Advice for New Faculty Members*. Without his insights into the academic profession, teaching, and writing, I would not have completed this book. I attribute a great deal of the satisfaction I experience in the academic profession to his guidance.

This book would not have been possible without the help of numerous manuscript reviewers, known and unknown. Special thanks to David Clinton, Michael Desch, and Benjamin Jensen. Thanks too to all the anonymous reviewers who helped me refine the ideas and evidence presented here.

The research conducted for this book would not have been possible without financial assistance from a number of sources. The graduate school at the University of Notre Dame provided me with funds to do archival research at the John F. Kennedy Library and the U.S. Army Heritage and Education Center. The center itself provided additional financial assistance through the General and Mrs. Matthew B. Ridgway Military History Research Grant. The Lyndon B. Johnson Library also provided financial support through the Moody Research Grant. Thanks also to Margaret Campbell, whose generous support came at a crucial time in my career.

I could not have asked for a better editor and publisher. Gary Kass and the people at the University of Missouri Press have been fantastic. Gary was an enthusiastic supporter of the project from the first. I am indebted to him for his keen editorial eye and his help in overcoming my timidity as a first-time author.

Of course, any errors that remain in this book are mine alone.

I have dedicated this book to my parents and my wife. Sadly, my father, Oliver, did not live to see this book into print, but his constant example of integrity, hard work, and kindness equipped me to bring this project to fruition. My mother, Anne Campbell, continually stormed heaven with prayers to ensure the success of this project and instilled in me a lifelong love of learning.

Finally, none of what I have accomplished would have been possible without the incredible and steadfast support and love of my wife, Angela Campbell. She intrepidly raised three small children as I worked through two graduate degrees. She has made numerous sacrifices and been my rock. Thanks also to my children, Mary, Oliver, and Walter, for being a constant source of joy and pride and a continual reminder of what really matters.

ABBREVIATIONS

AAN	Army After Next
ADP	Army Doctrine Publication
ADRP	Army Doctrine Reference Publication
BCT	Brigade Combat Team
BNSP	Basic National Security Policy
CAC	Combined Arms Center
CENTCOM	U.S. Central Command
CGSC	U.S. Army Command and General Staff College
COIN	counterinsurgency
CONARC	Continental Army Command
DCSOPS	deputy chief of staff for military operations
DPG	Defense Planning Guidance
DSCA	Defense Support of Civil Authorities
FM	Field Manual
IN/COIN	insurgency and counterinsurgency
ISIS	Islamic State in Iraq and Syria
JCS	Joint Chiefs of Staff
LIC	low-intensity conflict
LID	light infantry division
MNF-I	Multinational Force Iraq

MOOTW   military operations other than war

NSAM   National Security Action Memoranda

NSSUS   National Security Strategy of the United States

ODSS   offense, defense, and stability and support operations

OIDP   Overseas Internal Defense Policy

OOTW   operations other than war

RMA   revolution in military affairs

ROAD   Reorganization Objectives Army Division

SACEUR   Supreme Allied Commander Europe

SAMS   School of Advanced Military Studies

SBCT   Stryker Brigade Combat Team

SF   U.S. Army Special Forces

SOP   standard operating procedure

TRADOC   U.S. Army Training and Doctrine Command

ULO   Unified Land Operations

MILITARY REALISM

INTRODUCTION

WHY DID THE United States Army, which had said "never again" to counterinsurgency (COIN) after Vietnam, embrace it as a solution to recent wars? In the aftermath of Vietnam, senior army officers promised never again to "quietly acquiesce in halfhearted warfare for half-baked reasons."[1] After Vietnam, COIN was "a mistake to be avoided."[2] Analysts of organizational behavior and military affairs have used theories of bureaucracy and military culture to explain why the U.S. Army rejected COIN in Vietnam. Some argued, from a bureaucratic perspective, that COIN did not provide the increased resources, organizational autonomy, and predictability that bureaucracies crave.[3] Others contended that COIN contradicted the conventional-warfare mind-set at the heart of U.S. Army culture.[4] As one army officer in Vietnam stated flatly, "I'll be damned if I permit the United States Army, its institution, its doctrine, and its traditions to be destroyed just to win this lousy war."[5] In short, in Vietnam, despite the unconventional circumstances, the U.S. Army fought the war it wanted to fight.

However, others maintain this did not have to be. Forceful civilian leadership could have compelled the army to change.[6] Indeed, fifty years later, advocates of such civilian intervention argue that during the recent war in Iraq, civilian leaders did just that. The Bush administration forced the U.S. Army in Iraq to adapt a COIN doctrine and strategy despite its bureaucratic and cultural proclivities.[7] This is one solution to the initial puzzle: the U.S. Army changed because civilians forced it to change. However, as neat as this explanation appears, it does not square with the evidence presented in these pages. In actuality, senior army leaders at home and in Iraq began developing COIN doctrine long before civilian leaders became enamored with the idea. In fact, when the army began developing COIN doctrine for Iraq, civilian leaders were opposed to using a COIN strategy there.[8] Therefore, the presence or absence of civilian intervention does not solve the puzzle. If anything, this evidence reinforces the puzzle because the army adopted a doctrine contrary to its supposed bureaucratic interests and cultural traditions. Another popular explanation, military mavericks within the army driving innovation, also proves problematic. Upon closer examination, the army officers who advocated COIN in Iraq were far from maverick outsiders; they had stellar army careers.[9] Officers like General David Petraeus were more products of the institution than popular accounts suggest.[10] Moreover, these accounts neglect other senior army leaders who began the push for COIN prior to Petraeus's highly publicized efforts.

Even more strikingly, the army's focus on COIN did not wane after the surge in Iraq. The army codified COIN as a central mission in the 2008 edition of its most important war-fighting doctrine, *Operations*. Later, President Obama and his closest advisers worried that U.S. military leaders were conspiring to "box in" the president and force him to adopt a COIN strategy for Afghanistan as well.[11] According to extant theoretical approaches, the army should use doctrine to justify its bureaucratic desires and express and instill its cultural identity. Making COIN a central part of army doctrine and operations serves neither goal. This is why, these theorists contend, COIN has not been central to doctrine in the past. The army's about-face on COIN is astonishing.[12] It confounds available theories and popular views of military organizations as incapable of change. Even when one looks into the details of the case, the puzzle not only remains but extends beyond the confines of Iraq. So the question remains: Why did the same U.S. Army that had said "never again" to COIN after Vietnam adamantly recommend it as a solution to recent conflicts and even infuse COIN into its main war-fighting doctrine?

Explaining the puzzling rebirth of COIN remains important. Doing so, however, requires a new theory of change and continuity in military doctrine. Military doctrines are the authoritative expressions of the theories of victory, mission priorities, and standard operating procedures (SOPs) that militaries use to prepare their forces for present and future conflicts. At their highest level, doctrines express how a military organization thinks about using force to address international threats and support national security. COIN is one among a number of mission priorities set out in doctrine. Therefore, solving the central puzzle of this book means answering a more general question: Why do military organizations change or preserve their doctrines?

To answer this question, I introduce the theory of military realism. This new theory argues for a military realist mind-set among senior military officers shaped by a deep appreciation for the escalatory logic of force and the physical friction that always limits its use. This mind-set leads to significant caution about the use of force and a threat assessment largely based on the balance of material capabilities, which then inform doctrinal continuity and change. Senior military officers direct the most important changes in military doctrine. They make these changes when they perceive that the mission priorities and theories of victory expressed in doctrine do not address the most dangerous threats to national security. Contrary to popular expectations and previous theorizing, these leaders can overcome or adapt to bureaucratic, cultural, and civilian opposition to these changes. For instance, according to military realism, military officers' caution about the use of force can lead to doctrines that are often less aggressive than popular opinion might expect, bureaucracy and culture might prefer, or civilian leaders might demand. In the pages that follow, I use the development of U.S. Army doctrine from 1960 to 2008 to evaluate military realism against competing approaches to military innovation. I argue that military realism often provides a better explanation of military doctrine than competing theories. At the same time, because this work focuses on the U.S. Army from Vietnam to Iraq, it offers a solution to our central puzzle.

After the withdrawal of U.S. forces from Iraq in 2011 and the sweeping offensive of the Islamic State in Iraq and Syria (ISIS) into territory liberated by U.S. COIN strategy, we might be tempted to dismiss as irrelevant the U.S. Army's experiment with COIN because it failed to secure Iraq. However, the revival of COIN in the U.S. Army and its powerful effects on U.S. Army thinking and doctrine remain one of the most puzzling cases of military innovation to date. More generally, regardless of the outcome in Iraq, military innovation in the form of change and continuity in military doctrine has important consequences for international relations, national security, and civil-military relations.

This recent case of military innovation is inextricably tied up with the story of the U.S. Army before, during, and after Vietnam. The recent revival of COIN in the army is only puzzling if we assume we know what happened to the U.S. Army and its doctrine in this earlier period. This book begins with the U.S. Army under President Kennedy and follows the development of army doctrine from the jungles and rice paddies of Vietnam to the scorching desert and sand-blown streets of Iraq. Using recent historical scholarship and the new theory of military realism, the analysis here shows that our understanding of this critical earlier period in the history of the U.S. Army and its doctrine is incomplete.

Just as important is our understanding of what happened to the army after Vietnam. This study indicates that the post-Vietnam narrative about the army is also incomplete. In places, in fact, the army itself misinterprets the history of its post-Vietnam doctrine. Finally, we cannot understand the army's recent adoption of COIN outside of the doctrinal ferment that accompanied the end of Cold War. The army was in the process of "transforming" its forces and doctrine when terrorists struck the United States on September 11, 2001. Only with this post–Cold War background can we understand the recent doctrinal shift toward COIN.

Armed with this reassessment of the process and content of army doctrine from the previous five decades, this book is able to examine its central puzzle with fresh eyes. There are so many comparisons made between the U.S. Army's experiences in Vietnam and Iraq, but these are often not informed by a real appreciation for the important differences between these two conflicts or an accurate assessment of previous army doctrine. When we examine the revival of COIN in the army from the clearer perspective provided here, the picture looks very different. The resulting account of the recent rebirth of COIN in the U.S. Army shows that the story of this innovation too is flawed. But many of these flaws are discernible only from the broader doctrinal perspective provided by the previous chapters. Only by following army doctrine from Vietnam to Iraq can we honestly assess doctrinal change and continuity in the latter case.

This book facilitates this broader perspective on army doctrine because it does not focus exclusively on the changing ideas about COIN therein. It also examines army officers' views of the wider threat environment they confronted from 1960 to 2008, their understanding of the changing roles of conventional and nuclear forces, and their changing perspective on the relationship between attack and defense in their most important doctrine. Together with COIN, these represent the three key areas of doctrine considered in these pages. Taking this broader doctrinal perspective helps place the army's experience in Vietnam and after squarely within its Cold War context, and not in isolation, as other works tend to do. Most important, as discussed below, the broader doctrinal view provided by consecutive case studies of army doctrine helps evaluate the competing theories of military innovation examined here.

The analysis concludes in 2008 because this is the moment of truth for the army's recent relationship with COIN. In this year the army publishes its first *Operations* manual in the wake of General Petraeus's famed 2006 COIN manual, which he then implemented through the surge in Iraq. Did the army as an institution then embrace COIN? We can determine the power and extent of that embrace by the scope of its influence on the pinnacle of army doctrine, the 2008 *Operations* manual. Additionally, although the case studies conclude in 2008, the analysis there can provide some insight into more recent changes in U.S. Army doctrine, and I do so in the concluding chapter.

Finally, the findings of this study have broader implications for civil-military relations, foreign policy, international relations, and of course the study of military innovation. For instance, the theory of military realism provides a different perspective on the mind-set of military officers. Today understanding this mind-set is more important than ever, because former military officers James Mattis and John Kelly inhabit some of the most important and powerful positions in the administration of President Trump.

What Is Doctrine, and Why Does It Matter?

Military doctrines are authoritative expressions of the main missions, theories of victory, and SOPs that militaries use to prepare their forces for conflict. But why should anyone but military professionals care about the development or content of military manuals? One can grasp the broader importance of doctrine by contemplating the circumstances of soldiers in battle. Consider a famous photograph from the trenches of the First World War.

Figure 1. British officer leads soldiers "over the top" on the western front in World War I. Photograph by John Warwick Brooke. Courtesy of the National Library of Scotland.

The picture captures a squad of infantryman moving down a trench about to go over the top. In the frame are eight British soldiers, still in the trench, their bodies tense, their heads ducking in response to a nearby artillery burst, the smoke from which still lingers in the air. Their body language conveys their natural desire to stay where they are, in the safety of the trench, on the cusp of no-man's-land, the cusp, for some, of life or death. A soldier at the front of the squad is frozen in midstumble over the lip of the trench. Already out of the trench, standing among the barbed wire and fresh shell craters, is a solitary figure, a British officer with his back to the trench, shoulders bent. He is perhaps about to look back to ensure that his young charges are following his frightening example.

They did follow, and this scene was replayed over and over again in the Great War. It is repeated to some extent in every war. Soldiers, struggling against all their natural inclinations to self-preservation, put themselves in harm's way. When we consider the unnatural requirements of war, we come to appreciate the observation of military historian John Keegan: "Inside every army is a crowd struggling to get out."[13] The vast majority of human beings flee from death and wounds. To overcome these natural inclinations, militaries train and indoctrinate their soldiers extensively and continually. Training imposes order on and inspires unity of effort in individuals engaged in an activity that naturally causes fear, paralysis, and flight.[14] "No one," wrote Samuel Huntington, "is more aware than the professional soldier that the normal man is no hero." Consequently, "the military profession organizes men so as to overcome their inherent fears and failings."[15] Doctrine and training play an important role in this organizing of men by providing theories of victory, mission priorities, and SOPs.

However, the foot soldier is not the only one who experiences the friction, uncertainty, and fear of war. The commander who orders them to fight at a specific time and place is also subject to these forces, though in a different way. While the soldier at the front needs physical courage to act, the commander needs moral courage to make often irrevocable decisions. Like the soldier at the front, the commander too must overcome his natural inclination not to take risks. As the soldier would like nothing better than to stay in his trench, often the commander would like nothing better than to keep him there and not risk the uncertainty of action. Moreover, besides the physical friction that resists the smallest movement in war, the commander has the enemy to consider. War is not the use of violence against an inanimate object, but its use against a reactive enemy.[16] A misstep in a battle or a theater of war can expose a unit or an entire army to destruction at the hands of the enemy or the elements. The pressure for decision only increases with rank. Although most memorable, highly aggressive commanders, like George S. Patton Jr. and Douglas MacArthur, are the exception to the rule. General George McClellan's hesitancy to come to grips with the Confederate forces in the Civil War is a case in point.

The conditions of command inspired Carl von Clausewitz, the military veteran and theorist, to argue that it took a special kind of "military genius" to overcome the mental friction of war and make decisions in the midst of grave danger and constant uncertainty.[17] But military geniuses are rare. Doctrine is one tool that can help officers navigate these perils and make decisions amid uncertainty, friction, and fear. What tactical training and doctrine do for individual soldiers, operational doctrine can do for the officers who lead them. Thus, doctrine is important because it can prepare military officers to lead more effectively.

The hopes and fears of nations often rest with the forces in the field and their doctrines. The quality of training and doctrine can either allay those fears or shatter those hopes. The highly effective training and doctrine of the German army in World War II led to the shattering of Europe. The effectiveness of German forces was in part the result of changes in training and doctrine based on the lessons of the First World War and the invasions of Poland and France.[18] In the case of France in 1940, continuity in French doctrine was as important as innovation in German doctrine.[19] French forces failed to stem the German tide because their doctrine of controlled battles was a perfect target for a German doctrine that undermined French cohesion through penetration. The quality of doctrine, like the quality of training, can determine how effectively a military will fight once engaged.[20] The performance of the Wehrmacht is a stark reminder of what can happen when an effective doctrine serves an ideology bent on the breaking of nations and peoples.

However, the import of military doctrine is not limited to combat and command effectiveness. Change and continuity in military doctrines can have additional consequences for international relations and domestic politics. In international relations, for instance, variation in the offensive or defensive thrust of doctrine can increase or decrease the likelihood of war. Doctrines with highly offensive theories of victory can signal hostile intentions and lead to apprehension among other nations. The threatened states might increase their military capabilities and develop offensive doctrines of their own. In the language of international relations theory, offensive doctrines can exacerbate the security dilemma—that fearful condition among states caused by the uncertainty of intentions and the ever-present possibility of the use of force in an anarchic international system. By increasing the intensity of the security dilemma, offensive doctrines make states feel less secure and increase the likelihood of crises, miscalculation, and war.[21] Conversely, clearly *defensive* military doctrines can produce the opposite effect. Defensive doctrines can signal benign intentions and thereby reduce international apprehension and promote peace.[22]

However, the above argument ascribes to the spiral model of warfare, that is, that neither side in a conflict wants war but that armed conflicts erupt out of crises that spin out of control due to miscalculation.[23] Other scholars argue, conversely, that wars arise out of a failure to deter those who seek to use war as a means of policy.[24] For instance, the failure of the British to devise a continental strategy in the 1930s, with the forces and military doctrine to support it, meant that they could not effectively deter Adolf Hitler's continental strategy. This deterrence failure contributed to the outbreak of war.[25] Although adherents to the spiral and deterrence models disagree about the origins of war, they agree, along with the present work, that understanding change and continuity in military doctrine is an important component in the causes of war.

Domestically, military doctrines can have repercussions on foreign policy and civil-military relations. To employ a negative example, foreign policy can be undermined when military doctrine contradicts that policy.[26] For instance, when the foreign policy of a state seeks international accommodation to further its goals, the retention of a highly offensive military doctrine can undercut this policy. Developing military doctrines consistent with a pacific foreign policy will be a constant struggle if military organizations favor aggressive doctrines. Those who use a bureaucratic or military cultural perspective often argue that aggressive, war-winning doctrines are most attractive to militaries. When they are free from civilian control, as they were in Germany prior to World War I, such doctrines reign supreme. The resulting cult of the offensive drove crisis toward war. On the other hand, when civilian leaders keep a watchful eye on their militaries, as in pre–World War I Britain, doctrines that contradict a pacific foreign policy are less likely to grow in the shadows of civilian ignorance.[27] The failure of a state military to integrate its doctrine with foreign policy can also foster distrust between civilian and military leaders and fracture civil-military relations. As I show in the chapters that follow, civil-military distrust was a recurring theme in U.S. national security affairs, in part because civilian leaders ascribed to bureaucratic and cultural accounts of what motivates military organizations.

While civilian leaders may distrust their military organizations, they are also dependent on their professional advice. This advice is indispensable for the protection of political communities, but especially in modern democracies where elected leaders increasingly lack military experience and knowledge of military affairs.[28] The complexity of the modern state and modern war makes the civil-military division of labor necessary. Therefore, determining whether military officers are motivated by bureaucratic interests, cultural norms, or military realism can make civil-military relations more effective. Conversely, an erroneous understanding of what motivates military organizations can unnecessarily fracture civil-military relations and separate civilian leaders from much-needed military advice.

Finally, military doctrines can lead to the misallocation of precious national resources. If, for instance, a military organization designs its doctrine solely to increase its share of national resources,[29] then they will squander the contents of the national treasury on doctrines that do not further national security. Moreover, the resulting increase in defense spending can make the state less secure by inspiring fear in other states and exacerbating the security dilemma. Understanding the extent to which organizational and cultural biases, rather than practical needs, guide the development of doctrine can help preserve limited national resources and reduce international provocations.

These few examples show that military doctrines, which might at first seem of concern to only a few experts, have important consequences. Change and continuity in military doctrine can affect military effectiveness, international relations, the quality of civil-military relations, and national resources and security. Doctrinal innovation and stagnation can also powerfully affect the security and prosperity of political communities. Thus, explaining the causes of doctrinal variation and continuity is important. Unfortunately, existing theoretical explanations do not provide a complete picture of these phenomena. Consequently, I put forward military realism as an alternative explanation.

Military Realism and Military Doctrine: The Argument in Brief
Military realism contends that senior military officers initiate major innovations when the theories of victory and mission priorities of existing doctrine do not plausibly address the most dangerous threats. However, bureaucratic priorities or cultural norms are not the only shapers of this threat assessment. The experience of and preparation for warfare produces a two-part military

realist mind-set in military officers. First, these military realists appreciate that the use of force has an escalatory logic that is only partially under the control of each belligerent. No matter the political object, failure to resist or surpass an opponent's escalation results in defeat or the abandoning of that object. Thus, the interactive, escalatory logic of force exerts influence independently of the political situation. Rather than imposing control, the use of force brings about an uncertain, interactive logic that dictates behaviors and limits choices. When it comes to the use of force, as the saying goes, "the enemy gets a vote." Second, and at the same time, military realists have a deep appreciation for how the friction of the physical world limits the use of force. Amid the constant friction of war, the simplest thing is very difficult.[30]

Bureaucratic and military cultural explanations take theories developed in other areas, like business and government bureaucracies, and then impose those theories on military organizations.[31] Such analysis, however, does not get at what makes military organizations unique, their close relationship to the logic and limits of violence and the resulting effects on the assessment of threats and doctrine. The military realist perspective leads senior officers to assess international threats based on material capabilities, the doctrines of potential adversaries, and the physical frictions theirs and opposing doctrines must overcome. The doctrines that arise from this threat assessment will prioritize dealing with the most dangerous threats and will overcome bureaucratic inertia and cultural taboos to do so. Contrary to Barry Posen's theory of military doctrine—referred to here as civilian realism—military realists are close observers of the international threat environment and can overcome bureaucratic and cultural barriers to change in the absence of civilian intervention. Moreover, while military realists prefer offensive doctrines because they enact escalation, in the presence of a physically superior adversary they will develop defensive theories of victory that enlist friction to offset imbalances in capabilities. In the absence of a state-based threat, senior military officers will prioritize the protection of the vital material interests of the state that generate military capabilities. Moreover, even in such a permissive threat environment, friction is a constant obstacle to the deployment and operation of military forces. This constant fight with friction will temper doctrinal optimism about, for instance, offensive military options.

Despite bureaucratic and cultural opposition, according to military realism, senior officers will embrace revolutionary forms of warfare if they are the key to addressing the most dangerous threat. The advent of nuclear weapons represents just such a revolution in warfare. While bureaucratic and cultural perspectives expect militaries to compel these weapons to conform to bureaucratic imperatives and cultural norms, military realism anticipates that military officers will alter doctrine in significant ways to accommodate these weapons if demanded by the threat environment. They can accept these changes even if they are inconsistent with their formative military experiences. Missions like COIN will often be a lower priority for military realists, not because of bureaucratic or cultural constraints, but because in general insurgencies constitute a less dangerous threat than the major conventional and nuclear capabilities of other states. At the same time, however, military realists can adopt solutions to the problem of insurgency that contradict bureaucratic and cultural preferences. In a threat environment where insurgencies represent one of the gravest threats, military realists will alter doctrine in significant ways to address the threat of insurgency. However, as greater threats emerge in the environment, doctrine will gravitate toward them and away from lesser threats, like insurgency. The military realist perspective can also influence threat assessment during conflicts. In the theater of war, as in the international system, military realists will often prioritize dealing with the most dangerous threat of physical escalation.

These predictions should make it clear that military realism, as the name implies, is a realist theory of military innovation that contends with bureaucratic, cultural, and other realist alternatives. While military realism shares some aspects with international relations realism conceived more broadly, it is also distinct from this realist tradition. There are many variants of realism in international relations theory, but they all contend that the realm of international relations is in a condition of anarchy, in which the use of force is always a possibility due to the absence of any authority above states. Striving for survival in a dangerous world, states can truly rely only on their own material capabilities to secure themselves. Fear casts a constant shadow over the realist international system as states increase their capabilities in an environment in which they are uncertain of one another's intentions. Rather than assuming other states have benign intentions, states in a realist world assume hostile intentions and judge which states are most threatening by their material capacity to carry out those intentions. In this environment the most powerful states are the most consequential. In the international systems, as Thucydides has the Athenian delegation say to the weaker Melians, "the strong do what they can and the weak suffer what they must."[32] Military realism is realist in the sense that material capabilities, or the lack thereof, are one of the main drivers behind threat assessments by military officers, assessments that then inform doctrinal innovation or continuity. However, in this new theory, the term *military* modifies *realism* because the concern with capabilities among military officers is grounded in their preparation for or direct experience of war. The realism of military realism is not grounded, for instance, in the structure of the international system—as structural realists would have it—but rooted in the experience and practice of military officers and the military realist mind-set it produces. As already noted, at the core of this mind-set is a concern with the escalatory and uncertain character of the use of force and the multifarious frictions that always obstruct it. It is the contention here that this mind-set provides an explanation for change and continuity in the doctrines of military organizations.

It should be made clear from the outset, however, that this work does not deny that military cultures and bureaucratic interests exist. The cultural traditions of militaries have affected their combat performance and doctrine. World War I provides many well-worn examples. For instance, cultural preferences for cavalry charges and the bayonet influenced the way that militaries prepared for the fighting. Moreover, there was a marked preference for offensive operations in the prewar doctrines of the European militaries.[33] To deny the import of bureaucracy and culture would be to deny the historical record. However, the historical record also shows that when those bureaucratic preferences and cultural preconceptions ran into the cold, hard realities of the World War I battlefield, they were more flexible than expected. More recent studies of tactics and doctrine in World War I show that this was one of the most tactically innovative wars in modern history. Those innovations resulted in the combined-arms doctrine, which still fills the pages of the military manuals of all major armies. Such tactics were completely alien to military officers and cultures at the outbreak of the war.[34] Though bureaucratic and cultural preferences initially sidetracked and stifled innovation, in order to survive on the modern battlefield, militaries on the western front developed a new system of fighting that contradicted many of those preferences. The élan of the cavalry and bayonet charge gave way to stealthy infiltration and the methodical creeping barrage. Thus, bureaucratic and cultural factors do have an effect on doctrine. However, military realism argues that conditions exist under which these factors are overridden and thereby provides a fresh account of change and continuity in military doctrine.

Finally, the doctrinal adaptations that result from the threat environment can actually change military culture, as one recent work on the U.S. Army in Vietnam and Iraq has shown.[35] The present work contends that these adaptations and the resulting changes in military culture are attributable to a military realist response to the threat environment. Here the present work is consistent with Patrick Porter's critique of the "cultural turn" in the study of war.[36] Porter provides a number of historical instances in which the evidence contradicts the expectations of Western versus Eastern military culture, and his alternative explanation is highly consistent with military realism. The relative strength and weakness of military forces, Porter contends, are much better predictors of military innovation than their diverse cultures. Both Western and Eastern militaries adopted unconventional and defensive modes of warfare when they were weak and more aggressive and conventional modes when they were strong. Porter argues, therefore, that military cultures are more changeable than their advocates expect and that, like military realism, the origins of those changes are found in realist variables like power and weakness.[37] While bureaucratic and cultural variables can explain some continuities and change in military doctrine, they have their limits. Realist variables, like available capabilities, often determine those limits. The military realist perspective is the conduit through which such variables and others effect military innovation.

The military realist perspective also limits civilian intervention in doctrine. Civilian support can accelerate major doctrinal changes already put under way by senior military officers, but civilian leaders do not determine the essential characteristics of doctrine. Rather, the threat assessment of military realists governs these characteristics. However, assuming regular civil-military relations, civilians exercise significant influence over doctrine. Military officers adapt their doctrine to current material circumstances. For instance, political leaders will not always furnish the forces necessary to implement the logic of force and overcome friction in the face of the most dangerous threats. Doctrine is not simply a list of military preferences. Senior military officers plan to address the most dangerous threats in the near term with the means at their disposal. When political leaders constrain resources, preferences for offense and resources give way to calculations of relative capabilities, opposing doctrines, and friction. The military realist's simultaneous appreciation of friction conditions his preference for offensive doctrines. Defensive theories of victory result, which seek to overcome disparities in material capabilities with the assistance of friction. Therefore, the amount of resources civilian governments provide to their militaries can have a powerful effect on doctrine, precluding some kinds of doctrinal innovation. Thus, civilians can influence doctrine through the allocation of resources, but they will not determine how doctrine responds to those allocations. Instead, a military realist assessment of the threat environment will dictate the plausible doctrinal responses.

This is only a brief sketch of the logic of military realism and the theoretical alternatives. The origins and implications of that logic and how it relates to existing theories of military innovation will be set out in more detail in the next chapter.[38]

Why Only America's Army?

If military realism is a general theory of doctrinal change and continuity, why choose to analyze it through a single military organization, the U.S. Army, from 1960 to 2008? I design the investigation in this way for four reasons. First, this structure gives the best chance of solving the important puzzle that gave birth to this book. The first two and the last case-study chapters, the U.S. Army before and during Vietnam and the U.S. Army in Iraq, are bookends that address the army's love-hate relationship with COIN. However, this is not just a rehashing of worn-out debates about Vietnam. I draw on new histories of the U.S. Army in the Cold War and Vietnam that challenge previous historical accounts that buttress many bureaucratic and cultural explanations.[39] The analysis provides better context than studies focused solely on the army in Vietnam.[40] It does so by considering the broader 1960s threat environment, rather than focusing only on the dilemma of Vietnam. Therefore, to provide a solution to its motivating puzzle, this book follows the doctrinal process of the U.S. Army all the way from Vietnam to the insurgent wars of the post-9/11 era. This structure gives the richest possible context to recent developments in U.S. Army doctrine, shaped amid the memories of Vietnam and two raging insurgencies. The detailed analysis ends in 2008 because this was the year that the army published its first *Operations* manual after the publication of its new 2006 COIN manual and the surge of forces and COIN strategy in Iraq. If the U.S. Army really did make COIN a key part of their most important doctrine during this period, *Operations 2008* is the place to look. There have been some significant changes in army doctrine since then, which I discuss at some length in the concluding chapter. Nonetheless, given the main puzzle that motivated this book, the detailed case-study analysis concludes in 2008.

Second, in addition to setting the stage for solving this puzzle, the structure of the book forces military realism to run a theoretical gauntlet. The alternative theories should easily explain the doctrinal behavior of the U.S. Army. The powerful bureaucracy and culture of the U.S. Army make it a prime candidate for theories focused on those variables. Indeed, a number of works on military innovation use bureaucratic and cultural approaches to do just that.[41] Providing a better explanation is a challenge for military realism. If military realism is up to this challenge, it deserves consideration as an alternative explanation of doctrinal change and continuity, and we need to take its implications for policy seriously.

The case of the U.S. Army is also fertile ground for testing the strengths of military realism against those of civilian realism. According to civilian realism, civilian leaders assess international threats based on a realist calculus of the balance of power, design a strategy in response, and then impose the necessary changes in military doctrine on a recalcitrant military bureaucracy. Civilian realism argues that military organizations must be compelled to change in response to the threat environment, while military realism argues that they will change voluntarily in response to variation in the most dangerous threats. In terms of timing, therefore, changes in civilian realist strategy should instigate and precede changes in U.S. Army doctrine. On the other hand, military realism expects senior officers to change doctrine in response to major changes in the threat environment, with or without civilian prodding. From 1960 to 2008, major shifts in the nature of international threats and U.S. strategy, especially after the Cold War and 9/11, make it possible to test these competing predictions. In short, the structure of this work forces military realism to give battle to its theoretical adversaries on the ground of their choosing. Military realism is a powerful explanation of doctrinal innovation if it passes this difficult test. At the same time, the alternative explanations are less convincing if they fail to explain what should be an easy series of cases.

Third, despite concerns about generalizability, conducting consecutive case studies of one military organization over an extended period has a number of advantages. Looking at one or two consecutive cases of organizational behavior is insufficient. Such an analysis would get at only the short-term causes of doctrinal innovation or stasis. For instance, an examination of the development of the German blitzkrieg doctrine that began in the 1930s or '40s would fail to take into account the influence of the lessons of World War I, which the German Army had begun to distill during the 1920s.[42] With this additional context, we see blitzkrieg as an evolutionary change rather than a doctrinal revolution brought about, for instance, by the intervention of Adolf Hitler.[43] In addition, consecutive case studies allow for the tracking of military culture over time. Indeed, cultural theorists argue that across the period examined here, U.S. Army culture remained unchanged.[44] In this way, we can determine whether military culture is as influential as these theorists contend, whether it is subject to change, and why.[45] In short, comparing a military organization to itself over time is an effective means of tracking short- and long-term causes of change and continuity in military doctrine.[46]

The final reason for focusing exclusively on fifty years of U.S. Army doctrine is that it has important implications for contemporary international relations and U.S. national security. The United States has a disproportionate impact on international relations. The U.S. Army represents a large proportion of the U.S. defense establishment. Thus, the U.S. Army, its leaders, and its doctrine will continue to play an important role in shaping American strategy and foreign policy. For instance, as noted above, military doctrines can have both positive and negative effects on international relations. Military doctrines can lead to international distrust, arms racing, and even war. While defensive doctrines may be a source of reassurance and cooperation, they may also contribute to war by failing to present a convincing deterrent to revisionist powers. If this book can clarify the origins of offensive or defensive theories of victory in the U.S. Army, it could shine another light on the path to reducing international tension and conflict into the future.

The period in which America and its army now find themselves is one of great uncertainty. After more than a decade of counterinsurgency operations and fighting nonstate actors, the United States is now confronted with rising state-based threats in the form of a bellicose Russia and a rising, and increasingly assertive, China. However, this is not the first time the U.S. Army has had to adapt to a changing world and diverse threats. From 1960 to 2008, the U.S. Army confronted a changing and uncertain threat environment more than once. Sometimes the resulting innovations helped the army adapt to that environment and sometimes not. The lessons of doctrinal innovation and continuity presented in these pages can help the U.S. Army navigate yet another period of uncertainty. In the concluding chapter I examine U.S. Army doctrine since 2008 to give the reader a sense of how that process of adaptation is proceeding so far.

Perhaps most important, the case studies in this book show that civilian leaders often view military officers as bureaucratic or cultural partisans who will change only when compelled by outsiders. I argue that this view is problematic. As international relations scholar Stephen Walt points out, when leaders have mistaken theories, disaster can result.[47] Mistaken views about the motivations of military officers, and the policies guided by those views, can undermine civil-military relations and, thereby, national security. Conversely, a correct understanding of military motivations can help leaders get the most out of military advice while appreciating its limitations. While it is true that war is too important and destructive to leave to the generals, especially in the nuclear age, discounting their advice cuts civilian leaders off from their real insights about the logic and limits of force. I argue that seeing military officers as military realists provides a better theoretical foundation for judging their advice and can contribute to better strategy and policy. A sound view of the motivations and perspective of military officers is especially important when considering the Trump administration. At the time of writing, veteran military officers inhabit the positions of secretary of defense, chief of staff, and, until recently, national security adviser. The epithet "Mad Dog" sometimes used to describe President Trump's secretary of defense, James Mattis, nicely encapsulates the prejudice that military officers are champing at the bit to unleash the nation's dogs of war. Bureaucratic and military cultural perspectives on military innovation provide a theoretical explanation for and help perpetuate this view among policy makers, scholars, and the public. In these pages I argue that this prejudice and the theories that support it are often unfounded. Policy makers and observers of national security affairs accepting such theories risk being misinformed. Worse, policy makers risk making bad policy and undermining civil-military relations. By showing that military realism is a powerful explanation of change and continuity in military doctrine, this work seeks to establish it as an alternative perspective on the motives of military officers that can strengthen civil-military relations and improve strategy and foreign policy. Even if the findings here are applicable only to the U.S. and its army, the implications for U.S. national security and international relations today should not be underestimated.

The Plan of the Book

After beginning with a concise definition of military doctrine and how it can change, the next chapter sets out the origins and logic of military realism and its implications for military threat assessment, doctrine, and doctrinal innovation. Next, I explain how military realism differs from the established theories of military innovation. Examining every element of U.S. Army doctrine over fifty years would fill the pages of multiple books. Therefore, three key areas of army doctrine are isolated and tracked over five decades and eight editions of *Operations*. The chapter will then justify the focus on these three areas of doctrine by explaining their suitability for evaluating the alternative theories. Briefly, the first key area is the importance of conventional versus nuclear missions, the second is the degree to which doctrinal theories of victory are offensive or defensive, and the third is the treatment and priority given to the COIN mission. As I will explain, in these three areas the predictions of military realism directly contradict alternative explanations, in terms of either doctrinal process, timing, or content. Therefore, this tripartite division of doctrine provides the starkest possible contrast between explanations. The book then uses five case-study chapters to evaluate military realism and the theoretical alternatives. This systematic setup also allows for the most rigorous assessment of the strengths and weaknesses of military realism. As previously mentioned, the outcome of this theoretical contest has implications beyond theoretical debates in the ivory tower. In addition to contributing to the theoretical debate, examining the role of COIN in U.S. Army doctrine over five decades provides a solution to the puzzle that incited this work, the U.S. Army's recent, unexpected embrace of COIN.

The action in the first case study, "Flexible Response, the Nuclear Battlefield, and Counterinsurgency: Kennedy and Army Doctrine in the 1960s," surrounds *Operations 1962*. The U.S. Army published this manual amid the change in U.S. strategy from massive retaliation to flexible response and in the shadow of insurgent "wars of national liberation." *Operations 1962* dealt with all three key areas of doctrine, and civilian strategy was demanding change across all three. The next chapter, "Army Doctrine in the Shadow of Vietnam: *Operations 1968*," delves into the development of army doctrine during the critical year in Vietnam, 1968. This chapter assesses the wartime expectations of military realism and the alternative theories. The story of the army in Vietnam is a model case of bureaucratic and cultural forces stifling military innovation. If this work can revise our understanding of the U.S. Army in Vietnam, it could deprive bureaucratic and cultural explanations of one of their paradigmatic cases. At the same time, this analysis can significantly strengthen military realism if the new theory provides a stronger explanation of important aspects of this important case.

Chapter 4, "From Active Defense to AirLand Battle: The Cold War Doctrine of the '70s and '80s," follows the development of army doctrine while the service licked its wounds from Vietnam. Scholars of military innovation often cite the development of Active Defense and AirLand Battle doctrines, expressed in *Operations 1976, 1982*, and *1986*, as doctrinal responses to defeat in Vietnam.[48] These manuals were the doctrinal expressions of the mantra "No more Vietnams." The U.S. Army itself still considers *Operations 1976* and *1982* two of the most consequential doctrinal changes in its history.[49] Moreover, the army developed these manuals during important fluctuations in U.S. foreign and national security policy, from the rise of détente under Nixon to its demise under Reagan.

The first post–Cold War chapter, "The Power Projection Army: Doctrine in the Post–Cold War Era until the Eve of September 11," follows the development of *Operations 1993* and *2001*, two manuals forged during one of the most uncertain periods in the history of American national security policy. Senior civilian leaders and army officers were grappling with a world revolutionized by the disappearance of the threat that had guided U.S. strategy and army doctrine since the 1950s. *Operations 1993* was the army's first post–Cold War capstone manual. *Operations 2001* was an update of *Operations 1993* that sought to draw on the lessons of the post–Cold War operational environment. However, just when the army was coming to grips with the "new world order," the strategic landscape seemed to transform beneath its feet.

The army published *Operations 2001* only a few months before the September 11, 2001, terrorist attacks on the United States. According to international historian John Lewis Gaddis, in the aftermath of the attacks on New York and the Pentagon, President Bush "presided over the most sweeping redesign of U.S. grand strategy since the Presidency of Franklin D. Roosevelt."[50] By the time the U.S. Army wrote another *Operations* manual, the United States had invaded two countries as part of a Global War on Terror and was embroiled in COIN campaigns in both. The army released *Operations 2008* during what some were calling the "new counterinsurgency era."[51] Two years before, the army had published its new COIN manual. While doctrine writers were at work on *Operations 2008*, the army was surging troops into Iraq under the guidance of the ideas set out in that new COIN manual. This is the climactic chapter of the book. The previous chapters provide the context for understanding why the army seems to have latched on to COIN at this point in its history. If the army had truly made COIN a core mission in its doctrine, the proof would be in the pudding—its most important manual, *Operations 2008*.

The concluding chapter brings together all of the parts of this complex story. First, and most important, it assesses how well the competing explanations stood up under scrutiny, answering questions like this one: Does the evidence support the claim that military officers are just bureaucrats in uniform? Second, the final chapter confronts this question: How well can military realism explain the changes in U.S. Army doctrine after 2008? Third and finally, the conclusion asks: What are the implications of military realism for military innovation studies, international and civil-military relations, and national security policy? This chapter proposes answers to all these questions and more. However, it also sets out the limits of this work and points out the additional research required to establish military realism as a strong alternative to the theories that currently dominate the literature on military innovation.

1 MILITARY REALISM

A New Perspective on Military Innovation

THE INTRODUCTION ESTABLISHED that military doctrine is not only of concern to military professionals and international security scholars. Change and continuity in the ways that militaries think about war and prepare for it can have important consequences for military effectiveness, international peace and security, economic prosperity, and civil-military relations. Variation and stagnation in military doctrines have meant the difference not only between life and death for soldiers but for nations. This chapter fleshes out the theoretical reasoning behind military realism and its explanation of doctrinal change and continuity.

Deck Chairs on the *Titanic*? Military Doctrine and Degrees of Doctrinal Change

A clear understanding of military doctrine and doctrinal change begins with their definitions. We need to know what doctrine is and what it is not. We also need to know if doctrinal changes are significant or insignificant. Does a new doctrine fundamentally change the way that a military organization thinks about war and its missions, or is doctrinal change simply akin to rearranging deck chairs on the *Titanic*? Defining military doctrine enumerates its parts and the degree to which doctrine can change. This definition also helps evaluate the predictions of the competing theories. Different theories expect different degrees of change in military doctrine. Clear definitions can also help assess popular expectations of military organizations. If, for instance, militaries are always "fighting the last war," we should expect minimal doctrinal change despite important changes in threats to national security or the strategies for dealing with them.

Doctrine and How It Changes

Military doctrine is an authoritative expression of the theories of victory, mission priorities, and standard operating procedures that a military organization uses to prepare its forces for conflict.[1] However, these three parts are not equal in importance; some make up the core of doctrine, while others are on its periphery.[2] The theories of victory and mission priorities are the core of doctrine. On the periphery of that core are the SOPs used to execute those theories and missions. The core of doctrine is like its brain and vital organs, and the SOPs are like the extremities that protect them and execute their will. An example will help illustrate the distinction and the relationship between the two parts.

During World War II, the main mission of the Allied air forces was long-range bombing informed by a theory of victory through strategic bombing campaigns. According to this theory of victory, the bombing offensive would cripple the German economy, crush its people's will to fight, and end the war.[3] Strategic bombing was the doctrinal core of these World War II air forces. It took priority over air-defense operations or close air support of ground forces.[4] Peripheral SOPs supported this doctrinal core. Peripheral changes might include the addition of a new arm to the service to execute core missions more effectively.[5] New arms enable new SOPs. For instance, the Allied air forces employed new fighter technology to increase the effectiveness and survivability of their long-range bombers.[6] For most of the war, there was variation in the SOPs of these air forces, but their core theory of victory and mission priority remained.

Because the periphery of doctrine serves the core, changes on the periphery of doctrine will not change its core. However, changes to the core will reverberate out to the periphery. Core changes might include a shift from an offensive to a defensive theory of victory or the deletion, addition, or shuffling of missions. Changes in mission priorities or theories of victory recast the way that a military sees its central role and the paths to victory. For instance, abandoning an offensive for a defensive theory of victory would necessitate reducing SOPs for major offensive operations and the offensive spirit they demand. Thus, current SOPs and subordinate arms may be ill-suited to new missions and theories of victory. Military organizations will have to alter these peripheral elements of doctrine to enact its new core. Militaries will also have to school their forces in these new SOPs.

Changes in theories of victory may mean changing the imperatives of leadership in war. For instance, a highly offensive doctrine rewards an officer's initiative and regards inaction as an evil to be avoided. A defensive doctrine, on the other hand, encourages more caution and deliberation among officers. Veterans of the old way of warfare will have to revise their hard-won combat instincts to make it in the new system. The same, of course, is true when the shift is from a defensive to an offensive theory of victory.

Considering the consequences and extent of core changes, one can appreciate why military organizations are sometimes reluctant to make major changes to their underlying theories of victory and mission priorities, especially while fighting. Few sports teams would change their defensive or offensive scheme midseason for fear that adaptation might be slow and lead to defeats. How much more real is this concern when the lives of people and nations are in the balance. Because of their disruptive character, core changes will be especially difficult in wartime. The slow change in ground-combat doctrine in World War I, despite the horrendous costs of persisting with existing theories of victory and SOPs, is a classic example.[7]

Nevertheless, core changes in wartime do happen, the most comprehensive being to the theory of victory. For instance, in the Korean War, the transition from taking territory through maneuver to inflicting casualties through firepower, measured in body counts, was due to a transition from an offensive to a defensive theory of victory. Gone were the days of General MacArthur's dashing offensives—sometimes against the wishes of his civilian masters. Grinding attrition orchestrated methodically by General Ridgway took their place. Ridgway placed greater emphasis on the destructive advantages of the defense and the risks of offense. Such changes require a change in the mind-set of the whole army and reached out from the center to affect the doctrinal periphery. The army had to replace SOPs designed to support a war of movement with those that furthered a strategy of attrition in an increasingly unpopular war, using firepower to maximize enemy casualties while minimizing friendly losses.[8] In wartime core changes in doctrine lead to major uncertainty and risk defeat. Militaries understandably enact them with great trepidation. Nevertheless, they do enact them.

So military doctrines are authoritative expressions of a doctrinal core, made up of a theory of victory and mission priorities, and a doctrinal periphery of SOPs to execute those theories and missions. Doctrinal change can happen either in the core or on the periphery. But not all doctrinal changes are created equal. Some are adaptive, peripheral changes that serve the doctrinal core, while others transform theories of victory and rearrange mission priorities. We now turn to military realism and its explanation of change and continuity in military doctrine.

Military Realism: Explaining Doctrinal Change and Continuity

The experience of and preparation for war produces in military officers a two-part military realist mind-set. The first part is an appreciation for the logic of force. When two people or groups come into conflict, one or both can choose to use violence to impose their will on the other. If the target of the violence resists, an interaction comes into being. This interaction of violent forces has a logic. In order to impose its will on the unwilling, each party must either escalate its use of force or relinquish its object. Warfare is highly dependent on the reactions that one's actions inspire in the adversary and vice versa. Colloquially, officers express this idea of war as inescapably interactive with the adage: "The enemy gets a vote." Not surprisingly, Carl von Clausewitz, an experienced military officer and theorist expressed it best. "I am not in control," the author of *On War* explained. "[My enemy] dictates to me as much as I dictate to him."[9] This escalatory interaction is the logic of force.[10] Relatedly, for military realists, because an unpredictable enemy heavily influences this violent interaction, they also appreciate that the initiation of force always produces major uncertainty. The experience of and preparation for war inculcate these realities into the minds of military officers.

The second part of the military realist mind-set is an appreciation for the way in which the physical world limits the use of force. Time, friction, and available means all place limits on the use of force in war. For instance, states cannot uproot fortresses to take part in an invasion.[11] Even societies completely mobilized for war face physical limits. Workers manufacturing the weapons of war cannot simultaneously use them on the battlefield. In addition, powerful physical forces hinder the use of military forces in the field. The simplest maneuver is difficult amid constant friction.[12] Difficult terrain, weather, and that persistent force gravity can bring the machine of war to a grinding halt.[13]

There has been no discussion thus far of the political nature of war. This is not an oversight. Wars do indeed serve a political purpose, the value of which determines the amount of force exerted in its pursuit.[14] The total mobilization of a society to serve a limited political objective would be absurd.[15] For this reason, states often do not employ all of the force at their disposal.[16] However, the military realist mind-set focuses primarily on the logic and physical limits of force and less so on its political nature.

They emphasize these two aspects of force over the political for two reasons. First, according to the logic of force, once a state initiates a coercive interaction, no matter the political object, failure to resist or surpass an opponent's escalation results in defeat or the abandoning of the political object.[17] The logic of force, therefore, exerts influence independent of the political situation.[18] It is not necessary for us to assume, as some do, that the military officer "forgets that other means can also be used" because of their fixation on military operations.[19] Rather, they are concerned with the reality that, no matter the political object, escalation requires counterescalation to attain the object or resist its imposition. That master of political persuasion Cicero was confronted with this brutal logic in the avengers of Julius Caesar: "I cannot even for myself find out what must be done; for what can be done against force, without force?"[20] According to the logic of force, when one side to a dispute appeals to force, the other must reciprocate or be overcome.

The second apolitical constant in war is friction. No matter what political object a state or group seeks through force, it will always take place in the resistant medium of the physical world. Friction will always limit what is possible in military operations and war. Clausewitz, who witnessed his first battle at thirteen, provides a particularly vivid picture of battle and its difficulties. He describes the young officer approaching his first battlefield.[21] He takes us from the distant sound of artillery, past the command post, where shells are falling among the staff attempting to direct the battle, up to the front line, where the apparent chaos of the combat, the screams of the dying, and the snap of bullets move the novice of battle to pity and horror.[22] This natural human inclination to recoil from the pity and horror of battle, like our World War I soldiers on the cusp of no-man's-land, is another form of natural friction. Human beings will always flee from death and wounds, and war will always ask them to overcome this natural inclination and act.[23] For military officers, the experience of and preparation for combat put the physical limits on force in sharp relief. Changes in the political objects that lead to wars will not alter the friction encountered by the forces sent to attain those objects.

It makes sense that military officers would focus on these two elements because when they prepare for war in times of peace, they do not know what political disagreements will lead to war. Therefore, they focus on what they do know: that force has a logic and that friction makes the simplest thing in war very difficult. Below I set out how the military realist appreciation of the logic and limits of force influence those preparations for conflict known as military doctrines. However, one additional consequence of the military realist outlook bears mentioning.

One further aspect of the military realist mind-set is a keen awareness of the great uncertainty involved in war. The use of force produces major uncertainty because its repercussions are often determined by the responses of an unpredictable enemy. As already mentioned: "The enemy gets a vote." Military plans can try to anticipate the responses of the enemy but cannot predict them with certainty. The physical world, with its changeable weather and unknown terrain, adds to this ever-present uncertainty. The uncertainty violence breeds helps explain why military officers are often much less optimistic about the use of force than their civilian counterparts.[24] As General Stanley McChrystal recently warned, "War is sort of like something radioactive that you shouldn't touch unless you've done a tremendous amount of understanding of just the damage that it will do."[25] Robert Gates, former director of the Central Intelligence Agency (CIA) and later secretary of defense under Presidents George W. Bush and Obama, put it this way:

> It was my experience over the years that one of the biggest misimpressions held by the public has been that our military is always straining at the leash, wanting to use force in any situation. *The reality is just the opposite.* In more than twenty years of attending meetings in the Situation Room, my experience was that the biggest doves in Washington wear uniforms. And perhaps that is as it should be. Our military leaders have seen too many half-baked ideas for the use of military force advanced in the Situation Room by hairy-chested civilians who have never seen combat or fired a gun in anger.[26]

These observations and examples line up nicely with Richard Betts's research. In all the Cold War crises that Betts examined, U.S. military leaders were never more aggressive than their civilian counterparts when it came to the decision to initiate the use of force.[27]

Betts illustrates this point nicely with an episode from the Cuban missile crisis. Many consider this event a classic case of more cautious and reasonable civilian leaders holding at bay overly aggressive military officers. Sometimes, however, the roles were reversed. During the crisis, commandant of the U.S. Marines, David Shoup, was concerned with the casual way in which civilian officials were discussing the option to invade the island. In a meeting with these officials, Shoup set out a map of the United States. He then superimposed a map of Cuba over it, showing how the island extended from New York to Chicago. He then placed a final transparency on top of the other two. This time no one in the room could tell what the minuscule dot dwarfed by Cuba was. When asked, Shoup replied, "That, gentlemen, represents the size of the island of Tarawa, and it took us three days and 18,000 marines to take it."[28] Shoup was keenly aware of the friction and uncertainty involved in even the smallest military operations. Moreover, this military caution held into the post–Cold War. Generals Colin Powell and Norman Schwarzkopf were hesitant to initiate the use of force against Iraq in the 1990s, and Secretary of Defense Richard Cheney had to press them to develop more offensive options.[29]

But this military caution is not limited to American officers. German generals opposed Hitler's plans of attack for France and Poland because of the uncertainty and friction involved. The blitzkrieg on France succeeded because Heinz Guderian disobeyed his cautious commanders, including Hitler, who were nervous about tanks advancing with insufficient infantry support. As historian Anthony Beevor concludes, "Thus what was erroneously described as a Blitzkrieg strategy was to a large degree improvised on the ground."[30] After Guderian's success, Hitler was more open to his ideas and replaced other senior officers with "men who were entirely [Hitler's] creatures."[31]

In Great Britain during World War II, Field Marshal Alanbrooke tempered Churchill's most ambitious strategic initiatives. He noted of Churchill, "He knows no details, has only got half the picture in his mind, talks absurdities and makes my blood boil to listen to his nonsense."[32] As a case in point, Churchill was concerned with the political capital the Allies could gain with Stalin from opening a second front or launching operations that would compel the Germans to draw forces away from the eastern front. Alanbrooke, in military realist fashion, was concerned less with the political repercussions of such operations and more with the problems of supply and the numerical disadvantages that the troops would face in executing Churchill's operations.

Other scholars too have noticed military realist caution. However, none of these theorists or practitioners traces the origins of this military caution to the logic and limits of force as the present work does. Bernard Brodie noted, "Bold commanders have usually been harder to find than cautious ones."[33] Samuel Huntington came to similar conclusions about the "military mind" in *The Soldier and the State*.[34] It seems then that theorists who advocate civilian intervention as a means of restraining the ingrained aggression of military officers have it backward.

The general character of the military realist mind-set is also evident in how military officers think about restrictions on the use of force in war. Somewhat paradoxically, although they are cautious about the initial use of force, military realists prefer rapid escalation to win once civilians have decided to use force. As one scholar put it, "Generals prefer using force quickly, massively, and decisively to destroy enemy capabilities rather than rationing it gradually to coax the enemy to change his intentions."[35] This preference springs from a counterintuitive truth about warfare appreciated by military realists. Often the best way to end wars rapidly is to exert oneself as much and as quickly as possible. The most certain means of ending war quickly, assuming you refuse to surrender, is to exert yourself to the utmost. In short, use all the force at your disposal to enact the logic of force and impose your will on your opponent. For instance, for our World War I soldiers the quickest way to end their harrowing experience was to exert themselves, to break cover against all their rational and natural inclinations, and assault the enemy defense, subdue it, and thereby end the engagement. From the military realist perspective, what was true for those soldiers is true for war in general. Chairman Powell expressed it this way: "Use all the force necessary, and do not apologize for going in big if that is what it takes. Decisive force ends wars quickly and in the long run saves lives."[36] Next, we turn to how this military realist perspective affects military officers' assessment of international threats and the doctrines they design to confront those threats.

Military Realism, Threat Assessment, and Mission Priorities

A military realist perspective grounded in the logic and limits of force assesses threats based on relative material capabilities and the military doctrines of potential adversaries. Material capabilities include available troops, weapons and resources, population, and economic potential for war fighting. However, from the perspective of military realism, states with immediately available troops and weapons, rather than long-term potential capabilities, are more threatening.[37] States can use their forces in being in the short term to render an adversary helpless. Military organizations design doctrine to address the range of threats, but resources are always limited, so doctrine tends to focus on the gravest threats.[38] Doctrine prioritizes those threats that can martial overwhelming physical force and destroy material capabilities. State-based militaries are usually the source of threats of this kind. The most important missions in doctrine will be those that are essential for addressing the gravest threats. Not surprisingly, military realism also expects military officers to pay close attention to geography. Geography can increase or decrease the relative friction confronting military forces and their doctrine. Geography and the friction it produces are a constant enemy that hinders military forces even when no menacing state-based threats are on the scene. Given this prioritization of threats, senior military officers change theories of victory and mission priorities when they no longer plausibly address the material capabilities and doctrine of the most dangerous threats.

In the absence of looming threats from powerful states, military realists will shift the emphasis in doctrine toward protecting the vital material interests of the state, which generate and sustain its material capabilities. The securing of fossil fuels is the most straightforward example. But such a permissive threat environment does not automatically lead to doctrinal optimism among military realists. Even in the absence of powerful enemies, friction dogs the deployment and operation of military forces. When the securing of vital material resources requires the traversing of major geographical obstacles, military doctrine will take this into account, even if doing so cuts against parochial preferences.

Powerful state militaries are not the only threats to national security, however. Guerrilla, insurgent, and terrorist groups can also threaten homeland security and important foreign interests. Nevertheless, from the military realist perspective, unconventional threats are rarely as dangerous as powerful state militaries. In some cases, however, insurgents can pose an existential threat to states, their allies, or their interests. In such situations, defeating irregular enemies like insurgents can become an important, if not the primary, mission in military doctrine. In general, however, unconventional threats are simply less dangerous than those emanating from states. Consequently, when a military organization faces threats of overwhelming force from other state militaries, missions like COIN become a lower priority in doctrine.

These, then, are the mission priorities associated with military realism. Now it is time to consider the implications of the military realist perspective for the second part of the doctrinal core, its theory of victory.

Military Realism and Theories of Victory:
Offensive versus Defensive

Doctrinal theories of victory can have numerous characteristics.[39] However, the focus in this work is on the degree to which doctrinal theories of victory are offensive or defensive and why. The introduction argued that the offensive or defensive character of military doctrines has important international and domestic political consequences. Additionally, military realism and the alternative theories of military innovation offer competing explanations for variation between offensive and defensive theories of victory. For our purposes, we can think of theories of victory as existing along a continuum, with the most offensive theories of victory on one end and the most defensive theories of victory at the other.[40] The most offensive theory of victory would be one that considered offensive operations the only positive means to victory and defensive operations as a temporary expedient until the attack can be taken up again. The most defensive theory of victory would advocate pure resistance through defensive operations, allowing the enemy to dash himself to pieces on the shoals of an impregnable defense—essentially, allowing the enemy to wear themselves out rather than destroying their capabilities through a major counteroffensive. Competing explanations of change and continuity in military doctrine make predictions about which end of this continuum military organizations prefer, why, and in which direction doctrine should tend.

Bureaucratic and military culture theories argue that militaries often prefer offensive theories of victory.[41] To a certain extent, military realism agrees. The logic of force implies a preference for an offensive theory of victory. Offensive action is the most direct path to successful military operations. Through offense, military forces destroy the physical capabilities of the enemy and occupy their territory, ensuring the enemy raises no more forces. In this way, the enemy is disarmed and subdued and the war concluded as rapidly as possible. We observe this preference in the calls of General Powell and others to employ overwhelming force quickly to reach a decision and terminate wars. This argument assumes offensive action.

Conversely, the logic of force does not recommend a passive, defensive theory of victory. For the defender to win without transitioning to the offense, the attacker, after meeting resistance and before he has exhausted his material capabilities, must choose to give up his objective and settle for a negotiated peace. Defense by itself cannot produce victory but relies on the wearing down of the opponent's will to fight.[42] Defensive doctrines, therefore, are more dependent on the willingness of the opposing side to continue fighting. Thus, military officers prefer offensive theories of victory because they enact escalation and are the most certain path to victory. Purely defensive theories of victory, conversely, place the fighting forces in a dependent position vis-à-vis their opponent.

However, the preference for the offense recommended by the logic of force does not exhaust military realism's expectations for theories of victory. According to military realism, military officers are also keenly aware of the ever-present and multifaceted friction that besets all attempts to use force. This friction gives the defensive form of warfare advantages over the offense.[43] While the soldier or the army in the attack must overcome friction, the defender can exploit friction, allying with it to wear down the attacking force. For instance, in combat the defender can fire from behind cover. Attackers, on the other hand, must break cover, exposing themselves to defensive fire, to close with and subdue the defender. Recall again our World War I soldiers huddled in their trench. In the defense, these soldiers would only raise their heads above the lip of no-man's-land and cut down the advancing enemy. In the attack, however, they must move to reach the defender and expose themselves to its fire and friction. Besides physical friction, the psychological friction is less for the soldier in the defense, who does not have to expose himself to a wall of unrelenting steel to accomplish his mission. This mismatch between attack and defense has led to the rule of thumb that an attacker should have a three-to-one superiority over the defender to succeed.[44] Nor have the advantages of the defense diminished in modern warfare. Stephen Biddle has argued convincingly that a defense organized in depth has consistently blunted offensive operations in modern military history. This is even so on twenty-first-century battlefields, where dug-in opponents remain extremely difficult to dislodge without the use of infantry, even when the attacking force has all of the might of the U.S. Air Force at their disposal.[45] There are further defensive advantages, as the case-study chapters will illustrate, but this suffices for the present purpose.

From the military realist perspective, the limits that the physical world places on the use of offensive force lead to a recognition that the defense has significant advantages over offense and that under some conditions a defensive doctrine is preferred. The advantages of the defense allow a numerically inferior foe to resist a superior attacker. Therefore, when confronted with a potential foe enjoying material superiority, militaries can develop defensive doctrines to offset the imbalance of capabilities. Increases in adversary capabilities are not the only source of an imbalance of resources, however. Obviously, reductions in available resources by political leaders can also cause an imbalance of capabilities. Under major resource constraints, militaries must exploit all of the advantages inherent in a defensive theory of victory to have a hope of resisting. In short, the military realist appreciation of friction conditions the preference for offense recommended by the logic of force and can lead to the promotion of a more defensive theory of victory.

However, it should be noted, even defensive theories of victory will have some offensive elements, at the very least at the tactical level.[46] No defense is completely passive, especially in modern war. While the overall theory of victory might be defensive, to win local engagements the defender must often make use of local counterattacks. As an astute observer of the power of the defense pointed out, the defense "is not simply a shield, but a shield made up of well directed blows."[47] However, according to military realism, the doctrine of a force at a material disadvantage will not recommend extending local counterattacks into a general offensive that its inferior capabilities could not sustain.

In short, although the logic of force leads military realists to prefer an offensive theory of victory, the physical limits on the use of force, and the consequent advantages that accrue to the defender, temper this preference. When the most dangerous threats enjoy significant material superiority, militaries can place defensive theories of victory at the heart of doctrine. Such doctrines might not promise victory, but they do make survival more likely.

This is not the first work on military innovation to argue that militaries will voluntarily adopt defensive doctrines. In *Imagining War*, Elizabeth Kier argues that militaries select defensive doctrines when they are consistent with their military culture.[48] Below, I set out how military realism differs from Kier's cultural approach. Before that, however, a discussion of military realism's explanation of doctrinal continuity and change is necessary.

Military Realism and Doctrinal Innovation

Military realism makes predictions about the likely threat assessment of military officers, the mission priorities that flow from those threats, and the circumstances under which theories of victory are more or less offensive or defensive. Now we turn to a discussion of how military realism explains changes in doctrine. According to military realism, senior officers initiate changes in either or both the established mission priorities and the degree of offense or defense in their theory of victory when they cease to plausibly address the most dangerous threats. Such changes might cut against bureaucratic imperatives, cultural traditions, and civilian intervention. Nevertheless, senior officers will champion these changes. Surprising changes could include removing or reinterpreting cherished doctrinal concepts associated with offensive theories of victory and deeply held cultural traditions. In addition, while the focus of doctrine will be the most dangerous threats, when the threat environment allows, the doctrinal focus can shift to less dangerous unconventional threats, even when the doctrinal alterations required cut against bureaucratic and cultural preferences. In permissive threat environments, that is, in the absence of a state-based threat, senior military realists will focus doctrine on securing the vital material interests of the state and overcoming friction. Senior officers should also be able to look beyond their limited personal experience and adapt to forms of warfare that challenge the relevance of that experience. Although the focus here is on changes in core missions and theories of victory, these changes should cascade outward to the doctrinal periphery and give birth to new SOPs that serve the new doctrinal core. Doctrinal changes, then, arise from a perception among senior officers of an incompatibility between changes in the threat environment and the nucleus of doctrine.

This is not to say, however, that the threat assessments of military officers will be correct or that the changes they make to doctrine will be effective or wise. The French Army prior to 1940 saw the specter of German aggression on the horizon. While they made some doctrinal changes, these were largely peripheral because they saw their doctrine as essentially appropriate for addressing the threat. Initially, they possessed a numerical advantage.[49] By the time the French military recognized the inappropriateness of their prewar doctrine, it was too late. The belief that French doctrine, stiffened with a sprinkling of the new tank units, was up to the task stifled appropriate adaptations. The same is true of doctrinal innovations examined here. The close integration of tactical nuclear and conventional army forces in Cold War army doctrine might have made nuclear war more likely. The embrace of the "revolution in military affairs" and military "transformation" after the Cold War led to doctrinal innovations that likely weakened the force for the conflicts to come. The military realist perspective seeks to explain doctrinal continuity and change, but the contention is not that the result is always better doctrine or battlefield success.

Military Realism and U.S. Army Doctrine from 1960 to 2008

The chapters that follow test the predictions of military realism against three theoretical alternatives across three key areas of U.S. Army doctrine from 1960 to 2008. The doctrinal focus is the U.S. Army *Field Manual (FM) 100-5* (later *3-0*), *Operations. Operations* manuals are the most important expression of army doctrine because they outline mission priorities and theories of victory to which subordinate manuals must conform. As one scholar of military innovation put it, *Operations* "contains the Army's conception of war and how it intends to fight war."[50] The three areas analyzed for continuity and variation are the importance and relationship between conventional and nuclear missions in doctrine, the degree to which the theory of victory is offensive or defensive, and the treatment and relative priority given to COIN missions. First, military realism expects army doctrine to make conventional or nuclear missions central to doctrine when necessary to address the most dangerous threats. Senior army leaders will push bureaucratic or cultural preferences for conventional forces to one side if a doctrine centered on the nuclear mission is necessary. Second, senior army leaders will prefer offensive theories of victory. However, I expect senior officers to push for a more defensive theory of victory in the face of major negative imbalances of capabilities vis-à-vis the most dangerous threats. Contrary to cultural explanations, senior U.S. Army officers will push through doctrinal changes even when they require a break from nostalgia for the army's World War II finest hour, the source of its culture. Senior leaders and the doctrine writers they employ will also reinterpret doctrinal concepts tied to the cultural traditions of the U.S. Army to address the most dangerous threats. When necessary, senior army leaders will bypass army bureaucracy to push through doctrinal innovations.

We should also see senior army officers rejecting calls to make doctrine more offensive when the threat environment dictates a more defensive theory of victory. When the threat environment is relatively permissive in terms of state-based threats, army doctrine will shift its focus to the protection of vital material resources that generate and sustain material capabilities. But the absence of hostile and powerful nation states will not automatically lead to doctrinal optimism and highly offensive theories of victory. Senior army leaders will ensure that doctrine keeps in mind how the friction caused by geography impedes the deployment and operation of military forces, how it hinders offense and facilitates defense.

Typically, the threat of insurgency will not be severe enough to warrant a central place in doctrine. However, this does not mean that army officers will chiefly propose conventional military solutions to insurgency, as bureaucratic and cultural interpretations expect. Their doctrinal imagination is not bounded by parochial considerations. Moreover, when insurgency represents one of the gravest threats facing America, then it can become a central part of U.S. Army doctrine. Typically, however, in the presence of grave state-based threats, COIN will have a subordinate role in doctrine.

The simplest way to identify change or continuity in U.S. Army doctrine is to compare it to its doctrinal predecessor, which the new manual supersedes. However, sources like *Military Review*, the flagship journal of the U.S. Army Command and General Staff College (CGSC), provide additional evidence of army thinking across time.[51] There are of course limitations to focusing primarily on one professional publication within the U.S. Army. The editors of these publications have significant latitude.[52] Nevertheless, *Military Review* is widely recognized as seminal to U.S. Army thinking about warfare. It is the main publication of the CGSC, which military-innovation scholars have called "the center of army culture" and a hub of cultural indoctrination.[53] In his recent comprehensive history to U.S. Army doctrine, Walter E. Kretchik calls *Military Review* a "sounding board" for doctrinal ideas in the army.[54] Historian

Brian McAllister Linn also uses *Military Review* to gauge doctrinal ideas in a U.S. Army poised for the nuclear battlefield.[55] Whenever the U.S. Army promulgated a new version of *Operations*, it usually introduced it to the force in an article in *Military Review*. This is a recognition that *Military Review* and the CGSC were the home of high-level army doctrine and doctrinal thinking. The content of *Military Review* is especially important in the 1960s, when the record of doctrinal development in the army is sparse.

Professional military institutions like the CGSC, and their publications, are a means of transmitting organizational culture.[56] The doctrinal ideas expressed therein, therefore, should be largely consistent with U.S. Army culture. If, instead, they are consistent with military realism, this strengthens the new theory. Tracing doctrinal thinking through *Military Review* also helps establish the timing of doctrinal change and continuity, a key to evaluating the theories. For instance, when civilian leaders abruptly impose doctrinal innovations contrary to bureaucratic and cultural preferences, these innovations should not figure prominently in *Military Review* prior to the attempted imposition. Similarly, if contrary innovations are included in doctrine only to placate civilian demands, contributors to *Military Review* should not regularly discuss them prior to the civilian intervention. However, should doctrinal innovations appear often in *Military Review* prior to civilian initiatives in their favor, this supports military realism, especially when these innovations cut against bureaucratic and cultural preferences.

Next, a comparison of military realism and competing theories delineates their differing expectations and previews the findings of the case studies that follow.

Military Realism and the Alternative Explanations
Civilian Realism and Military Realism

A number of theorists argue that to overcome rigid military cultures and bureaucracy, civilian leaders must intervene to promote doctrinal change.[57] Barry Posen's realist variant of this argument is the seminal work in studies of military innovation.[58] Posen argues that civilian leaders are more attuned to the international threat environment than their military subordinates, who are blinded by their bureaucratic biases. This work refers to Posen's theory as civilian realism because civilian assessments of international threats drive doctrinal change.

In Posen's telling, civilians formulate strategy to deal with national security threats and then use handpicked military mavericks to resist the machinations of military bureaucrats and help make military doctrine consistent with the civilian leaders' new strategy.[59] Thus, the impetus for innovation first arises among civilian leaders, who then impose it on the military through a maverick officer.[60] Across the three key area of doctrine, then, civilian strategy will determine whether the U.S. Army prioritizes conventional forces over nuclear forces, offensive or more defensive theories of victory, and the COIN mission. Posen includes a caveat, however. If the complexity of managing international alliances distracts civilian leaders, then military bureaucrats can capture the doctrinal process and bend it to their parochial will. In this scenario, army priorities across the three areas of doctrine will be identical to those expected by the bureaucratic perspective discussed below.

According to military realism, in contrast, unless they are willing to purge the officer corps, as Hitler and Stalin did, civilian leaders are unlikely to force changes to the core of doctrine, even with the support of a military maverick. Senior military leaders often see such mavericks as outsiders within their military services. Consequently, mavericks lack the influence necessary to change military organizations.[61] However, civilian leaders can support core changes initiated by senior military realists and thereby increase the speed of change.

Military realism and civilian realism also diverge in other ways. For instance, civilian realism argues that civilian leaders are more mindful of the international balance of power than their military subordinates, whose bureaucratic or cultural biases stifle innovation until civilians and their mavericks impose it. The theory assumes that civilian leaders are not subject to biases that distract them from a clear assessment of international threats. However, civilians also suffer from bias. The most obvious example, in democracies, is the desire for election and reelection.[62] Like the distracting international alliances that can short-circuit civilian realism, these biases can also distract civilian leaders from assessing international threats and monitoring their militaries. At times like these, parochial interests should dominate doctrine.

The case studies presented here show that parochial interests do not always keep military officers from accurately assessing international threats. For instance, and on the contrary, U.S. Army officers were highly attuned to their threat environment. Even in the absence of civilian intervention, senior leaders changed army doctrine in ways warranted by changes in the threat environment but contrary to hypothesized bureaucratic and cultural preferences. These changes included, for instance, the adoption and preservation of a defensive theory of victory at the core of U.S. Army doctrine. Even when left to their own doctrinal devices, the army preserved this defensive doctrine. This is contrary to the preference for the offense that should be in evidence in the U.S. Army bureaucracy and that civilian realism expects to dominate in the absence of civilian oversight.

The above reasoning shows that civilian and military realisms also have different predictions when it comes to the timing of doctrinal innovation. Civilian realists should initiate innovations, which they then impose on an unwilling military bureaucracy. Changes in civilian strategy, therefore, should precede major doctrinal changes. Military realism, on the other hand, expects the most important doctrinal changes to originate within the military, often prior to or in the absence of changes in civilian strategy. The timing of changes in U.S. Army doctrine follows the expectations of military realism. Civilian leaders often took credit for doctrinal and organizational changes that originated within the army. To be clear, the implication is not that all of these innovations were sound, but that they originated within the army and often broke the bonds of parochialism. For instance, the final two case studies show that the U.S. Army embraced the military transformation agenda earlier and more enthusiastically than previously appreciated and prior to civilian interest in transformation. However, this led to doctrinal and organizational innovations that introduced vulnerabilities into the force when the new technologies did not fulfill their promise. The timing of these innovations is inconsistent with civilian realism. Moreover, the innovations were often contrary to bureaucratic interests, which civilian realism assumes should dominate internal doctrinal developments. Instead, the embrace of transformation was an organizational response to a changing post–Cold War threat environment undertaken in the midst of major resource reductions.

Regarding military mavericks, civilian leaders do employ them, but the results are more consistent with military than civilian realism. Stephen Peter Rosen is correct that established military leaders see mavericks as outsiders, which curtails their influence.[63] The weakness of the maverick mechanism may also be due to the self-contradiction within it. Civilian leaders do lack the military expertise to audit their military organizations. Indeed, scholars have documented the decline in civilian knowledge of military affairs, especially in the United States.[64] This is why they need mavericks. However, the contradiction arises when civilian realism assumes that civilians *do* possess the military expertise necessary to select a military officer that reflects their strategic vision. The case studies here show that military mavericks often represent a military realist perspective on doctrine more consistent with the views of senior army officers than would-be civilian innovators. In the U.S. Army under Kennedy and under Bush II, the military mavericks that civilians selected either worked at cross-purposes with civilians or persuaded civilians to adopt innovations preferred by the U.S. Army's senior leadership. They often did so because civilian initiatives neglected or were inconsistent with the range of threats confronting the United States.

Military Realism and Rosen's Theory of Military Innovation

Scholars of military innovation will object that there appears to be little difference between military realism and Stephen Peter Rosen's theory of military innovation. Both theories agree that innovation originates in the military; that military mavericks will have limited influence;[65] that civilian leaders can accelerate, but not impose, major innovation;[66] and that the international security environment is the stimulus for military innovation.[67] However, important differences remain.

Rosen's groundbreaking work in military innovation studies, *Winning the Next War*, focuses on innovations in existing combat arms or the creation of new combat arms within a service. While such innovations are extremely important, I focus on change and continuity in the mission priorities and the offensive or defensive orientation of theories of victory in military doctrine.[68] In addition, military realism argues that the military realist appreciation for the logic and limits of force shapes the lens through which senior military officers assess international threats and develop doctrinal solutions. Rosen makes no such claims. Rosen's book also argues that the process of innovation will be slower and generational, as the military organization promotes officers who then use their power to champion military innovation.[69] In contrast, military realism expects officers to be more mentally flexible, leading to more rapid changes than Rosen anticipates. Here I show that U.S. Army officers bloodied in its finest hours, from World War II to the Gulf War, advocated nuclear and unconventional warfare doctrines that called into question the very relevance of their formative experiences. Innovation does not have to wait for the military organization to cycle these officers out of its ranks. Under the right conditions, these very officers can be the champions of change.

Looking at the three key areas of doctrine reveals additional difference with Rosen. Rosen acknowledges that his work does not explain the military innovation brought about by the nuclear revolution. He argues, "This innovation was unique, and is outside the scope of the explanations laid out in this book."[70] It is an "anomalous" case, Rosen contends, because military officers do not possess the relevant "professional expertise" to pursue independent military innovations in this area.[71] In contrast, the present book does examine the effects of the nuclear revolution on the doctrine of the U.S. Army. Here I argue that it is not an "anomalous" case for military realism, but one consistent with its expectations. Rosen also focuses on theories of victory,[72] but here the primary concern is with the degree to which these theories are offensive or defensive. Military realism makes specific predictions as to when doctrines should be more or less offensive. Military realists prefer offensive doctrines but adopt defensive doctrines to redress imbalances of material capabilities. Rosen argues only that they vary, contrary to bureaucratic explanations.[73]

Rosen also focuses on military innovation during wartime. He is concerned with whether militaries can use wartime experience to improve their wartime performance.[74] However, he develops a different theory based on intelligence and "strategic measures of effectiveness" to explain the presence or absence of wartime innovation.[75] For Rosen, learning in wartime can occur when "feedback" from the battlefield exposes the problems with established missions. However, wartime innovation is extremely difficult when established missions are failing and armies need new missions to succeed, because feedback from the battlefield is relevant to established missions and not the new mission. In short, according to Rosen, in warfare it is difficult for armies to recognize that they are failing.[76] In the last case study of this work, however, the U.S. Army adapts to the threat of insurgency at a pace and in ways contrary to Rosen's expectations. Senior leaders in the army perceived the disjunction between operations in Iraq and existing doctrine and training, in the absence of significant feedback. They began the relevant doctrinal innovations prior to the change in mission under General Petraeus and his new "strategic measure of effectiveness": securing the population. COIN ideas in the U.S. Army go on to powerfully influence the 2008 edition of *Operations*, the U.S. Army's main war-fighting manual. At least in this case, Rosen is mistaken when he contends, "Wartime innovation is likely to be limited in its impact."[77] Military realism offers a solution to the puzzle that prompted this study, and it is contrary to the expectations of Rosen's approach.

There are additional differences discussed in the case studies, but I will conclude with a final one in the interest of brevity. Both works also examine some of the same historical cases. Rosen discusses the U.S. Army's failure to innovate toward COIN both under pressure from President Kennedy and then in Vietnam.[78] The present work too deals with both of these cases. Thanks to new evidence from primary and secondary sources, I present a picture of the U.S. Army under Kennedy and in Vietnam that is inconsistent with Rosen's assessment. The new perspective of military realism and new evidence provide support for a new interpretation of these key cases.

However, it is not the contention here that Rosen's theory has been invalidated. It would be impossible to make such a claim based on a study of one military organization over time. Many aspects of Rosen's theory remain extremely valuable for understanding military innovation more generally. However, in a number of cases that Rosen claims to explain, military realism actually provides a better explanation and establishes itself as a powerful alternative explanation of doctrinal innovation. In the end, military realism does not supplant Rosen's important work but is distinct from it and challenges it in some areas and cases.

Military Realism and Military Bureaucracy

Bureaucracies by their very nature are supposed to preserve routines and be resistant to change.[79] Prominent bureaucratic theorists argue that militaries are just like other bureaucracies, seeking to avoid uncertainty and increase resources and autonomy.[80] Civilian leaders and others often lament the powerful influence of bureaucratic imperatives on their militaries. In their view, militaries assess threats in light of bureaucratic interests rather than objective national security needs. If they change doctrine, they do so largely to serve bureaucratic objectives.[81] Theorists who use the bureaucratic approach to explain military doctrine argue that military bureaucrats command the doctrinal process, not civilian leaders.[82]

Bureaucratic imperatives have implications for all three of our areas of doctrine. When it comes to the question of nuclear versus conventional missions, military bureaucracies prefer conventional ones. Conventional missions require more resources and generate less uncertainty than untested nuclear missions. Indeed, the economic savings involved was a main attraction of nuclearized Cold War strategies, like massive retaliation, which slashed U.S. Army budgets.[83]

Conversely, some theorists of bureaucracy contend that organizations care more about preserving autonomy than increasing resources.[84] In the U.S. case, making nuclear weapons central to army doctrine undermines its autonomy because nuclear authority rests with civilian leaders.[85] The advent of tactical nuclear weapons exacerbated this problem because civilians, fearful of nuclear escalation, were more likely to interfere with battlefield decisions. Moreover, making the success of doctrine dependent on weapons that civilians might not permit a commander to use generates widespread uncertainty. Thus, to protect their autonomy and avoid uncertainty, army bureaucrats should be especially eager to minimize their reliance upon tactical nuclear weapons.

One might argue, on the other hand, that the army would adopt nuclear missions to attain those new resources in addition to or instead of resources related to conventional forces.[86] To avoid uncertainty, the army would simply integrate nuclear forces into its existing theory of victory. Such integration could also be a bureaucratic means of exerting maximum control over nuclear weapons to preserve autonomy.[87] However, army bureaucrats should not revolutionize the core of doctrine to suit the new weapons because of the resulting uncertainty. Instead, in the case studies of the Cold War U.S. Army that follow, U.S. Army doctrine embraced the nuclear revolution, and especially tactical nuclear weapons, in response to the rising Soviet threat. Bureaucratic concerns were secondary to developing a doctrine that would give the army a fighting chance in the face of shrinking budgets and a powerful enemy.

Regarding offense and defense, the bureaucratic desire for resources, autonomy, and certainty all recommend an offensive theory of victory. In the absence of civilian intervention, Steven Van Evera argues, military bureaucracies "almost invariably purvey offensive ideas, and develop offensive solutions."[88] From a bureaucratic perspective, this aggressive tendency in military doctrine is perfectly rational. If it requires three attackers to subdue one defender, then offense can garner three dollars while defense nets only one. Offensive theories of victory provide more resources than defensive ones. The complexity of offensive doctrines also preserves autonomy by making them opaque to the prying eyes of civilian nonexperts. The offensive also increases certainty by maintaining the initiative in military operations. If a military bureaucracy is imposing its SOPs on its opponent, that is, attacking, it dictates the tempo and direction of combat and places the enemy in an uncertain, reactive position. Conversely, defensive theories of victory cede the initiative to the enemy. Contrary to military realism then, no matter the circumstances, military bureaucrats should push for offensive doctrines.[89] Yet again, however, in the case studies that follow, the U.S. Army adopts defensive theories of victory in their most important doctrine when they face an imbalance of forces vis-à-vis the most dangerous threats. Army doctrine even reinterprets traditionally offensive principles, like the initiative, to support a defensive theory of victory. Based on the imbalance of capabilities, senior army leaders rejected calls from inside and outside the army to make doctrine more offensive.

COIN missions, especially those based on securing the population, should also be anathema to military bureaucrats. COIN missions furnish fewer resources than conventional ones, are highly defensive, and require a combined civil-military strategy that dilutes military autonomy.[90] In this final area of doctrine, the one most closely related to the puzzle at the heart of this book, the U.S. Army again often defies bureaucratic expectations. While COIN is peripheral to doctrine in the face of the Soviet threat, army officers were on the cutting edge of developing concepts for dealing with insurgency. Far from recommending conventional military solutions to insurgency, army officers appreciated the limited applicability of such solutions in COIN operations. Unconventional threats took a central place in army doctrine with the receding of the Soviet threat and reached their zenith in *Operations 2008*.

Bureaucratic forces do exert influence on militaries. Military realism, however, sets out the conditions under which senior leaders will sideline bureaucratic preferences for resources, autonomy, and certainty to enable doctrinal change.[91] Military realism agrees that military officers prefer offensive theories of victory. However, the origin of this preference is the logic of force and not the thirst for resources. Moreover, this preference is not indomitable. When confronted with a materially superior foe, military realists will adopt a defensive theory of victory that exploits the advantages of friction that plague the attacker. Military realism also defines the conditions under which militaries will sacrifice autonomy. Senior military officers sacrifice organizational autonomy, if addressing the most dangerous threats demands a high degree of coordination with other military services, national militaries, or civilian authorities. In addition, when faced with doctrinal dilemmas, military leaders do not limit themselves to in-house solutions. They will reach outside of the organization for alternatives. Such alternatives come from other national militaries, for example. Military organizations will even sacrifice autonomy to produce a doctrine that can plausibly resist the most dangerous threats.

Military Realism and Military Culture

Military cultures are often the result of long and bloody experience. This institutional memory can have significant staying power and often informs the core of military doctrine. Military culture theorists argue that cultural norms shape military doctrine.[92] Cultural norms are intersubjective beliefs that come in two varieties: constitutive norms, which tell actors who they are, and regulative norms, which tell actors what they can and cannot do.[93] A military's unique historical experiences shape its norms and define the "essence" of its culture and the boundaries of doctrinal change.[94] The most important experience, however, is the organization's "foundational war" or "finest hour." The theories of victory and mission priorities at the essential core of doctrine originate here. According to the cultural approach, changes in doctrine are possible but limited to narrow cultural pathways. While doctrine changes, culture does not.[95] Thus, the cultural core of doctrine persists with only some peripheral changes. Senior officers, guardians of culture, exert strict control over any innovations to make sure they fall within cultural boundaries. In terms of threat assessment, the guardians of culture will focus on those threats and capabilities that preserve and promote their culture. The core of doctrine will focus on addressing these culturally approved threats.

A number of cultural theorists argue that across the period examined here U.S. Army culture and its doctrinal preferences are consistent.[96] The culture of the U.S. Army privileges conventional warfare where offensive operations achieve decisive victory.[97] These preferences have their roots in its finest hour, attacking across Europe to end World War II.[98] One of the icons of this experience, General George S. Patton Jr., expressed the army's cultural affinity for offensive theories of victory: "In case of doubt, ATTACK!" A preference for attack over defense became an unquestioned axiom in U.S. Army doctrine.

U.S. Army culture also affects the reception of nuclear and COIN missions in doctrine. Another important cultural norm within the U.S. Army is autonomy from civilian authority.[99] As already noted, civilian control of tactical nuclear weapons would constitute a significant blow to army autonomy. The army preference for autonomy, combined with one for conventional warfare, should ensure that the Cold War U.S. Army resists revolutionizing doctrine to incorporate nuclear weapons. U.S. Army culture should ensure that *Operations* manuals have an offensive theory of victory and favor conventional over nuclear missions. Cultural theorists have also argued that the U.S. Army is culturally opposed to preparing for unconventional forms of warfare, especially COIN.[100] Either the COIN mission will be absent from doctrine, or doctrine will recommend conventional military solutions to the challenge of insurgency.

Military realism anticipates that under certain conditions, the bounds of military culture will be broken. When core missions and theories of victory are inappropriate for addressing a dangerous threat, the U.S. Army will change doctrine accordingly, even if those changes violate its cultural norms. The heart of doctrine will come to reflect the most pressing threats. From 1960 to 2008, U.S. Army doctrine was more responsive to the threat environment than to cultural norms. Senior army leaders did not unreflectively adapt doctrine to the cultural norms of the U.S. Army. On a number of occasions, these leaders recognized the cultural traditions that new doctrines violated and went ahead with the changes anyway. Army doctrine even reinterpreted key doctrinal concepts to suit the threat environment. For instance, army doctrine continually reinterpreted the concept of initiative—a concept intimately linked with offensive warfare and cultural icons like Patton—first to support a defensive theory of victory and then a new COIN doctrine. When it came to COIN, even in the 1960s, U.S. Army officers were in the vanguard of theorizing and took COIN seriously as a solution to some of the problems facing U.S. forces in South Vietnam. In the post–Cold War, when the United States rose to preeminence and the spectrum of threats narrowed, the army gave unconventional warfare a more prominent place in doctrine. Moreover, the population-security variant of COIN that army doctrine espoused was the very type of COIN doctrine that its culture should have rejected. Finally, although the focus here is not on cultural change, it does appear that doctrinal and organizational innovations undertaken to address the most pressing threats changed U.S. Army culture.

The present work challenges other expectations among theorists of military culture. For instance, Long argues that where threats and opportunities are ambiguous, military culture will be at its most powerful.[101] For the U.S. Army, the post–Cold War threat environment was highly ambiguous. Nevertheless, senior U.S. Army leaders began taking unconventional forms of warfare seriously in this period despite their incongruity with U.S. Army culture. Despite the ambiguity of the threat environment, these leaders laid the intellectual groundwork that would support the shift toward COIN in recent wars and recent army doctrine, shifts at odds with U.S. Army culture.

This work also presents a challenge to Elizabeth Kier's *Imagining War*, an exemplary work on the effects of military culture on the choice between offensive and defensive doctrine.[102] Kier argues that the offensive or defensive character of doctrines is determined not by civilian intervention or bureaucratic imperatives but by a military cultural response to civilian military policy.[103] Civilian leaders, moreover, are motivated not by the international balance of power but by the domestic political balance of power, in which the place of the military in society is a vital consideration.[104] However, civilian policy does not decide whether doctrines will be offensive or defensive. Instead, within the bounds set by military policy, the unique culture of the particular military determines whether doctrine is offensive or defensive. Kier argues that culture "consists of many assumptions that are rarely debated and seem so basic that it appears impossible to imagine that things could be different."[105] Military culture sets the bounds within which doctrinal innovation occurs: "The officer corps imagines only certain alternatives."[106] For instance, the French Army before World War II adopted a defensive theory of victory because civilians had reduced the tenure of conscripts from three years to one year. French Army officers could not imagine one-year conscripts executing offensive operations. The result, in the French case, was a defensive theory of victory.

Military realism agrees with Kier's contention that militaries can choose defensive doctrines, contrary to bureaucratic and civilian realist perspectives. However, military realism argues that the resulting defensive doctrine can contravene a military's culture. Cultural traditions, like long-standing doctrinal concepts, are actually open to reinterpretation in the face of dangerous threats. Military realists can imagine and implement countercultural doctrines. The evidence presented here shows a U.S. Army able to move beyond its cultural boundaries in response to the threat environment. In short, the doctrinal imagination of the officer corps was not limited to culturally approved alternatives. However, I agree with Kier's contention that, contrary to civilian realism, civilian leaders are often distracted from the international balance of power by their battles to shift the domestic political balance of power in their favor.[107] Kier convincingly shows that this was the case in France and Britain between the world wars.

The present work also challenges Kier's interpretation of a specific case of doctrinal innovation in the U.S. Army. Drawing on U.S. Army doctrine during the Cold War to make her point, Kier contends that in the 1980s, U.S. Army culture reasserted itself through AirLand Battle doctrine. For Kier, the shift from Active Defense to AirLand Battle, *Operations 1976* and *1982*, respectively, represented a change from a defensive to a culturally approved offensive theory of victory.[108] On the contrary, in the fourth chapter, I show that Active Defense and AirLand Battle had more similarities than differences and that, contrary to cultural expectations, AirLand Battle preserved the defensive theory of victory in army doctrine. During the Cold War, the Soviet threat to Europe grew in relative terms due to reductions in U.S. Army resources and simultaneous increases in Soviet capabilities. To cope, the U.S. Army adopted doctrinal innovations that incorporated nuclear weapons and a defensive theory of victory. At the time, senior army leaders knew these changes were contrary to U.S. Army traditions but championed them regardless. They continually argued that nostalgia for the army's World War II finest hour had to be set aside.

Kier's work remains one of the best examples of cultural theorizing on military innovation, with much to offer military innovation studies. This work does not systematically challenge her insights into the origins of civilian military policy. However, a cursory examination suggests that military realism may also provide an explanation for French Army doctrine before World War II. Reducing the conscript term of service from three years to one year, whatever the domestic political reasons, meant that the French Army would shrink dramatically in the near term while the German Army was growing. A defensive theory of victory would be an appropriate military realist response to this looming imbalance of capabilities.

Cultural theorists like Kier argue that U.S. Army culture has a powerful preference for conventional, offensive doctrine and an aversion to COIN.[109] In these pages, military realism challenges the cultural explanation in each of these areas of doctrine. It argues that under the right conditions, senior leaders in the U.S. Army will transform its doctrine in countercultural ways to address the most pressing threats. As mentioned in the introduction, here military realism supports Patrick Porter's criticism of the "cultural turn" in the study of war and military innovation. Porter argues that the relative material strength or weakness of military forces has a more powerful influence on their choice between conventional or unconventional military strategy than culture. The present work argues that the origin of this unexpected cultural flexibility is the military realist mind-set.

Conclusion

From the discussion above, it should become clear why I selected these three areas of U.S. Army doctrine to evaluate military realism against the alternatives. In each area military realism makes different predictions than the alternatives, in terms of either the innovation process or outcome or both. Both bureaucratic and cultural perspectives expect the U.S. Army to favor conventional military forces and missions over nuclear ones. Conventional forms of warfare promise more resources, autonomy, and certainty to the U.S. Army and hark back to its World War II finest hour. Therefore, the army should not revolutionize its doctrine to make room for these new weapons. On the contrary, if required by the imperatives of the threat environment, military realism anticipates that the army will make major changes to doctrine to accommodate nuclear weapons. These accommodations will be in evidence in doctrine through the revision or removal of culturally approved and bureaucratically beneficial principles of war and doctrinal concepts. Even doctrinal concepts rooted in the cultural traditions of the U.S. Army will be open to revision. If the threat environment demands it, senior army officers will promote doctrinal innovations that call into question the relevance of their formative experiences in the U.S. Army. In other words, they should be able to resist the temptation to fight the last war.

According to many, one of the most sacrosanct doctrinal traditions of the U.S. Army is its preference for the offense. Both bureaucratic and cultural explanations of military innovation expect U.S. Army doctrine to show a persistent preference for an offensive theory of victory, despite changes in the threat environment. Instead, military realism expects the degree to which U.S. Army doctrine is offensive or defensive to oscillate with changes in the threat environment. Military realism concurs that such a preference exists and will find its way into doctrine when the army possesses the material capabilities necessary to execute offensive operations. But senior officers in the U.S. Army will pursue a more defensive theory of victory when the force faces a materially superior foe. The calls for a defensive doctrine will be louder still when geography introduces additional obstacles to the execution of operations against powerful enemies. When menacing nation-states do not populate the threat environment, army doctrine will focus on protecting vital material resources. But even in relatively permissive threat environments, the military realist appreciation for friction should temper doctrinal enthusiasm. In the absence of dangerous enemies, military realists in the army should dwell on the physical friction caused by geography, its deleterious effects on offensive operations, and the advantages it gives to defenders.

Bureaucratic and cultural perspectives also share expectations regarding the reception that the COIN mission will receive in the U.S. Army and its doctrine. COIN missions, especially when they entail an extensive population security role for the army, satisfy few bureaucratic desires. Their emphasis on infantry provides few of the resources that accompany preparations for conventional warfare. The defensive nature of COIN places army forces in a reactive position vis-à-vis the insurgent enemy, thereby increasing uncertainty. Finally, the highly political nature of COIN wars undermines military autonomy through political interference. Culturally, COIN missions are not part of the essence of U.S. Army culture. Such missions do not draw on the cultural traditions of the U.S. Army established during its finest hour. Instead, these traditions favor offensive, conventional warfare. COIN, in contrast, especially when based on population security, is a defensive and unconventional form of warfare abhorrent to the norms of U.S. Army culture.

The military realist mind-set disposes military officers to see insurgency as less threatening than the large military forces of states. Military realism expects, therefore, that in the presence of grave state-based threats, senior officers in the U.S. Army will give the mission of countering insurgents a minor role in its main doctrine. However, when an insurgency represents the most pressing threat facing the United States and its critical material resources, army leaders should adapt doctrine to address this threat, even at the expense of bureaucratic and cultural preferences. For instance, army doctrine will not automatically recommend conventional military solutions to deal with an insurgency.

For civilian realism, the preferences of civilian authorities, rather than those of the institutional army, often shape military doctrine. This theory argues that civilian authorities change national security strategy in response to rising international threats. Civilian officials then reach down into their military organizations, with the help of a military maverick, to overcome the military bureaucracy and make military doctrine consistent with their strategy. Civilian realism assumes that military officers are more concerned with their narrow bureaucratic interests than the international threat environment, whereas civilian leaders are clear-eyed assessors of the international balance of power. Keep in mind, then, when the evidence presented here contradicts bureaucratic explanations, as military realism argues it will, it also contradicts part of the civilian realist explanation.

From 1960 to 2008, civilian realist leaders in the United States should have to actively subvert parochial forces within the American military to make military doctrine respond to international threats. If strategic changes demand changes in U.S. Army doctrine, civilian leaders and mavericks will collaborate to integrate national strategy and U.S. Army doctrine. The present work expects, instead, senior U.S. Army leaders to initiate doctrinal changes when existing doctrine is ill-suited to the gravest threats that face the United States. These leaders perceive dangerous alterations in the threat environment and, when necessary, begin to adjust doctrine prior to intervention by civilians. Moreover, if civilian leaders attempt to impose major doctrinal changes that undermine the ability of the U.S. Army to deal with what its leaders see as the severest threats, the army will resist the imposition. Army doctrine might pay lip service to these innovations—perhaps through peripheral doctrinal changes—to placate civilian authorities, but will not alter the core of its most important doctrine. That being said, civilians can use their authority to accelerate changes already under way in the U.S. Army. Thus, military and civilian realism have different expectations when it comes to the sources and timing of doctrinal change in the U.S. Army.

Through fifty years of U.S. Army innovation across these three areas of doctrine, military realism has expectations contrary to those of the theoretical alternatives. This theoretical opposition is ideal for evaluating the competing explanations. The case-study chapters to follow uncover the forces that shaped, or failed to shape, the U.S. Army's way of warfare over five decades. The findings, I argue, are more consistent with military realism than the theoretical alternatives. Along the way, the story told about the U.S. Army and its doctrine contradicts a number of accepted narratives about America's Army, even narratives widely held within the U.S. Army itself.

2 FLEXIBLE RESPONSE, THE NUCLEAR BATTLEFIELD, AND COUNTERINSURGENCY

Kennedy and Army Doctrine in the 1960s

SCHOLARS OF FOREIGN policy and international relations, and the general public, have been fascinated by the story of the Kennedy administration, of the rise of Camelot and its tragic end. In addition to its spellbinding narrative, however, the Kennedy administration also provides a fertile test bed for theoretical explanations of military innovation. Perhaps no American administration had cast itself as so innovative, as so desirous of discovering "New Frontiers," as so youthful and flexible in mind and body.[1] One look at the U.S. Army of the early '60s, and one can see why theorists of military innovation have attributed its behavior to the management of bureaucrats, the guardians of army culture, or the relentless intervention of civilian realists. The conditions were ripe for army bureaucracy and culture to take the reins of doctrine and twist it to their own ends. However, these internal army forces met a worthy adversary in the person of President Kennedy, who came into office with eyes wide open to the proclivities of bureaucrats and other defenders of the national security status quo. Under these conditions, we would expect one of these theoretical perspectives to win the day. On the contrary, I contend that military realism explains the doctrinal behavior of the U.S. Army under Kennedy better than these alternatives. The international environment that confronted army bureaucracy, culture, and President Kennedy sets the stage.

The International Environment of the Early 1960s

In 1960 John F. Kennedy and his army confronted a threat environment shaped by the bipolar Cold War conflict. According to Kennedy and his predecessors, the central strategic goals of the United States were to secure Europe from Soviet domination and Asia from Chinese domination.[2] The Warsaw Pact and NATO forces were arrayed against each other in Europe, where both sides assumed the Soviets enjoyed major conventional military superiority and where they certainly had numerous geographical advantages. Here Kennedy hoped above all to avoid an inadvertent war leading to a nuclear holocaust.

The thorny problem of how to protect West Berlin, a democratic island in a hostile communist sea, still confronted the U.S. president. During Kennedy's tenure, the Soviets would continue to put pressure on Berlin. Kennedy's response was to call up 150,000 army reserves and increase defense spending. The crisis ended with the building of the Berlin Wall. On the periphery, the Soviets were sponsoring wars of national liberation, insurgent movements like the one that had overtaken China.

To confront these threats, Eisenhower had relied on massive retaliation, an asymmetrical strategy that threatened a devastating nuclear response for actions that threatened vital American interests, such as a Soviet invasion of Western Europe. Kennedy preferred a more symmetrical approach that would confront Soviet aggression at and below the nuclear threshold.[3] Such a strategy was possible because Kennedy believed the U.S. economy was less fragile than Eisenhower had assumed, enabling increased defense spending.[4] To achieve symmetry in Europe, the United States and NATO would have to increase their conventional capabilities.[5] New lower estimates of Soviet military strength emanating from the office of Kennedy's new secretary of defense, Robert McNamara, a member of Kennedy's new "ministry of talent," raised hopes for an effective conventional defense of Europe. These estimates showed near parity between NATO and Warsaw Pact forces in Europe.[6] Limited wars, like Korea, would also require effective conventional forces.

At the nuclear level, despite the election rhetoric surrounding the "missile gap," the Kennedy administration determined that the United States had a marked advantage in strategic nuclear weapons.[7] Kennedy also placed greater emphasis on the periphery than his predecessor did because he thought conflicts there could disturb the balance of power.[8] Kennedy wanted to confront this "monolithic and ruthless conspiracy" by increasing U.S. unconventional and counterinsurgency capabilities.[9] U.S. military advisers would help allies on the periphery resist communist insurgencies. As John Lewis Gaddis characterized it, Kennedy's strategy exposed his "zero-sum" view of international relations in which a gain for communism anywhere was a loss for the United States.[10] In this threat environment, each theoretical alternative has certain expectations for the U.S. Army and its doctrine.

Bureaucracy and Army Doctrine in the Early 1960s

According to bureaucratic explanations of military innovation, militaries are just like other bureaucracies, always seeking to avoid uncertainty and increase resources and autonomy.[11] Militaries assess threats in light of bureaucratic interests and not objective national security needs. If they change doctrine, they do so to serve bureaucratic objectives. The bureaucratization of the U.S. Army had reached its zenith in the 1950s and '60s. Army officers were trading in their "black boots" for the "black shoes" of Wall Street and Madison Avenue.[12] However, the service was adopting more than the attire of the business world. It was also adopting many of its management principles. Under Eisenhower, American land forces had been depleted by the president's preference for nuclear weapons as the guarantor of national security. For the most part, the delivery of such weapons would fall to the U.S. Navy and Air Force, leading to the slashing of army budgets.[13] In some respects, Kennedy's arrival presented army bureaucrats with a perfect opportunity to recover from the damage inflicted by President Eisenhower. With stronger conventional forces, Kennedy argued, the United States could confront the creeping aggression of the Soviets, especially in places such as Berlin, where Soviet actions had harried American leaders and would harry Kennedy, too. In theory, this revival of the conventional mission was a perfect opportunity for army bureaucrats to replenish their coffers after the lean Eisenhower era.[14]

Army bureaucrats should not have been enthusiastic about all of Kennedy's innovations, however. Adding an offensive theory of victory to Kennedy's conventional warfare initiative could increase resources still further.[15] In fact, an offensive theory of victory was already present in the army's most important doctrine at the time: *Field Manual 100-5, Operations 1954,*[16] which was in force when Kennedy took office. It praised the attack and considered all defensive operations as temporary, until the initiative could be seized again by attacking. However, Kennedy wanted the army to be prepared to use conventional forces in a *defensive* role. This aspect of Kennedy's strategy should be one of the hardest to impose on army bureaucrats.

A conventional mission and an offensive theory of victory would also increase army autonomy and reduce uncertainty, two key goals of bureaucracies.[17] Making nuclear weapons central to army doctrine undermined military autonomy because nuclear authority rested with civilian leaders. Kennedy in particular intended to place nuclear weapons, especially the tactical kind, firmly in the hands of civilian leaders.[18] Therefore, making tactical nuclear weapons central to U.S. Army doctrine increased the likelihood of civilian interference in doctrine and tactical decisions. Thus, army bureaucrats should be especially eager to minimize the reliance upon tactical nuclear weapons. If the army holds on to the nuclear mission under Kennedy to secure both conventional and nuclear budgets,[19] to reduce uncertainty the army should simply integrate nuclear forces into traditional conventional missions. This integration would also exert maximum control over those weapons, thereby preserving autonomy while maximizing resources.[20] Such integration avoids the uncertainty of revolutionary change and preserves autonomy. The army should not revolutionize the core of its doctrine to suit the new means because of the uncertainty generated by drastic change. A more conventional doctrine would also reduce uncertainty because the army could draw on its extensive experience fighting conventional wars. Conversely, it had never fought a nuclear war. So based on the implications of the bureaucratic model, army bureaucrats should welcome Kennedy's new strategy of flexible response, with its revival of the conventional option, additional resources, restoration of autonomy, and reduced uncertainty.

At the same time, Kennedy championed one more strategic initiative with consequences for army doctrine. Kennedy wanted the U.S. foreign policy and defense establishment to confront communist insurgencies in the developing world. Militarily, COIN is an unconventional mission that fulfills few bureaucratic desires.[21] For instance, COIN forces are infantry intensive and do not require expensive mechanized platforms. As a 1960s authority on COIN, David Galula, pointed out, "The less [technologically] sophisticated the counterinsurgent forces, the better they are."[22] *Operations 1954* hardly mentioned COIN-like missions. If they make an appearance in the army's most important manual, then army doctrine will advocate conventional military solutions to insurgency. Little innovation should occur. If *Military Review* or *Operations 1962* mention insurgency, they will recommend highly conventional military solutions, rather than unconventional solutions such as civic action and population security or "hearts-and-minds" COIN.[23] Transforming the army to confront guerrillas in the countryside would not improve its finances, strengthen its bureaucracy, or relieve it from the uncertainty of the nuclear age.

Army Culture and Army Doctrine in the Early 1960s

Under the corporate army's three-piece suit, however, its cultural heart still beat. That heart, the essence of army culture, was born in the crucible of its finest hour: *attacking* across Europe to end World War II.[24] Scholars have already used cultural approaches to explain the U.S. Army in the 1960s. John Nagl argues that the British army adapted to COIN in Malaya because colonial policing, which was similar to COIN in a number of ways, shaped its organizational essence. This was not the case for the U.S. Army in the 1960s, whose culture entailed defeating conventional forces in offensive combat reminiscent of World War II.[25] For Andrew Krepinevich, the "army concept" that stifled army adaptation in the 1960s had its origin in the army's finest hour.[26]

When Kennedy became president, the army was fewer than twenty years from that finest hour. Indeed, the vast majority of senior army officers had participated directly in the defeat of Hitler's Germany or Tojo's Japan. In World War II, massed conventional forces in the attack defeated America's enemies and raised army prestige to its pinnacle. For the U.S. Army and its senior leaders in the 1960s, this had been a formative experience, one that defined their identity, telling them who they were and what they could and could not do. The essence of army culture extolled conventional missions and offensive theories of victory in the core of doctrine.[27] Although there is room for tinkering around the edges of doctrine, its core must reflect the cultural essence.[28]

Ironically, one of the most celebrated participants in the army's World War II finest hour, Dwight Eisenhower, threatened its culture with extinction in the 1950s. By making nuclear weapons the focus of U.S. strategy, President Eisenhower undermined an army culture rooted in conventional warfare. In 1957 S. L. A. Marshall argued, "Nuclear munitions were a passing fad," and "the Army must not deny its cultural heritage." To do so, he warned, "flew in the face of the American military experience and invited cultural collapse."[29] In addition, U.S. army culture especially values its autonomy from political interference. Tight civilian control of tactical nuclear weapons represented a significant blow to that autonomy, another cultural rationale for reducing doctrinal reliance on tactical nuclear weapons.[30]

Under Kennedy, flexible response provided the U.S. Army with a perfect opportunity to fulfill some of its cultural goals, such as greater emphasis on conventional over nuclear forces and the concomitant increases in autonomy. If military culture is as strong as its proponents expect, Kennedy's conventional-forces initiative should have suited army culture down to the ground. However, an army culture steeped in offense should resist Kennedy's desire to cast those conventional forces in a defensive role. Therefore, along with army bureaucrats, army cultural custodians should have held on to the offensive theory of victory in *Operations 1954*, preserving it into *Operations 1962* under Kennedy. For different reasons, though, army culture and bureaucracy should also push to downplay the nuclear mission and return to its conventional-warfare roots. As the bureaucratic explanation expects, if the army does retain the nuclear mission, it should integrate these new weapons into a highly conventional doctrine consistent with its culture.

Army culture and bureaucracy are united in not only what they approve but also what they reject. Along with its bureaucrats, the stewards of army culture should see to it that COIN did not become a mission priority in army doctrine. COIN missions are contrary to the conventional essence of army culture.[31] COIN concepts that emphasize the importance of civic over military action would be especially open to ridicule from a culture that praised aggression and taking the initiative through attack. The army's most important war-fighting manual, *Operations*, would be least likely to give such missions pride of place. If COIN makes an appearance in the *Operations* manual, the manual will advocate conventional military solutions to insurgency consistent with the cultural essence of the army. Therefore, Kennedy's demands to make COIN a main mission of the army should have run aground on the shoals of army bureaucracy *and* army culture. The army might meet Kennedy's COIN initiatives with token peripheral changes but would never allow it to infiltrate the core of army doctrine. Cultural artifacts, like *Military Review*, should reflect these cultural priorities. The army should resist Kennedy's COIN initiatives as contrary to its cultural essence.[32] There were numerous reasons to believe that U.S. Army culture would win the day in the struggle over early 1960s army doctrine.

Civilian Realism and Army Doctrine in the Early 1960s

As set out in the previous chapter, civilian realism argues that civilian leaders are careful observers of the international threat environment, unlike their military subordinates who are blinded by bureaucratic self-interest. Civilians formulate new strategy based on the international balance of power. Through handpicked military mavericks, civilians impose their strategy on a resistant military bureaucracy, which inevitably opposes the elements of civilian strategy that do not further bureaucratic priorities.[33] In terms of timing, civilian strategic ideas are the catalyst for doctrinal change, which civilians impose on their military organization with the help of a military maverick.[34]

According to civilian realism, the bipolar structure of the Cold War should simplify Kennedy's task because of the absence of the complex, multipolar diplomacy that bedeviled heads of state prior to both world wars. Kennedy intervened in the U.S. military to make its organization and doctrine consistent with his new strategy of flexible response. He targeted the U.S. Army in particular for change. Kennedy's strategy had implications for each key area of army doctrine. Kennedy sought to increase conventional and COIN capabilities in the army. A conventional military capability would give the United States a step on the escalatory ladder before nuclear use, thereby strengthening deterrence through more credible threats.[35] Kennedy would resort to nuclear weapons only once conventional means failed.[36] The young president did not ignore nuclear weapons but wanted conventional preliminaries to be available. Kennedy advocated a more defensive, scalable military strategy that would provide time for diplomacy to function prior to scaling up to an all-or-nothing nuclear exchange. However, to avoid inadvertent escalation, Kennedy would reduce U.S. dependence on *tactical* nuclear weapons.

Thinking like a civilian realist, Kennedy saw bureaucracies as the biggest obstacle to his new strategy. "Damn it," he railed, "[National Security Adviser McGeorge] Bundy and I get more done in one day at the White House than they do in six months at the State Department."[37] Kennedy also felt like he was combating cultural forces in the army. As historian Robert Dallek put it, Kennedy shared the popular conception that "generals always prepare to fight the last war."[38] Interestingly, to overcome the army's bureaucracy, Kennedy employed exactly the mechanism civilian realism expects: a military maverick.[39] Kennedy enlisted retired general Maxwell D. Taylor to help him make the U.S. government and defense establishment capable of flexible response.[40] At the same time, however, Kennedy wanted the army to counter communist insurgencies in the developing world. Kennedy saw communist insurgencies as a threat to the balance of power.

Under the watchful eye of Kennedy's maverick, *Operations 1962* should emphasize both conventional and nuclear missions, have a defensive theory of victory, and make COIN a priority. These innovations in civilian strategy should precede innovations in the military, which they impose on the army bureaucracy. The most difficult changes should be forcing a defensive theory of victory and COIN mission on the army; both these forms of warfare are contrary to bureaucratic interests and cultural preferences.[41] Army bureaucrats and cultural guardians presented a unified front opposed to Kennedy's initiatives. If civilian realism is correct, *Operations* manuals and *Military Review* should advocate offensive, conventional doctrine prior to Kennedy's arrival but then shift toward a defensive doctrine focused evenly on both conventional and nuclear weapons. *Operations 1962* should also make COIN a priority after its neglect in previous manuals. COIN innovations should begin in civilian circles and then infiltrate the military bureaucracy.

Military Realism and Army Doctrine in the Early 1960s

According to military realism, military realist concerns for addressing the most dangerous threats should guide continuity and change in the core of U.S. Army doctrine under Kennedy. The most dangerous threat at the time was the USSR. The Soviets possessed both conventional and nuclear capabilities and enjoyed numerous material advantages, in terms of forces in existence and geography. To overcome these advantages, military realism anticipates that *Operations 1962* will keep the nuclear mission at the core of army doctrine. Military realists will make tactical nuclear weapons a key part of army doctrine if needed to address the most dangerous threat, even if adopting such weapons requires major doctrinal innovations contrary to army culture and bureaucratic desires. The military realist perception of the balance of material capabilities should determine the degree to which 1960s doctrine has an offensive or defensive theory of victory. If senior army leaders perceive a material mismatch between NATO and Soviet forces in Europe, for instance, army doctrine should move toward a more defensive theory of victory.

Finally, military realists should not make COIN a mission priority. Army resources were limited, and insurgencies did not represent the most dangerous threat in the early '60s. However, insurgencies were capturing territory in the Cold War, most notably China. So military realists should not dismiss them out of hand. Military realism does not imply, as bureaucratic and cultural theories do, that discussions of COIN in *Operations 1962* will propose conventional military solutions to insurgencies. To preserve or change doctrine, senior officers should bypass bureaucratic and cultural obstacles. Military realism expects that articles in *Military Review* should discuss the implications of nuclear weapons, defensive theories of victory, and unconventional solutions to insurgency as much as or more than conventional warfare and the army's finest hour. Regarding the timing of doctrinal innovations, military realists can implement major doctrinal changes before civilian realists and their military mavericks step in.

These then are the expectations of military realism for army doctrine in the shadow of "Camelot's Court."[42] Bureaucratic, cultural, and civilian realist forces often push doctrine in directions contrary to the expectations of military realism. Indeed, as argued above, the conditions in the early 1960s were ripe for the competing explanations to triumph. If, on the other hand, military realism wins the day, this case study is strong evidence in favor of this new explanation of military innovation.

Nuclear and Conventional Missions in the Early 1960s

By the early 1960s, nuclear weapons had drastically changed how people thought about war and peace. It had taken the mobilization of entire societies and five years of global war to level the metropolises of Germany and Japan. With the advent of nuclear weapons and advancements in their means of delivery, the destructive power greater than that which had set the Axis states ablaze could be unleashed in hours instead of years.[43] In the 1950s and '60s, technological developments moved nuclear weapons from the realm of strategy, targeting enemy cities, to the realm of tactics, targeting enemy formations on the battlefield. Footage from training exercises at the time shows American soldiers huddled in trenches while the blast wave from a tactical nuclear weapon passes over their heads. Like their World War I predecessors, these soldiers then went over the top, but this time they advanced under the shadow of a mushroom cloud reaching thousands of feet into the air.[44] Significant disagreements about the meaning of the nuclear revolution for national security overshadowed the foreign policy of the new Kennedy administration. Early in the administration, civilian and military leaders had very different views of the utility of nuclear weapons and the role that they would play in the new strategy of flexible response.

President Kennedy was extremely critical of the strategy of massive retaliation. To implement his new strategy, executive power had to overcome bureaucratic inertia.[45] To combat the partisans of massive retaliation, Kennedy brought fresh blood into his administration, ranging from the former chief executive officer of Ford Motor Company Secretary of Defense Robert S. McNamara to a former Harvard dean, National Security Adviser McGeorge Bundy.[46] Kennedy hoped this "ministry of talent" would shake up the administration of American government.[47] His government would bring civilian and military bureaucrats to heel. Kennedy was pessimistic about professional military recommendations because he believed they represented parochial interests and did not consider the broader political context of the Cold War. Moreover, he did not consider military officers particularly intelligent.[48] Said Kennedy of military officers in the Pentagon: "They haven't any brains."[49]

The failure of his military advisers to predict the outcome of the Bay of Pigs debacle had soured the president on the military subordinates he had inherited from Eisenhower.[50] For his strategic transformation, Kennedy enlisted a stalwart critic of massive retaliation and advocate of flexible response: former army chief of staff Maxwell D. Taylor.[51] Like the president, Taylor backed increases in conventional forces.[52] Taylor helped design the pentomic division and was army chief of staff from 1955 to 1959. However, he had retired in protest because of how massive retaliation had degraded the land army.[53] In a new position, military representative to the president, Taylor had great influence and audited military advice for Kennedy.[54] Robert Kennedy argued, "Every decision that the President made on foreign policy was cleared through Maxwell Taylor. . . . He was in seeing the President continuously."[55] Kennedy had selected his maverick.

Flexible response was also attractive for domestic political reasons. In the 1960 presidential election, Kennedy was running against Eisenhower's vice president, Richard Nixon.[56] Flexible response was a clear departure from Eisenhower's—and by implication Nixon's—strategy of massive retaliation. Kennedy wanted to give the American people a clear choice between staying with massive retaliation and setting out for a "new frontier" with a new strategy.[57] Contradicting civilian realism but corroborating Kier's argument, domestic political concerns influenced Kennedy's assessment of national security strategy.[58]

In February 1961, Secretary of Defense Robert McNamara informed Kennedy that U.S. forces overseas were oriented toward "nuclear war . . . at the expense of their ability to wage" conventional war. Instead, their "*primary* mission" should be "non-nuclear warfare."[59] McNamara also argued that previous estimates of 175 Soviet divisions facing NATO were inflated. With additional conventional capabilities, but not additional units, NATO forces could mount a conventional defense of Europe.[60] McNamara blamed the overestimation of Soviet strength on low-level military bureaucrats trying to gain "more forces and higher budgets."[61] McNamara and his staff dismissed subsequent army demands for more conventional forces partly on these grounds. McNamara used theories of bureaucratic motivations to dismiss military advice that was contrary to the president's policy initiatives.

However, the president could not ignore nuclear weapons. Indeed, Kennedy ordered a strategic missile buildup, even after he recognized the "missile gap" as a fiction. However, Kennedy feared inadvertent nuclear escalation, especially by field commanders using delegated launch authority to fire tactical nuclear weapons.[62] In 1962 the Basic National Security Policy (BNSP) drew an analogy between nuclear crises and the July crisis of 1914, in which military plans overtook critical diplomacy. To avoid a nuclear July crisis, these weapons had to be tightly controlled by civilian leaders.[63] Moreover, distinctions between tactical and strategic nuclear weapons were meaningless. Using battlefield nuclear weapons, the BNSP stated, would "rapidly lead to general nuclear war."[64] Other civilian advisers thought their use "was politically un-thinkable and would destroy NATO."[65] In June 1961, McNamara concurred, saying, "Once you use them, you use everything else. You can't keep them lim-ited. You'll destroy Europe, everything."[66] Consequently, civilian leaders in the early 1960s restricted the deployment of tactical nuclear weapons.[67]

Under massive retaliation, the army had developed a nuclear-centric orga-nization and doctrine through the "pentomic divisions" and *Operations 1954*, respectively. The new regime would revise both. In May 1961, McNamara recommended an alternative divisional organization to replace the pentom-ic divisions: the Reorganization Objectives Army Division. ROAD increased conventional firepower and mobility, facilitating flexible response through the application of "measured force without threatening nuclear devastation." Each ROAD division included three brigades that commanders could tailor to their mission with different types of infantry, airborne, or armored battalions. Tailoring would increase flexibility and ready the army for a "wide variety of worldwide requirements," that is, for a flexible response.[68] After receiving this report, Kennedy announced ROAD to Congress as a decisive move away from massive retaliation and toward flexible response, thereby fulfilling an import-ant campaign promise.[69]

Consistent with civilian realism, civilian authorities sought to change the army's main mission to suit civilian strategy. They even employed a military maverick, General Taylor, to assist. Yet what appears to have been a slam dunk for civilian realism is less convincing when one examines the *process* and *tim-ing* of doctrinal change and continuity. The U.S. Army actually initiated the ROAD redesign prior to Kennedy's initiatives, and it represented a refinement of army organization for the nuclear battlefield, not a departure from past doc-trine and organization.

Kennedy's Army and Nuclear and Conventional Missions

Senior army officers considered the defense of Europe their central mission and failure there the most dangerous threat. According to Army Chief of Staff George Decker, "Our primary interest must be in Europe. . . . [T]o lose in Europe would be fatal."[70] However, senior officers were not as optimistic as McNamara about a *conventional* defense of Europe. Decker thought such a de-fense would require several additional divisions, increases McNamara reject-ed.[71] Without additional forces, stopping a Soviet conventional assault would require tactical nuclear weapons.[72] Only by these means, senior army officers argued, could NATO counter the offensive armored thrust at the core of Soviet military doctrine. Soviet doctrine also assumed its commanders could use tactical nuclear weapons to support the maneuver of their armored units.[73] Moreover, the Soviets had the forces to execute this doctrine, possessing 50 percent more tanks than NATO forces. McNamara's new conventional-forces assessment acknowledged this disparity in armor but dismissed it because NATO forces were stronger in other areas.[74] Later, Alain Enthoven, one of the architects of the Office of the Secretary of Defense estimates, recognized that simply counting forces was insufficient for formulating a strategy for NATO. Moreover, the OSD estimates included all NATO reserves, which, even by 1968, the alliance could not integrate into fighting units in Europe.[75] Geographically, the closer proximity of Soviet reserves and the great distances army reserves would have to travel made it likely that early in a European conflict, the Soviets would have significant advantages. From the military realist perspective, the Soviets possessed the forces in being (that is, readiness), the doctrine, and the geographical advantages to execute decisive escalation through offensive operations. NATO conventional forces in Europe did not have the strength to resist them. Unlike military realists in the army, McNamara's civilian realist assessment of the military balance did not consider Soviet military doctrine.

Army officers also disagreed with civilians about the escalatory potential of battlefield nuclear weapons. Civilians' arguments that the use of tactical nuclear weapons was "politically unthinkable" and would "destroy Europe" could not prevent their use. After all, in the living memory of civilian and military leaders, Europe *had* been destroyed. Moreover, World War II had shown clearly that people could fight on even when the enemy reduced their cities to smoking ruins. From a military realist perspective, the destruction of Europe may have been "politically unthinkable," but it was not impossible. Indeed, it had happened in living memory. Nor were military realists alone in their assessment of the utility of tactical nuclear weapons. At the time, foreign policy intellectuals such as Henry Kissinger and Raymond Aron argued that military forces could use tactical nuclear weapons without its leading to general nuclear war.[76] Moreover, the doctrine of the most dangerous threat, the Soviet military, assumed its forces could use tactical nuclear weapons in a limited way to support battlefield maneuver. Because of the imbalance of forces in Europe, tactical nuclear weapons were the only plausible means of responding if the Soviets enacted their doctrine. For the leaders of the army, nuclear weapons were not a "passing fad" but a dangerous reality.

This did not mean that the army was satisfied with its present organization and doctrine. As early as 1956, long before civilian officials sought to replace them, senior army leaders considered the pentomic division and *Operations 1954* failures and began designing alternatives. According to Kretchik, Generals George Decker, Hamilton Howze, Donald V. Bennett, and Paul L. Freeman considered the pentomic concept "farcical" and tried to reduce the nuclear focus in army instruction and doctrine.[77] General Decker saw the weaknesses of the pentomic system in the late 1950s while in command in South Korea. In response, when he became army chief of staff, Decker began developing its replacement with the help of his vice chief of staff and former deputy chief of staff for military operations (DCSOPS), General Clyde Eddleman.[78] Prior to joining Decker, Eddleman had helped stand up the new West German Army. This new force, which would help meet the first waves of a Soviet assault on Europe, employed an innovative organization. The Bundeswehr, as the new army was known, tailored its divisions through interchangeable brigades of infantry, armor, and mechanized infantry.[79] Eddleman brought this tailoring concept to the development of ROAD.

Whereas five pentomic battle groups made up a pentomic division, three brigades with three to five interchangeable battalions made up a ROAD division. This was a return to the triangular divisional structure of World War II. Andrew Bacevich and others have argued that the adoption of ROAD was a return to a conventional-warfare doctrine consistent with the preferences of army bureaucrats and cultural guardians. With the rise of flexible response, the army no longer needed a nuclear doctrine to compete for massive retaliation dollars.[80] However, this claim is not borne out by the evidence.

After World War II, the army began revising its understanding of warfare to accommodate the advent of nuclear weapons. As CGSC faculty member Colonel Victor Hobson wrote in 1957 in *Military Review*, although the experience of World War II had been a valuable guide to doctrine in the past, new doctrine had to recognize that "the battlefield of the future must be viewed in the light of an environment which is completely new, novel, and different."[81] At the beginning of Hobson's piece, a note from the editors of the CGSC journal assured its readers that this piece was consistent with army doctrine. As another *Military Review* article of the previous year noted, "We can no longer quote the drills and tactical moves of the last war."[82] This echoes Chief of Staff Taylor's contention at the beginning of the pentomic reorganization that "the Army is burning its military text books."[83] The result was an army doctrine and organization that focused on the ability to disperse and reconcentrate rapidly in the face of nuclear attack. Gone were the days when massed army formations sought the enemy for decisive battle; forces organized in this way would now be vulnerable to wholesale destruction by battlefield nuclear weapons. Unexpectedly, the army establishment was pointing out the limited applicability of experience gained from its World War II finest hour. However, in the end, senior army leaders thought the pentomic concept overreached by placing too much stock in nuclear weapons. This resistance among senior officers likely sprang in part from the unilateral way in which Taylor imposed the pentomic reorganization on the army.[84]

Instead of ignoring them in favor of a conventional organization, the new ROAD divisions would help to overcome the doctrinal dilemmas of the nuclear battlefield, which had given birth to the pentomic division. For instance, a ROAD division was more survivable than a pentomic battle group. The ROAD divisions had better dispersion, a key to survival on a battlefield scorched by nuclear weapons. If one pentomic battle group was destroyed, 20 percent of the entire division would be lost, while one lost ROAD battalion would mean only 11 percent attrition.[85] General Decker also pushed for the mechanization of infantry because the added mobility would increase dispersion and enable army forces in Europe to fight outnumbered.[86]

Helicopters in particular would increase mobility and dispersion, facilitate intelligence gathering, and strengthen command and control of dispersed units. In 1957 General Hamilton H. Howze, the father of the airmobile concept, advocated the use of helicopters in an antiarmor role on the nuclear battlefield in Europe. The 1963 Howze Board reiterated this role for the helicopter.[87] Like mechanized infantry, helicopter mobility was ideal for fighting against a materially superior foe in Europe whose doctrine called for major armored thrusts, supported by tactical nuclear weapons if necessary. Therefore, though often associated with guerrilla warfare in the popular imagination, the army originally developed helicopters with the nuclear battlefield in mind.[88]

On April 4, 1961, Continental Army Command (CONARC) briefed the ROAD concept to General Decker. Decker was only partly satisfied. He ordered a third Davy Crockett tactical nuclear weapon for each infantry battalion and reconnaissance squadron. Decker thereby increased rather than decreased the role of nuclear weapons in ROAD, showing that ROAD was not a renunciation of battlefield nuclear weapons as some contend.[89] In addition, although Decker recognized the value of tailoring for flexible response, the army had to balance "strategic mobility" with "tactical utility."[90] Light forces that could go anywhere in the world on short notice were not heavy enough to counter Soviet armor in Europe. Here the U.S. Army confronted a problem it would struggle with perennially. Its forces were either "too light to fight" or "too fat to fly."[91]

Given the gravity of the Soviet threat, the majority of army divisions would be fixed, heavier divisions without tailorable battalions. CONARC made all of the changes Decker ordered.[92]

For Decker, the ROAD reorganization was important, but organization without doctrine was like bricks without mortar. Decker described doctrine as the "cement that binds a military organization into an effective fighting unit."[93] In the early '60s, *Operations* manuals were developed and written at the CGSC, where army leaders closely integrated them with the instruction meant to prepare aspiring senior officers for conflict.[94] *Operations 1962* was the doctrine for ROAD and a repudiation of massive retaliation in favor of a version of flexible response. General Harold K. Johnson was commandant of the CGSC when officers there wrote *Operations 1962*. According to Johnson, massive retaliation had placed too much emphasis on destruction. The effective use of military force did involve destruction by firepower, but fire was useless without maneuver. Only maneuver supported by fire could take control of territory.[95] Fire alone could not achieve a decision.[96] Massive retaliation put too much faith in firepower at the expense of maneuver. In remarks clearly aimed at massive retaliation, *Operations 1962* argued that the army of the 1960s was ready "to defend land, people, and resources *without destroying them*," had "alternatives other than total nuclear war or inaction," and could not, therefore, "be blackmailed into accepting marginal or creeping [Soviet] aggression."[97] But army criticism of massive retaliation was not new. The U.S. Army chief of staff from 1955 to 1959 was none other than General Maxwell Taylor, a well-known critic of massive retaliation and advocate of the pentomic divisions, flexible response, and tactical nuclear weapons. During Taylor's tenure, the CGSC conducted a study on limited nuclear war. A 1957 *Military Review* article summarized its finding that such "creeping aggression" was "difficult to deter with a thermonuclear threat."[98] However, army doctrine was not consigning nuclear weapons to the dustbin of history. The "alternatives" to massive retaliation included the use of tactical nuclear weapons.

For the army, tactical nuclear weapons were central to flexible response. As early as 1957, General Clyde Eddleman, then DCSOPS, before helping Decker design ROAD as vice chief of the army, argued that "flexibility in the application of atomic weapons" was essential to a flexible "strategic concept" for the U.S. Army.[99] This link between tactical nuclear weapons and flexible response persisted into the Kennedy era. According to the 1962 edition of *Operations*, battlefield nuclear weapons had many advantages. Tactical nuclear weapons increased combat power and enhanced capabilities.[100] Moreover, the army had optimized ROAD divisions to exploit these advantages.[101] Contrary to the views of civilian leaders, for the army the limited use of battlefield nuclear weapons was an essential part of flexible response because they could resist an overwhelming conventional attack and enable the maneuver of ground forces.[102]

From a bureaucratic and cultural perspective, one might expect the army to keep tactical nuclear weapons on board to garner additional resources. However, the army should co-opt nuclear weapons into traditional doctrine. The army should not allow these weapons to revolutionize their doctrine and organization, because that would produce major uncertainty and result in a doctrine that did not reflect army culture. But the U.S. Army did just that, changing doctrine and organization in major ways to make the most of tactical nuclear weapons, first with the pentomic concept and then with ROAD. As evidence, the trends of articles published in *Military Review*, the journal of the CGSC where *Operations '62* took shape, shows the priority given to solving the dilemmas of the nuclear battlefield over the reliving of the army's finest hour. According to faculty at the CGSC, "The atomic battlefield picture provide[d] the framework for the entire doctrinal effort."[103] At no time in the relevant period did the number of articles discussing the army's finest hour ever approach the number of articles discussing the implications of strategic and tactical nuclear weapons. In fact, from 1958 to 1961 there were no articles published about World War II in *Military Review*. Some might claim that the Civil War, and not World War II, was the formative experience of the army.[104] However, contributors to *Military Review* wrote only slightly more articles on the Civil War than they did on World War II: 6 in total between 1957 and 1962. Most revealingly, 2 of the 6 pieces discussed how the advent of tactical nuclear weapons would have drastically changed the conduct of the Civil War.[105] As the CGSC faculty pointed out, "There [was] no room for nostalgia" when it came to understanding warfare in the nuclear age.[106]

In his most recent treatment of the U.S. Army and the atomic battlefield, Brian McAllister Linn points out that the number of articles on nuclear weapons in *Military Review* declined over time, supporting his contention that the army turned away from the nuclear battlefield in the 1960s. Between 1954 and 1959, Linn points out, the journal published 142 articles on atomic warfare, but only 43 between 1960 and 1969.[107] These numbers are somewhat misleading, however. Tracking proportion of articles rather than number is a more accurate way of assessing this trend because the number of articles per issue varied from year to year, with a high of 168 articles published in 1957 and a low of 136 in 1962.[108] While the number of articles declined, the proportion of articles on nuclear weapons, which peaked at 20 percent in 1958, still constituted roughly between 10 percent and 15 percent between 1959 and 1962, the period during and just after the development of ROAD and the publication of *Operations 1962*. This trend even followed the army into the Johnson era and Vietnam, with articles on nuclear weapons accounting for 8 percent in 1964, 7 percent in 1966, and 10 percent in 1967. In contrast, articles on World War II were absent from 1959 to 1961 and peaked at just 2 percent in 1962. Between 1963 and 1968, articles dealing with World War II hovered between 3 percent and 0.5 percent. Admittedly, discussion of the doctrinal implications of nuclear weapons in *Military Review* gradually declined after 1958. But this marks the period already mentioned when senior army leaders recognized that the pentomic concept had gone too far and needed revision. In response, however, as subsequent trends in *Military Review* show, the army did not abandon preparations for the nuclear battlefield for World War II conventional-warfare nostalgia.

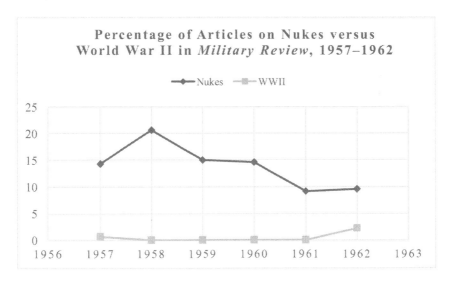

The observed trend in *Military Review* is much more consistent with military realism, which expects nuclear weapons to be central to army thinking. This trend does not show an army set in its ways but reveals one that strove to adapt doctrine to a revolutionary form of warfare that was the most plausible means of countering the most dangerous threat. There was a decline in pieces on nuclear weapons beginning after 1958 once the army had decided on dispersion and mobility as the answers to the challenges of the nuclear battle-field. Contrary to civilian realism, this downward trend began before Kennedy's conventional-forces initiatives.

In summary, long before Kennedy became president, the army perceived the weaknesses of the pentomic concept and began working to replace it to better address the most dangerous threat. The army agreed with civilian officials that the pentomic division and *Operations 1954* were problematic.[109] However, ROAD and *Operations 1962* did not seek to downplay the nuclear mission in favor of a conventional one. Instead, tactical nuclear weapons remained central to army organization and doctrine. General Decker increased the number of tactical nuclear weapons assigned to each ROAD division, further evidence that the army was not putting these weapons to one side in the 1960s. Contrary to civilian realism, civilian realists did not impose doctrinal and organizational innovation on a recalcitrant military bureaucracy. Military realists in the army clearly saw the threat posed by Soviet forces in Europe. They changed organization and doctrine before civilian realists intervened. Moreover, they did not accept elements of civilian strategy that removed the means to address that threat—tactical nuclear weapons—even though a more conventional mission would have been consistent with bureaucratic preferences and army culture.[110] Interestingly, the U.S. Army of the 1960s confronted a similar challenge to the land armies of World War I: developing doctrine to "conduct meaningful military operations in the face of radical firepower."[111] In response, Stephen Biddle argues, World War I commanders developed the modern system of combined arms. The U.S. Army also innovated in the face of this radical challenge. Given the imbalance of capabilities, military realists in the army embraced the nuclear mission and changed doctrine in surprising ways to integrate these weapons into war fighting. In short, when Kennedy and McNamara ordered the replacement of the pentomic concept, they were pushing against an open door, one the army began to open almost five years before Kennedy's election. Moreover, the U.S. Army interpretation of flexible response guided the resulting innovations more than the civilian version.

Kennedy's Military Maverick

Where was Kennedy's "military maverick," General Taylor, in all this? According to the maverick mechanism, Taylor should have headed off the disintegration of civilian and army views of flexible response. In fact, army officers were concerned that Taylor might disrupt the ROAD reorganization.[112] Although well placed to intervene, Taylor had almost no role in ROAD.

According to Decker, Taylor did have "several questions" about ROAD, but instead of answering them McNamara "just let the matter drift" and Taylor did not persist.[113]

If Taylor was not an effective maverick with ROAD, he was even less so with tactical nuclear weapons. As army chief of staff, Taylor oversaw the design of the pentomic divisions and doctrine and promoted tactical nuclear weapons in doctrine. Like senior army officers and *Operations 1962*, Taylor thought battlefield nuclear weapons were an essential part of flexible response and that the United States should increase their numbers. Under Kennedy, Taylor objected to drafts of the BNSP because they dismissed tactical nuclear weapons. The Joint Chiefs of Staff (JCS) agreed, arguing that the strategic thinking embodied in BNSP drafts downplayed tactical nuclear weapons in a way that was "unjustified."[114] Taylor used his considerable influence with the president to persuade Kennedy of the utility of these much-maligned weapons. In addition, Taylor pointed out to Kennedy that the army had been developing doctrine and forces suitable for the nuclear battlefield since the 1950s.[115] Other senior military officers, like General Lauris Norstad, also confronted Kennedy with the need for tactical nuclear weapons as an escalatory step prior to a general nuclear war.[116] Therefore, Taylor did not interfere with ROAD because he approved of its determination to preserve the tactical nuclear mission for the army. Contrary to the logic of civilian realism, Kennedy's military maverick was more in step with army senior leadership than with his civilian patron.

The persistence of Taylor and other senior officers paid off. In May 1962, four months after the publication of the new *Operations* manual, McNamara ordered a study of tactical nuclear weapons.[117] In fact, the army officer whom McNamara chose to conduct the study was none other than General Harold K. Johnson, fresh from leading the army's Command and General Staff College, where he oversaw the writing of *Operations 1962* and was in charge of developing new nuclear battlefield doctrine.[118] From July to October 1962, he conducted the study for McNamara and argued, like *Operations 1962* and Generals Decker, Norstad, and Taylor, for the continued utility of tactical nuclear weapons. Johnson also concurred that the United States should increase the number and variety of tactical nuclear weapons in its arsenal.[119] By 1964 McNamara had accepted the close integration of conventional and tactical nuclear forces at the heart of ROAD and *Operations 1962*. The administration increased the number of U.S. tactical nuclear weapons, and even the State Department withdrew its objections to expanding tactical nuclear weapons in Europe.[120] Francis Gavin argues that Kennedy agreed to these changes to reassure NATO allies disconcerted by his conventional-forces initiative.[121] However, military realists in the U.S. Army were an integral part of making flexible response more acceptable to NATO allies by ensuring that it retained tactical nuclear options. In the end, Kennedy's military maverick did more to bring civilian strategy into line with army doctrine than vice versa. Here again, as with ROAD, military realism's expectations of the timing of doctrinal change are supported, while those of civilian realism are not. Rather than being compelled to respond to the threat environment by clear-seeing civilians, military realists convinced civilian leaders to change their strategy to reflect the threat environment, reversing the causal relationship proposed by civilian realism. The revolutionary means of violent escalation ushered in by the nuclear revolution could not be uninvented. In fact, tactical nuclear weapons might have been the only means of overcoming the numerous material advantages enjoyed by the most dangerous adversary.

Offense, Defense, and the Principles of War in *Operations 1962*

There is significant evidence that military officers prefer offensive doctrines. Recall General George S. Patton Jr.'s remark: "In case of doubt, ATTACK!" This simple statement expressed what many consider a permanent truth of warfare: grasping the initiative through attack has many advantages. One of those advantages is that attack forces the enemy into a reactive position. Forcing the enemy to fight for his survival with an unexpected attack obliterates any plans that he was hatching. For those outside the military profession, this faith in the attack and in aggressive action can be alarming. Pronouncements like Patton's reinforce the popular view that military officers are highly aggressive and constantly looking for opportunities to ply their bloody craft.

For President Kennedy, Patton's advice was particularly alarming for an army armed with nuclear weapons. In the 1960s, the army's World War II finest hour was still fresh in the memory of its leaders, most of whom had participated in it directly. Indeed, Kennedy was replacing Patton's commanding officer, Dwight Eisenhower, as commander in chief. If it had not been for his premature death in a car accident not long after the surrender of Germany, General Patton would have had a powerful influence on the post–World War II U.S. Army. Even in his absence, however, Patton's aggressive spirit should still animate U.S. Army culture and appeal to army bureaucrats. These forces should mount a formidable attack against Kennedy's promotion of a more defensive strategy. If the army of the 1960s preferred an offensive theory of victory, the surest place to look for it is in the *Operations* manual.

The 1962 manual discussed offense and defense in its chapters "Principles of War" and "Conduct of Battle." The principles had guided army doctrine since the 1920s and had expressed a distinct preference for offense.[122] Both *Operations 1954* and *1962* discussed the principles of war. The first principle of war states that all military operations "must be directed toward a clearly defined, decisive and attainable objective." The "ultimate military object" is the physical destruction of enemy capabilities. The second principle, the principle of the offense, enacts this "ultimate military object." According to the principles of war, *only* offensive action achieves "decisive results," that is, the destruction of enemy capabilities. The defense, on the other hand, is only a "temporary expedient" until offense is possible.[123] Therefore, the principles of war are an expression of the military preference for offense. In fact, based on the inclusion of the principles of war, Ingo Trauschweizer recently argued that the 1962 manual had an offensive theory of victory.[124]

However, stating the principle of the offense and advocating an offensive theory of victory are not the same thing. While the principles of war express the military preference for offense, in the next chapter, "Conduct of Battle," *Operations 1962* tempers this preference and highlights the power of defense. Here, the military realist preference for offense meets its appreciation of friction and the power of defense. Following the principles of war, *Operations 1954* had argued that defense was a temporary expedient until conditions favored the offense.[125] The 1962 manual, on the other hand, shifted away from a focus on the principles of war.[126] In fact, it argued against blind adherence to the principles. For instance, contrary to the principle of the offense, the new manual argued that defensive operations could "prevent, resist, or *destroy* an enemy attack."[127] In addition, forces engaged in the defense could actually repel an attacking force by "*destroying* or ejecting the enemy from the defender's position."[128] I highlight the terms *destroy* and *destroying* because destruction was previously reserved for the offense. Indeed, recognizing its break from tradition, the manual stated that commanders must make it clear to their subordinates that "an effective defense is an opportunity to *destroy* the enemy."[129] Destroying the enemy no longer required a transition to offense. Robert Doughty, a historian of U.S. Army doctrine, notes these changes in *Operations 1962* with surprise.[130]

But this was not simply aggressive language smuggled into doctrine under the guise of defense. Doctrine did not advise commanders to follow up a stalwart defense with a sweeping offensive to seize the initiative. Breaking with tradition again, *Operations 1962* argued it was not even necessary to transition to the offense to gain the initiative. *Operations 1962* attributed a degree of initiative to defense, a concept unheard of in previous army doctrine. Defenders could gain the initiative by selecting the area of battle, forcing the enemy to react to their defensive plan, and exploiting enemy weakness and error. Nor was the defensive always imposed on the commander. Contravening the principles of war again, the commander might "*deliberately* undertake defensive operations . . . to destroy the enemy."[131] Although army thinking traditionally reserved the initiative for the attacker, army doctrine reinterpreted the concept of the initiative to co-opt it into a defensive theory of victory.

All this is contrary to supposed bureaucratic and cultural preferences. Nevertheless, *Operations 1962* took it a step further when it heaped praise on commanders who mastered the defense. "The conduct of defensive operations under adverse conditions," the manual argued, "is the *supreme test* of the field commander," and "the *highest order of leadership* and tactical skill is demanded."[132] This is high praise in the army's most important manual for a form of warfare supposedly anathema to army culture and contrary to its bureaucratic interests. However, conducting defensive operations under adverse conditions was exactly the challenge that U.S. Army commanders faced in Europe.

One might see here more confirmation of civilian realism. Kennedy desired a more defensive doctrine, and the army complied. However, the timing tells a different story. All of these defensive concepts were present in the army prior to Kennedy's arrival. For example, in 1957—when Senator Kennedy won the Pulitzer Prize for *Profiles in Courage* and was three years from the White House—Lieutenant General Clyde Eddleman, DCSOPS and Decker's future vice chief of staff, argued for the virtues of defensive operations. Eddleman was not just a voice crying in the wilderness; DCSOPS is a highly sought position in the army, a consistent path to the highest commands. In the same year, Lieutenant Colonel Mitchel Goldenthal set out Eddleman's views in *Military Review*, in another piece that the editors said was "in consonance with current doctrine as taught at the CGSC."[133] Like *Operations 1962*, the piece imbued defense with the initiative by making the enemy respond to the defensive plan and the great capacity of tactical nuclear weapons for destroying the enemy.[134] Friction, both natural and man-made, played a key role here. According to Goldenthal, the commander of a defense organized in depth channels the heavily armored attacker into position using natural and man-made barriers. Like senior army leaders and General Taylor, Goldenthal saw battlefield nuclear weapons as an integral part of the mobile defense.[135] "The use of atomic weapons greatly facilitates defense against numerically superior forces."[136] In addition, that superiority made a transition to a general offensive unwise. Only "limited offensive actions" were feasible, given the material advantages Soviet forces enjoyed.[137] Prior to the Kennedy presidency, the most senior army officers were advocating a more defensive theory of victory, which *Operations 1962* subsequently expressed in doctrine. Moreover, the officers responsible for this defensive theory of victory were not military mavericks but army officers on traditional career paths.

In fact, some civilian leaders were concerned with the overly defensive orientation of the U.S. Army in this period. During committee hearings on defense appropriations in 1959, Senators Stuart Symington and Dennis Chávez raised concerns that the U.S. Army was thinking too defensively. They were concerned that the army was "planning a Maginot line complex" instead of an offensively oriented "blitzkrieg . . . complex." In the exchange, Senator Chavez pointed out that the great Carthaginian general Hannibal was never on the defensive but always on the offensive. Major General Robert Wood, the target of this line of questioning, responded in typical military realist fashion: "If I remember the Punic Wars he won the battles but lost the wars."[138] Given the balance of capabilities in Europe, the army was preparing and refining a defensive theory of victory and was wary of those inside and outside of the army who advocated a risky offensive approach.

Operations 1962 represented a change in army doctrine. On the spectrum of theories of victory, it moved away from the offensive pole and toward its more defensive end. This was contrary to the principles of war, part of army culture and doctrine since the 1920s. The principles of war express the preference for the offense noted by military realism and other theories. However, Kennedy refused to provide the additional forces needed to right the imbalance of capabilities, never mind enable the offense, and geography put the United States and its NATO allies at an additional disadvantage. Available resources, geography, the balance of capabilities in Europe, and likely Soviet doctrine recommended a more defensive theory of victory. So an appreciation of limited means and friction restrained the offensive preference that flows from the logic of force. When the principles of war, which support bureaucratic interests and represent a cultural icon, contradicted these doctrinal needs, army doctrine reinterpreted them to suit the threat environment.

Kennedy's Guerrillas: Counterinsurgency and Army Doctrine

For President Kennedy, insurgency was a means of spreading communism that could not be arrested by large conventional forces or nuclear weapons. Indeed, its immunity to conventional forms of deterrence and coercion is one of the reasons insurgency was so popular among communist revolutionaries in the 1960s. This immunity is why it remains so prevalent today, from ISIS insurgents in Iraq and Syria to Russian "volunteers" in the Ukraine; low levels of force can conquer territory without inciting large-scale military counterintervention. Though communist insurgencies occupied the global periphery, they were bringing states into the communist camp. These insurgent victories on the periphery, Kennedy thought, could disturb the balance of power.[139] Robert Kennedy, Kennedy's closest adviser, argued that countering communist subversion, especially spearheaded by Castro's Cuba in America's backyard, was essential.[140] Here, as historian Robert Dallek points out, Robert Kennedy was likely expressing his brother's views, as he had done on numerous other occasions.[141] As Kennedy prepared to take office, Soviet premier Nikita Khrushchev professed his country's support for "wars of national liberation," making insurgency and counterinsurgency (IN/COIN) a part of the superpower struggle.[142] The premier knew firsthand the struggles the Kennedy administration would face in trying to counter these insurgent movements. As the chairman of Ukraine's Council of Ministers in the late 1940s, Khrushchev had fought nationalist insurgents in Western Ukraine.[143] To respond to the Soviets' unconventional offensive, Kennedy argued, the United States had to engage in COIN.[144]

However, Kennedy opposed purely military solutions to insurgency. The president argued, "No amount of arms and armies can help stabilize those governments which are unable or unwilling to achieve social and economic reform and development."[145] Here Kennedy was echoing his deputy national security adviser, Walt Rostow, a modernization theorist.[146] Rostow argued that the root cause of communist insurgency was "social injustice and economic chaos."[147] These conditions made the mass of the populace either indifferent or attracted to communist insurgents. This theory of modernization shaped U.S. COIN strategy, which the Kennedy administration articulated in its Overseas Internal Defense Policy (OIDP). In it, economic aid and development, political reform, and military assistance constituted "preventive medicine" used to inoculate the populace against subversion.[148] States with active insurgencies would receive military equipment and advisers to provide a security umbrella under which economic and political reforms could proceed.[149]

Kennedy promulgated twenty-three National Security Action Memoranda (NSAM) on COIN, each demanding specific changes, from requiring COIN experience for officer promotion to ordering the U.S. Agency for International Development (USAID) to prioritize indigenous police training.[150] He increased the number of U.S. military advisers in South Vietnam "to expose them to the . . . conditions of guerrilla warfare."[151] Kennedy also expanded the U.S. Army Special Forces to be a specialized COIN force. SF units trained local forces in COIN techniques and promoted modernization through local "civic action" in sanitation, roads, medicine, and economic development.[152] In January 1962, Kennedy established the Special Group (Counter-insurgency) (SG[-CI]) with NSAM 124 and put General Maxwell Taylor at its head. This body would coordinate COIN efforts across departments and agencies.[153] Kennedy ordered McNamara to make sure army organization and training incorporated COIN. "The effort devoted to this challenge," the president wrote, "should be comparable in importance to preparations for conventional warfare."[154] All of this represented, in the words of one scholar, "a major effort to produce a coherent doctrine for counterinsurgency in the U.S. government."[155] In hindsight, a number of authors argue that Kennedy's development-based approach to COIN was prescient, if only the army had listened.[156]

However, hindsight has colored this rosy image of Kennedy's single-minded commitment to COIN. Many argue that the United States failed in Vietnam because the army did not adopt a COIN strategy that emphasized local forces and civic action.[157] Some, including theorists of military innovation such as Rosen, point to a November 30, 1961, meeting between Kennedy and army leaders in which Kennedy supposedly pressed the army to make COIN a priority.[158] In reality, however, the meeting was not even Kennedy's idea but that of Ted Clifton, Kennedy's senior military aide, and Elvis Stahr, the secretary of the army. Although Kennedy pushed COIN, he also told the generals "that he wanted . . . the Army to be able to fight at the lowest end of the spectrum [of conflict] . . . as well as right on up [the spectrum]." Stahr said the meeting was primarily to boost army morale after the lean Eisenhower years.[159]

Moreover, while he did see population security and "hearts and minds" as part of COIN, Kennedy placed just as much emphasis on U.S. military advisers training local guerrillas to *start* insurgencies inside communist regimes. For instance, the president lamented that the Vietnamese communists had thousands of guerrillas operating in South Vietnam but the United States had none operating in North Vietnam.[160] In fact, one of the attractions to the Bay of Pigs operation for Kennedy was the assertion by advisers that if the invasion failed, the attackers could melt into the countryside and start an anti-Castro insurgency. For Kennedy, organizing insurgency movements inside communist countries would be an additional task for Special Forces. Special Forces and irregular units also had to be prepared to contribute to conventional and nuclear combat operations. In a European war, SF would infiltrate Soviet satellites and organize local guerrilla bands to conduct raids on Soviet lines of communication, attacking targets behind enemy lines and calling in nuclear strikes on enemy reserves.[161]

Kennedy's more nuanced view of COIN helps explain why the president was not as disappointed in army COIN efforts as some have suggested. True, initially Kennedy was not pleased with army progress.[162] However, as General Decker's COIN initiatives began to take hold, the president remarked, "They're beginning to recognize the nature of the problem, and what they're doing at Fort Bragg is really good."[163] In March 1962, Kennedy received a progress report from the SG(CI) that cited extensive progress in COIN efforts.[164] However, Kennedy did lament the failure of *civilian* agencies, such as the State Department and USAID, to make COIN a priority. A later review of COIN efforts throughout the government concurred, concluding that only the army and Marines had developed a COIN doctrine and pushed it down their ranks.[165] Critics of the U.S. Army cite Kennedy's initial dissatisfaction but fail to note his later approbation.[166]

The army and the administration also agreed that the army's role in COIN would be advisory and that only a small portion of its force, Special Forces, would become COIN specialists. Accordingly, individual but not unit training and education in COIN expanded.[167] This absence of unit training has been cited as proof the army did not take COIN seriously. However, this was consistent with the priorities of civilian leaders. When we recognize that Kennedy wanted the army to retain its capabilities for the full spectrum of warfare and appreciate finer distinctions in the president's conception of COIN, army initiatives look much more consistent with civilian wishes and much less like bureaucratic or cultural foot-dragging. Although COIN was important to Kennedy, it was not as high a priority as some contend. This interpretation of Kennedy's COIN initiatives undermines theories of military innovation that depend on the previous problematic analysis for support.[168] Nevertheless, despite this coincidence between civilian demands and army COIN efforts, it would be a mistake to attribute these results solely to civilian intervention as civilian realism might expect.

Kennedy's Army and Counterinsurgency

In the early 1960s, U.S. Army leaders considered the defense of Europe to be their main mission and designed their forces and doctrine accordingly. In spite of this, army leaders did not ignore the threat of insurgency.[169] After all, from the military realist perspective, insurgency worked. In 1949 it had toppled the government of the most populous country in the world, China. In the 1950s and '60s, it continued to threaten U.S. allies and interests. Critics argue that senior army officers, hoping to preserve their conventional culture and the more abundant resources they provided, thought specific COIN expertise was not essential and that conventional forces could deal with guerrillas.[170] On the contrary, army leaders appreciated the unique skill set required for COIN.[171] According to Army Chief Decker, "Obviously [regular army] units are not the proper response to a band of guerrillas which in a flash will transform itself into a scattering of 'farmers.' Neither are they best geared to move into a weak country and help it move up the development ladder by training local forces to improve the people's health, transportation, and building programs."[172] By 1962 there were four thousand SF in the U.S. Army. According to Decker, they were prepared for nation-building duties that would address the popular grievances that insurgents fed on.[173] Decker clearly understood development-based COIN.

Because COIN is contrary to its bureaucratic and cultural preferences, the last place we should see it is in the U.S. Army's most important war-fighting manual of the period, *Operations 1962*, especially considering civilians did not push COIN as hard as previously believed. The army could have easily buried COIN in subordinate manuals. Instead, the army changed its most important manual to reflect the insurgent threat. Although it listed COIN as the fifth of five mission priorities, *Operations 1962* nonetheless dealt extensively with irregular warfare and COIN.[174] Though this change might seem minor, its predecessor, *Operations 1954*, discussed guerrilla warfare for a grand total of two pages as part of a catchall chapter titled "Special Operations."[175] *Operations 1962*, on the other hand, dedicated two entire chapters—a total of forty-six pages and more than a quarter of its content—to these types of operations. The chapters were titled "Unconventional Warfare" and "Military Operations against Irregular Forces." Moreover, the manual did not advocate conventional military solutions to insurgency. The discussion of COIN was surprisingly consistent with a development-based approach.[176] Only when a COIN campaign escalated to the stage of mobile guerrilla warfare did civic action take a backseat to offensive counterguerrilla operations.[177] Lest one think this was the militarization of COIN under the noses of civilians, civilian COIN strategists approved this prioritization. NSAM 119, "Civic Action," written by National Security Adviser McGeorge Bundy, argued, "In countries threatened by external aggression, local forces should participate in civic action projects which *do not materially impair performance of the primary military mission.*"[178]

In addition, this prioritization was also recommended by the father of insurgent strategy, Mao Zedong, and David Galula's counterinsurgent response. Mao argued that guerrilla forces could not achieve decisive results without the assistance of more conventional forces and that guerrilla units could not operate in the presence of strong conventional forces.[179] Galula argued that the counterinsurgent needed strong conventional forces to dislodge guerrilla units prior to using civic action to win over the population.[180] The army prioritization of counterguerrilla operations prior to civic action was consistent with these views and those of civilian COIN strategists.[181]

Based on this evidence, some might argue that the story of COIN in Kennedy's army is consistent with civilian realism. However, the congruence between army doctrine and civilian COIN initiatives was not the result of civilian intervention in the army that compelled army officers to change their thinking. The process and timing do not square with this interpretation. The army was at the cutting edge of development-based COIN theorizing before Kennedy even took office. Recent histories of the U.S. Army in the 1950s and '60s have documented a very marked interest in COIN among army officers. As Gregory Daddis shows, in the same way army officers considered Soviet doctrine, they were also diligent students of insurgent doctrine.[182] The army's COIN doctrine showed an appreciation for subversive strategy and was not simply the application of conventional warfare approaches to COIN. As early as 1957, officers at the CGSC recognized the link between modernization and "the growth of major social, economic, and political problems," maintaining that "such social injustice invites exploitation by Communists."[183] The proper response, a 1957 *Military Review* article continued, was "bettering economic conditions"[184] and restoring "political and economic stability."[185] From 1957 to 1961, between 5 percent and 7 percent of articles published in *Military Review* were on COIN, an average of nine articles per year.[186] This compares favorably with the 10 percent to 20 percent of articles on nuclear warfare, an average of twenty-two articles per year. This evidence does not support bureaucratic and cultural expectations that contributors to *Military Review* would largely ignore COIN. Moreover, as exemplified by the article just cited, COIN articles in *Military Review* did not prescribe conventional military solutions to insurgency, either.

The army's ideas about COIN were codified in *Field Manual 31-15, Operations against Irregular Forces*, developed at the CGSC prior to Kennedy's election.[187] According to this manual, insurgency is an "outward manifestation of public disenchantment with certain political, social, and economic conditions." It concluded, as Kennedy and Rostow would, that "military action, unaccompanied by meaningful reforms, could at best suppress, but never completely eradicate, a heartfelt revolutionary movement."[188] *Operations 1962*, also developed at the CGSC, echoed this conception of COIN. Contrary to civilian realism, the army's interest in COIN preceded Kennedy's COIN initiatives. In fact, army COIN doctrine actually influenced civilian strategy.

When the National Security Council set out the Overseas Internal Defense Policy, which the administration called its "Counterinsurgency Doctrine," it drew extensively from the Joint Chiefs' joint concept for COIN. Before that, the COIN ideas emanating from the CGSC had heavily influenced the joint concept.[189] As in the case of tactical nuclear weapons, the U.S. Army first articulated important doctrinal innovation, which civilian officials then adopted. *Operations 1962* reflected the fact that the army had been developing COIN concepts and doctrines in response to low-level communist aggression since the late 1950s. Civilian pressure was not the reason for the inclusion of COIN in army doctrine.

One might argue that the army embraced the COIN mission during the Kennedy administration as yet another way to ensure additional resources. If this were the case, the army bureaucracy should have ignored COIN until it became bureaucratically advantageous under Kennedy. As shown above, however, the army began to think about and adapt to COIN in unconventional ways well before Kennedy's COIN initiatives made it lucrative.[190] The army certainly highlighted and expanded these efforts under Kennedy, but they did not originate with Kennedy's COIN initiatives.

The army was not opposed to the nation-building aspects of COIN, as bureaucratic and cultural theorists argue. In fact, unconventional COIN concepts expressed by civilians often had their origin in army thinking. Not surprisingly, therefore, *Operations 1962* discussed COIN extensively. The army took the insurgent threat seriously because of its demonstrated ability to conquer states. Still, for the Cold War U.S. Army, the more serious threat of Soviet forces in Europe meant that it would not make COIN its primary mission.[191] The Soviet threat, rather than parochial interests or historical culture, explains COIN's lower priority in U.S. Army doctrine.

Conclusion

At the opening of a new decade, Kennedy wanted to explore a "New Frontier" in U.S. Cold War foreign policy and strategy.[192] Unexpectedly, military bureaucracy, military culture, and civilian realism do not explain Kennedy's army as well as military realism. As military realism expects, the army transcended bureaucratic interests and cultural norms to design a doctrine capable of addressing the threat environment. Military realists in the army, including the military maverick handpicked by civilian leaders, resisted civilian initiatives incompatible with the necessary doctrinal changes. Regarding conventional versus nuclear missions, bureaucratic and cultural theories predict that *Operations 1962* would favor the former. They were mistaken. The army kept and refined the nuclear mission in both organization and doctrine. It would not let go of tactical nuclear weapons, even though they promised fewer resources, were a significant threat to its autonomy, and caused major uncertainty. Culturally, Kennedy's army should have downplayed the nuclear mission in new doctrine and sought to relive its conventional "finest hour." Instead, army thinking in *Military Review* and *Operations 1962* was rooted in the operational implications of the nuclear battlefield. When it came to army doctrine and nuclear weapons, analogies from the past were irrelevant. Instead, "doctrine" had to "be based more on theory than in the past."[193] Senior army officers spearheaded these necessary changes, which contradicted bureaucratic interests and cultural preferences.

Contrary to civilian realism, military realists in the army made organizational and doctrinal changes, such as the ROAD reorganization, *prior* to changes in civilian strategy. Civilian leaders took credit for these changes after the fact. In the controversy over the utility of tactical nuclear weapons, General Maxwell Taylor, Kennedy's military maverick—a key causal mechanism for civilian realism—worked against his civilian patrons to align civilian strategy with army doctrine, rather than the other way around. In the end, you can take the maverick out of the military, but you can't take the military out of the maverick.

When it came to deciding on an offensive and defensive theory of victory, *Operations 1962* tempered the offensive emphasis of *Operations 1954* and espoused a more defensive theory of victory. Army doctrine shifted to a more defensive theory of victory, which could enlist friction to offset Soviet advantages and counter its offensive doctrine. This confounds bureaucratic and cultural explanations because defensive theories of victory do not serve organizational preferences or army culture. Nor was the shift to a more defensive theory of victory driven by civilian realists. The army was advocating a more defensive theory of victory before Kennedy took office because of the imbalance of capabilities it faced. For military realists, the logic of force recommends an offensive theory of victory. However, in the U.S. Army of the early 1960s, the balance of capabilities, enemy doctrine, lack of resources, and ever-present friction tempered this preference and resulted in a more defensive theory of victory. The army imposed on itself one of the doctrinal changes that its bureaucrats and cultural guardians should have resisted tooth and nail.

Finally, the history of Kennedy's push for COIN in the U.S. Army has been mischaracterized. This incomplete narrative has provided unwarranted support for bureaucratic and cultural perspectives on military innovation. Critics of the army's COIN efforts under Kennedy fail to note his eventual satisfaction with those efforts. Army Chief Decker—a supposed conventional-warfare dinosaur—understood the unique skills required for development-based COIN. *Operations 1962* vastly expanded the place of COIN in army doctrine. Moreover, civilian realists did not impose this COIN concept on the army. The timing of COIN innovation in the army is more consistent with military realism. Prior to the Kennedy era, the real, but secondary, threat of insurgencies led to innovative thinking and doctrine in the army. In fact, these COIN ideas of the army informed civilian strategy, reversing again the causal expectations of civilian realism. Nevertheless, for the army, the degree of physical danger posed by Soviet forces in Europe, rather than bureaucratic or cultural factors, made COIN a lower priority in doctrine.

In the early 1960s, military realism provides an explanation for change and continuity across all three areas of army doctrine. Moreover, the evidence often contradicted the expectations of the alternative theories. Military realists adapted army missions and the theory of victory in unexpected ways, even in the realm of irregular warfare. Unbeknownst to them, in Vietnam the army was about to be consumed by one of those irregular conflicts.

3 ARMY DOCTRINE IN THE SHADOW OF VIETNAM

Operations 1968

IN 1965, THREE years after it published *Operations 1962*, the U.S. Army went from advising to engaging directly in combat in Vietnam. After three years of fighting in Vietnam, the army published a new edition of *Operations* in 1968. By this time, more than nineteen thousand U.S. military personnel had been killed, and troop levels had peaked at more than five hundred thousand. Elements of nine of the army's seventeen active divisions took part in the fighting. The brunt of fighting fell on the ground forces, with the army and Marines suffering 75 percent of the total casualties.[1] Both the public and scholars of military innovation consider the U.S. Army in Vietnam a paradigmatic case of narrow bureaucratic interests and cultural bias stifling military innovation. The story of the U.S. Army in Vietnam is a particularly good opportunity to test the competing explanations of military learning in wartime. A number of scholars have argued that the failure of the army to learn in Vietnam was the result of bureaucratic resistance or maladaptive military culture.[2] However, the bureaucratic and cultural explanations of this case actually rest on a weak foundation. A discussion of the army's treatment of COIN in the 1960s— begun in the previous chapter—the actual conduct of the war in Vietnam, and the broader Cold War context confronting the army in 1968 expose the cracks in that foundation. In its place, a new foundation based on recent historical analysis and military realism takes shape. The result is a new perspective on the U.S. Army in Vietnam and its doctrine in the late 1960s.

Much like the previous chapter, this one begins by setting out the predictions of the competing explanations across the three key areas of doctrine: the import of conventional versus nuclear missions, the offensive or defensive character of theories of victory, and the import and treatment of the counterinsurgency mission. In the first two areas, doctrinal continuity was the order of the day in the late 1960s. Continuing to contravene bureaucratic and military cultural expectations, the army preserved and elaborated on its nuclear mission in *Operations 1968*. The late 1960s manual also preserved a more defensive theory of victory that broke bureaucratic and cultural boundaries. As will be made clear below, from the military realist perspective, the threat environment the army confronted in the late 1960s recommended this continuity in the core of army doctrine.

However, in the areas of COIN and wartime innovation, this chapter breaks new ground. As shown already, bureaucratic and cultural interests did not blind the U.S. Army to the threat of insurgency. True, COIN had a relatively minor role in the army's most important war-fighting manual, but doctrine writers had greatly expanded its place in the *Operations* manual between the mid-1950s and 1960s. This concern with COIN did not stop when army units became entangled in the fight to save South Vietnam. In fact, figures formerly associated with the anti-COIN camp, such as William Westmoreland, had a deep understanding of the dilemmas of COIN and did not ignore them when prosecuting the war. In addition to this new perspective on the U.S. Army and COIN in the 1960s, I argue below that we need not invoke bureaucratic and cultural biases to explain the army's focus on large-scale conventional operations in Vietnam. Rather, the enemy the army faced in Vietnam included a large conventional military force and was not primarily small bands of guerrillas in black pajamas. Part of the reason bureaucratic and cultural theories seem so well supported by this case is a historical narrative of the war that mistakenly focuses on conflict at the village level. When we apply the logic of military realism to the theater of war and the threats therein, and arm ourselves with a more complete historical context, the strategy the army adopted in Vietnam makes sense. Military realism helps explain both why the army came to take COIN seriously and why it responded as it did to the challenges of the war in Vietnam. The contention here is not that the army was correct to adopt this strategy or the doctrine it did in the late 1960s. Rather, the contention is that a military realist outlook shines more light on these decisions than an exclusively bureaucratic or cultural viewpoint.

In addition, neither does the civilian realist approach to military innovation explain the doctrinal behavior of the U.S. Army in this period. In 1968, after deciding not to seek reelection, President Johnson was preoccupied with leaving a legacy as a peacemaker by ending the war in Vietnam. The Johnson administration did not engage in the kinds of civilian interventions in the army that had characterized the Kennedy White House. According to civilian realism, while the civilian cats are away, the bureaucratic mice will play. The distraction of civilian leaders should open the door for military bureaucrats to capture the doctrinal process and shape it to serve their interests. However, much of the evidence presented below contradicts these expectations. In the end, military realism, in conjunction with new historical scholarship, brings fresh eyes to this crucial period in the history of America and its army. Moreover, by challenging one of the paradigmatic cases in military innovation studies, this chapter calls into question bureaucratic and cultural understandings of military organizations.

Army Bureaucrats, Army Doctrine, and Vietnam

The previous chapter argued that army doctrine of the early 1960s undermined the priorities of army bureaucrats, especially in the areas of nuclear versus conventional missions and offensive versus defensive theories of victory. Let us assume this was an anomaly and that bureaucratic forces will ascend to their rightful place atop the army during the Vietnam War. Under President Johnson, then, bureaucratic forces within the army will rehabilitate the core of army doctrine, reviving an offensive theory of victory. These same forces should reverse the revolutionary and disruptive nuclear weapons doctrine concocted in the late 1950s and early 1960s. As argued in the previous chapter, these changes would ensure increased resources and autonomy for the army and reduce uncertainty. Evidence of a resurgent army bureaucracy should also be evident in the pages of *Military Review*, where there should be a revival of the import of conventional warfare and a denigration of the early 1960s obsession with nuclear weapons, especially at the tactical level. Articles in *Military Review* will hark back to the army's World War II finest hour as part of its effort to shed the nuclear mission. Discussions of attack and defense in the pages of the Command and General Staff College's flagship journal will also work to reinstate offense as the dominant form of warfare.

A resurgent army bureaucracy will also put COIN in its proper place. Three years after the U.S. Army hit the ground in Vietnam, its doctrine should exorcise the COIN fad of the Kennedy years. A number of scholars argue that the U.S. Army refused to change its doctrine to fight more effectively in Vietnam because it was contrary to its bureaucratic interests. Unlike the Wehrmacht, during the army's finest hour, the elusive Vietnamese guerrilla would not stand and fight, making it impossible for the army to impose the SOPs of conventional warfare on them. Undaunted, the story goes, the army persisted in trying to impose conventional military solutions on the unconventional problem of insurgency in Vietnam.[3] Articles in *Military Review* will recommend mostly conventional military solutions to the problem of insurgency. Articles on the ongoing war in Vietnam will portray that war in conventional military terms and draw on the conventional experience of the army to suggest paths to victory there. In the absence of Kennedy's COIN initiatives, there should be a reduction in the number of *Military Review* articles on COIN. *Military Review* should cull "hearts-and-minds" COIN from its pages now that civilians are no longer championing the COIN fad. The conventionalization of the war in Vietnam will facilitate this culling process.

U.S. Army Culture in Vietnam

Let us assume too that early 1960s army doctrine was a momentary aberration when it came to U.S. Army culture. The organizational and doctrinal focus on nuclear missions, defensive theories of victory, and COIN flew in the face of that culture. Consequently, in the latter part of the decade, cultural forces within the army will press for a return to a culturally consistent doctrine. The guardians of army culture, like its bureaucrats, will revise the core of army doctrine, downplaying the nuclear mission and resurrecting an offensive theory of victory. In short, U.S. Army doctrine in the late '60s should return to its World War II finest hour and its conventional, offensive roots. In this way, the guardians of army culture will make the doctrinal core conform once again to the cultural norms of the U.S. Army. Issues of *Military Review* from this period should reflect this process of turning away from the faddish nuclear and COIN missions of the Kennedy era and returning to a focus on conventional warfare and offensive theories of victory.

In terms of wartime innovation, cultural theorists, like their bureaucratic forerunners, see the army in Vietnam as a paradigmatic case of military culture undermining organizational learning. Army culture blinkered it to the lessons of COIN operations in Vietnam. It was too busy trying to impose its norms of conventional, offensive warfare on the conflict, even if the enemy refused to cooperate.[4] Therefore, the army of the late 1960s is an easy case study for military culture. The institutional animosity toward COIN will manifest itself in army doctrine through a reduction in the role of COIN in *Operations 1968*. Articles in *Military Review* on the war in Vietnam will reinforce the conventional-warfare focus that so many scholars have argued dominated army thinking in this period. COIN based on hearts and minds and social, economic, and political reform will fade into the background or disappear altogether as army culture reasserts itself during Vietnam. If army doctrine discussed COIN at all, it will propose conventional military solutions to the problem of insurgency.

Civilian Realism and the Vietnam Era U.S. Army

According to civilian realism, when civilian leaders are preoccupied with complex diplomacy, they are less concerned with monitoring and intervening in their military organizations. Under these conditions, bureaucratic and cultural forces are free to shape doctrine.[5] In 1968 there was indeed a high level of civilian preoccupation with matters other than battling government bureaucrats, a favorite pastime of the Kennedy regime. There was significant policy continuity between the Johnson and Kennedy administrations. After all, Johnson kept on much of the Kennedy cabinet. Robert McNamara and Dean Rusk remained in their positions as Secretaries of Defense and State, respectively, while Johnson promoted Walt Rostow to national security adviser.[6] He said of McNamara, "That man with the Stay-Comb hair is the best of the [Kennedy] lot."[7] "McNamara's got more brains than anybody I'm dealing with. . . . I wouldn't want to be President if he weren't here. . . . You could have the damn job—tomorrow."[8] The distrust of the military establishment that had permeated the Kennedy White House lived on in the members of the "ministry of talent" that Johnson had kept on.[9] Johnson shared Kennedy's suspicion of the motives of his military advisers. Referring to their requests for more troops and aggressive actions in Vietnam, Johnson said, "It's hard to be a military hero without a war. Heroes need battles and bombs and bullets in order to be heroic."[10] Nevertheless, Johnson had different priorities than Kennedy when it came to national security because he faced different circumstances.

The year 1968 witnessed extensive domestic political unrest in the United States, the Tet Offensive—with consequences in Vietnam and at home—and a presidential election. In this year, President Johnson sought a negotiated end to the war in Vietnam and strategic arms talks with the Soviet Union. These two issues dominated discussions between the president and his foreign policy team, even when international events, such as France's withdrawal from NATO and the invasion of Czechoslovakia, might have called this prioritization into question. Johnson, unlike Kennedy, did not employ a military maverick to change the army. Johnson had moved General Taylor from the chairmanship of the JCS to the post of U.S. ambassador to Vietnam in 1964. However, initiatives like the Special Group (Counter-insurgency), initially under Taylor's oversight, "withered away" under Johnson.[11] Johnson later reenlisted Taylor to become special consultant to the president and chairman of the Foreign Intelligence Advisory Board from 1965 to 1969. However, in this capacity Taylor, like the rest of the administration, was preoccupied with Vietnam policy, especially in 1968.[12] In retrospect, Taylor called 1968 "the climactic year" for the

United States in Vietnam.[13] Despite the continuing role of Kennedy's military maverick, Johnson and his civilian advisers were far less concerned with the minutia of military doctrine than his predecessor had been. Civilian distraction leaves the door open for organizational interests and cultural preferences to dominate the doctrinal process. It would not be surprising, therefore, if *Operations 1968* reflected the bureaucratic interests and cultural preferences set out in the previous two sections.

Army doctrine under Kennedy had been compelled to pay lip service to Kennedy's COIN push, but the 1968 manual would remove the emphasis on COIN and return the army to its conventional roots. If it discussed COIN, *Operations '68* would propose conventional military solutions to the problem of insurgency. Indeed, many argue that this tendency played out in General Westmoreland's focus on "search-and-destroy" operations in Vietnam, which sought the large conventional units of the enemy. In Vietnam the army fought the war its bureaucrats and cultural guardians wanted to fight, and the results were disastrous.[14] Articles published in *Military Review* during this period should reflect the conventionalization of the war in Vietnam and should make little mention of the COIN ideas that were in the air during the Kennedy years. Instead, the pages of *Military Review* will reflect a focus on conventional, offensive warfare consistent with the interests of army bureaucrats and the norms of army culture.

Military Realism and the Vietnam Era U.S. Army

Military realism anticipates little change in U.S. Army doctrine in the late 1960s. In stark contrast to the alternative explanations, it predicts that *Operations 1968* will preserve the nuclear and defensive focus of *Operations 1962* because the most dangerous threat to the United States remained unchanged. As shown in the previous chapter, prior to U.S. engagement in Vietnam, Soviet forces enjoyed numerous material advantages over U.S. Army and NATO forces, especially in the early stages of a potential European war. As I argue below, in the late 1960s this danger increased and reinforced the import of the nuclear mission and the defensive theory of victory at the core of army doctrine. These priorities should be evident in the trends in writings in *Military Review*. If military realism is correct, the trends established in the early 1960s issues of *Military Review* should persist into the late 1960s and vary with the gravity of the Soviet threat. Military realism does not share the expectation of the bureaucratic and cultural alternatives that *Military Review* will see a revival of conventional warfare, the army's World War II finest hour, or offensive theories of victory.

Regarding COIN, military realism predicts that even after their extensive experience in counterguerrilla warfare in Vietnam, COIN will have a subordinate role in army doctrine. However, as with *Operations 1962*, there is no reason the army will not develop fresh thinking about COIN, thinking that contradicts supposed bureaucratic and cultural imperatives. In addition, innovative thinking about COIN should be present in the pages of *Military Review* during the army's engagement in Vietnam, and there should be an increase in articles on COIN as the army's involvement in South Vietnam deepens. As already noted, a number of scholars consider the U.S. Army in Vietnam a paradigmatic case of bureaucratic and cultural forces crushing organizational learning. However, recent scholarship has seriously undermined the traditional historical narrative of the army in Vietnam. Once we have a clearer picture of the kind of war and enemy the army faced in Vietnam, the bureaucratic and cultural explanations are undermined and military realism sheds new light on one of the most important episodes in the history of the post–World War II U.S. Army. Finally, to reiterate, civilian realism expects bureaucratic forces in the army to guide doctrine in this case, so the expectations of military realism here also contradict civilian realism.

Vietnam and Europe: Threats and Priorities
Vietnam in 1968: Civilian and Military Perspectives

By the time the army revised its keystone doctrine for the second time in the 1960s, much had changed. The year was 1968. The extent and intensity of army operations in Vietnam had greatly expanded. In the summer of 1962, there were 16,500 U.S. advisers in Vietnam, and U.S. and South Vietnamese Special Forces were conducting covert raids into North Vietnam.[15] By the spring of 1965, the South Vietnamese were losing one battalion and one district capital per week to large Vietcong units.[16] In response, Lyndon B. Johnson increased Kennedy's escalation to include U.S. Marine and U.S. Army combat units in 1965.[17] Soon Johnson authorized the U.S. commanders to seek out the enemy in offensive operations. Eventually, General William C. Westmoreland, U.S. commander in Vietnam, requested more troops, and Johnson provided them, 500,000 by 1968.

Westmoreland chose to employ many of these forces in seeking major Vietcong and North Vietnamese units that had infiltrated South Vietnam with increasing frequency, especially after the insertion of U.S. combat troops.[18] In this way, Westmoreland hoped to keep the main force units from disrupting the pacification and COIN campaigns at the village level, as they had done in

1964 and 1965. The view that Westmoreland focused on search and destroy, while ignoring the pacification campaign, is incomplete. Westmoreland saw the pacification campaign and his large-unit operations as intimately linked. He did acknowledge that "my battlefield strategy was to grind down the enemy."[19] However, he saw this as complementary to the pacification campaign. Westmoreland thought it would be impossible to establish population security, a key to any successful COIN campaign, while large enemy units roamed the countryside with impunity, ready to smash with brute force any gains made in pacification.

In part, the Johnson administration's "strategy of gradualism," adopted in 1965 and championed by Secretary McNamara, dictated Westmoreland's military strategy. The tactical engagements brought about by search and destroy would serve the overall strategic objective of "graduated pressure," causing such overwhelming attrition in the communist forces that they could not replace their losses. Civilian strategists coupled the pressure of these ground operations with a bombing campaign against carefully selected targets inside North Vietnam.[20] This pressure, so the logic went, would inspire the leaders of the insurgency in the North to seek a negotiated peace rather than continue the war.[21] A similar strategy, McNamara argued, concluded the Cuban missile crisis.[22] As during that crisis, civilian officials had to control the use of force as a tool for signaling intentions. Consequently, civilian officials carefully selected and reviewed bombing targets inside North Vietnam.[23] This limited use of force had additional audiences. It would signal to the Soviet Union and China that U.S. goals in Vietnam were limited, forestalling counterinterventions.[24] McNamara was confident in this strategy, and Johnson was very confident in McNamara. Moreover, the strategy seemed to be working.

At the beginning of 1968, many, especially U.S. military commanders in Vietnam, were speculating that the tipping point sought by gradualism was near. Communist resistance was about to crack. Upon his return from Vietnam in May 1967, Major General William E. DePuy said the following about the likelihood of success there:

> What they were doing to us in 1964 and 1965 we are now doing to them. I would not want to speculate how long it will take. It is moving in the right direction, and the main forces are generally back in the jungle. The general organization, morale and effectiveness of the local forces are steadily—not fast enough, mind you—going downhill. I just cannot help but see success at the end of that road. There will be setbacks, and it will take a long time, but I do not see how you can lose once that is set up.[25]

Even Army Chief Harold K. Johnson, often portrayed as an opponent of Westmoreland's strategy, saw "clear and concrete evidence of progress" and argued that the enemy was losing at a ratio of four to one in combat engagements in Vietnam.[26]

The Tet Offensive shattered this optimistic speculation. Launched on January 30, 1968, the offensive saw 87,000 North Vietnamese and Vietcong troops attack thirty-six of the forty-four provincial capitals of South Vietnam.[27] Communist cadres also infiltrated the American embassy in Saigon. This massive and coordinated attack put the lie to any speculation that the insurgency and its North Vietnamese director were on the ropes. However, from a military perspective, the Tet Offensive was a lopsided defeat for the Vietcong and their northern allies. In April 1968, Westmoreland told President Johnson that "since Tet [the] enemy has suffered colossal military defeat. He has lost 60,000 men and 18,000 weapons." U.S. and South Vietnamese forces had completely destroyed many main-force North Vietnamese units and numerous Vietcong cadres, who had exposed their shadow-government apparatus to destruction to execute Tet. Consequently, after 1968, the North Vietnamese had to provide the majority of communist insurgents. Operationally, the U.S. and South Vietnamese counterattack was a complete success and set back the communist insurgents for many months, if not years.[28] The military consequences of Tet shook the communist leadership in Hanoi.[29] In addition, COIN operations after Tet met with greater success because of the absence of main-force enemy units. The commander of one of the most successful COIN operations in Vietnam after Tet acknowledged that "the absence of threat by large, well-trained, well-equipped NVA [North Vietnamese Army] forces" made COIN success possible.[30] President Johnson asked Westmoreland if "the light at the end of the tunnel is any nearer," to which Westmoreland responded, "Yes." The change in communist tactics had "accelerated the attrition inflicted on the enemy. He has suffered a military defeat of major magnitude."[31]

Nevertheless, many, including civilian officials in Washington, saw the Tet Offensive as the beginning of the end of America's war in Vietnam.[32] Similar to Dien Bien Phu, which had not defeated the French in Vietnam militarily but had crippled public support for the war, Tet had undermined public confidence in the war effort and fractured the will of the U.S. leadership to continue fighting.[33] According to General Bruce Palmer, who would become vice chief of staff under Westmoreland, by the summer of 1968 it was "clear that President Johnson had lost any stomach for the war and was determined to negotiate a political settlement with Hanoi."[34] Westmoreland's assurances that

Tet was a victory fell on deaf ears. The offensive had destroyed his credibility by exposing his previous assessments as overly optimistic.[35]

On March 31, 1968, two months after the beginning of Tet, President Johnson announced his intention not to run for reelection. Instead, he would dedicate all his energies to seeking a peaceful solution to the war in Vietnam.[36] The year 1968 would see the first steps in a process of de-escalating the war that would proceed unabated until the United States withdrew all of its ground forces from Vietnam. For the remainder of his presidency, efforts to get a cease-fire and peace terms in Vietnam consumed Johnson.

Europe in 1968: Civilian and Military Perspectives

While America was embroiled in the critical year of the Vietnam War, 1968 also saw important developments in Europe. Although Kennedy had been popular in Europe, many European allies disliked Johnson and disapproved of his escalations in Vietnam.[37] European leaders were worried that Vietnam was overshadowing their concerns.[38] While Vietnam was distracting the United States from European affairs, the shadow of the Soviet threat to Europe loomed larger than ever, as the Soviets modernized and expanded their military capabilities. Secretary of Defense Clark Clifford, McNamara's replacement, noted these increases in Soviet defense spending. As early as October 1967, when McNamara was still secretary of defense, the Supreme Soviet had decided to increase defense spending by 15 percent.[39] Despite increasing Soviet strength in Europe, Johnson was advocating the removal of some U.S. troops from the Continent.[40] This was in part to get the West Germans to resume their "offset" payments (West German purchases of U.S. military hardware) so the United States could recoup the expense of keeping its forces in Europe. However, it was also an attempt on Johnson's part to de-escalate Cold War tensions. In 1967 Johnson returned thirty-four thousand U.S. troops to the United States from West Germany.[41] For some U.S. lawmakers, however, Johnson's reductions had not gone far enough. The Symington Amendment in the U.S. Senate sought to reduce U.S. troops in Europe from three hundred thousand to fifty thousand.[42] Despite these demands, Johnson refused any further troop reductions near the end of his time in office, stating, "I want to negotiate with the other side—not throw in the towel as I go out."[43]

When it came to nuclear weapons, Johnson was seeking accommodation with the Soviets through strategic arms-limitation talks, especially in 1968. He also pursued a nuclear nonproliferation agreement with the Soviets and the West Germans, though the Germans correctly perceived that the treaty was a means of assuring the Soviets that the West Germans would not develop their own nuclear weapons.[44] Like other civilian leaders in the 1960s, Johnson also rejected the concept of "limited nuclear war" and the devolving of nuclear authority to ground commanders.[45] Rusk pushed Johnson to arrange a summit with Soviet premier Aleksey Kosygin to send a signal to the "military industrial complex" that "getting an agreement to limit offensive and defensive missiles is the national policy of the United States." The arms race, the secretary continued, was a "rat hole" consuming "tens of billions."[46] Historian Thomas Schwartz argues that reducing the risk of nuclear war was "the overriding imperative of the Johnson presidency."[47]

As with the early Kennedy administration, however, civilian leaders and senior army officers did not see eye-to-eye on Europe or the role for nuclear weapons in its defense. Even while the war in Vietnam entered its critical year, senior army leaders still saw defending NATO Europe as their central mission.[48] They agreed with Army Chief of Staff Decker's earlier assessment that to lose in Europe would be "fatal" for the United States.[49] Decker continued, presciently, "We could lose in Asia without losing everything."[50] Nevertheless, the army's options for defending Europe were limited.

As chronicled in the previous chapter, civilian and military leaders disagreed about the balance of capabilities in Europe. Decker and other senior army officers were skeptical of civilian plans for a conventional military defense of Europe. The Office of the Secretary of Defense produced its new estimates to show there was a rough equality between NATO and Warsaw Pact forces in Europe. Indeed, recently released records of the Warsaw Pact states show that McNamara's estimates were far more accurate than 1950s assessments.[51] However, senior army officers argued that counting units was not enough. The Soviets had an offensive military doctrine predicated on massive armored thrusts in the event of war in Europe, supported by tactical nuclear weapons if necessary. McNamara's estimates acknowledged that the Soviets had 50 percent more tanks than NATO, the very instrument for executing their doctrine.[52] By 1968 the situation NATO was facing in Europe had deteriorated further.

In 1968 senior army and NATO leaders were even more skeptical of their capacity to resist Soviet aggression in Europe. U.S. troop reductions, its commitment to Vietnam, and Soviet force increases and modernization undermined the defense of Europe in the late 1960s.[53] By this time, Soviet forces outnumbered NATO forces and were better prepared for a fight.[54] Soviet forces constituted more than forty-five divisions and twenty-nine hundred tactical aircraft. Conversely, the U.S. government had reduced the U.S. Army in

Europe from 272,000, during the Berlin crisis, to 170,000 by the end of 1970. During Vietnam, the U.S. military presence in Europe dropped by more than 100,000 personnel, from 420,000 to 315,000 by September 1968.[55] Regarding readiness, Soviet units were at 90 percent readiness, as compared to 75 percent among NATO units. Moreover, as always, because of their shorter lines of communication, Soviet reserves would reach the front far more quickly. Numerous units in the United States would take months to achieve sufficient readiness.[56] Not only were U.S. military forces outnumbered, but their strategic reserves would be subject to much more friction than those of the Soviet Union in the event of war.

To make matters worse, many troops slated for the defense of Europe were already engaged in Vietnam, or the army had scavenged them to provide troops for the war.[57] For instance, the 101st Airborne Division was a rapid-reaction force for a crisis in Europe. However, the whole division and part of the 82nd were in Vietnam. According to the Army vice chief of staff, General Bruce Palmer, General James K. Polk, commanding general of the U.S. Army Europe, wanted out of his post early in 1968 because "he saw the 7th Army destroyed by the [Vietnam] war and there was nothing he could do about it."[58] General James Gavin of the U.S. Army viewed Vietnam as undermining the security of Europe by depleting U.S. military resources in this more important theater. Gavin was retired at the time but expressed this opinion to those he knew on active duty.[59] In light of these conditions, General Lyman Lemnitzer, Supreme Allied Commander Europe (SACEUR) and former U.S. Army chief of staff and chairman of the Joint Chiefs, concluded that NATO would have no choice but to rely on tactical nuclear weapons to defend Europe from a Soviet attack in the late 1960s.

The U.S. Army's troubles in Europe did not stop here, however. France withdrew its forces from NATO's integrated command structure and requested that all NATO forces leave its territory. With this decision, NATO lost five divisions and the main lines of communication through France to West Germany. The new lines of communication were located much closer to the West German border, and a Soviet attack would likely overrun them.

The situation in Europe deteriorated still further between August 20 and 21, 1968. During these two days, the Soviet Union deployed between 190,000 and 250,000 of their newly modernized forces in an invasion of Czechoslovakia. The Soviets were reacting to the political liberalization of the Czech leader Alexander Dubcek,[60] which they saw as a threat to the socialist movements in their satellites.[61] Secretary of Defense Clark Clifford and Earle Wheeler, chairman of the JCS and former army chief of staff, called the invasion a "quick, efficient, effective, and sophisticated" operation.[62] In the aftermath of the invasion, there was concern that Romania, Yugoslavia, or Austria might be next.[63] The invasion "shattered" the apparent "predictability" of East-West relations. At the time, many, including President Johnson, were touting the rise of détente and the end of the Cold War. Initially, senior civilian officials had discounted a Soviet military move against Czechoslovakia.[64] Secretary Rusk thought that the "political costs" of such a move would be too high.[65] After the apparent success of his efforts to conciliate the Soviets, the surprise of the invasion prompted President Johnson to call it a "bombshell"[66] and say, "The Cold War is not over."[67] According to Secretary Clifford, Moscow was "letting the world know" that it could "deliver its forces wherever it might choose to" and that Soviet foreign policy had not lost its teeth.[68]

The invasion caught civilian officials off guard, despite the fact that SACEUR Lemnitzer had informed Washington that Warsaw Pact exercises on the Czech border in July and August "exceeded anything that had ever been carried on in Europe."[69] They were so large that military leaders thought that they might be a "cover" for operations against NATO.[70] If it was a cover, Lemnitzer observed later, "they were hitting us at one of our weakest spots because France had just pulled out of the military integrated structure . . . in Southern Bavaria . . . where Bavaria runs along West Germany . . . along the Czechoslovakian border."[71] In his assessment of the consequences of the invasion, General Wheeler pointed out that the invasion increased the threat to NATO in three ways: Warsaw Pact troops had moved west, Warsaw Pact states had partially mobilized, and there were more Soviet troops in the satellite states.[72] In addition, U.S. Army commanders in Europe told Wheeler that they would need weeks or months to prepare and deploy to Europe.[73] General Wheeler informed President Johnson, "There is no military action we can take."[74] Although Johnson subsequently warned the Soviets not to act against Romania, Secretary of Defense Clifford, echoing Wheeler, told his Pentagon staff that the United States could do nothing to stop them.[75] The invasion highlighted and increased the vulnerabilities of NATO forces in Europe, making an already dire situation worse.

Despite the crisis atmosphere precipitated by Soviet aggression, Johnson was not prepared to make any direct declarations of America's commitment to Europe and continued to seek accommodation with the Soviets.[76] Clifford, Rusk, and Wheeler argued that the United States needed to do something to reassure the NATO allies, like a crisis meeting. Johnson would not approve such a meeting, however, until he had assurances from NATO allies that they would announce increases in their own military spending and preparedness.[77] Johnson would not increase U.S. commitments to NATO. To do so would increase the balance-of-payments issues associated with U.S. troops in Europe and undermine his attempts to de-escalate the Cold War. Domestically, such expenditures would undermine his Great Society programs. In the face of this increased threat to NATO and U.S. forces, the president still wanted to push ahead with strategic arms talks.[78] He also continued to seek Senate approval for the Non-Proliferation Treaty, arguing that failure to do so would be "ruinous."[79] In his last months in office, Johnson was determined to leave a legacy as a peacemaker in both Vietnam and the Cold War arms race. Unfortunately, in the end, he would accomplish neither.[80]

The reductions of U.S. troops in Europe, the strain of operations in Vietnam, the modernization and expansion of Soviet forces, the withdrawal of France from NATO, and the Soviet invasion of Czechoslovakia represented a perfect storm that threatened to overwhelm the U.S. Army in Europe. In Czechoslovakia the Soviet military had shown that it could move large numbers of troops rapidly and effectively, exactly what was required to execute their doctrine based on armored thrusts. According to senior army officers, and from the military realist perspective, the most dangerous threat had increased. Soviet forces in being outnumbered and outgunned NATO forces and were well placed to overcome the friction of war and execute their offensive, armored doctrine. This was the threat environment that confronted the writers of *Operations 1968*.

Army Doctrine in the Shadow of Vietnam and Czechoslovakia
Europe, Nuclear Weapons, and
Attack and Defense in Operations 1968

By the time the army was developing *Field Manual 100-5, Operations of Army Forces in the Field, 1968*, the former commander of all U.S. forces in Vietnam, General Westmoreland, was army chief of staff. The army published *Operations 1968* on September 6, 1968, three weeks after the Soviet invasion of Czechoslovakia. From the outset, there was an obvious difference between *Operations 1962* and *1968*. This difference reflected international circumstances. Displayed in bold below the titles of each major chapter were the Standardization Agreements (STANAGs) the United States had with its NATO and other allies and with which the new manual was compatible. Consistent with the views of its senior leadership, the central mission of army doctrine remained the defense of NATO Europe.[81] Although Johnson refused to make overt declarations of renewed U.S. support for NATO, by placing the STANAGs front and center in its most important doctrine, the army had done just that.

Despite this new doctrinal wrinkle, the inclusion of the STANAGs simply reinforced the European focus already at the core of army doctrine. As anticipated by military realism, the core content of army doctrine went largely unchanged between *Operations 1962* and *1968*. An examination of *Operations 1968* bears this out. Literally whole sections of *Operations 1962* and *1968* were identical.[82] For instance, the 1968 edition preserved the "spectrum of warfare," which required a flexible response instead of massive retaliation. This flexible response might still include tactical nuclear weapons. This made sense given that in January 1968, the same month the Tet Offensive kicked off, the NATO allies made flexible response their official defense policy. Initially, under the previous administration, European leaders were worried that Kennedy's conventional-defense initiatives signaled that the United States was unwilling to use nuclear weapons to defend Europe. American reluctance to authorize nuclear use was frightening because senior European commanders agreed with their U.S. Army counterparts that, given the balance of forces and material advantages enjoyed by the Warsaw Pact, tactical nuclear weapons would be necessary to hold back a Soviet assault on Europe. The German commander of Allied Forces Central Europe thought that selective use of tactical nuclear weapons would be required to hold off the Soviets, though he doubted that political authorization would come in time.[83] By 1968, however, partly through the influence of military realists both inside and outside the U.S. Army, flexible response included tactical nuclear weapons and the possibility of limited nuclear war, as advocated by *Operations 1962* but originally rejected by the Kennedy administration. *Operations 1968* argued nuclear use was subject to "scaling," that is, the United States could use nuclear weapons in a limited way.[84] Thus, the European allies signed on to flexible response once it started to look more like army doctrine and allayed their fears of American reluctance to engage in nuclear war to save Europe.

Along with the spectrum of warfare, *Operations 1968* also preserved the introductory chapter, "The Conduct of Battle: The Comparison of Nuclear and Nonnuclear Warfare."[85] Like its predecessor, the 1968 edition stated that commanders must have a keen awareness of the difference between conventional and nuclear operations and be constantly considering the consequences of a transition from one to the other. The 1968 edition of *Operations* continued to contend that the limited use of tactical nuclear weapons could facilitate the maneuver of conventional forces on the nuclear battlefield.[86] This continuity made sense considering that Soviet doctrine in 1968 continued to emphasize the use of nuclear weapons and maintained that they could use their conventional forces, which they were increasing dramatically, to exploit gaps in the enemy lines created by nuclear strikes. The nuclear mission remained at the core of doctrine. As historian Ingo Trauschweizer points out, U.S. forces in Europe "had to be prepared for nuclear, conventional, and mixed warfare" and "trained for small-unit tactics on the nuclear battlefield."[87] Understandably, then, *Operations 68* continued to advocate the close integration of conventional and nuclear forces and operations and listed the numerous advantages to be gained through nuclear use.[88] Furthermore, dispersion remained the primary means of minimizing the vulnerability of forces to nuclear attack. High mobility through mechanization, including helicopters, would enable dispersion.[89] The U.S. Army designed its forces and *Operations 1962* for just this kind of war. This effort continued into *Operations 1968*. The 1968 edition's sole addition was a discussion of "radiation effects and combat efficiency" that set out the acceptable and unacceptable levels of radiation to which commanders could expose their combat units.[90]

The army's continued interest in nuclear weapons was not limited to the pages of its most important doctrine. Articles on nuclear weapons made up a significant proportion of the editions of *Military Review* from 1962 to 1968.

There was variation from year to year in writing on nuclear weapons in *Military Review*, but this variation is inconsistent with bureaucratic, cultural, and civilian realist expectations. As civilian authorities became more preoccupied with Vietnam, these alternative theories expect a return to conventional warfare and World War II finest-hour thinking in the army. The opposite occurs. In this period, army interest in nuclear weapons is highest in 1967 (10 percent) and significant in both 1964 (8 percent) and 1966 (7 percent) under Johnson, returning to levels seen in 1961 and 1962. In contrast, articles on World War II peaked at 3.6 percent in 1963 and never rose above 1 percent from 1964 to 1968, being completely absent from the pages of *Military Review* in 1967 and 1968. While these trends are not consistent with the expectations of the alternative theories, they are consistent with military realism. As Vietnam began to degrade U.S. forces in Europe and the expansion and modernization of Soviet forces became clear, army interest in nuclear weapons increased. France's withdrawal from NATO in 1967 likely contributed to this trend. The army could not sweep nuclear weapons aside in the name of bureaucratic expediency or cultural norms. Especially given the even greater imbalance of capabilities in the late 1960s, the use of tactical nuclear weapons remained the only plausible means of resisting a Soviet advance into Europe. Interestingly, although this struggle would take place on some of the same battlefields where World War II had raged, the army was not harking back to its cultural finest hour for the keys to victory. The continuity between *Operations '62* and *'68* was not due to laziness on the part of the army's doctrine writers. The need to devise a doctrine that could plausibly address the most dangerous threat in the early 1960s had placed nuclear weapons firmly at the core of U.S. Army doctrine. By 1968 domestic political decisions and international circumstances had intensified the danger. As military realism expects, the result was a doctrine that leaned heavily on tactical nuclear weapons.

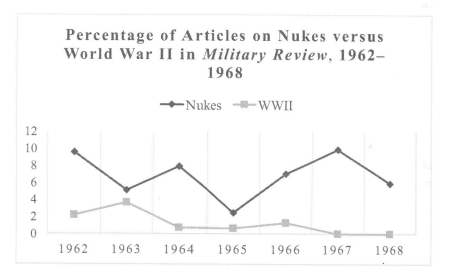

Percentage of Articles on Nukes versus World War II in *Military Review*, 1962–1968

The same doctrinal continuity was present when it came to offensive or defensive theories of victory. Like its predecessor, *Operations 1968* included "the principles of war," but with the same caveats.[91] Commanders were not to apply these principles blindly but adjust them to conditions on the ground. The changes in the army understanding of the relationship between attack and defense introduced by *Operations 1962* remained in the 1968 edition. The imbalance of capabilities that had precipitated these changes had increased in the intervening six years. Thus, defensive operations remained a means of destroying an attacking force and thereby contributing to the ultimate objective of the war.[92] As with *Operations 1962*, the defender continued to enjoy the initiative. Nor was the defense simply a fallback position when offense was impractical. A commander, argued the 1968 edition, could select the defensive deliberately, "particularly under fluid nuclear battlefield conditions."[93] Therefore, the authors of army doctrine passed on the more defensive theory of victory that originated in *Operations 1962*. This is contrary to Trauschweizer's contention that both *Operations 1962* and *1968* had an offensive theory of victory because they included the principles of war.[94] The threat environment of 1968 made adherence to the principles of war a fool's errand.

Finally, there was also continuity in the organization of the army units expected to execute doctrine. The ROAD divisional organization remained ideal for carrying out the core of army doctrine. The increased mobility provided by the ROAD divisions would facilitate rapid dispersion in the face of nuclear attack and mobile defensive operations against a materially superior foe.[95] Because senior army leaders saw the ROAD divisions as an essential component of the core mission, the army preserved ROAD and their doctrine throughout the course of the war in Vietnam. Army leaders also fought to retain a force in Germany able to resist a Soviet attack.[96] Some criticize this prioritization in light of the failure in Vietnam. However, at the time, as Trauschweizer points out, echoing the military realist view, "the specter of nuclear war in Europe was much more threatening than defeat in a peripheral war."[97]

In the end, contrary to the expectation of bureaucratic or cultural explanations, army doctrine in the late 1960s did not return to the glory days of World War II and conventional warfare. In 1968 the army continued to wrestle with the operational dilemmas of fighting on the nuclear battlefield and kept nuclear weapons at the core of its doctrine. Conventional warfare did not usurp the place of nuclear missions, and an offensive theory of victory did not overthrow the more defensive orientation of *Operations 1962*. This continuity is unexpected when civilian preoccupation with Vietnam and problems at home had left army bureaucrats and cultural guardians to their own doctrinal devices. However, this continuity is perfectly consistent with military realism. The dangerous threat presented by Soviet material capabilities, which had inspired the doctrinal innovations of the early 1960s, was more menacing in the late 1960s. Tactical nuclear weapons and a defensive theory of victory were essential components of a plausible response to this threat, no matter how much they conflicted with the interests of army bureaucrats and the norms of army culture.

The Lessons of Conflict: Vietnam,
Counterinsurgency, and *Operations 1968*

The war in Vietnam undercut the ability of the army to defend Europe. However, this did not mean *Operations 1968* ignored COIN or the lessons of Vietnam. In order to understand the lessons the army drew from Vietnam, however, we must begin with a clear picture of how the army thought about COIN in the 1960s and then what the army experience in Vietnam looked like. We must also evaluate this understanding in the context of the Cold War threat environment just set out. Only then can we evaluate what lessons the army did or did not incorporate into *Operations 1968*. The contention here is that taking these steps will weaken bureaucratic and military cultural explanations of the army in Vietnam. Conversely, this approach strengthens military realism as an explanation of army strategy and learning in Vietnam and of the role of COIN in *Operations 1968*.

As the previous chapter argued, COIN was more prominent in the 1962 edition of *Operations* than it had been in any previous edition.[98] Moreover, this prominence was not the result of civilian leaders forcing change on a reluctant bureaucracy or ossified army culture. From the late 1950s to the early 1960s, the U.S. Army was taking the threat of insurgency seriously. In practical, military realist terms, insurgency was a successful means of defeating an opponent and taking control of the state. Insurgents had defeated American allies and were threatening to do so again in Southeast Asia. However, the army's solutions to this threat were not limited to bureaucratically driven or culturally accepted methods, like offensive combat operations. Army officers recognized the importance of civic action and development in countering insurgencies. They also considered conventionally trained and thinking forces inadequate to the task. The pages of *Military Review*, the flagship journal of the Command and General Staff College, a supposed bastion of army culture and tradition, also reflected a concern with COIN. Moreover, the majority of the articles on insurgency and COIN in *Military Review* did not recommend conventional military solutions to insurgencies. The question is whether the U.S. Army's concern with COIN ended with the Kennedy era. The chart below compares the proportion of articles written on insurgency and counterinsurgency in *Military Review* from 1962 to 1968 to articles on the use of tactical nuclear weapons and World War II.[99]

Clearly, the concern with COIN in *Military Review* did not end with the Kennedy administration, as bureaucratic and cultural theories expect. This

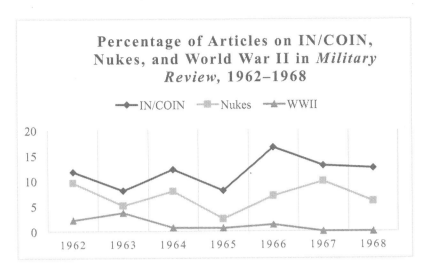

Percentage of Articles on IN/COIN, Nukes, and World War II in *Military Review*, 1962–1968

continuity is surprising given that there was no longer a need to pay lip service to COIN to placate civilian leaders. The army continued to wrestle with the problem of insurgency into the Johnson administration. Though there was a sharp increase in IN/COIN articles during the Kennedy administration, topping out at 11 percent, there was no precipitous drop in IN/COIN articles after Kennedy's assassination, when army bureaucracy and culture should have reasserted themselves under a Johnson administration less interested in the topic. In fact, the highest proportion of articles on IN/COIN was 16 percent in 1966, the year after army combat units touched down in South Vietnam. From then until 1968, the proportion of articles dealing with COIN never drops below 13 percent, a greater proportion than at the height of Kennedy's COIN push.

Bureaucratic and cultural theorists might counter by pointing out that we would expect an increase in articles on IN/COIN after the engagement in Vietnam, but their content will reflect army preferences for conventional-warfare solutions to the problems of insurgency. This is to be expected, too, because many of these pieces were written by students of the CGSC, where they were being indoctrinated in the cultural and bureaucratic priorities of the army. However, the evidence does not support this interpretation. The following chart summarizes the number of articles published about Vietnam in *Military Review* from 1963 to 1968. It then divides the articles based on whether they were primarily about conventional engagements and warfare in Vietnam or IN/COIN-type operations involving civic action and other unconventional methods of COIN.

There was not a particular emphasis on conventional military solutions to the insurgency in Vietnam. In fact, many of the pieces linked success in COIN operations there to civic action and population security. Beginning in 1966, the first full year U.S. troops were engaged in Vietnam, the number of articles on COIN versus conventional operations was equal. In 1967 there were more articles on COIN than conventional operations in Vietnam. Finally, in 1968, the only year when articles on conventional operations outnumbered COIN articles, there were six articles on COIN in Vietnam and seven on conventional military operations. This hardly represents a resounding rejection of COIN. This evidence contradicts bureaucratic and cultural expectations. The fact that CGSC instructors and students wrote a high proportion of these COIN articles reflects the degree to which COIN was part of the curriculum there and that CGSC did not primarily recommend conventional military solutions to insurgency. Moreover, the above data show us that the army was not simply drawing lessons for conventional warfare from Vietnam. Students and instructors at the CGSC consistently contemplated the lessons from COIN operations in Vietnam in the pages *Military Review*. The CGSC, a supposed bulwark of army culture, promoted deep thinking about a form of warfare that is supposedly abhorrent to that culture.

There was an even higher proportion of articles on IN/COIN than there was on nuclear weapons from 1962 to 1968. Articles on nuclear weapons had reached their peak in 1958, topping out at 20.7 percent and with an average of 16.1 percent between 1957 and 1960. It was in this period that the army

Military Review Articles on Vietnam, 1963–1968

wrestled with the dilemmas of the nuclear battlefield and then settled on its interpretation of the consequences of nuclear weapons for its operations. In contrast, the army continued to wrestle with IN/COIN into the 1960s, especially as it became directly involved in Vietnam. Still, between 1962 and 1968, *Military Review* dedicated an average of 6.8 percent of each issue to nuclear weapons. However, the proportion of articles on nuclear weapons began to increase between 1966 and 1968, possibly due to revelations about Soviet forces' modernization and expansion in the midst of American involvement in Vietnam and the French withdrawal from NATO.

Contrast the treatment of IN/COIN and nuclear weapons with the proportion of articles on World War II, and it becomes clear that the army of the 1960s was not dwelling on its cultural finest hour. From 1962 to 1966, articles on World War II constituted 1.7 percent of *Military Review* issues and made no appearances in either 1967 or 1968. Meanwhile, IN/COIN, a form of warfare supposedly anathema to military bureaucrats and U.S. Army culture, was consistently discussed in *Military Review*.

Army officers did not confine their thinking about IN/COIN within the walls of Fort Leavenworth, however. One officer keenly aware of the challenges of COIN, and who thought a great deal about Mao Zedong's strategy of the People's War, was none other than William Westmoreland. According to many, General Westmoreland was the archetypal army officer in Vietnam, obsessed with finding conventional military solutions to the insurgency. However, Westmoreland had thought extensively about the problems of COIN even in the years leading up to the war in Vietnam, as the army itself had done. While in charge of West Point, Westmoreland had increased the number of hours cadets would spend studying COIN and encouraged the development of a summer program on COIN operations.[100] Westmoreland was a product of an army system that took COIN seriously.

However, when Westmoreland and the army arrived in Vietnam in 1965, they were not confronted by a low-level insurgency. Instead, they joined a war that employed both low-level subversion and main-force units that were annihilating South Vietnamese security forces. As one army officer noted, "We were constantly running into strong NVA and VC units, well equipped, well armed, well organized and always from regimental to division strength."[101] Some have argued that the army obsession with destroying enemy main-force units in Vietnam was favored because it was more consistent with army culture than development-based COIN operations. On the contrary, as shown above, the army took COIN seriously. However, in Vietnam, the army did not face the kind of war that COIN theories of the 1950s and '60s were designed to counter. The main-force units of the enemy were not a figment of Westmoreland and the army's cultural imagination. By December 1965, 160 Vietnamese Communist battalions, of which 55 were North Vietnamese regulars, were operating in South Vietnam and in the border areas of Cambodia and Laos.[102] Things were no better in 1966 and 1967, when forty-five hundred and six thousand enemy infiltrated South Vietnam *per month*, respectively.[103] Therefore, between these two years, approximately 126,000 enemy combatants flooded into Vietnam. Add to this that NVA main-force units began infiltrating into South Vietnam as early as 1963, and one gets a sense of the extent of the forces arrayed against U.S. and South Vietnamese ground forces. In this early phase of the war, these infiltrating units were linking up with Vietcong units, forming battalions or larger formations, and destroying South Vietnamese forces.[104] Indeed, the strength and tactical proficiency of these units precipitated direct American intervention.

Most important, the Vietnamese Communists saw these units not as part of a low-level subversion campaign but as engaged in the annihilation of South Vietnamese and U.S. military units. The purpose of these forces, according to Vietnamese Communist leaders, was "to conduct battles of annihilation to shatter a significant portion of the enemy's regular army."[105] Strategically, according to the leadership in Hanoi, although the political struggle was important, it was secondary to the main-force battle, which "had to follow the laws of war, which are to destroy the enemy's combat strength."[106] As Gregory Daddis notes, "U.S. Army tactics sometimes were reliant on firepower and large-unit operations because of the enemy's own commitment to winning the war militarily."[107] This advocacy of battles of annihilation might seem surprising coming from the Vietnamese Communists, who are often seen as the heirs of Mao's strategy of the People's War. However, Mao stressed continually that guerrilla operations by themselves could not be decisive.[108] The father of modern revolutionary insurgency argued that only when guerrillas transitioned to a more conventional style of fighting and destroyed the enemy in direct combat could they achieve a decision.[109] The Vietnamese Communists were in the midst of this transition when Johnson inserted U.S. forces into the war.

In response to this state of affairs, Westmoreland had to develop a strategy that would both address subversion and low-level insurgent activity and confront main-force units trying to annihilate the South Vietnamese security forces. Westmoreland used U.S. forces in large operations to attack large enemy formations to keep them away from areas where COIN activities were combating subversion and lower-level violence.[110] In August 1966, he expressed the relationship between COIN and enemy main-force units in the following way: "Essential tasks of revolutionary development and nation building cannot be accomplished if enemy main force units can gain access to the population centers and destroy our efforts."[111]

Westmoreland was not alone in considering the North Vietnamese large units the best target for U.S. forces and a priority for the war effort as a whole. Some have argued that General Harold K. Johnson, army chief of staff from July 1964 to July 1968, was dissatisfied with the way Westmoreland was running the war. The evidence for this claim is his commissioning of the PROVN report in March 1966. The PROVN study supposedly called for a COIN strategy and a turning away from Westmoreland's obsession with accumulating "body counts" in the fight against main-force units. The PROVN study is often used as a bludgeon to indict Westmoreland's strategy and laud Chief of Staff Johnson's better, but tragically ignored, appreciation of COIN in Vietnam.[112]

But in fact, General Johnson agreed with Westmoreland's assessment that pacification could not be undertaken successfully unless enemy main-force units were destroyed or at least kept off balance. As Johnson stated, "The enemy's larger military formations must be driven away from the population. . . . If we were to adopt a strategy which emphasizes only clear and hold operations, enemy base areas would become reasonably secure again. Any change in emphasis away from search-and-destroy operations would free the enemy to operate with relative impunity around and between the peripheries of our enclaves."[113]

In addition, upon closer examination, the PROVN study provided few novel recommendations and in the end agreed with the prioritization of the destruction of main-force units.[114] As historian Andrew Birtle points out, the report "repeatedly stressed that the 'bulk' of allied regular forces should be directed against the enemy's main forces while the 'remainder' guarded the people, since 'the primary role' of US armed forces in Vietnam was 'to isolate the battlefield' by curtailing significant infiltration, demolishing the key war zones, and fully engaging PAVN [People's Army of Vietnam] main force VC units wherever and whenever they are located. Unrelenting pressure must be imposed upon these major enemy combat forces."[115]

Thus, senior army leaders agreed that COIN operations were on the low end of the conflict spectrum, and army commanders could not conduct them in the presence of an enemy force capable of major escalation. It would appear, then, that the military realist perspective also expressed itself in army strategy in Vietnam. So long as the United States sought to impose its will by force, U.S. commanders could not ignore an enemy that could appeal to the escalatory logic of force. Given the limited forces at Westmoreland's disposal, these forces had to be the focus of his operations.

This did not mean that Westmoreland completely neglected COIN in Vietnam or pacification. Gregory Daddis convincingly documents Westmoreland's continual concern with the pacification program in South Vietnam. American commanders, with the support of Westmoreland, repeatedly adapted their tactics for dealing with the problem of the politico-military conflict they were fighting.[116] "Throughout his term," Daddis points out, "pacification remained an integral part of Westmoreland's strategy."[117] Westmoreland's dilemma, attempting to balance major military operations with COIN in Vietnam, reflected the broader thinking in the army revealed in the pieces on Vietnam in *Military Review*, where there was an almost equal proportion of articles on COIN as there was on conventional engagements and solutions.[118] In public comments on Vietnam, Westmoreland continually reminded his listeners, "Viet Nam is not only a military operation, but a 'political and psychological' struggle as well."[119] The commander of Military Assistance Command, Vietnam, understood the importance of civic-action programs as a means of winning over the people. He encouraged subordinate commanders to undertake such programs in addition to seeking out large enemy formations. As Daddis concludes, arguments that Westmoreland did not appreciate or try to implement a COIN strategy in Vietnam "fall flat" when confronted with the historical evidence.[120]

Senior army leaders were not the only army officers who came to Vietnam with their heads full of COIN theories, which the facts on the ground then upended. Army commanders who came to Vietnam critical of what they saw as Westmoreland's overly conventional approach, at the expense of a COIN strategy, confronted starker realities on taking command. Despite their best efforts to engage in civic action and COIN operations, the conventionally powerful enemy drew them into violent engagements. For instance, Major General William R. Peers, commander of the 4th Infantry Division, had a clear understanding of the imperatives of COIN: "Killing the Viet Cong alone can't achieve the goal of defeating the enemy. The concept of nation building ties together the military, political, economic, social and educational programs which aim to liberate the people from Viet Cong control."[121]

The result of this outlook was the Good Neighbors initiative, which placed a ten-man civic-action team in villages to work with locals. Despite his best efforts to focus on COIN, by November 1967 Peers was "immersed in more conventional operations": "Peers's intelligence staff soon determined that the entire 1st North Vietnamese Army Division was preparing for an assault near Dak To. Meanwhile, NLF [National Liberation Front] main force units unleashed diversionary attacks against such targets as Kontum City. On 3 November, the 4th Infantry Division made its first significant contact with the NVA and for the remainder of the month became consumed in a bloody struggle for the borderlands. In all, over 370 Americans were killed in battle. Estimates of enemy losses ranged between 1,000 and 1,600 dead."[122]

Although Peers appreciated the importance of COIN for winning over the populace, he could not ignore the reality and threat of escalation presented by major NVA and Vietcong units. Westmoreland and the U.S. Army in Vietnam were not imposing their cultural essence on the war. Rather, they were responding to the enemy strategy that they confronted on arrival. Moreover, the army's response to the actual enemy they faced in Vietnam was consistent with military realism. The army in Vietnam prioritized dealing with main-force units because otherwise attacks by these forces would undermine any COIN efforts. Army commanders could not ignore the ability and willingness on the part of the Vietnamese Communists to appeal to the escalatory logic of force. Civic action and economic and political development could not stem that tide.

Recent cultural interpretations of the army's behavior in Vietnam neglect this conventional aspect of the war and indict army culture based on the assumption that the war was predominantly one against small groups of shadowy guerrillas. Austin Long uses Army Special Forces and U.S. Marine operations in Vietnam as examples of strategic roads not taken because of the army's wrongheaded obsession with conventional fighting. Long uses the army takeover of the Montangard indigenous forces, established by the Army Special Forces, and their subsequent transition to more conventional offensive operations as an instance of army culture overriding sound military innovation. However, no mention is made of the major escalation in conventional forces undertaken by the North Vietnamese at the time of the transition, a threat that local defense forces doing population security and civic action could not address.[123] Instead, Long attributes this move to army cultural norms and its obsession with large-unit operations, which precluded it from adopting the supposedly more effective small-unit approach of the Special Forces.[124]

Long argues that the U.S. Marines also had a better organization for COIN in Vietnam, the Combined Action Platoons. Other scholars too cited the CAPs as an example of COIN done right in Vietnam.[125] These squads of Marines would insert themselves into a Vietnamese hamlet and run combined security operations with the local Popular Forces (PFs) to secure and win the hearts and minds of the local populace. The Marines' openness to this mode of operations, Long contends, was due to their military culture, which was traditionally rooted in COIN-type operations. In fact, however, main-force enemy units overran the majority of the CAPs and compelled the Marines to transition to less vulnerable "mobile" CAPs.[126] Moreover, in 1966, major Vietnamese Communist forces infiltrating into South Vietnam forced even the culturally predisposed Marines to shift much of their force away from COIN to confront these forces.[127] Prior to this the Marines were able to concentrate on COIN and CAPs in places like Quang Ngai Province because they were not in the direct path of main-force PAVN units infiltrating from Cambodia or Laos.[128] Long uses heavy conventional fighting as an explanation for the Marines' departure from the norms of a military culture that promoted COIN, but makes little mention of the similar circumstances that confronted the U.S. Army. If military culture is so central to the explanation, why did the Marines abandon population security when confronted with the powerful conventional forces of the PAVN? In the case of the Marines too, the logic of force dictated military operations more than military culture. As Daddis notes at the end of his work, "Simply put, war is about interaction."[129] As military realism expects under such conditions, commanders prioritized the more dangerous threat because escalation required counterescalation.

In sum, though the army took COIN seriously, the highly conventional threats it encountered in Vietnam led Westmoreland and the army to prioritize the fight with the main-force enemy. Nevertheless, as Daddis shows, even in the teeth of the conventional fight, Westmoreland did not abandon efforts at COIN. Daddis concludes, "Though a gripping tale, the story of Westmoreland and the army losing Vietnam because of a foolhardy devotion to conventional operations and a zealous pursuit of high body counts is quite simply fiction."[130] The analysis here shows that it is not the case, as Long contends, that the army or Marine Corps' behavior in Vietnam "indicates a powerful role for organizational culture in determining the actual conduct of counterinsurgency."[131] The army focused on main-force units not for cultural or bureaucratic reasons but because these units were a dangerous source of escalation. Thus, the military realist tendency to focus on the most dangerous threats may not be limited to international threat assessment but can also express itself within a theater of operations.

As I have pointed out already, however, the military realist focus on the logic of force does not necessarily lead to optimal doctrine or, in this case, military strategy. The focus on main-force units may have made it difficult for the military realists in the U.S. Army to shift their attention from them when conditions on the ground changed. When the Vietnamese Communists backed away from their conventional unit strategy later in the war, Westmoreland and his predecessor, General Creighton Abrams, continued to seek out the most dangerous threat in the theater of war.[132] By then, enemy main-force units had dispersed and shrunk from direct combat.[133] Military realists are not purely rational strategic thinkers but strategists who tend to focus on the escalatory logic of force when an opponent appeals to it. In this way, the military realist perspective may have hindered adaptation in military strategy later in the Vietnam War.

The prioritization of main-force units was not without its advantages, however. After the initial shock of Tet, the preparedness of army units to counter such main-force units enabled them to deal a major military blow to the Vietnamese Communists, from which they would take years to recover. Consequently, because the Communists had been so devastated by the Tet *counteroffensive*, COIN efforts after 1968 met with greater success.[134] From the army perspective, therefore, just at the point when their mode of operations had dealt a devastating blow to the enemy, civilian leaders denied them the resources to follow up the post-Tet victories.[135] In short, the conduct of the war did not disprove the army focus on enemy main-force units, which influenced the lessons learned.

Westmoreland's Lessons and Operations 1968

Armed with a more accurate picture of the actual conduct of the war in Vietnam and an appreciation of the army's concern for COIN in this period, we can better evaluate the doctrinal lessons the U.S. Army drew from that war and which of the competing theories of military innovation best accounts for the results. Once he became army chief of staff, some argue, General Westmoreland was obsessed with justifying his and the army's role in Vietnam. Westmoreland was so distracted, Lewis Sorley argues, that the general was not the chief of staff during this period; rather, his vice chief, Bruce Palmer, was actually running the army.[136] Palmer himself vehemently denied this assessment, however. "That's not true at all," Palmer stated in his army oral history. "Westy knew what was going on and held the reins firmly."[137] Westmoreland did spend a great deal of time traveling and speaking on the war.[138] However,

110

his travels around the country were an attempt to remedy the fact that "the difficult task of 'Nation Building' fails to receive the public attention that is accorded to combat actions in Vietnam."[139] Westmoreland's justification is no doubt surprising to those who see him as a narrowly conventional soldier. In short, Westmoreland, the highest-ranking officer in the U.S. Army, was working to dispel the narrative of the Vietnam War that bureaucratic and cultural theorists argue it was in the interest of the army to perpetuate.

While he was trying to change the national narrative about Vietnam, Westmoreland was also concerned with drawing lessons from the war. While the army's experience in Vietnam did not lead to core changes in its doctrine, the lessons learned in Vietnam did appear in the pages of *Operations 1968*, published during Westmoreland's tenure as army chief of staff. According to Westmoreland, the lessons the army needed to preserve from Vietnam were the following: the important advancements in airmobile operations;[140] better techniques for controlling artillery fire and locating "enemy mortars, artillery, and long range rockets";[141] the utility of tanks and mechanized forces, at first deemed inappropriate for Vietnam;[142] and the need for increased bomb accuracy, especially in a tactical role.[143] Other technical innovations included the sensor, which Westmoreland thought would enable the "soldier of the future" to defend more economically because of better awareness of the enemy's location. This was an important consideration for a force on the defensive facing a materially superior foe, like the army in Europe.[144] According to Westmoreland, this "embryonic" sensor technology could revolutionize future warfare.[145] Westmoreland established the STANO program (surveillance, target acquisition, and night observation) at Fort Hood, Texas, to study the battlefield implications of new sensor technology.[146] In many ways, Westmoreland was right. Sensor technology would become a key aspect of the revolution in military affairs (RMA) that swept through the U.S. military in the 1990s. Electronic communications also saw significant advancement in Vietnam.[147] Reflecting the observations of the chief of staff, *Operations 1968* discussed the effects of this new technology at length.

Westmoreland also ordered the commandant of the Command and General Staff College, Lieutenant General John H. Hay, to study the tactical lessons learned from engagements in Vietnam. Westmoreland had selected Hay based on his Vietnam combat experience.[148] If we accept the argument that unconventional guerrilla bands dominated the Vietnam War, incorporating these highly conventional lessons into army doctrine appears shortsighted and parochial, consistent with a bureaucratically and culturally stunted military organization. However, when we appreciate the more conventional aspects of the enemy highlighted earlier, these lessons are much less surprising and we need not attribute them to parochialism.

Of all the operational lessons of Vietnam, however, Westmoreland gave pride of place to the experience of airmobile infantry. In Vietnam the tactics of helicopter-borne assault were refined to facilitate rapid concentration of forces against the main forces of the enemy. Westmoreland promoted army aviation extensively, even receiving his helicopter pilot certification while army chief of staff. In his memoir, *A Soldier Reports*, he wrote effusively of the virtues of the helicopter. "Most impressive of all," he wrote there of the helicopter in Vietnam, "for the first time in military history . . . a true airmobility on the battlefield" was achieved.[149] "The military man of the future will," he continued, "truly think, live, and fight in the three dimensions of ground, sea, and air."[150] Like Hamilton Howze, Westmoreland identified helicopters as a new breed of cavalry. "It was with some satisfaction and keen awareness of change," the general wrote, "that . . . my first mount in the army had been a horse and my last a helicopter."[151]

Not surprisingly, then, airmobile forces figured prominently in *Operations 1968*. In *Operations 1962*, airmobile operations had shared a chapter with *airborne* operations. In keeping with the chief of staff's enthusiasm for air mobility and the extensive use of the helicopter in Vietnam, *Operations 1968* gave airmobile operations their own chapter. The new manual set out how airmobile forces contributed to each of the principles of war. However, the manual made little mention of the role that air mobility could play in counterguerrilla operations. Rather, it lauded these forces for the same reasons expressed in the 1962 edition. Airmobile forces vastly increased the "mobility" and ability of units to "disperse" rapidly for defense and attack.[152] Moreover, their ability to gather intelligence and communicate over longer distances could help mitigate the disadvantages of a widely dispersed force.[153] A focus on the ability to move troops rapidly by helicopter was nothing new to army doctrine. *Operations 1962* argued that the added mobility of helicopters was essential for success in fighting a much more powerful Soviet foe in Europe. Helicopters would enable the mobile defense necessary to counter a Soviet doctrine of armored penetration. In 1968 Westmoreland and the army were following in the intellectual footsteps of Hamilton Howze, the father of airmobility. Howze had recommended helicopters for an antiarmor role in Europe.[154] Airmobile forces would also be more survivable on a battlefield irradiated by tactical nuclear weapons. It is worth noting again that while helicopters are often associated with hunting down elusive guerrillas in Vietnam, all through the 1960s the U.S. Army saw them primarily as a means of defending Europe against a Soviet attack, especially if tactical nuclear weapons had to be used. The use of air-mobile forces in Vietnam reinforced the army view that helicopters could be a powerful tool of warfare. Westmoreland was determined that those lessons, and others from Vietnam, be codified in the army's most important doctrine.

Counterinsurgency and Operations 1968

Although Westmoreland wanted some of the more conventional lessons of Vietnam codified in doctrine, this did not mean that *Operations 1968* abandoned COIN. According to all three of the alternative theories, once the civilian COIN initiatives dried up under Johnson, the army should use the opportunity to excise COIN from its most important doctrine. Indeed, when it came to COIN-type missions, there appear to be important differences between the early and late 1960s manuals. In *Operations 1962*, the chapter on unconventional warfare was followed by one on "military operations against irregular forces."[155] This rather lengthy chapter was *not* included in *Operations 1968*. Rather, doctrine writers subsumed discussion of operations against irregular forces into a new chapter titled "Cold War Operations."[156] This section describing operations at the lowest end of the conflict spectrum joined operations against irregular forces with "parades, maneuvers, demonstrations, police and patrol duty . . . or reinforcement of a threatened area."[157] With this stroke of the pen, doctrine writers seem to have relegated COIN in army doctrine. In fact, however, the *Operations* manual of the Vietnam War continued to reserve space in its pages for COIN missions, although under a different name.

Operations 1968 replaced the term *counterinsurgency* with the concept *stability operations*. The use of the term *stability operations* instead of *COIN* was intentional. "Within the U.S. Army," *Operations 1968* stated, "use of 'stability operations' or 'internal defense and internal development' is preferred to 'counterinsurgency.'"[158] Stability operations received their own chapter in *Operations 1968*.[159] General Harold K. Johnson, army chief of staff from July 1964 to July 1968, championed this new designation for COIN-type operations.[160] Again, some paint General Johnson as an advocate of COIN who was, according to one recent account, "deeply disturbed" by the army's COIN performance in Vietnam and was trying to use the concept of stability operations to change the institution.[161] However, as shown in the debate surrounding military strategy in Vietnam, Johnson did not repudiate the way the army was fighting in Vietnam. Moreover, the Kennedy administration established the concepts of stability operations and internal defense; they were not innovations of the Vietnam-era army. The COIN doctrine of the Kennedy administration was titled the "Overseas Internal Defense Policy," literally called the "Counterinsurgency Doctrine" of the administration.[162] The definition of *stability operations* in *Operations 1968* bears out the relationship between stability operations and OIDP. Stability operations were "internal defense and internal development operations and assistance provided by the Armed Forces to maintain, restore, or establish a climate of order within which responsible government can function effectively and without which progress cannot be achieved."[163]

As Kennedy and the army of the early 1960s advocated, the focus of these operations was political and social development, without which military operations would be fruitless. In such missions, *Operations 1968* stated, the army must "assist, through the Military Assistance Program, in developing military strength and economic and political stability of selected friendly nations."[164] However, according to *Operations 1968*, commanders had to discontinue stability operations in the presence of an enemy prepared to escalate the use of force. This too was consistent with army doctrine and thinking in the early 1960s. Confronting main-force enemy units while trying to conduct pacification operations in Vietnam bore out this doctrinal insight and was consistent with the military realist perspective on the power of escalation to dictate military operations. In the end, by favoring the terms *stability operations* and *internal defense and internal development* over *counterinsurgency*, *Operations 1968* was invoking the internal-defense plan developed under Kennedy rather than rejecting COIN.[165] In fact, after the war, Colonel Harry G. Summers, an army officer and vociferous critic of COIN in Vietnam, lambasted the army for retaining the COIN concept in *Operations 1968*. Summers "noted that [*Operations 1968*] contained wooly definitions of the purpose of the Army centered in notions of providing stability and development throughout the world."[166] COIN remained in army doctrine because the army took the threat of insurgency seriously, even if it did not alter the core of its doctrine. *Operations 1968* rejected COIN in name only, not in substance.

The lessons the U.S. Army doctrine drew from Vietnam make more sense when one appreciates that operations there were not limited to countering shadowy insurgents at the village level. There was a constant threat of attack by forces capable of real escalation, which undermined pacification. The army focus on these forces and the doctrinal lessons drawn from the Vietnam experience seem much less like bureaucratic or cultural foot-dragging when we recognize their context and understand the military realist perspective. The alternative theories expect the army to stop paying lip service to COIN in their doctrine when Kennedy's COIN initiatives faded. In fact, however, COIN remained an important part of army doctrine. The historical evidence does not support the idea that the army's "written doctrine . . . was merely a smoke-screen."[167] Army military strategy in Vietnam and the doctrine it developed in the heat of fighting there do not support bureaucratic and cultural theories as well as previously thought. Moreover, military realism provides a strong alternative explanation of the U.S. Army in Vietnam and the army doctrine born in the climactic year of that war.

Conclusion

This chapter took the theory of military realism and its theoretical competitors from a peacetime to a wartime context. But this was not just any war. Scholars of military innovation see the story of the U.S. Army in Vietnam as a model of what happens when bureaucratic and cultural forces inhibit military innovation, even while the bullets are flying and soldiers are being killed. However, we should not examine the conflict in Vietnam in isolation, as is too often done. While the army was embroiled in Vietnam, the Cold War provided the broader strategic context for innovation and continuity across the three key areas of U.S. Army doctrine. As the previous chapter showed, the gravity of this threat guided army doctrine in the early 1960s. By 1968 the threat from the Soviet Union had increased, especially in Europe, the Soviets expanding and modernizing their conventional forces and increasing defense spending. The Soviet invasion of Czechoslovakia and the "defection" of France from NATO[168] made the already difficult job of defending Europe more challenging. As this threat rose, the demands of the war in Vietnam and the withdrawal of U.S. troops from Europe depleted the army's physical capabilities to address it. This frightening state of affairs validated the threat assessment and doctrinal decisions made in the early 1960s. The result was doctrinal continuity. *Operations 1968* upheld and expanded the emphasis on the nuclear battlefield in army doctrine. In addition, *Operations 1968* preserved the more defensive theory of victory that was developed in the late 1950s and early 1960s. This doctrinal continuity is contrary to the expectations of bureaucratic and cultural theories. Rather than maximizing autonomy and resources and fleeing uncertainty, the army continued to base its force structure and doctrine on the very weapons that endangered these bureaucratic priorities. Even peripheral changes in army doctrine, like airmobile tactics tested in Vietnam, continued to serve the requirements of the nuclear battlefield. Although nuclear weapons and a defensive theory of victory were contrary to U.S. Army culture, they remained at the center of doctrine, as required by the threat environment and as military realism anticipated.

The evidence presented here is also problematic for civilian realism. Army leaders should have taken advantage of civilian preoccupation with Vietnam and domestic politics to pursue a conventional doctrine consistent with bureaucratic preferences and cultural norms. In the absence of oversight, they could have given nuclear weapons a much lower profile and adopted an offensive theory of victory. As already noted, they did neither. In this case, senior leaders in the army kept sight of the international threat environment, while civilians were preoccupied elsewhere.

A number of scholars have argued that the U.S. Army tried to conventionalize the war in Vietnam to suit its cultural and bureaucratic preference for conventional warfare and its distaste for COIN operations. However, as this and the previous chapter argued, throughout the 1950s and '60s the army took the threat of insurgency seriously. Senior army officers recognized that COIN operations were not like conventional military operations and that conventional forces were not well suited to COIN. Had the army confronted only a shadowy insurgent force in Vietnam, it would have conducted a classic COIN operation that might have been the pride of Galula and other COIN theorists. However, the enemy that the army faced in Vietnam was actually highly conventional and had been since before 1965. In many ways, the Vietnamese Communists conventionalized the war in Vietnam, not U.S. Army bureaucrats or cultural guardians. That the army drew conventional-warfare lessons from Vietnam for *Operations 1968* is unsurprising.

The deteriorating situation in Europe, exacerbated by Vietnam, ensured COIN would be a low-priority mission for the army in 1968. *Operations 1968* placed COIN, what it called "stability operations," squarely at the low end of the conflict spectrum. The COIN mission continued to be a low priority in the army's most important manual. Nevertheless, army doctrine did not forget about COIN, and its pages preserved the insights about COIN expressed in *Operations 1962*.

Although not the main focus of this chapter, military realism also provides a plausible explanation for army strategy in Vietnam. The army focused on the main-force units of the NVA and Vietcong because if their power had gone unchecked, they would have undermined any COIN efforts with their attacks, as major enemy units had done in 1964 and 1965, helping to trigger American intervention.[169] The army did not go after large enemy units for cultural or bureaucratic reasons, but did so because these units were capable of over-turning COIN efforts with their superior forces. Indeed, this was the enemy's strategy. The army in Vietnam based its strategy in part on the escalatory logic of force and the way in which force had to be met with force.

The case of the U.S. Army in Vietnam has shaped our understanding of military bureaucracies and culture. However, the narrative of the U.S. Army in Vietnam is flawed, calling into question the theories that enlist this narrative for support. Alternatively, military realism helps us understand the unexpected flexibility of the U.S. Army that fought in Vietnam. Military realism helps explain why the army focused on both Europe and the Soviet threat but also took COIN seriously and did not simply recommend conventional military solutions to the problem of insurgency. Communist insurgencies represented a real threat but were less dangerous than the specter of Soviet aggression. In the end, the communist insurgency in Vietnam forced the United States to accept defeat there and overran its South Vietnamese ally. Many have argued that defeat in Vietnam left an indelible mark on America's army and haunted it and its doctrine into the 1970s and '80s.

4 FROM ACTIVE DEFENSE TO AIRLAND BATTLE

The Cold War Doctrine of the '70s and '80s

ALMOST A DECADE passed between the publication of *Operations 1968* and its successor *Operations 1976*. The army published the new manual the year after the fall of Saigon marked the end of the Vietnam War and of South Vietnam as a political entity. After its central role in the victories of World War II, America had experienced its first serious military defeat. That defeat left an indelible mark on all those who experienced it and on American politics and foreign policy. The U.S. Army was one of the institutions rocked to its foundations by the experience. In its grief over the loss, many argue, the U.S. Army went into denial. Its leaders turned their backs on the Vietnam experience and refocused their attention on familiar and comfortable ground: the defense of Europe. One of the chief proponents of this intentional amnesia, says the conventional wisdom, was General William E. DePuy, who had commanded the First Infantry Division in Vietnam.[1] As the quotation from him in the previous chapter showed, DePuy was one of those army officers in Vietnam who were optimistic about the prospects for victory there in 1967. He went on to found the new U.S. Army Training and Doctrine Command (TRADOC). There he decisively shaped the post-Vietnam U.S. Army through the development of *Operations 1976*.

The development of *Operations 1976* under DePuy, known as Active Defense, and *Operations 1982* and '86, known as AirLand Battle, have received more attention than any other doctrinal changes in the U.S. Army. Both doctrines were key drivers of change in the U.S. Army after Vietnam. Thus, the case of doctrinal development in the U.S. Army of the 1970s and '80s is perfect for assessing the factors that shape military doctrine and drive military innovation. However, this chapter will make the case that the accepted narrative about the development of these doctrines, even within the U.S. Army itself, is incomplete and often inaccurate. As in the two previous chapters, here I work to place the U.S. Army doctrine of the period within its broader Cold War context. The previous two chapters also provide a broader doctrinal context, which allows us to determine if army thinking and doctrine after Vietnam were as revolutionary as some want to claim. I again test the expectations of military realism against those of its three competitors across the three key areas of doctrine. This chapter provides an additional opportunity to evaluate the extent of doctrinal innovation because it encompasses the transition between two crucial editions of *Operations*, in which many of the same players took part. The result is a story about the post-Vietnam U.S. Army that cuts against the accepted narrative both inside and outside that army.

Civilian Leaders and U.S. Army Doctrine in the '70s and '80s

To tell this story, we need to define the cast of theoretical characters. Here this means again beginning with the expectations of the competing theories of military innovation in a different civil-military and international context. Civilian realism argues that civilian leaders will be keenly aware of the international balance of power and will intervene in their militaries to ensure that military doctrine integrates properly with the strategies civilians adopt to manage the international balance of power. The U.S. government at the end of the 1960s and leading into the 1970s epitomized a civilian leadership with its eyes fixed on the international balance of power. The Nixon administration, and especially its chief figures President Nixon and Henry Kissinger, represented one of the most conscientiously realist administrations in American history.[2] As historian Francis Gavin points out, "They believed that world politics was driven, as it had been for centuries, by geopolitical competition between great powers."[3] From the realist perspective, the Nixon administration brought rationality back to U.S. foreign policy after the anomaly of Vietnam. According to Kenneth Waltz, the father of structural realism, the realist policies of Nixon and Kissinger constituted a "maturation of the bipolar world," and "the Nixon doctrine announced the shift."[4] According to the Nixon Doctrine, continued by President Ford through Secretary of State Kissinger,[5] the United States would no longer attempt to contain communism everywhere in the world.[6] The Nixon Doctrine also shifted from a two-and-a-half-war strategy under Kennedy and Johnson to a one-and-a-half-war strategy.[7] The United States would concentrate on deterring or being able to fight a war against its great-power rival, especially in NATO Europe.[8] They would do so with nuclear weapons if necessary, but in a retaliatory capacity.[9] According to civilian realism, this change in strategy in response to the threat environment will lead to a refocusing of army doctrine on the European theater and away from the de-escalating war in Vietnam.[10] Indeed, some have argued that it was this change in strategic outlook between the Johnson and Nixon administrations that drove the development of Active Defense, the 1976 edition of *Operations*.[11]

According to civilian realism, therefore, *Operations 1976* will have a defensive theory of victory with nuclear weapons playing an integral role. The rejection of Vietnam-type interventions by the Nixon Doctrine ensures that COIN-type missions will have a minor role in *Operations 1976*.[12] Nixon and Kissinger will implement these changes through a military maverick to ensure that army doctrine reflects their strategic outlook. A maverick will be key because a defensive theory of victory is contrary to the preferences of military bureaucrats, the key impediment to doctrinal innovation, according to civilian realism. In terms of timing, therefore, alterations in army doctrine will occur in the aftermath of the strategic shift under Nixon.

In contrast, the Cold War strategy of the Reagan administration rejected the Nixon Doctrine. It called for abandoning détente with the Soviet Union and winning the Cold War. Reagan increased U.S. defense budgets to enact this strategy and sought to develop offensive options for fighting in Europe.[13] According to Barry Posen, father of the civilian realist school of military innovation, and Steven Van Evera, writing in 1983, the Reagan administration placed more emphasis on "offensive missions and tactics."[14] This was of concern to these international relations scholars, who saw such missions and tactics as a major cause of wars.[15] If civilian realism is correct, and *Operations 1976* conformed to the Nixon Doctrine, *Operations 1982* will undergo a core change from the more defensive theory of victory espoused by the Nixon administration to a more offensive theory of victory consistent with Reagan-era strategy. Bureaucratic and cultural forces in the army should accelerate the transition from a defensive to an offensive theory of victory, which, according to civilian realism, suits their parochial preferences. Nuclear weapons would continue to be central to *Operations 1982* because if it had to fight a nuclear war, the Reagan administration thought that it was wise to prepare to win.

Reagan also differed from Nixon when it came to unconventional warfare missions like COIN. Reagan wanted the U.S. military to prepare for low-intensity conflicts (LICs), which included the COIN mission, in response to communist subversion around the globe and especially in the Western Hemisphere. Reagan's LIC initiatives should result in a revival of COIN-type missions in *Operations 1982* and *1986*. Here, though, the bureaucratic and cultural forces within the army should resist Reagan's innovations. Regarding timing in the Reagan case, these core changes in army doctrine should occur after the ascendancy of Reagan and his declaration of a new strategy for the Cold War.

As Posen's analysis of the Reagan administration at the time shows, Reagan's initiatives played into the hands of military bureaucrats and were a recipe for escalating the Cold War.

Military Bureaucrats and Army Doctrine in the '70s and '80s

In the 1970s, the U.S. government significantly depleted army resources, especially with the establishment of the all-volunteer force.[16] According to the bureaucratic perspective, an offensive, conventional doctrine is the best way of restoring these lost resources, while maintaining autonomy and avoiding uncertainty. At the same time, Nixon and Kissinger advocated a high degree of autonomy for the military services.[17] This was not due to their faith in bureaucracies. According to Kissinger, "The spirit of policy and that of bureaucracy are diametrically opposed."[18] When it came to *military* bureaucracies, Kissinger considered them narrowly parochial: military bureaucrats always seek greater resources, no matter the threat environment. For instance, he once noted, "When [military bureaucrats] want money, no matter what country we're in war against, including Switzerland, that we're going to lose."[19] In general, Kissinger was skeptical of the military and their advice.[20] Consequently, Nixon and Kissinger sought to bypass U.S. government bureaucracies, including military bureaucracies. Instead, the White House and the National Security Council would direct foreign policy.

In the 1970s, therefore, civilian leaders largely left the army to its own doctrinal devices. Under these permissive conditions, army bureaucrats will capture the doctrinal process to serve their parochial interests. Consequently, senior army leaders will seek a major doctrinal change through *Operations 1976*. The 1976 manual should reestablish the preeminent place of offensive over defensive theories of victory. *Operations 1976* should be highly conventional and downplay nuclear missions because of their adverse consequences for the army bureaucracy. The danger posed by the Soviet Union and its conventional force modernization in the 1960s and '70s can be used to justify this conventional emphasis.[21] Moreover, the Nixon Doctrine, which sought to extricate the United States from Vietnam and refocus national security policy on the defense of Europe, would support a focus on NATO Europe. Although an offensive doctrine would be inconsistent with Nixon's policy of détente, the army should develop such a doctrine, even if Nixon did not provide the resources to make it a reality. Finally, in the absence of any demand from civilians to develop a COIN capability, COIN will drop almost completely out of the army's doctrinal lexicon. After all, according to bureaucratic and cultural theorists, the only reason the army had mentioned COIN in the past was to placate civilian authorities. This would not be necessary under Nixon. Thus, the 1970s should provide a perfect opportunity for the U.S. Army to enact its bureaucratic preferences through *Operations 1976*.

In the 1980s, Reagan's aggressive Cold War strategy and defense spending increases should give bureaucratic priorities a boost.[22] Reagan opposed détente and was more confrontational with the Soviet Union. As already noted, the Reagan administration also promoted more "offensive missions and tactics."[23] These new demands of civilian strategy coalesced with bureaucratic preferences for an offensive theory of victory. Moreover, although the Reagan administration sought to prepare for nuclear war with the Soviets, Reagan himself wanted to downplay U.S. reliance on nuclear weapons. This dovetails nicely with the military bureaucrats' preference for conventional missions.[24] Army bureaucrats should use the new Reagan-era strategy and resources to pursue their doctrinal preferences as expressed in *Operations 1982* and *1986*.

However, army bureaucrats should not welcome all Reagan-era initiatives. Even under pressure from the Reagan administration to develop doctrine and forces for LICs in places such as Central America, army doctrine should continue to downgrade COIN-type forces and missions or at most use these forces to promote conventional missions and offensive theories of victory. In short, we should observe doctrinal continuity in the 1980s manuals when it comes unconventional missions, like COIN. As they had done under Nixon, army bureaucrats should relegate such missions to the doctrinal backwater of subordinate manuals.

U.S. Army Culture and Army Doctrine in the '70s and '80s

A powerful cultural narrative has built up around the development of *Operations 1976* and *1982*, known respectively as Active Defense and AirLand Battle. A number of scholars have used the post-Vietnam army as a paradigmatic example of the power of military culture. The dirty war in Vietnam was anathema to U.S. Army culture, which favored offensive, conventional operations reminiscent of its World War II finest hour. After its defeat in Vietnam, the army ceased to focus on the infantry tactics central to the fighting in Vietnam and shifted its attention from Asia to the defense of Europe.[25] The army of the 1970s sought solace in a kind of war to which it was culturally predisposed and at which it had historically excelled.[26] The army should defend Europe with a "totally new doctrine . . . Active Defense."[27] The Nixon Doctrine reinforced this culturally approved shift. "The focus on Europe," argued Lock-Pullan, "thus blended the World War II identity of the Army and the strategic orientation of the United States after Vietnam."[28] By reasserting its traditional culture, this new clarity of mission was the rallying cry that helped to pull the army out of its post-Vietnam doldrums.[29] There should be clear evidence of the reassertion of army culture in *Operations 1976*. In fact, many consider the Active Defense doctrine espoused by the 1976 edition as one of the central engines of change in the post-Vietnam army. Gone were the faddish nuclear missions of the 1960s. The army should replace them with an offensive, conventional-warfare mission consistent with army culture. As James Q. Wilson pointed out, "Traditionally the Army had always taught the superiority of offensive maneuvers."[30] Finally, *Operations 1976* will exorcise COIN, an artifact of Vietnam, from army doctrine.

Progress toward these cultural goals in the army will not even have to break its stride with the ascendancy of Ronald Reagan. With his opposition to détente and preference for *winning* the Cold War, Reagan's defense buildup would provide the additional resources to maintain an offensive, conventional doctrine consistent with army culture.[31] As a result, the 1976, 1982, and 1986 editions of *Operations* should share the same doctrinal core while incorporating some new technologies on the doctrinal periphery. However, the guardians of army culture—whose mantra was "No More Vietnams!"—will resist pressure from the Reagan administration to prepare for COIN-type LICs.[32] The process of change in the '70s and '80s will be shepherded by these cultural guardians. A number of scholars already argue that in the aftermath of Vietnam, the U.S. Army reasserted its culture, shaped in the crucible of World War II. Its post-Vietnam doctrines played a key role in this drama of cultural resurrection.

Military Realism and U.S. Army Doctrine in the '70s and '80s

Many see the post-Vietnam period as representing a sea change in the U.S. Army and its doctrine. Indeed, according to this dominant narrative, doctrine was key to instigating and proliferating major changes in the army. This is a problem for military realism because it expects a significant amount of doctrinal continuity in the aftermath of Vietnam. If, unexpectedly, the evidence supports military realism, this success under adverse conditions will strengthen it further and call the accepted narrative into question again. In the 1960s, Soviet forces in Europe already enjoyed many material advantages. The establishment of the all-volunteer force in 1973 and additional cuts to the force significantly reduced the size of the U.S. Army. These cuts to the army increased the relative material superiority of the most dangerous threat. Moreover, the USSR did not stand still in the 1970s. It continued to modernize and expand its conventional forces and increased its lead in forces in being. Under these conditions, military realists in the army should recommend that *Operations 1976* retain a defensive theory of victory and continue to integrate nuclear weapons into its doctrine. While this doctrinal continuity is contrary to the expectations of the alternative theories, military realism agrees with the alternatives when it comes to COIN. COIN will be an especially low priority in *Operations 1976*. However, the relegation of COIN is a response to the threat environment and not necessarily an organizational and cultural backlash from Vietnam. As the previous two chapters have shown, theorists of military innovation have overblown the U.S. Army's aversion to COIN before and during Vietnam. They then use this presumed aversion to explain the turn away from COIN after Vietnam, without taking into account the changes in the threat environment. According to military realism, throughout the doctrinal process, senior army leaders, acting against bureaucratic interests and army culture if necessary, should defend this doctrinal continuity.

With the Reagan-era Cold War strategy and defense buildup, military realism predicts changes in army doctrine under certain conditions. If the increases in resources from the Reagan administration provide the army with enough forces or equipment to overcome its material inferiority in the European theater, then doctrine should begin to shift toward a more offensive theory of victory. However, if the increases are not sufficient, and only begin to make up for the major cuts inflicted in the 1960s and '70s, then the existing defensive theory of victory will remain at the core of army doctrine. This will be so despite civilian, bureaucratic, and cultural pressures to the contrary. Nuclear weapons should continue to be important in *Operations 1982*, given the physical dangers and tactical opportunities that they present for NATO forces in Europe. Finally, the army will make a significant commitment to COIN-like missions only if Reagan's LIC initiatives provide sufficient forces. Throughout, senior military realists in the army should guide the doctrinal process.

Once again, the deck is stacked against military realism. The new theory's explanatory power is formidable indeed, if it can explain the army after Vietnam as well as it did the army before and during that war. If so, scholars, policy makers, and the public at large should seriously question accepted explanations of the U.S. Army. A poor performance in what should be an easy case calls these theories into question more generally.

Military Threat Assessment and Doctrinal
Development after Vietnam and Beyond

The development and writing of *Operations 1976* occurred in a different institutional context than all previous army doctrine. In 1973 the U.S. Army Training and Doctrine Command was established, and General William E. DePuy became its first commander.[33] Early in his tenure, DePuy saw that the army was in need of a new training system and war-fighting doctrine; the one would have to be closely linked to the other.[34] The key to this doctrinal and training reformation was the rewriting of *Field Manual 100-5, Operations*. DePuy considered 100-5 the "how to fight" manual.[35] The fact that DePuy saw the rewriting of *Operations* as the key to changing training reinforces a main contention of this book: senior army officers took doctrine, and especially 100-5, very seriously. DePuy, the father of these changes, was an exemplar of the post–World War II army officer corps. His formative combat experience came as a major commanding a battalion of the U.S. Army's 90th Infantry Division in World War II. Before the breakout from Normandy, the Wehrmacht severely bloodied the 90th. In these engagements, 100 percent of the 90th's soldiers had to be replaced and 150 percent of its officers.[36] The first head of TRADOC also led soldiers in Vietnam. DePuy, molded in the crucible of the army's finest hour, would now be in charge of its post-Vietnam doctrine.

Although the context of doctrinal development had changed, the threat had not. Like many army commanders before him, DePuy saw the defense of Europe as the "principle and directed mission" of the U.S. Army and argued that doctrine should be primarily "oriented towards Europe."[37] A study commissioned by Army Chief of Staff Creighton Abrams in 1973, known as the Astarita Report, had come to the same conclusion, advocating that army doctrine and force posture focus on the defense of Europe and other great-power relationships.[38] The Astarita Report also argued that the conventional imbalance in favor of Soviet forces in Europe meant that tactical nuclear weapons would be required to blunt an assault on Europe.

However, these were hardly novel conclusions. As noted in the previous chapter, with the inclusion of the relevant STANAGs at the beginning of each chapter, *Operations 1968* had strongly signaled the army's intention to focus its doctrine on the major alliances. That manual also kept nuclear weapons at the heart of army doctrine. Unfortunately, in the 1970s, the army was in an even more tenuous position vis-à-vis the Soviet threat in Europe than in the previous decade. As we have seen, throughout the 1960s the army suffered from major material disadvantages in relation to Warsaw Pact forces in Europe.

Civilian decisions to cut army forces on the Continent exacerbated these disadvantages. In the mid- to late 1960s, while the army commitment to Vietnam consumed men and material,[39] the Soviets expanded and modernized their forces arrayed against NATO Europe.[40]

According to historian John Lewis Gaddis, in spite of these already adverse conditions, the Nixon and Ford administrations presided over "the most substantial reductions in American military capabilities relative to those of the Soviet Union in the entire postwar era."[41] As Gaddis points out, U.S. ground forces were cut by 207,000 between 1970 and 1977. In the same period, following the 1960s trend, Soviet forces *increased* by 262,000 men.[42] Even those previously skeptical of army concerns of being outnumbered in Europe, such as Alain Enthoven, who helped McNamara develop his new estimates of Soviet strength, thought the Nixon-era cuts were too deep.[43]

General DePuy described the resulting imbalance of power in stark military realist terms. In Europe there was at least "a two-to-one or three-to-one enemy superiority."[44] Numbers were not the only problem, however. Due to the proximity and size of Soviet reserves, as any war in Europe progressed the situation would get "worse, not better."[45] Language barriers, different training regimens, and lack of readiness would also hinder NATO's response time.[46] In 1972 the army considered only four of its thirteen active divisions combat ready.[47] Meanwhile, Soviet forces were increasing not only in numbers but also in quality. By 1973 the Soviets had developed new and better tanks, added five tank divisions to the forces facing NATO, and increased the number of tanks in all of its motorized rifle divisions. This buildup had begun in 1965.[48] This state of affairs was especially worrying from the military realist perspective, which bases threat assessment on material capabilities for war fighting *and* the doctrine used to coordinate those capabilities. The modernization and expansion of Soviet tank forces further increased the Soviet advantage in armor, which even McNamara had acknowledged, and enabled the execution of their doctrine based on massive armored thrusts.

In the early 1970s, it was clear to General DePuy that the army needed a new doctrine to address the progressively worsening threat environment. In October 1973, a major war broke out in the Middle East that reinforced the need for the new *Operations* manual.[49] The October War between Israel, Egypt and Syria demonstrated that the range and lethality of modern weapons had increased massively.[50] The rate of loss among Israeli and Arab ground forces "approached a destructiveness once attributed only to nuclear arms."[51] Man-portable antitank guided missiles made the modern battlefield especially lethal for tank crews.[52] As DePuy noted, the total tank losses in the three weeks for the Egyptians and Syrians alone, between fifteen hundred and two thousand, exceeded the number of U.S. Army tanks in Europe.[53] Because Israel and their adversaries were equipped with some of the most sophisticated weapons that their respective great-power patrons could provide, the loss ratios were especially concerning to NATO and the U.S. Army.[54] Moreover, captured Soviet equipment showed that they were well ahead of the United States in some combat vehicle technology.[55] Soviet air defenses protecting ground forces were also more advanced and prevented the Israelis from dominating the air, as they had in the Six-Day War. Mobile air-defense units advanced with attacking ground forces to protect them from air attack. The lack of air superiority increased their losses on the ground. This was a new element of Soviet doctrine adopted by the Arab armies in the 1973 war.[56] Warsaw Pact units in Europe were equipped with these modern weapons and air defenses.[57]

The October War was of particular interest to the U.S. Army because the force ratios between Israeli and Arab forces were similar to those between NATO and Warsaw Pact forces in Europe. Nevertheless, the superior training of Israeli tank crews allowed them to achieve loss ratios as high as fifty to one in some cases.[58] The October War demonstrated the importance of extensive training to overcome numerical inferiority.[59] DePuy pointed out, "There is no way that we can get the same degree of improved performance out of some small change in weapons as we can get through . . . the training of leaders and units."[60] DePuy used the lessons of the October War not to justify more resources, as bureaucratic theory expects, but to emphasize that training was more important than capital-intensive weapons programs. DePuy was well aware of the tendencies of bureaucracy. In fact, DePuy and Army Chief of Staff Abrams established TRADOC to create "the institutional space required to enable change in the bureaucracy."[61] In the end, the lessons of the October War reinforced the soundness of the changes under way at TRADOC, which the army had founded three months before the outbreak of the war, but were not the cause of these changes, as some argue.[62] As DePuy himself argued, "It would be incorrect to say that the Arab-Israeli War was the sole foundation upon which that doctrine was built."[63]

Cut down in size, DePuy feared, army forces in NATO Europe could be rapidly and decisively defeated.[64] Therefore, the army had to "fight outnumbered" and "win the first battle of the next war."[65] Enabling this capability would require qualitative superiority in training over all potential adversaries, especially the Warsaw Pact.[66] It is not surprising then, that *Operations 1976* was one of the most tactically focused manuals produced by the army. It did not include the spectrum of warfare or a discussion of the strategic context, as previous manuals had. Instead, it concentrated on *how to fight*, especially how to fight the Soviets in Europe.[67] The solution to the quandary the army faced in Europe was Active Defense. After proceeding through a number of drafts and commanders' conferences, TRADOC published the new *Operations* manual in July 1976.[68] The look of the new manual, with numerous pictures, graphs, and charts, certainly gave the impression that its content was revolutionary.[69] However, as an analysis of the three areas of doctrine will show, while *Operations 1976* included important peripheral changes, these changes reinforced the core of army doctrine established in the 1960s.

However, both the officers who shaped it and the army at large were not satisfied with Active Defense. *Operations 1976* was the most publicized manual in the history of the army and, therefore, was the target of much criticism. Importantly for the current analysis, army officers took issue with the emphasis on the defensive over the offensive in the manual. Many saw this as contrary to army traditions of offensive operations.[70] The central place of weapons systems in *Operations 1976* also drew fire because it "tore at the very fabric of the Army's cultural beliefs."[71] By 1981 a number of senior officers thought that *Operations 1976* "had to go."[72] DePuy had controlled the doctrinal process very tightly, and critics hoped that when he went, so would his doctrine.[73]

General Donn A. Starry succeeded DePuy at TRADOC in 1977. He worked closely with DePuy on *Operations 1976* and wrote significant portions of that manual. The army then sent Starry to West Germany to lead U.S. Army V Corps. There he implemented the concepts in *Operations 1976* into unit training and convinced other commanders to do the same.[74] Through this process, he too came to see a number of the flaws in *Operations 1976*. As TRADOC commander, Starry spearheaded its revision and replacement with *Operations 1982*. With this revision, which began in the late 1970s, the army replaced Active Defense with AirLand Battle doctrine.

The threat environment that the army faced in the late 1970s and early 1980s was graver still than in the immediate aftermath of Vietnam. In the years after Vietnam, due to Soviet defense budget increases and U.S. cuts, there was approximately a $40 billion difference between U.S. and USSR defense spending. By 1978 the gap had grown to approximately $65 billion. The Soviet Union retained and expanded its heavy armored force and its "tactical doctrine of rapid armored thrusts."[75] More worrying still, the Soviets were increasing their formations' capacity for attacking on short notice.[76] However, Soviet doctrine had also shifted, this time away from a single armored main effort to multiple efforts by first-echelon forces that powerful second-echelon units would then exploit. As in the past, deep thrusts into the rear areas of NATO defenses would undermine mobilization and lead to the general collapse of the NATO defense. The Soviet military thought, if executed rapidly enough, it might be possible to defeat NATO's military forces without nuclear weapons.[77] However, the Soviets were not neglecting the nuclear balance. This balance in Europe was shifting against NATO with the deployment of the Soviet SS-20 intermediate-range nuclear missile system.[78] These changes undermined important elements of Active Defense, and the army would need to adapt.[79]

Some argue that AirLand Battle was a "rejection" of DePuy's doctrine.[80] On the contrary, while trying to address its flaws, General Starry would retain and expand on large parts of *Operations 1976*.[81] This was because Starry was motivated, as DePuy had been, by the need to "solve the problem" the army "faced in Europe" of fighting outnumbered.[82] Many then and since criticized the army for focusing on the Soviet threat to Europe because it was a very unlikely scenario. Starry argued, echoing General George Decker two decades before, that although it was less likely, it was clearly the most dangerous threat to the "survival" of the United States and its allies.[83] Like good military realists, DePuy and Starry focused on the most dangerous threat. In fact, Active Defense and AirLand Battle, often portrayed in oppositional terms, were actually closer to fraternal twins born of a similarly dismal threat environment. This is borne out by their approaches to the three key areas of doctrine.

Conventional and Nuclear Forces in Operations 1976

At the core of *Operations 1976* was the use of an Active Defense against a Soviet attack on Europe. In Active Defense, a covering force would move out to meet the advancing enemy, while the main force retained its mobility to respond to the enemy's main effort.[84] Through a combination of their initial and stubborn resistance and advances in sensor technology, developed under Army Chief of Staff William Westmoreland, the covering force would discover the location and direction of the main effort.[85] Once this force located the enemy's main effort, the main force would use its superior mobility to move laterally across the battlefield and place itself in defensive positions in the path of the advancing enemy. In position, the main force would use its superior training and the increased lethality of modern weapons systems to destroy the attacker.[86]

On its face, *Operations 1976* was a highly conventional doctrine. It emphasized the importance of cover, concealment, and suppression, essentials of conventional warfare. It also emphasized highly precise tank gunnery and coordination among a combined arms team of conventional weapons.[87] These were the hallmarks of army tactics in World War II. Indeed, scholars and many in the army itself see *Operations 1976* as a return to the traditional doctrines of the army. This doctrine was a salve for an army culture scorched by the nuclear revolution and the Vietnam War.[88] However, a closer look reveals that the forces and methods espoused by *Operations 1976* were actually a peripheral refinement of previous army doctrine. Active Defense was highly consistent with the missions and theories of victory at the heart of 1960s doctrine.

The post-Vietnam cultural narrative claims that the army had become obsessed with conventional infantry tactics in Vietnam.[89] Consequently, the narrative continues, *Operations 1976* replaced this emphasis with a focus on mechanization and the use of weapons systems.[90] However, as already shown, even at the height of fighting in Vietnam, *Operations 1968* continued to promote mechanization, especially helicopters, as initiated by the Reorganization Objectives Army Division and *Operations 1962*. Throughout the war, the army worked to preserve the mechanized forces and organization needed to fight in Europe. In fact, before being sent to Vietnam, General DePuy had commanded the army's first mechanized infantry regiment in the early 1960s.[91] Army Chief of Staff Decker had developed these mechanized infantry units for ROAD. They would make the army more mobile and survivable on the nuclear battlefield. Helicopters were also part of this mechanization trend; they would facilitate the lateral movement essential for an Active Defense.

However, DePuy was not satisfied with the state of mechanized infantry tactics in the U.S. Army. Improvements in these tactics through training would enable the kinds of lopsided loss ratios the Israelis enjoyed in the 1973 war and that were essential for the outnumbered force that would fight the first battle of the next war. As with the ROAD design,[92] the West German Army played a key role in the development of these tactics. DePuy considered the Germans far more capable than U.S. Army units at coordinating armor and mechanized infantry units.[93] He attributed this to German *panzergrenadier* techniques,[94] which used mounted infantry in conjunction with tank assault in defensive operations. The West Germans set out these techniques in a basic statement of doctrine: the Bundeswehr's HDv 100/100 manual, published in September 1973.[95] DePuy actually sent copies of *Operations 1976* to the leaders of the West German Army for comment and used HDv 100/100 as a constant reference during the writing of the 1976 manual. He also brought the chief of German combat arms and the chief of staff of the West German Army, General Horst

Hildebrant, to the United States to discuss doctrine.[96] Bundeswehr techniques helped to refine the mechanization concept central to *Operations 1976* and its 1960s predecessors.[97] Instead of a radical doctrinal departure, the mechanized force espoused by *Operations 1976* was perfectly consistent with the 1960s manuals.[98] Rather than revolutionary changes, DePuy's tactical initiatives were refinements to the core of army doctrine established in the early 1960s.

In terms of equipment, the new suite of vehicles ushered into army service by DePuy—the main battle tank, the armored personnel carrier, and the helicopter—were all present in the 1960s. The advent of the M1 main battle tank, the M2 mechanized infantry fighting vehicle, and the Apache attack helicopter[99] were improvements of the mechanized warfare team espoused by *Operations 1962* and preserved in *Operations 1968*. This modernized equipment was part of peripheral, *evolutionary* change in army doctrine. DePuy made these peripheral changes to doctrine to make the army more effective at enacting its core mission and theory of victory, resisting a Soviet assault on Europe by exploiting the advantages of the defense.[100]

However, the West German Army was not the only service with which the army collaborated. The Active Defense hinged on close coordination between U.S. Army and U.S. Air Force units.[101] The latter was so essential because in any war in Europe, the United States would not enjoy the air superiority to which it had grown accustomed in previous wars.[102] The tank, center of the army's combined arms team, could not survive on the modern battlefield without tactical air forces.[103] Nor could vulnerable helicopters, with their mobility and tank-killing power, operate without air force aircraft attacking the Soviet air-defense system.[104] In addition, the air force could not mount its operations to achieve air superiority unless ground troops suppressed the missiles that threatened its aircraft from the ground. In the October War, the Israeli Air Force had lost 73 percent of its aircraft to ground-based systems, not opposing aircraft. This situation produced a mutual dependence that required close integration between the U.S. Army and the U.S. Air Force.[105] Chapter 8 of *Operations 1976* described the "AirLand Battle" in which army and air force units would cooperate closely to overcome enemy mobile air defenses and unleash the close air support the army needed to make up for its deficits in manpower and machines.[106] "The Army," *Operations 1976* admitted, could not "win the land battle without the Air Force."[107] According to army doctrine, therefore, the army could not fulfill its central mission without the air force. DePuy did not want to spend army resources on areas of the battlefield other than the "close-in battle" because, he argued, "We don't have enough money to duplicate Air Force systems—in fact, we don't have enough money to do what we need to do in the immediate battlefield."[108] Even in private correspondence between DePuy and Army Chief of Staff Abrams, DePuy acknowledged the need to work closely with the air force and showed no desire to battle the air force for resources, as bureaucratic theories of interservice rivalry would expect.[109] From the bureaucratic perspective, the AirLand Battle concept was a major and voluntary abridgement of organizational autonomy. For senior military realists in the army, this abridgment was necessary to enable a plausible response to the threat environment that the army faced.

Operations 1976 could not and did not ignore nuclear weapons. In addition to refining conventional tactics, *Operations 1976* recognized that in the 1970s, army forces must be dual capable, that is, able to fight on a nuclear as well as a conventional battlefield. The Soviets had continued to develop such forces throughout the 1960s and '70s. In fact, one justification for Soviet-force modernization and expansion was to produce an armored thrust so rapid that NATO could not use tactical nuclear weapons against it without endangering their own troops.[110] In some cases, the Soviets had surpassed the United States in dual-capable equipment.[111] For instance, Soviet vehicles captured in the October War had more advanced air-filtration and decontamination systems than U.S. and NATO vehicles.[112] These sealed tanks and armored vehicles could cross terrain contaminated by nuclear use.[113] Despite the army emphasis on the nuclear battlefield throughout the 1960s, Soviet forces were better prepared for it than the U.S. Army by the early 1970s.[114]

In Europe U.S. Army forces had to possess the ability to fight on a nuclear battlefield to remain compatible with the NATO strategy of flexible response. As shown in previous chapters, though it initially focused on increasing conventional forces, flexible response under Kennedy and Johnson increasingly incorporated tactical nuclear weapons in the defense of Europe. NATO allies in Europe adopted flexible response only once it incorporated a stronger tactical nuclear component. European allies worried that previous iterations of flexible response, with a focus on conventional forces, signaled an unwillingness on the part of the United States to use its nuclear arsenal to defend Europe. *Operations 1976* noted that NATO's doctrine of flexible response required "the capability to employ nuclear options at various levels of conflict . . . in combined conventional-nuclear operations."[115] Echoing their predecessors from the previous decade, senior army officers argued that the use of such weapons would not automatically lead to general nuclear war. According to *Operations 1976*, as with 1960s doctrine, limited use of nuclear weapons was possible and would lead to the "conventional-nuclear" phase of combat, where properly organized ground forces could survive and maneuver.[116] *Operations 1976* noted the advantages of battlefield nuclear weapons and dedicated an entire chapter to the consequences of their use on maneuver forces. In fact, the effects of radiation on troops received an even more detailed treatment than it did in *Operations 1968*.[117] In the 1970s, *Operations 1976* noted, although parity existed in strategic nuclear weapons, the United States possessed a marked advantage in tactical nuclear weapons.[118] Moreover, new smaller nuclear weapons reduced the "potential damage to friendly forces or nearby communities."[119] Tactical nuclear weapons could be a "means to concentrate overwhelming combat power and to decisively alter force ratios" at a time and place of the commander's choosing. These weapons "could mean the difference between victory and defeat."[120] Commanders could use battlefield nuclear weapons against Soviet reserves moving to the front to take pressure off forces engaged with the armored spearheads.[121] The 1976 manual also retained the doctrinal innovations for the nuclear battlefield set out in earlier manuals. For instance, dispersion and organization in depth would increase survivability on such a battlefield.[122] High mobility and mechanization would enable commanders to rapidly concentrate and disperse their forces, offering them more protection.[123] Again, helicopters were a vital source of this mobility.[124] Army forces had to retain the dual capability espoused by army leaders in the previous decade because this capability might be the only means of stalling a Soviet advance.[125]

Some have argued that General DePuy was opposed to making tactical nuclear weapons a major part of army doctrine because they were contrary to army culture.[126] As the above evidence shows, however, nuclear weapons were an important part of DePuy's new doctrine. Moreover, if nuclear weapons received a less detailed treatment in *Operations 1976*, it was because of circumstances rather than cultural bias. *Operations 1976* somewhat downplayed tactical nuclear war because the inclusion of classified tactical nuclear doctrine in the manual, which DePuy and Starry both initially favored, would have made it classified and reduced its circulation.[127] For *Operations 1976* to influence the training of the whole army, it had to have the widest distribution possible. Tactical nuclear doctrine was set out in more detail in its own capstone manual, *Field Manual 100-5-1, Conventional-Nuclear Operations*.[128] The 1976 edition dealt less with nuclear weapons than its authors would have liked to enable wide dissemination, not to assert army culture.

In sum, *Operations 1976* did not change the core of army doctrine regarding conventional and nuclear forces or the relationship between them. Instead,

Operations 1976 undertook peripheral changes in doctrine to make army units more effective at repelling a Warsaw Pact attack in Europe through a combination of conventional and tactical nuclear forces. For senior army officers, the dramatic increases in the relative size and sophistication of Soviet forces in the 1970s reinforced the need to integrate conventional and nuclear forces in army doctrine. The consistency between *Operations 1976* and 1960s doctrine may also explain why senior officers did not simultaneously pursue a reorganization of the army, as they had done with *Operations 1954* and the pentomic system and *Operations 1962* and ROAD.[129] The dual-capable forces established by the ROAD divisions, with their emphasis on mobility and dispersion, had continued relevance in the 1970s.

Therefore, *Operations 1976* was not the "dramatic" doctrinal change that some would have us believe. Both bureaucratic and cultural expectations that the army would shift decisively away from nuclear toward conventional weapons is not borne out by the evidence. Tactical nuclear weapons continued to be a vital part of army doctrine, despite bureaucratic and cultural reservations. Nor were the doctrinal developments in the army of the 1970s driven by changes in civilian strategy. While the Nixon Doctrine did call for a turning away from Vietnam and a focus on Europe, the army had never taken its eyes off the most dangerous threat, even during the height of its commitment in Vietnam. The timing of doctrinal change does not support civilian realism in this case, either. Only military realism expected this doctrinal continuity when it came to the treatment of conventional and nuclear missions. *Operations 76* entailed evolutionary, peripheral refinements to make the army more effective at carrying out the conventional-nuclear aspects of the core of its doctrine.[130] Senior army officers had shaped this doctrinal core in the 1960s to provide the army with a plausible means of countering the most dangerous threat. The recent work of Benjamin Jensen on the post-Vietnam U.S. Army fully corroborated this expectation of military realism.[131] However, because Jensen's investigation begins in the 1970s, his analysis does not fully appreciate how consistent *Operations 1976* was with its doctrinal predecessors. The established core of army doctrine remained relevant in the 1970s, as the characteristics of the threat environment persisted and worsened in the post-Vietnam era.

Conventional and Nuclear Forces in Operations 1982

The U.S. Army would revise its most important doctrinal manual twice under Reagan, providing another opportunity to examine change and continuity in the army's treatment of conventional and nuclear forces and missions.

The army published the first revisions, *Operations 1982*, during the early years of the Reagan administration. Reagan was skeptical of détente and pursued a more confrontational Cold War strategy, accompanied by a major defense buildup.[132] At the same time, Reagan's strategy expanded the number of missions for which the army would have to prepare. In this way, it returned to the more expansive strategy of the Kennedy era.[133] When it came to the Soviet conventional threat in Europe, Reagan understood that recent history had seen the "overwhelming growth" of Soviet conventional forces.[134] By the 1980s, he argued, "no one denies they have assembled an offensive force of tanks [and] mobile artillery, support aircraft and armored personnel carriers on the Western front in Europe that are superior to our forces and those of our NATO allies."[135] In addition, the Reagan administration knew that the United States had lost strategic nuclear superiority. The administration acknowledged that the U.S. Army did not have sufficient resources to enact its missions and that this lopsided situation might require the use of theater nuclear weapons to defeat a major conventional attack.[136] Moreover, Reagan did not think that the use of theater nuclear weapons would automatically lead to general nuclear war. Advocates of nuclear deterrence and disarmament alike were concerned that the administration thought it could win a nuclear war.

General Donn Starry spearheaded the revision of *Operations 1976* and its replacement with *Operations 1982*. Starry had worked very closely with General DePuy to develop the 1976 edition and succeeded him as TRADOC commander in 1977. Starry was in favor of many of the doctrinal concepts that DePuy had developed. He saw the revision of *Operations '76* as his most important task when he came to TRADOC in July 1977. He wrote major parts of *Operations 1982* with the help of Colonel Huba Wass de Czege at Fort Leavenworth.[137] Some in the army had criticized *Operations 1976*. Officers criticized the manual's laser-like focus on Europe. In its introduction, the authors of *Operations 1982* reassured their readers that they designed the doctrine for conflicts worldwide. However, the manual dealt with contingency operations other than the defense of Europe for only four pages.[138] Despite their attempts to reassure critics, Starry and his team clearly continued to focus doctrine on the Soviet threat to Europe. As Starry admitted later, he meant the changes he made to the army's most important doctrine, such as the operational level of war and deep attack, to "solve the problem" the army "faced in Europe."[139] Addressing the Soviet threat was still the focus of *Operations 1982*.[140] Moreover, as per Reagan's assessment above, the character of the threat had not changed significantly. Soviet forces in Europe were prepared to use their continually growing conventional superiority as part of an offensive armored thrust. Like a good military realist, Starry drew these conclusions from the Soviet literature on their military doctrine: "If you read the Soviet literature over the last 15 years or so . . . [t]hey have always believed that you could fight successfully at the theatre level and win. . . . I maintain that that's why the Soviets have undertaken such an enormous improvement in their conventional forces."[141] Indeed, in the 1980s, the Soviets were exporting more tanks than the United States had built over an extended period, while still modernizing and increasing the size of their own tank forces.[142] Their growing superiority in tanks, already substantial in the early 1960s, prior to Nixon's deep cuts, would be the backbone of their offensive armored doctrine.

To understand the role of conventional and nuclear weapons in *Operations 1982*, we must first familiarize ourselves with the basic doctrinal dilemmas that the manual set out to solve. Only then can we appreciate the potential role of conventional and nuclear forces therein. The army came to know the 1982 manual as "AirLand Battle doctrine," even though the AirLand Battle concept originated as part of Active Defense.[143] The TRADOC writers of *Operations 1982* thought the concepts in *Operations 1976* went a long way toward preparing the army to fight outnumbered, but the manual did not fully resolve the problems facing the army in Europe. When the authors of doctrine raised their eyes to take in the enemy forces beyond the initial meeting battle, new dilemmas arose. Even while writing Active Defense, Starry and its other authors recognized it did not pay sufficient attention to the danger of Soviet second-echelon forces.[144] The problem was that while NATO forces resisted the first echelon of the Soviet attacker with Active Defense, the second-echelon forces of the Warsaw Pact would strike. The mass, velocity, and ferocity of this strike would overwhelm the NATO units already engaged with the first echelon. In total, the Soviets had *four* echelons arrayed against NATO in Europe.[145] Despite these unresolved dilemmas, TRADOC decided that it was best to define the doctrine for the close-in tactical battle first and then resolve the issue of the second echelon in a later edition. After all, if the close-in battle were lost, the plan for the second echelon would be irrelevant. The alternative was to delay the publication of *Operations 1976*, which DePuy considered unwise because of its close relationship with the training reforms already under way.[146] Therefore, the germ of *Operations 1982* originated in this previous doctrinal process and the dilemmas it left unresolved.

To deal with the second-echelon danger, Starry and the TRADOC writers "fully fleshed out"[147] the concept of AirLand Battle. Under the new concept, army artillery and air force units would do more than destroy the air-defense system that shielded the assault of the first echelon.[148] In order to reduce the mass and velocity of the second echelon, artillery and air force units would strike at these forces en route to delay and attrite them before they could overwhelm the NATO defenders engaged with the first echelon.[149] Recent technological advances in sensors and observation would facilitate this mission.[150] These actions had to occur simultaneously with the close-in fight.[151] Consequently, the army expanded and deepened its doctrinal ties to the air force in *Operations 1982*, reinforcing the dependence between the services established by *Operations 1976* and again contradicting the logic of bureaucratic and cultural theories.[152] In September 1980, Air Force Tactical Air Command and TRADOC signed a joint memorandum that made the army corps commander the principal decision maker for the targeting of tactical air assets on the battlefield.[153] The air force would help launch strikes on the second echelon and give the main NATO force a much better chance of mounting a stout defense, even against a major Soviet effort.[154]

Nuclear Forces in AirLand Battle

Now that the basic concept of operations in the new manual is clear, we can examine the role of nuclear forces in AirLand Battle. While *Operations 1976* acknowledged the need for dual capability, *Operations 1982* was even more explicit about the need to integrate conventional and tactical nuclear forces. General Starry sought to deal more directly with nuclear weapons than had been permissible in the 1976 edition.[155] Starry was convinced that the situation in Europe "depended on the use of tactical nuclear weapons at some point in the battle."[156] According to *Operations 1982*, if authorized by civilian authorities, nuclear weapons could be a major asset to the commander in the field.[157] Most important for AirLand Battle, the strikes on the second-echelon forces could include tactical nuclear strikes, which would positively affect the outcome of the first-echelon battle.[158] Moreover, tactical nuclear strikes against second-echelon forces would confine much of the negative side effects of nuclear weapons, like radiation, to enemy-controlled territory.[159] However, to be prepared to execute such operations on short notice, the army had to design its doctrine to rapidly transition from a conventional to a nuclear-conventional battlefield. Therefore, echoing its doctrinal predecessors, AirLand Battle argued that army forces had to be dual capable. Army units had to be able to "operate without interruption even if the enemy resorts to nuclear weapons."[160] They had to determine the exact ratio of dispersion and concentration to fight conventionally or transition to conventional-nuclear operations.[161] Starry wanted these two modes of operations so closely linked that he counseled getting rid of the concept of "integrated" operations and assuming that the word *operations* included both conventional and tactical nuclear operations.[162] This degree of integration was essential to enable synchronization between the first-echelon fight and deeper strikes on the second echelon.[163] As Jensen notes, for Starry and *Operations 1982*, "There was no such thing as a non-nuclear battlefield."[164] Moreover, *Operations 1982* recognized that this level of integration was not novel. Both the NATO strategy of flexible response and Soviet doctrine called for dual capability. Both equipped and trained their forces accordingly.[165] In addition, the doctrinal solutions that Starry proposed for the integrated battlefield resembled concepts of dispersion, concentration, and then dispersion, devised in the pentomic era and refined thereafter. In the AirLand Battle army this sequence was renamed "scan, swarm, strike, scatter,"[166] but the basic idea was the same, though greatly facilitated by advanced sensor and information technology. In short, like Active Defense, AirLand Battle preserved the nuclear mission as part of the core of army doctrine. Nuclear weapons were an essential component of a doctrine that could allow the army to address the most dangerous threat.

The central doctrinal innovation of *Operations 1982*, destroying Soviet second-echelon forces with deep attack by artillery and air forces before they struck, possibly to include tactical nuclear weapons, did not constitute a core change in army doctrine. Rather, according to the authors of AirLand Battle, the new edition corrected a doctrinal weakness of which they had been aware since they helped write its immediate predecessor, *Operations 1976*. Nor did the 1982 edition change the way the army saw the relationships between the conventional and nuclear battlefields. For doctrines from the post-Vietnam era, *Operations 1976* and *1982* agreed with a great deal of pre-Vietnam army doctrine, which had called for the close integration of conventional and nuclear forces. Although it was contrary to bureaucratic interests and cultural preferences, the nuclear mission had to remain in the core of army doctrine. Doctrinal developers in the army could not ignore the dilemmas and opportunities that battlefield nuclear weapons produced. Even with a stalwart and well-coordinated defense, the combat power of these weapons might be the only means of prolonging resistance in Europe.

In this case, the timing of the doctrinal change within the army again contradicts the predictions of civilian realism. The new elements of 1980s army doctrine did not have their origin in the more robust Cold War strategy of the

Reagan era. Rather, AirLand Battle sought to solve doctrinal dilemmas left unresolved by Starry's mentor, General DePuy, and his doctrine of Active Defense. As already shown, the army had been consistently developing doctrine for fighting on a nuclear battlefield for decades prior to the rise of Reagan. Like Nixon's refocusing of U.S. strategy on Europe, Reagan's conception of the use of tactical nuclear weapons in a war-fighting rather than simply a deterrence capacity fell into line with, rather than shaped, army doctrine. Again, the timing of doctrinal innovation does not support the civilian realist argument that innovation arises *after* civilians develop a new strategy that requires doctrinal change in the military.

Attack and Defense in the Post-Vietnam Army
Attack and Defense in Operations 1976

In the early 1960s, the incapacity of the pentomic divisions and *Operations '54* for dealing with the most dangerous threat began a shift in the core of U.S. Army doctrine from an offensive to a more defensive theory of victory. Given the material advantages enjoyed by Soviet forces in Europe, the army had to call into question its traditional promotion of offensive operations.[167] Therefore, as chronicled by the two previous chapters, flying in the face of previous army doctrine, *Operations 1962* argued that defense could contribute to the ultimate object of warfare, the destruction of the enemy. Following the principles of war, earlier doctrine had reserved this decisive role to offense alone. This defensive emphasis persisted into *Operations 1968* because the threat that inspired the shift to a defensive theory of victory in the early '60s worsened later in the decade. This period saw further reductions in army forces in Europe, the depletion of those forces to fill the ranks fighting in Vietnam, the withdrawal of France from NATO, and the Soviet invasion of Czechoslovakia. All this occurred while the Soviet Union continued to expand and modernize its conventional forces arrayed against Europe.

From 1968 to 1973, U.S. government policy further depleted army forces in Europe when the shift to the all-volunteer force cut the size of the army by half.[168] General DePuy recognized that army doctrine had to have a defensive theory of victory for the army to fight outnumbered and win even the *first* battle in Europe, never mind the war. Contrary to the expectations of bureaucratic and military culture theories, the pages of *Operations 1976* discussed defensive operations much more than offensive operations.[169] When discussing the new lethality of modern weapons, it stressed the advantages they gave to the defender.[170] The defense had become so powerful, *Operations '76* argued, that a commander could succeed on the defensive with one defender for every three attackers. However, a successful *attack* required six attackers to subdue one defender armed with modern weaponry.[171] So modern weapons in conjunction with good use of terrain and obstacles by the defender meant that the traditional three-to-one ratio had to be *doubled* to six to one.[172] Senior army leaders observed these force ratios in the October War. More worrying still, the rate at which tanks were knocked out of action had increased dramatically. If the U.S. Army lost tanks at the same rate in a war with the Warsaw Pact, it would rapidly lose all of its armored capability in Europe.[173] According to army doctrine, the advantages of the defense had *increased* and made attack much more difficult.[174] Bureaucratic and cultural perspectives would expect the army to use technological advancements to promote offensive doctrine. The opposite happened. Benjamin Jensen describes the catalysts for this doctrinal innovation in starkly military realist terms. The factors that shaped Active Defense were "the effects of enemy doctrine, weapons capabilities, and the effects of terrain."[175]

Even more surprisingly, the principles of war were not even included in *Operations 1976*. As we have seen, these principles, the second of which argued for the superiority of offense over defense, had been a foundational part of army doctrine since 1921.[176] Instead of stating the principles and then limiting their doctrinal influence through caveats, as *Operations 1962* and *1968* had done, *Operations '76* removed them altogether. Moreover, this was no accident. In 1979, on the exclusion of the principles from *Operations 1976*, General Starry said, "We deliberately left the principles out," because "any leader who adheres inflexibly to one set of commandments is inviting disastrous defeat from a resourceful opponent."[177]

More surprisingly from the bureaucratic and cultural perspective, DePuy rejected an alternative draft of *Operations '76* that had the principles of war as its foundation. Major General John H. Cushman, head of the Command and General Staff College, submitted the draft for consideration, but DePuy rejected it as too abstract and impractical.[178] After this incident, DePuy took the responsibility for drafting the manual away from the CGSC, its traditional home, and brought it directly to TRADOC.[179] DePuy wanted to base doctrine on the "cold hard facts" of potential combat in Europe.[180] These "cold hard facts" painted a bleak picture of an outnumbered and outgunned NATO force. These adverse conditions required a defensive theory of victory freed from the constraints of the principles of war. As the six-to-one force ratio for successful attack made clear, a commander's outnumbered force would be destroyed if he adhered mindlessly to the principle of offense. Therefore, except under ideal conditions, defense was to be preferred to attack.[181] The traditional purpose of the defense, to delay until offense was possible, was listed *sixth* out of eight purposes of the defense in *Operations '76*.[182] The inclusion of the principle of offense in *Operations '76* would have contradicted the defensive theory of victory required to give the army a fighting chance against its most dangerous adversary. Therefore, in spite of army tradition and the supposed offensive bias of military bureaucrats, doctrine writers in the army left out the principles of war to make room for a highly defensive theory of victory.

Even Active Defense, however, had an offensive component, the counterattack. In fact, DePuy noted, "The counterattack to destroy an enemy force which has been stopped by defensive fires is the *essence* of the 'active' defense."[183] But this offensive element of the doctrine was restricted. "Sweeping counterattacks," DePuy stipulated, "which expose our forces to heavy losses as they surrender the advantages of the defender must be the exception."[184] Here DePuy was underlining a key relationship between attack and defense that constituted yet another advantage of the defense. Local counterattacks retain all of the advantages of the defense while invoking the destructive power of the offense. This is because defensive counterattacks strike at the attacking force before it can transition to the defense. In this way, the defensive counterattack enjoys the advantages of the defense and the initiative of attack. The counterattacking defender gets the best of both worlds, and the attacker gets neither. This is the best tactical situation in which an outnumbered force can find itself, and this was the key to Active Defense.[185] However, NATO forces could not undertake a general counteroffensive because they lacked the resources, ammunition, and "the ability to sustain it."[186] Under the Cold War circumstances of the 1970s, a general counteroffensive was unthinkable. As DePuy thought, offensive ideas of "large forces sweeping across the front [were] sheer bunk, or at least simply romantic."[187]

Since 1905 the army had instructed its officers to persist in the offense and pursue the enemy to destruction.[188] According to *Operations 1976*, however, commanders should undertake offensive operations with a heavy dose of caution and in conjunction with the "built-in" advantages of defense.[189] Yet this defensive emphasis did not mean that General DePuy was rejecting the military realist logic of force and its offensive implications. A disagreement DePuy had with General Alexander Haig, supreme NATO commander, bears this out.

General Haig criticized the defensive emphasis of *Operations 1976*. He wrote to DePuy, invoking the principles of war, that he would have liked to see "a more explicit reminder that in general, the ultimate purpose of any defense is to regain the initiative by taking the offense."[190] DePuy agreed, stating that Haig and other critics of *Operations 1976* "feel that success in battle only comes to the attacker. . . . I agree with all of that. . . . I don't think it is a formula for winning the war. At best, it is a formula for a stalemate or for deterrence. Unfortunately, however, the facts of life in NATO, and the correlation of forces as the Soviets call it, are such that we do not have a general offensive capability in Europe."[191]

Although DePuy and *Operations 1976* recommended local counterattacks to canalize and destroy a stalled attacker, the relative weakness of the army and its NATO allies meant that army doctrine had to have a defensive theory of victory. DePuy's emphasis on the power of the defense was nothing new to the army, however. The previous chapters place DePuy's decision in a doctrinal context broader than just the post-Vietnam army. Since the early 1960s, the army had been attributing greater power to the defense. This progression reached its peak in *Operations 1976* in response to the dire situation confronting the army in Europe. As military realism expects, the result of a great disparity of capabilities between the army and the most dangerous threat, a disparity that peaked in the 1970s, was a highly defensive theory of victory. Benjamin Jensen argues that Active Defense did constitute a new theory of victory because of its emphasis on suppression, movement to concentrate, and employing a heavier covering force than traditional army doctrine.[192] However, we are concerned here primarily with the offensive or defensive character of theories of victory for the purposes of theoretical testing. *Operations 1976* retained but refined the defensive theory of victory at the core of U.S. Army doctrine.

Nevertheless, we should not overlook those refinements. *Operations 1976* was far from identical to the 1960s manuals when it came to defense. According to *Operations 1962* and *1968*, commanders should not avoid the defensive form of warfare but should master it. The two specific defensive methods were the area and mobile defense. Mobile defense employed a covering force and kept the main force in reserve to counterattack. The area defense, on the other hand, was more static, used to hold territory. However, the manuals concluded, the defensive plan would likely be some combination of mobile and area defense.[193]

Active Defense was just such a combination. The Soviet military had designed its doctrine to execute a short-war strategy that would involve deep armored penetrations to defeat NATO quickly.[194] In Active Defense, a covering force would move out to meet this armored spearhead,[195] while the main force retained its mobility. When the covering force discovered the enemy's main effort, the main force would move laterally across the battlefield and prepare the ground to "ambush the advancing force."[196] Employing their perfected mechanized tactics, adapted from West German *panzergrenadier* techniques, in a defense in depth,[197] tanks, antitank guided missiles, and the rest of the combined arms team would "destroy the masses of enemy armored vehicles in the assault."[198] As advocated by Howze in the 1950s, helicopters would be a key antitank weapon so long as army artillery and air forces sufficiently suppressed the Soviet air-defense system.[199]

Yet DePuy recognized that this mode of operations might not be successful. In that case too, however, the advantages of the defense could be harnessed to great effect. As DePuy said in an interview, if the initial defense failed, "then the doctrine says that we have to trade a little bit of space for time and casualties. . . . [W]e can, in fact, fight a very stubborn action in a very small area, against a very large force . . . and then, move so that we are always fighting battles where they are most advantageous to us and least advantageous to the other side."[200]

This combat maneuver, delay, or "retrograde operations," received its own chapter in *Operations 1976*.[201] The delaying force seeks to inflict maximum casualties on the enemy as it disengages from the enemy attack.[202] As described in *Operations 1962* and by DePuy in the quote above, the defender could enjoy the initiative in this case by forcing the enemy to react to his defensive plan and by moving so that the defender is "always fighting battles where they are most advantageous to [him] and least advantageous to the other side."[203] The towns and villages of West Germany were particularly well suited to this type of fighting withdrawal that wears down the attacker.[204]

The import of retrograde operations translated into army infantry and armor training. At Fort Benning, the infantry school, and Fort Knox, the armor school, units "practiced moving rearward while simulating the destruction of an advancing enemy."[205] When DePuy visited Fort Benning at the beginning of his reforms, he was aghast to find officers untrained in the building of defensive positions and occupied instead with courses on management and leadership.[206] DePuy's focus on the basics of defensive tactics is interesting coming from an officer steeped in the army's finest hour and its offensive culture.

Again following in the footsteps of the 1960s manuals, *Operations 1976* praised the commander in the defense. *Operations 1962* stated, "The conduct of defensive operations under adverse conditions *is the supreme test of the field commander*" and "*The highest order of leadership and tactical skill is demanded.*"[207] The 1976 manual concurred, arguing that complex defensive operations were "*the most demanding of all ground combat operations.*" Those employing it had to be "highly competent" and "well trained."[208] According to *Operations 1976*, the most skillful commanders were those who could effectively employ the advantages of the defense and the opportunities for initiative therein.

The advantages of the defender would also transfer to the nuclear battlefield. As discussed in the previous section, *Operations 1976* acknowledged the advantages of battlefield nuclear weapons and the need to prepare for a nuclear-conventional battlefield. At the tactical level, the defender can shoot from behind cover, but the attacker must break cover and expose himself to deadly fire to close with and subdue the enemy. This same logic could obtain at the operational level on the nuclear battlefield, giving the defender additional advantages. *Operations 1976* recognized that the use of nuclear weapons complicated operations because they contaminate the battlefield.[209] However, if a retreating force employed nuclear weapons to complicate and disrupt the enemy's attack, then they would be moving away from the nuclear contamination. However, as at the tactical level, the attackers had to expose themselves to this hazard to come to grips with the defender. All the while, the active defender would be inflicting a heavy toll on the attacker with his lethal conventional weapons.

In sum, Active Defense would use the advantages of defense and local offense, in conjunction with advances in weapons technology and rigorous training of mechanized units, to achieve the lopsided loss ratios that the Israelis had enjoyed in the October War.[210] In this way, the U.S. Army in Europe, with the help of its NATO allies, and especially the West German Army, could fight outnumbered and win the first battle of the next war.[211] These defensive concepts echoed *Operations 1962* and *1968*. Like these predecessors, *Operations 1976* attributed much more extensive purposes to the defense than were traditionally recognized by the army. Foremost among these was to cause an enemy attack to fail.[212] Local counterattacks could then destroy the local attacking force without relinquishing the advantages of the defense.

The absence of the principles of war and, and therewith the principle of offense, was a clear signal of the defensive theory of victory in *Operations 1976*. Patton-like pursuits were out of the question.[213] Interestingly, DePuy had actually been present when Patton had slashed his way across Europe. However, his firsthand experience of the army's finest hour did not blind him to the "cold hard facts" of confronting the most dangerous threat in the 1970s. He did not seek to replicate this finest hour through an offensive doctrine, as military culture theory would expect, but expanded upon a defensive doctrine best suited for the imbalance of capabilities facing the army.[214]

Because of its refinements to the defensive emphasis of army doctrine in the 1960s, DePuy recognized, unlike some,[215] that *Operations 1976* "was not revolutionary" but "evolutionary."[216] While *Operations 1976* made clear that the theory of victory at the core of army doctrine was defensive, it was not a core change in army doctrine. The gradual doctrinal change toward a more and more defensive theory of victory originated in the 1960s and increased as the imbalance of forces increased and the physical obstacles to success mounted into the 1970s. Seen in this light, it is clear that civilian realists did not drive the defensive character of Active Defense; rather, conditions on the ground did. This result is also contrary to bureaucratic and cultural explanations, which expected a shift to an offensive theory of victory.

Offense and Defense in Operations 1982

Six years later, *Operations 1982* replaced *Operations 1976*. While the army published this doctrinal revision during the Reagan administration, army plans to revise *Operations 1976* began shortly after its publication. As already noted, Reagan increased the defense budget as part of a new Cold War strategy.[217] The five-year defense plan drawn up in 1981 called for an 8.1 percent increase in the U.S. defense budget, or an increase of 59 percent.[218] He abandoned détente and in some ways departed from the traditions of containment. Some considered his strategy aggressive to the point of irresponsibility, comparing it to the Cult of the Offensive that enthralled the militaries of Europe in 1914.[219] From a bureaucratic perspective, Reagan's aggressive foreign policy should be a plum opportunity for the army to increase its resources, autonomy, and certainty by shifting to an offensive theory of victory. This theory of victory would also be consistent with U.S. Army culture, which some argue recoiled at the defensive theory of victory espoused by DePuy and Active Defense. A cursory examination of *Operations 1982* would appear to confirm this prediction. Its emphasis on concepts such as "deep attack" appears highly offensive. However, a close analysis of *Operations 1982* paints a different picture.

DePuy and his doctrine team made great efforts to publicize *Operations 1976* throughout the army.[220] Their efforts made army doctrine a central concern, and point of contention, for more army officers than ever before.[221] Like General Haig, a number of army officers objected to the manual's emphasis on defense over offense.[222] However, as DePuy's response to this objection shows, the first commander of TRADOC thought that an offensive theory of victory was unrealistic and dangerous given the "correlation of forces" in NATO Europe.[223] *Operations 1976* was not purely defensive, however. DePuy's manual made it clear that NATO forces could destroy the numerically superior attacker only through exploiting defensive advantages, highly accurate fire, *and* local counterattacks with limited exploitation.[224] These counterattacks would canalize the attackers into positions that could facilitate and accelerate their destruction. However, if army commanders pushed these counterattacks too far, this would endanger their outnumbered forces and lead to defeat. DePuy's doctrinal collaborator and successor at TRADOC, General Donn Starry, was the primary author of the chapters on offense and defense in *Operations 1976*.[225] He worked out this use of the counterattack during the 1970s and wrote it into the 1976 manual. He also described the concept in an article in the journal *Armor*.[226] Other armor officers followed suit, publishing articles with titles such as "How to Defend Outnumbered and Win."[227]

Before moving on to a discussion of *Operations 1982*, a note on the role of Starry and armored forces in *Operations 1976*. Some have argued that rivalries between military arms, like armor versus infantry, drive doctrine, as each arm seeks to secure its own bureaucratic interests. There is little evidence of this in the story of Active Defense. DePuy, a traditional infantry officer, argued that armored units were the key to the army's theory of victory. He assigned General Starry, a career armor officer, to write major parts of *Operations 1976*. As Jensen points out, the problem of fighting outnumbered in Europe drove doctrinal development, not the parochial interests of the different arms within the army.[228] As military realism expects, senior army officers hurdled bureaucratic and cultural obstacles to design a doctrine that worked.

General Starry and the other writers of *Operations '76* were actually aware of many of the weaknesses that critics of the manual pointed to after its publication. DePuy and Starry justified the publication of the 1976 manual, even with its flaws, because the army needed a new doctrine to prepare it for the fight in Europe, especially with a much smaller all-volunteer force. The army needed *Operations '76* quickly. Once this manual was out and informing army training, the army could resolve its flaws in a later edition. This explains why the revision of *Operations '76* began the year after its publication. This revision was Starry's first priority as TRADOC commander.

In *Engaging the Enemy: Organization Theory and Soviet Military Innovation, 1955–1991*, Kimberley Zisk argues that civilian national security intellectuals play an important role in military innovation. Some have argued that such intellectuals were the driving force behind the abandonment of Active Defense for AirLand Battle. At the time of its publication, intellectuals, such as William Lind and Edward Luttwak,[229] were very critical of *Operations 1976*. Instead, they advocated "maneuver warfare," "a very offensive-minded defensive strategy."[230] In this concept, NATO forces would trade space for time and then strike a major blow against the exposed flank of the attacking force. Starry invited these public intellectuals to take part in the doctrinal debate. However, although their criticisms facilitated a fruitful debate within the army, Starry did not adopt the highly offensive maneuver-warfare option because of its lack of specificity. "Lind kept talking about maneuver warfare and so on," Starry noted later. "I don't know what he meant. He never said what he meant."[231] Some security studies scholars, including John Mearsheimer, shared Starry's confusion. Mearsheimer pointed out that there were major risks involved in such a concept of operations. "At best," he wrote, maneuver-oriented defense "is a vague prescription so lacking in substance that its impact on future policy will be negligible. At worst, it is a formula for disaster."[232] This rejection of maneuver warfare is surprising from the bureaucratic and cultural perspective because the kind of sweeping counteroffensive it envisioned was perfectly consistent with hypothesized bureaucratic interests and army culture. Instead of letting those interests and cultural norms guide him, Starry moved doctrine in the direction he saw as necessary to address the most dangerous threat. How much that doctrinal direction mimicked that of General DePuy becomes clear under close examination.

Many inside and outside of the army saw AirLand Battle as a return to a more offensive doctrine after the misguided Active Defense. *Operations 1982* was more explicit about the offensive elements of army doctrine. It argued that the army should inculcate officers in "the spirit of the offense."[233] However, this was a change in emphasis rather than substance. In fact, Starry argued in 1979 that *Operations 1976* already possessed this "spirit."[234] After all, as *Operations 1976* pointed out, through limited offensive operations, in the form of local counterattacks, army commanders could fully exploit the advantages of the defense and defeat the attacker. To inculcate this "offensive spirit," AirLand Battle doctrine resurrected the principles of war.[235] However, the principles were not the center of doctrine as they had been in the past. *Operations 1982* did not list the principles in its body and then use caveats to limit their offensive emphasis, as 1960s editions had. Instead, the 1982 manual put the principles at the back of the manual in an appendix. *Operations 1982* did discuss "the principles of AirLand Battle Doctrine" and "combat imperatives" but did not list all of the principles of war in its body.[236] The principles of AirLand Battle were initiative, depth, agility, and synchronization.[237] Moreover, in the discussion of "combat imperatives," where it was argued that each imperative was derived from one or more of the principles of war, the manual mentioned all of the principles *except* the principle of the offense.[238]

Nevertheless, in its chapter "Offensive Operations," *Operations '82* did call offense the "decisive form of warfare," because only offense "completely destroys the enemy."[239] Moreover, it contained a much more detailed discussion of offensive operations than *Operations 1976*. For instance, whereas *Operations 1976* spent only three paragraphs discussing exploitation and pursuit operations,[240] *Operations 1982* dealt with this aspect of offense through five full pages of detailed discussion. The 1982 manual discussed offense in general for thirty-three pages.[241] Moreover, *Operations 1982* also harked back to the finest hour of the army by mentioning such offensive commanders as MacArthur and Patton.[242] Despite these differences, though, the main points of the 1976 and 1982 manuals when it came to offense and defense were very similar.

More emphasis on "the offensive spirit" did not reverse the army's awareness, begun in the early 1960s, that defensive operations were much more than a temporary expedient. *Operations 1982* spent thirty pages discussing defensive and delaying operations, only three pages less than its discussion of offense. In its discussion of defense, *Operations 1982* echoed almost exactly *Operations 1976*.[243] The new edition noted the numerous advantages enjoyed by the defender, including better knowledge of the terrain and prepared positions, and that "the defender fights from cover against an exposed enemy" who is, therefore, more susceptible to highly lethal conventional and nuclear weapons.[244] Moreover, *Operations 1982* argued that the defense "is never purely reactive."[245] It does have reactive elements, but the defender also engages in offensive combat through defensive counterattacks.[246] "Offensive combat is as much a part of defensive operations as strongpoint defenses and delaying actions."[247]

As recommended by Active Defense, army commanders would use these techniques as part of a defense in depth to wear down the attacking enemy.[248] Starry and *Operations 1982* envisioned winning the close-in battle with the Soviet first echelon only after falling back to "the second or third [prepared] battle positions."[249] In such operations, the 1982 manual argued—contrary to the principles of war and army traditions, but consistent with *Operations 1962, 1968,* and *1976*—the defender could enjoy the initiative by constantly presenting the attacker with new situations that force him to react to the defensive plan.[250] Therefore, the principle of the initiative in AirLand Battle did not assume an offensive theory of victory. As an intellectual authority here, *Operations 1982* uses none other than Carl von Clausewitz:

> Clausewitz characterized the ideal defense as a "shield of blows." At the onset of the attack the defender yields the initiative. However, he uses his prepared positions and knowledge of the ground to slow its momentum and to strike the enemy with repeated, unexpected blows. He defeats the attacker's combined arms, degrades his strength and ability to concentrate, and destroys his force with effective maneuver supported by flexible firepower. He does not have to kill each enemy tank, squad, or combat system; he has only to destroy the ability of the attacking force to continue fighting.[251]

The excerpt clearly shows that, despite their nods to the power of attack, in the 1980s the writers of AirLand Battle preserved the defensive theory of victory at the core of army doctrine, introduced in the 1960s. Moreover, in their interpretation of Clausewitz, the writers of army doctrine did not emphasize his treatment of the offense, for which some have heavily criticized Clausewitz,[252] and focused instead on the Prussian officer's discussion of the power of the defense. Neither bureaucratic interests nor cultural norms blinded the authors of army doctrine to Clausewitz's arguments in favor of the power of the defense.

Regarding the relationship between attack and defense, therefore, Starry and *Operations 1982* agreed with much of *Operations 1976*. Discussing DePuy's "tactical perceptions," Starry stated, "In those perceptions . . . I found him to be exactly correct." Starry thought that DePuy and *Operations '76* were exactly right regarding the tactics required to win the close-in fight against the first echelon of a Soviet attack.[253] This agreement is hardly surprising because, as Starry pointed out later, "I wrote most of the defense and offense parts of that 1976 manual,"[254] although in the next breath Starry said, "and I knew something was missing—what to do about the follow-on echelons."[255] Where *Operations 1976* needed revision, as Starry and the other authors knew when they wrote it, was its failure to deal with the *second* and *third* echelons of a Soviet attack. The solution to this danger espoused by *Operations 1982* does appear highly offensive in orientation. Again, however, when we analyze the doctrinal process more closely, this element of AirLand Battle doctrine looks much less offensive.

Striking at the second echelon of the Soviet forces, or "deep attack," would slow and wear down those forces before they could contribute their numbers and firepower to the close-in fight at the first echelon. If NATO forces did not at least delay Soviet second-echelon forces on their trajectory toward the close-in fight, these Soviet reinforcements would overwhelm the outnumbered NATO defenders. The only way the defenders could prevent this, the authors of *Operations 1982* concluded, was through deep strikes by aircraft, artillery, unconventional forces, and, if necessary, tactical nuclear weapons against the follow-on echelons. These deep strikes would also disrupt and destroy Soviet command and control, undermining the attacker's plan.[256] Army and NATO commanders would synchronize these deep strikes with the close-in battle. This synchronization, another principle of AirLand Battle, led to the introduction of the "operational" level of war, between tactics and strategy.[257] Deep strikes would function at the operations level, positively shaping the conditions that would confront the defending forces at the first echelon, the tactical level.

However, the advent of deep attack did not signal a renewed faith in the power of the offense. The theory of victory at the core of 1980s army doctrine was still defensive.[258] The authors of *Operations 1976* knew that even if army commanders executed an active defense perfectly, the second echelon would still overrun them quickly. By striking these follow-on forces, combined with all the skills the army had honed under Active Defense, a NATO defense organized in depth could defeat the enemy "piecemeal—one echelon at a time."[259] In this way, NATO forces could "destroy the ability of the [Soviet] force to continue fighting" without having to match its numbers.[260]

Operations 1982 noted that the defensive framework would be made up of "continuous deep battle," a covering force to support the main effort, "a main effort in the main battle area," protection of the rear, and the use of reserves to support the main effort. In its description of covering-force operations, *Operations 1982* describes exactly Active Defense.[261] This description of the defensive framework attests that *Operations 1982* was advocating a combination of Active Defense, with its covering force and main effort, and deep strikes on second-echelon forces to enable the former.[262] In short, AirLand Battle doctrine made an impossible defensive task possible.[263]

Jensen argues that AirLand Battle's introduction of the operational level of war constituted a new "theory of victory."[264] However, it does not constitute a change in the offensive or defensive character of the theory of victory, which is the focus here. The actions prescribed by AirLand Battle at the operational level of war made a defensive theory of victory possible, but did not enable an offensive one. Jensen argues that AirLand Battle was a much more offensive doctrine than Active Defense. However, the evidence presented above shows that while AirLand Battle sought to inculcate "the spirit of the offense," it did not propose an offensive theory of victory. There were important differences in the doctrines, but AirLand Battle was not as a big a departure from Active Defense as sometimes thought.[265]

Rather than enabling a return to an offensive doctrine consistent with bureaucratic and cultural imperatives, deep strikes were a necessary precondition for *defensive* operations against a Soviet assault.[266] Moreover, the main source of deep attack was to be battlefield artillery and air interdiction and not mechanized forces slashing forward in a general offensive reminiscent of World War II. Though such proposals were recommended at the time, Starry rejected them as impractical.[267] The key innovation of *Operations 1982*, attacks on the Soviet second echelon, did not enable a return to an offensive doctrine but made a defense against the most dangerous threat plausible. These changes did not jettison a defensive for an offensive theory of victory. The 1982 manual placed more emphasis on the offensive elements of *Operations '76*, like local counterattack and "the spirit of the offense," but it did not reverse the defensive core of army doctrine. *Operations 1982* also echoed its predecessor and 1960s doctrine regarding the advantages of the defense.

Counterinsurgency and the Post-Vietnam Army
Counterinsurgency and Operations 1976

The total absence of COIN and stability operations from *Operations 1976* appears to support the dominant narrative of the post-Vietnam U.S. Army.[268] By jettisoning Kennedy- and Johnson-era COIN initiatives, the army was decisively turning its back on the Vietnam experience and focusing on the bureaucratically lucrative and culturally acceptable defense of Europe. This move was consistent with civilian Cold War strategy. Avoiding conflicts similar to Vietnam was one of the goals of the Nixon Doctrine.[269] Accordingly, Special Forces—the COIN experts—declined from thirteen thousand to three thousand from 1971 to 1974.[270] However, this is another case of civilian initiatives reinforcing, rather than causing, army initiatives. The army continued to consider the defense of Europe its most important mission, even during the height of Vietnam. Nixon did not inspire a sudden shift in mission priorities. Additionally, the previous two chapters show that the assumptions underpinning the bureaucratic and cultural story about the U.S. Army and COIN in the 1960s are problematic.

To review, before Kennedy came into office, the army was on the cutting edge of COIN theorizing and was working to prepare for the COIN mission.

The army then brought its COIN ideas to Vietnam. However, the powerful conventional capabilities of the NVA and Vietcong units they encountered there undermined much of their COIN efforts and led them to focus on the conventional fight. The cultural or bureaucratic antipathy toward COIN in the U.S. Army has been overstated and the supporting narrative of the Vietnam War incomplete.

From the military realist perspective, the turn away from COIN after Vietnam was inevitable. Due to the massive depletion of army forces in the 1970s and the concomitant increases in Soviet capabilities, DePuy removed COIN-type missions from *Operations 1976*. The army was at an even more serious material disadvantage in Europe than it had been in the 1960s. For the writers of the 1976 manual, the acuteness of the most dangerous threat eclipsed the need to prepare for COIN-like missions. As the new manual explained, "The Army's need to prepare for battle overrides every other aspect of the unit missions."[271] Military realists in the army had to concentrate all resources and training on producing a plausible defense against the Soviet threat. Not surprisingly, then, *Operations 1976* had no chapters or even sections on COIN, irregular warfare, or operations against guerrilla forces. Subordinate manuals on the subject had not been eradicated altogether, however. In the appendix, *Operations 1976* listed the subordinate manuals, among them *Special Operations Manual 90-8, Counter Guerrilla Operations*.[272] However, such missions were not part of the main *Operations* manual. *Operations 1976* was a "how to fight" manual, and COIN-type missions were not essential to that task. The increased gravity of the Soviet threat meant that the U.S. Army had to focus on preparing to confront it on the battlefield in Europe.

David Fitzgerald argues, however, that in subordinate manuals, the army's understanding of COIN and the role of Special Forces had fundamentally shifted after Vietnam, a symptom of resurgent army norms. Upon close examination, though, the army view of COIN appears quite consistent, even if it was no longer a key mission. First, Fitzgerald argues that after Vietnam, the mission of the SF shifted away from classic COIN, promoted by Kennedy, and toward attacking behind enemy lines in a European war.[273] However, from the foundation of the SF under General Decker, one of their main missions was to infiltrate behind Soviet lines in a European war and organize guerrilla bands to resist the Soviets and cut lines of communication. This suited President Kennedy, who encouraged the SF to become proficient in the fomenting of insurgency in target countries, an element of Kennedy's COIN initiative that Fitzgerald and other scholars neglect. The disruption caused by SF units in the Soviet rear would assist the outnumbered NATO troops fighting the main battle. Therefore, the European mission Fitzgerald describes was part of SF doctrine since their inception and was not a new mission.

Second, Fitzgerald argues that the 1972 subordinate manual *Field Manual 31-23, Stability Operations* represented a radical departure from previous army thinking on COIN missions.[274] However, the emphasis in the manual on the army taking an advisory role in COIN-like missions was not new or a radical departure from previous COIN thinking. As discussed in the previous chapter, army COIN theorizing always advocated this limited role for U.S. Army forces. Fitzgerald then points out that in 1974, the army replaced the term *stability operations* with *Internal Defense and Development*.[275] This language, rather than cutting itself off from COIN thinking under Kennedy, was reminiscent of "Foreign Internal Defense," the name given to the COIN doctrine of the Kennedy administration. Thus, the COIN thinking in the army in the 1970s had not changed radically.[276] Fitzgerald's argument appears to be based on an incomplete understanding of Kennedy's COIN initiatives that is widespread in the literature.

However, this consistency in subordinate manuals did not mean that General DePuy was an advocate of the COIN theorizing of the 1960s. General DePuy had a specific and prescient criticism of COIN doctrine in the aftermath of Vietnam. It echoes recent criticism of COIN doctrine in the aftermath of COIN revivals in the wars in Afghanistan and Iraq by authors such as Douglas Porch and Gian Gentile.[277] DePuy summed up the main COIN lesson from Vietnam as follows: "The whole thing [counterinsurgency], of course, was eventually sucked into the maw of Vietnam, but it was a very activist philosophy. It was premised on the assumption that if you were smart enough at all those things you could somehow thwart the efforts of the communists to subvert the third world. You could bring up some disadvantaged country in the image of America. Well, now after all these years we know better. We have a much more modest view of our capabilities."[278]

DePuy understood the logic of development-based COIN but thought Vietnam had demonstrated its limits. In his recent reevaluation of the army in Vietnam, Gregory Daddis comes to a very similar conclusion on the limits of COIN in Vietnam. The deteriorating situation in Iraq after the surge has led to similar criticisms of COIN doctrine today.

The overall point here, however, is that the balance of forces compelled the army to make COIN missions secondary to the defense of Europe in the 1970s. The army relegated COIN not for narrow bureaucratic or cultural reasons but because of its military realist assessment of how the army would resist the most dangerous threat under the severe resource constraints it confronted in the 1970s.

Counterinsurgency in the 1980s

Ronald Reagan renewed the interest in COIN in U.S. government circles, though under a different name, low-intensity conflicts. LICs interested Reagan because, like Kennedy, he wanted to counter communist subversion in the developing world. Reagan wanted to thwart insurgents in Angola, El Salvador, Ethiopia, and Nicaragua and support resistance movements in Eastern Europe and Afghanistan.[279] In El Salvador, sounding much like Kennedy, Reagan called for aid to the Salvadoran military to enable them to "launch a full scale country-wide *counterinsurgency* effort to include civic action and psychological operations."[280] Secretary of Defense Caspar Weinberger wanted to develop a U.S. response to LICs, which he considered one of "the most plausible [conflict] scenarios for the future."[281] Consequently, U.S. military and army SF funding was increased dramatically during the 1980s, rising from $440 million in 1981 to $2.5 *billion* in 1988.[282] However, Weinberger and the JCS were opposed to direct U.S. intervention using regular army units. They feared an incremental strategy that could slowly draw the United States into conflict, as had happened in Vietnam. U.S. military leaders through the early 1980s argued that the problems in Central America were not amenable to a military solution and that the injection of U.S. troops would make the problem worse, not better. Army officers recommended building up indigenous forces to deal with insurgents. In 1984 General Paul F. Gorman, commander of Southern Command, the command with responsibility for Central America, argued that he "could foresee no circumstances when it would be useful" for the United States to send combat troops to El Salvador. General John Galvin, Gorman's successor, held similar views,[283] as did the chief of staff of the army, General Edward Meyer.[284]

In the end, however, Reagan's concentration on this threat was more rhetorical than real. The administration restricted the number of advisers deployed to El Salvador to fifty-five at any given time, a very small number when compared with the more than ten thousand advisers deployed to Vietnam under Kennedy. As in the 1960s, in the Reagan era SF would be advisers to indigenous forces.[285] Like previous administrations, Reagan argued that the main effort against insurgents had to be local. The "military institutions in threatened states must become able to provide security for their citizens and governments."[286]

The best expression of the limited appetite civilian leaders had for any protracted COIN-like campaign involving U.S. forces was the 1984 Weinberger Doctrine, with its highly restrictive rules for deploying U.S. forces abroad.[287] The failure of the U.S. mission in Lebanon, which was undertaken against Weinberger and the U.S. military's advice, was the main catalyst for developing the Weinberger Doctrine. Reagan's decision to remove the troops after a suicide bombing that killed 241 Marines in 1983 was an indication of his less than sanguine view of limited engagements.[288] Nevertheless, later he would seek to make the army better prepared for such limited conflicts.

Despite the fact that the army had published *FM 100-20, Low Intensity Conflict* in 1981,[289] LICs were not discussed in *Operations 1982*. The first manual of the 1980s did have a section titled "Unconventional Warfare," designated an SF mission. As in the previous two decades, the SF continued to be an important addition to a European war. Working behind enemy lines to organize insurgents, SF units could contribute to the deep-attack aspect of AirLand Battle by gathering information and striking enemy units and facilities to disrupt the Soviet second echelon.[290] In the same section, *Operations 1982* defined guerrilla warfare as an adjunct to conventional operations.[291] The discussion of unconventional and guerrilla warfare took up one page of the manual, with another brief mention in the four-page chapter "Contingency Operations."[292] *Operations 1982* discussed COIN-like missions more than its doctrinal predecessor, but only as an additional means of executing AirLand Battle doctrine. Richard Betts points out that in the 1970s and '80s, "The Special Forces' mission was further conventionalized and largely taken over by World War II–style Ranger battalions."[293] Fitzgerald calls the conventional component of the SF mission in this period "surprising."[294] On the contrary, as previous chapters have shown, the use of the SF as part of the defense of Europe was actually part of the SF mission since their inception in the early 1960s.

The use of the SF in Europe was not necessarily a repudiation of COIN and the Vietnam War. In fact, the army had not forgotten the important COIN lessons of Vietnam. The debate surrounding COIN campaigns in Central America in the '80s showed that the army understood COIN and had not forgotten its tenets.[295] The reports generated about COIN in this period continually cited civic action and the establishing of government legitimacy as the keys to successful counterinsurgency. As Army Chief Meyer noted, "Unless you have the commitment of the people or the indigenous forces . . . you're not going to solve guerrilla warfare."[296] The army clearly understood COIN. Meyer and his army, however, had to prepare for these lesser contingencies "without compromising the decisive theatre of Central Europe."[297] From the military realist perspective, the army needed all its resources, including the SF, to have a chance of resisting the most dangerous threat.

The dominant narrative of the army in the '80s is that it was obsessed with Europe and had completely forgotten about COIN and LICs. Some army officers did think their institution was too concerned with the defense of Europe and not with the emergence of LICs. Interestingly, some of these critics grounded their criticisms in a misinterpretation of the conflict in Vietnam, a main theme in the previous chapter. As one officer noted, "The reason for the failure of American efforts in Vietnam is clear. The military managers of that era did not understand the kind of war facing them." These managers, the author continued, had undue faith in the "conventional approaches to combat, so successful in all theatres of operations during World War II."[298] As the previous chapter argued, however, the "military managers" of the war in Vietnam actually had a deep appreciation of the kind of war they were fighting. At issue was that it was not only a LIC but also an intense fight against conventionally proficient enemy formations. The presence of these formations undermined the COIN efforts that the "military managers" such as General Westmoreland *knew* were a key part of success. It appears, then, that the erroneous understanding of the war in Vietnam originated, in part, in the army itself in the 1980s.

However, these LIC advocates were not voices crying in the wilderness. There was a push in the 1980s by senior officers to ensure that the army took LICs seriously. Senior army officers, such as Generals John Galvin, Paul Gorman, and Fred Woerner, supported army preparation for LICs. Captain David Petraeus was Galvin's aide and allegedly wrote a speech for Galvin in which he lamented the army's discomfort with "internal wars," where "the societal dimension takes on crucial importance."[299] In light of recent events, these lines would seem to burnish Petraeus's COIN credentials. However, as we shall see below, Captain Petraeus also wrote an article in *Military Review* advocating the use of forces designed for LICs, the new light infantry divisions (LIDs), for the conventional defense of Europe. Like the army of the 1980s, Petraeus was pulled in two directions.

The concern with LICs also reached the CGSC and army doctrine. In one instance, the deputy commandant of the CGSC, Major General Gordon R. Sullivan, who agreed with assessments of the army in Vietnam that this book challenges, supported a push within the army to make two capstone manuals instead of just one, *FM 100-5 Operations* and another LIC capstone manual titled *FM 100-20, Military Operations in Conflicts Short of War*. However, the senior leadership of the army opposed this doctrinal initiative. Army Chief of Staff General Carl Vuono and the head of TRADOC, General Maxwell Thurman, rejected the idea of giving LICs their own manual.[300] Interestingly, one CGSC officer at the time based his objection to the separate capstone manual on a more accurate assessment of the army experience in Vietnam. Fitzgerald sums up Colonel John Landry's concerns as follows: "Landry worried that the Army might undertake an LIC mission but still find itself in a war, as it had done in Vietnam. In this case, Landry asked, which doctrine would the Army use: its doctrine for war or its doctrine for operations other than war?"[301] Landry's argument reflects a clearer understanding of the army's war in Vietnam and the real dilemmas it presented for advocates of COIN. Moreover, separating LIC doctrine from war fighting threatened to institutionalize the problem the army had in Vietnam, where it needed to be proficient in both COIN and conventional fighting and be able to coordinate both in a campaign. In the end, the attempt to separate LICs from *Operations* was unsuccessful.

However, later in his presidency, Reagan's interest in LICs had a direct impact on army doctrine when he established the light infantry divisions from 1984 to '85.[302] According to the administration, the purpose of the LIDs was as a rapid-deployment force for LICs. Although there was opposition within the army, five LIDs were eventually established. The army would form two of the light divisions by converting active infantry divisions into LIDs, two more would be new divisions, and a fifth would be a converted National Guard unit.[303]

To make room in army doctrine for the LIDs, LICs made an appearance in the new 1986 edition of *Operations*.[304] In these conflicts, the manual stated, army units would encounter "irregular and unconventional forces, enemy special operations forces, and terrorists."[305] Despite being designated to deal with such unconventional adversaries, LIDs also had an important role to play in any conflict over Europe. LIDs, the doctrine writers argued, could be a highly effective tool for fighting in "built-up areas."[306] *Operations 1976* and *1982* had argued that fighting in these "built-up areas" would be a vital part of a stubborn defense of West Germany.[307] In fact, in 1985, a retired General DePuy penned an article in *Army* titled "The Light Infantry: Indispensable Element of a Balanced Force." The article supported the concept of the LIDs by highlighting their role in defending Europe.[308]

DePuy was not the only officer who supported the use of LIDs in Europe. The year before DePuy's article appeared in *Army*, a young David Petraeus wrote an article in *Military Review* that argued for the use of LIDs in a European defense. Petraeus argued, "Given the terrain of Germany and the tactical doctrine of the Warsaw Pact . . . [t]he new lights [divisions] could effectively perform various missions: defense of urban areas or strongpoint, rear area combat operations, air assault operations, and dismounted operations during periods of limited visibility or in restrictive terrain."[309] Despite his support of the LIC missions and recent reputation as a COIN partisan, in the 1980s Petraeus argued that forces designated for COIN-like missions could be a force multiplier for the defense of Europe.[310] The training and doctrine of the LIDs reinforced this focus on supporting conventional operations.[311]

While the LIDs had a role to play in AirLand Battle, some proposals for their use were considered unrealistic.[312] The father of *Operations 1982* met proposals that the LIDs could also handle larger contingencies such as a Soviet invasion of Iran with ridicule. "That's preposterous!" exclaimed General Starry in one interview. "That's foolish! We're just deceiving ourselves."[313] Despite the versatility of LIDs, the army thought they certainly had their limits.

The addition of LIDs to army doctrine represented only a peripheral change. Doctrine writers in the army preserved the core of army doctrine in *Operations 1986*. As one of its primary authors noted, *Operations 1986* was "a second edition of current doctrine [*Operations '82*] rather than a revision," and it made "no changes to basic doctrine."[314] The authors of doctrine integrated the new LIDs into the army's main mission, addressing the most dangerous threat with AirLand Battle.[315] Like other unconventional forces in the 1960s, LIDs would contribute to the defense of Europe by an outnumbered force.[316]

During the Reagan era, U.S. civilian and military leaders faced the same problem that confronted Kennedy and his army in the early 1960s. How could the United States maintain heavy forces to defend Europe against a powerful Soviet attack and prepare lighter forces for smaller global contingencies, such as insurgency and regional conflicts, which also threatened U.S. interests? As in the 1960s, the army understood the unconventional threat and the imperatives of such operations. In fact, the army may have taken such threats more seriously than the Reagan administration, which did not match its strong LIC rhetoric with a strong LIC policy. Bureaucratic interests and cultural norms do not appear to have blinded army leaders to unconventional threats. However, these threats were less dangerous than the one that endangered the security of Europe. As Army Chief of Staff Meyer made clear, following his predecessors and military realism, the defense of Europe was the "decisive theater" and the doctrinal priority for the army.

Conclusion

Both inside and outside the army, a powerful narrative has formed about the army after Vietnam. Bloodied and demoralized, the army came out of Vietnam determined to forget the lessons of that war. This will to forget was most evident in army doctrine and training. Under the guidance of General William E. DePuy, the army refocused on the conventional defense of Europe against the Soviet threat. A return to a type of warfare reminiscent of the army's World War II finest hour blotted out the painful memory of the fighting in the rice paddies and jungles of Vietnam. Lending it still more strength, this narrative is consistent with the expectations of a number of the competing theories. Nevertheless, this narrative has many flaws. When we identify these flaws, and especially when we place the doctrinal changes of the '70s and '80s in the broader doctrinal context of the 1960s, military realism provides a better explanation of army doctrine in this period. For instance, one of the main assumptions underpinning this narrative is that the army had turned away from Europe during Vietnam. However, as the previous two chapters have shown, in the lead-up to and during Vietnam, the army remained focused on the threat from the USSR. This consistent focus on Europe and the threat from the Soviet Union undermines the established narrative of the post-Vietnam army and supports the expectation that military realists will focus on the gravest threats.

In terms of both outcome and process, the evidence presented in this case best supports military realism. According to this theory, given the balance of forces between the army and the Soviet adversary, senior army officers should preserve the defensive, conventional-nuclear core of army doctrine in the 1970s and '80s. With the 50 percent reduction in the size of the army through the all-volunteer force and other cuts, and the continuing modernization and expansion of Soviet forces, the power of the most formidable adversary greatly increased in this period. Consequently, as military realism would predict, General DePuy made the defensive emphasis in army doctrine even more definite than it had been in the 1960s. He developed Active Defense, a highly defensive theory of victory at the core of army doctrine. DePuy rejected drafts of *Operations* that were too offensive in character. Interestingly, General DePuy, considered a consummate military bureaucrat by many and an officer who participated in the army's World War II finest hour,[317] did not design doctrine in accordance with bureaucratic and cultural imperatives. He also retained the nuclear mission that some considered contrary to army traditions. DePuy forcefully directed the development of this culturally insensitive doctrine. Starry continued this trend through the addition of the deep attack, which would make Active Defense possible. Starry appreciated the need for an "offensive spirit" in army doctrine but refused to adopt highly offensive theories of "maneuver warfare" that would have served bureaucratic interests but produced an implausible means of resisting the Soviet threat. Starry was also more explicit about the vital role that nuclear weapons played in army doctrine, a role the authors of *Operations 1976* had downplayed due to doctrinal secrecy requirements.

As per the logic of force at the heart of the military realist perspective, both DePuy and Starry recognized that only offense could ensure victory by compelling a decision. However, both officers thought that a highly offensive doctrine was implausible because the Soviet enemy in Europe enjoyed too many material advantages. Consequently, they sought to exploit the "built-in" advantages of the defender to make up for what the army lacked in material capabilities. Exploiting the limits that the physical world placed on the attacker and the advantages of defense produced a credible doctrine. They developed this doctrine even though its core was contrary to the bureaucratic interests and the military culture of the U.S. Army. Senior military realists, in the persons of DePuy and Starry, spearheaded doctrinal development to produce a plausible means of resisting the most dangerous threat. While civilian decisions to cut available resources limited doctrinal options, DePuy and Starry engaged in doctrinal change to adapt to those conditions, much like their 1960s predecessors. Doctrine was more a tool for adapting to available resources than one for garnering more.

According to military realism, and contrary to bureaucratic perspectives, military organizations will limit their organizational autonomy to design a credible doctrine. In the two decades after Vietnam, the U.S. Army did just that. When formulating doctrine in the 1970s, the U.S. Army gave up a significant amount of its autonomy in two instances. First, the army arranged a very close relationship with the West German Army and sought a high degree of doctrinal consistency between the West German Army's *defensive* doctrine and *Operations 1976*. Second, the army inaugurated a major collaboration with the U.S. Air Force to enable the concept of AirLand Battle and took doctrinal cues from this competing service.[318] In an admission of deep interservice dependence, rather than rivalry, General DePuy argued that the army could not execute its main mission without the air force. General Starry made this army–air force collaboration even more central to army doctrine when he made AirLand Battle the key concept of *Operations 1982*. Starry also continued the effort to ensure doctrinal continuity with the West German Army. These doctrinal changes were necessary to combat the gravest threat, even if they undermined army autonomy.

Regarding COIN, military realism expects COIN to be a low-priority mission in this period, especially in the face of the threat from the Soviet Union. In *Operations 1976*, a U.S. Army reduced in size by half eliminated COIN from army doctrine. It could not spare the resources to prepare part of its force for these missions. The relegation of the COIN mission in the Nixon Doctrine made this alteration easier but was not its cause. The 1970s was the nadir of army strength and, therefore, the nadir of COIN in army doctrine. In addition, during the 1970s and '80s, the army enlisted SF and LIDs, forces designed for unconventional warfare, to assist in the defense of Europe. However, this was not a new mission for such forces. Since their inception, army leaders meant such forces to assist in the defense of Europe by sowing confusion and destruction in the Soviet rear and thereby facilitating a stalwart defense. Confronting the main adversary required all of the forces at the army's disposal. Finally, in the 1980s senior army leaders understood the threat of LICs and that conventional military operations could not resolve these conflicts. Nevertheless, such conflicts were much less threatening than the specter of a Soviet assault on Europe. Army bureaucracy and culture did not blind army leaders to the realities of LIC threats and missions, but the presence of the Soviet threat to Europe ensured they would remain on the doctrinal periphery.

Military realism explains doctrinal change and continuity in the army of the 1970s and '80s. The core of U.S. Army doctrine continued to focus on the defense of Europe and retained its nuclear mission and defensive theory of victory. The COIN mission continued to be peripheral to army doctrine, but not necessarily for the reasons hypothesized by the alternative explanations. Neither bureaucratic and cultural imperatives nor civilian intervention determined the core of U.S. Army doctrine. Despite changes in Cold War strategy between Nixon and Reagan, army doctrine demonstrated significant continuity. Although Jensen seeks to explain doctrinal development at a more micro level, he concurs with the assessment that the bureaucratic, military cultural, and civilian interventions in doctrine do not explain the development of Active Defense or AirLand Battle. Jensen argues that these doctrinal innovations in the army were "problem driven." I argue that the military realist perspective initiated and sustained that drive through the 1970s and 1980s. What Jensen's otherwise stellar analysis lacks, however, is the broader doctrinal context provided by the previous chapters, which exposes the high degree of doctrinal continuity between U.S. Army doctrine before, during, and after Vietnam. Military realism anticipated this surprising continuity, despite bureaucratic and cultural expectations to the contrary.

5 THE POWER–PROJECTION ARMY

Doctrine in the Post–Cold War Era until the Eve of September 11

BETWEEN 1989 AND 1991, the Soviet Union began to collapse and then ceased to exist. Not long after, the United States and its United Nations allies forced Iraqi forces from Kuwait. In August 1991, the U.S. Army chief of staff, General Gordon R. Sullivan, tasked Lieutenant General Frederick M. Franks Jr., his choice for commander of U.S. Army Training and Doctrine Command, with developing a new army doctrine for the changed strategic environment of the post–Cold War. Sullivan's ideas about changing the army were the "roots of the Army's effort to transform itself" after the Cold War, and they stretched into the first decade of the twenty-first century.[1] In June 1993, the U.S. Army published its first post–Cold War edition of *Field Manual 100-5, Operations*.[2] Army writing teams revised *Operations 1993* throughout the 1990s but did not publish its replacement until eight years later with *Field Manual 3-0*,[3] *Operations 2001*. The army distributed its first manual of the twenty-first century just three months before al-Qaeda terrorists smashed commercial airliners into the Twin Towers and the Pentagon and crashed another in a field in Pennsylvania.

With the fall of the Soviet Union, the threat that had shaped the core of army doctrine for decades disappeared. The development of army doctrine at the end of the Cold War and into the twenty-first century offers yet another opportunity to test the competing theories of military innovation. However, this time there is a radical shift in the international threat environment, the key factor, according to military realism. We begin as before by setting out the expectations of the competing theories across the three key areas of doctrine given the international context. I then evaluate how well the historical evidence supports each explanation, first by discussing the threat environment, as assessed by civilian and military leaders, then the doctrinal processes leading to both *Operations 1993* and *2001*. After the doctrinal process of each manual is outlined, each key area of doctrine is used to evaluate the performance of each theoretical perspective.

The U.S. Army after the Cold War made major changes to its doctrine by removing the nuclear mission from the core of doctrine and adopting an offensive theory of victory. However, the writers of army doctrine did not forget the lessons about the power of the defense so central to its Cold War doctrine. The transformation of the threat environment also resurrected the army's concern with threats at the lower end of the spectrum of conflict. To prepare itself for these "operations other than war" (OOTW), the army revived the ideas that had underpinned classic counterinsurgency doctrine and with which it had become so familiar in the 1950s and '60s. Army leaders also embraced a transformation agenda that required major changes in its World War II and Cold War ideas of warfare. While some of these doctrinal innovations catch the alternative theories off guard, they are consistent with military realism.

Civilian Realists and U.S. Army Bureaucracy at the End of the Cold War and into the Twenty-First Century

In a unipolar world, the dominant hegemon does not face any threats to its national survival. According to civilian realism, this period should see few major civilian interventions in military doctrine. The propitious balance of power means civilians will have little incentive to integrate military doctrine with strategy. Nor will civilian leaders need the services of military mavericks to reconcile military doctrine with their strategic vision. According to civilian realism, military bureaucrats, on the other hand, should be active under these conditions. These bureaucrats should capture the doctrinal process and shape it to meet bureaucratic goals. When civilians take their eyes off the military, its bureaucrats run the show.

In the post–Cold War, therefore, army bureaucrats will use doctrine to fill their coffers, shield themselves from outside interference, and reduce unpredictability. Offensive theories of victory and conventional missions are one means of achieving these goals. Consequently, despite the receding Soviet threat, the U.S. Army should continue to define the international threat environment in terms that justify an offensive, conventional doctrine. Senior army leaders should use army doctrine as one tool to justify maintaining large conventional military formations. These same leaders should see to it that doctrine washes away any residue of the defensive theory of victory left over from the Cold War. Further, the army should welcome the opportunity to renounce nuclear weapons and all the doctrinal uncertainty they produced. With the departure of nuclear weapons, moreover, the army will no longer rely on civilian authorization to implement a large part of its doctrine. Army bureaucrats should return their institution to its conventional-warfare roots. Senior army bureaucrats should also use doctrine to define the army's organizational turf, its unique skills and missions, to defend against the encroachments of other U.S. military services. The army bureaucracy should be especially powerful after two decades of professionalization under the all-volunteer force.[4]

These army bureaucrats will relegate counterinsurgency or low-intensity conflicts within doctrine, even while the post–Cold War threat environment witnessed a rise in LICs. They should not allow LIC operations, like peacekeeping, to become a main army mission because they do not serve bureaucratic interests. These are messy politico-military operations, involving major uncertainty and political interference and requiring few expensive military platforms. As one recent study put it, the army's lack of preparation for LICs, despite "the constabulary demands of civilian policy makers,"[5] "reflected an institutional bias that favored the familiar over the innovative and the quantitative over the qualitative."[6] Thus, bureaucratic preferences for preserving and acquiring new conventional weapons systems, ever more capable of destroying other weapons systems, hindered the army from adapting to a post–Cold War environment characterized by LICs.[7] Instead, military bureaucrats in the army used the lessons from post–Cold War operations, such as Desert Storm, to promote an offensive, conventional trajectory in doctrine that fulfills bureaucratic needs. Aware of this tendency, in the aftermath of Desert Storm one commentator counseled the army to forsake "the seductive urge to keep refighting World War II."[8]

Many inside and outside of the U.S. military saw the major advances in precision-guided weapons put on display during the Gulf War as the first shots in a revolution in military affairs.[9] However, under the watchful eye of army bureaucrats, the RMA should be anything but revolutionary. As Wilson pointed out, bureaucracies want the newest technology but "only when the new, sophisticated bit of technology is consistent with existing tasks." "If the new technology," Wilson continues, "requires a redefinition of core tasks it will be resisted."[10] This is reminiscent of the French Army's integration of tank forces in the interwar period. French military leaders peppered tanks throughout the force instead of organizing them into powerful striking forces as innovators such as Charles de Gaulle advised. Bureaucracies always seek to avoid revolutionary change. After all, the argument goes, innovation is a kind of "creative destruction" that undermines the established routines and power bases of military bureaucrats.[11] Analysts have made this very argument regarding the U.S. Army and the RMA.[12] According to this argument, the army undertook only "evolutionary" changes and incorporated elements of the RMA into existing doctrinal structures. The military bureaucrats leading the army sought to undermine RMA initiatives and were adept at "stifling innovation."[13]

Operations 2001 should continue the doctrinal trends established in *Operations 1993*. When it came to the relegation of LIC operations, army bureaucrats found a kindred spirit in the Bush administration. The distaste in the Bush administration for peacekeeping missions dovetails perfectly with what Avant and Lebovic characterize as the post–Cold War army's desire to focus on "large-scale, capital-intensive, high-technology operations."[14] *Operations 2001* should focus on the offensive use of technologically advanced conventional-warfare platforms. Such a focus promises the greatest bureaucratic payoff. At the same time, however, as Secretary Donald Rumsfeld lamented, the army resisted attempts by civilian leaders to transform doctrine in ways at odds with bureaucratic objectives.[15]

U.S. Army Culture after the Cold War and into the Twenty-First Century

Even in the uncertain post–Cold War, the culture of the U.S. Army should be the North Star guiding innovation. A capstone doctrine centered on conventional forces in a decisive offensive role would be consistent with that culture and the World War II finest hour that gave birth to it. Despite the disappearance of the Soviet threat, the army should seek to maintain its major Cold War forces and use doctrine as one tool to justify this continuity. Accordingly, through *Operations 1993* and *2001*, the army should prepare for culturally approved operations and shun their contraries, that is, defensive and *unconventional* modes of warfare. For instance, in the absence of a Soviet threat, the army should welcome the opportunity to renounce nuclear weapons as a major part of its doctrine. The army should also resist preparing for LICs, despite the fact that it was engaged in a number of them in this period. Indeed, arguing from a cultural perspective, Fitzgerald contends that *Operations 1993* did not represent a significant change from AirLand Battle doctrine.[16] Cassidy argues that the post–Cold War U.S. Army "marginalized" operations other than war, their term for unconventional tasks like COIN, because of its deep-seated culture.[17] Senior army leaders and doctrine writers should use the lessons from recent conflicts, such as the Gulf War, to justify a doctrine that conforms to army culture. Indeed, scholars have argued that the army saw the Gulf War as a vindication of Cold War doctrine and its traditional focus on conventional warfare and offensive operations.[18] These scholars blame the offensive, conventional mind-set of army culture for the institution's failure to adapt to a transformed international environment.[19]

Revolutionary changes in doctrine and organization can fracture the military traditions at the heart of military culture. In order to shield army traditions, senior officers should work to minimize the cultural disruption from the RMA. They will champion those elements of the revolution that facilitate the offensive, conventional essence of army doctrine and discard incongruous elements. Indeed, Chad Serena argues that the U.S. Army leadership simply plugged the components of the RMA into the kinds of operations for which they already had an "institutional penchant."[20] These guardians of army culture should resist Secretary of Defense Rumsfeld and his transformation agenda beginning in the year 2000.

Military Realism after the Cold War and into the Twenty-First Century

According to military realism, the post–Cold War period should be a period of major doctrinal change. From the military realist perspective, after the collapse of the Soviet Union there was no comparable threat waiting in the wings. Nevertheless, the United States still had vital material interests outside of its territory that were essential for generating force in defense of those interests. These included natural resources, such as oil, and open lines of communication as part of a globalizing liberal economic order that undergirded the U.S. economy. Regarding oil, the army had been eyeing this geostrategic concern since the 1970s, when the embargo by the Organization of Petroleum Exporting Countries underlined U.S. dependency on foreign oil. Deploying to and fighting in this region had received some treatment in doctrine, and conflicts there, such as the 1973 October War, had made U.S. intervention or counter-intervention a real possibility. Moreover, Soviet material support to countries in the Middle East had equipped them with highly advanced weaponry, even if it had not produced military victories.[21]

According to military realism, the balance between conventional and nuclear weapons in army doctrine should shift toward conventional and away from nuclear weapons beginning with *Operations 1993*. This should persist in *Operations 2001*. Army doctrine from the 1950s to the '80s had kept nuclear weapons at the core of doctrine because senior army leaders thought tactical nuclear weapons might be the only way to blunt a Soviet assault on Europe. In addition, Soviet doctrine called for dual-capable forces able to maneuver in the shadow of mushroom clouds. For these reasons, the U.S. Army adopted dual-capable forces that integrated conventional and nuclear doctrine and force structure. With the fall of the Soviet Union, the major nuclear and conventional threat that necessitated the nuclear mission in doctrine had dissipated. Moreover, Soviet leadership had greatly reduced the size and physical proximity to Western Europe of their conventional forces. With the disappearance of this dual-capable threat and the absence of a similarly equipped successor, *Operations 1993* should place much less emphasis on nuclear weapons than previous army doctrine. Conventional forces should come to the fore again in army doctrine. This should persist into *Operations 2001*. In all three areas of doctrine, there should be evidence that the army reinterprets its doctrinal concepts and even its history in order to prepare its forces to deal with the threat environment it confronts.

However, the conventional forces in army doctrine should have a different mission. With the passing of the Soviet threat, senior army officers should begin to see threats to vital material resources and the lines of communication to them as the most dangerous threat. In the absence of state-based threats, the friction of geography still presents a formidable obstacle to the deployment and operations of military forces. Therefore, even if it requires a core doctrinal change, senior army leaders should alter the forces' mission and doctrine to enable them to secure these vital material resources. Logically, in the U.S. case, a power-projection capability would be necessary to secure these distant resources. The army should place more emphasis on the ability to project conventional force over distance than it had in the past and to parts of the world other than Europe. Ironically, the global focus that civilian leaders often pushed for during the Cold War, but that the army saw as unrealistic given the imbalance of capabilities with the Soviets, should become a major part of army doctrine.

When it comes to the offensive or defensive orientation of army doctrine, military realism predicts that as part of the core change in mission, *Operations 1993* and *2001* will also have a more offensive theory of victory than Cold War army doctrine. Power projection necessarily involves an offensive capability. This is especially so when the force is projecting power to a geographical location where it does not have forward-deployed troops or established defenses and allies. In this situation, a military force must establish a foothold in the area through offensive operations, at times against a prepared defense. Consequently, military realists in the army should temper this offensive emphasis in doctrine with their appreciation for the increased friction that accompanies offensive action, especially if political leaders limit available resources. Friction remains the perennial enemy to overcome.

Finally, on the subject of COIN-like missions after the Cold War, military realism argues that militaries design their doctrines to deal with the range of international threats but that they prioritize the most dangerous. The removal of the Soviet Union as a threat, and the absence of a great-power replacement, narrowed the spectrum of conflict that had guided army doctrine since the 1960s. From 1962 to 1986, the lowest end of the conflict spectrum, where insurgency and LIC reside, had received the least attention in army doctrine. It disappeared from its pages altogether when the Soviet threat was at its peak in the '70s and '80s. Moreover, the army stretched the missions of forces designated for such conflicts to include the nuclear and conventional defense of Europe. However, in the threat environment of the post–Cold War, military realists within the army should pay more attention to this lower end of the conflict spectrum than they had in the 1970s and '80s. However, the availability of resources for the power-projection mission could temper military realist enthusiasm for unconventional missions. If forced to choose between the power-projection mission and COIN-like missions, military realists in the army should prioritize the former as most necessary for addressing threats to the vital material interests of America.

Civilian and Military Threat Assessment after the Cold War

According to civilian and army leaders, there were two important post–Cold War threats facing the United States: first, the need to secure resources and global lines of communication, which were "threatened by regional hegemons" in a number of places, and, second, regional instability that might threaten these resources and lines, the lifeblood of the economic prosperity of the United States and its allies.[22] Thinkers in the Pentagon articulated a regional strategy for securing oil and other vital resources at the end of the George H. W. Bush administration. Set out in the 1992 Defense Planning Guidance (DPG), the goal of the strategy, Secretary of Defense Richard Cheney argued, was to "preclude hostile, nondemocratic domination of a region critical to our interests."[23] In short, a regional strategy would prepare the United States to act against the kind of regional aggression that precipitated the Gulf War.[24]

The U.S. Army agreed with this regional focus, but not because it was imposed by their civilian superiors. In fact, the Joint Staff of the U.S. military began to focus on regional threats as early as 1987. The "Joint Strategic Capabilities Plan" differentiated between "the most dangerous threat," the Soviets in Europe, and "the most likely, regional conventional conflicts unlikely to involve Soviet forces."[25] Beginning in March 1989, these regional scenarios began to inform U.S. military force structure.[26] Between 1989 and March 1992, when the DPG emerged, Chairman of the Joint Chiefs of Staff Colin Powell was directing subordinates to develop forces for regional contingencies. With the fall of the Soviet Union, these regional threats became the primary threat. As in other cases covered here, the DPG is an example of civilian leaders latching on to strategic ideas developed within the military services, which civilians then promote as innovations.

Not long after the promulgation of DPG 1992, President Bush failed to win reelection and William J. Clinton succeeded him. The Clinton administration preserved this regional element of U.S. strategy. "The United States," as Secretary of Defense Les Aspin put it, "must have the capability to deal with regional bad guys."[27] The administration saw the post–Cold War as increasingly characterized by global economic interdependence. The United States, as the sole superpower, stood to gain or lose the most from that interdependence.[28] The Clinton administration thought that the best way to preserve the prosperous status quo was through democratic enlargement. As National Security Adviser Anthony Lake stated, "The successor to a doctrine of containment must be a strategy of enlargement—enlargement of the world's free community of market democracies."[29]

However, the Clinton administration also wanted to preserve global stability through peacekeeping operations. Like Kennedy's concern with communist insurgency, the Clinton administration argued that even minor threats to stability on the periphery could destabilize regions vital to the economic interests of the United States, threatening its unipolar position.[30] Therefore, the U.S. military had to be prepared to participate in the peacekeeping missions that would restore stability in peripheral areas.[31]

Army Chief of Staff Sullivan appeared to agree with this new focus on nontraditional military operations and their connection to U.S. economic interests. He argued that the army needed to prepare "to conduct operations, usually in conjunction with allies and friends, that aimed at creating or restoring conditions favorable to economic development and trade."[32] In order to preserve the "new world order" in the Clinton era, the U.S. Army would have to prepare for two simultaneous regional conflicts and for peacekeeping duties to shore up international stability.[33] These were very different missions but with one common characteristic: they would both require global power projection.[34]

A New Mission for the Army and the Doctrinal Process

In the 1990s, the army confronted the major uncertainty inherent in the "un-settled debris of the bipolar world."[35] The decline of the military remnant of the Soviet Union persisted and worsened.[36] As a 1990 NATO study conclud-ed, the Soviet Union "no longer was capable of threatening in practice the massive surprise attack that had for so long been the basis of NATO's mili-tary planning."[37] Given this major change in the threat environment, it was clear to senior army leaders that the main mission of the army would change and that doctrine would have to change with it. Interestingly, however, U.S. Army thinking about regional conflicts began before the fall of its perennial adversary. In 1988 Lieutenant General John Foss, the deputy chief of staff for operations and plans, brought together a number of army colonels and RAND Corporation thinkers to study the effects of a changing international environ-ment on the future of the army. The resulting Antaeus Study actually built on the concepts developed by TRADOC's September 1987 "AirLand Battle Fu-ture" study, which studied the effects of defense trends on army doctrine and organization. Antaeus concluded that the future army would need to be highly deployable and that this would likely require "'modular' division designs" for "deployability and flexibility."[38]

Senior army leaders decided early on that a change in doctrine would be the cutting edge for adapting the army to a post–Cold War characterized by region-al threats. The revision of *Operations 1986* began between 1990 and 1991. Army Chief of Staff General Carl E. Vuono[39] directed now general John W. Foss, the commander of Army Training and Doctrine Command, to update *Operations 1986* for the post–Cold War. Foss established a writing team for this purpose at the School of Advanced Military Studies at Fort Leavenworth. SAMS was the graduate school of the CGSC. The guides for doctrine were internal army documents that sought to marry precision weapons and information technol-ogy with elements of AirLand Battle.[40] Foss thought AirLand Battle doctrine was sound. However, the new doctrine had to reflect that the army, unlike in the Cold War, would often be conducting operations into areas where few or no troops were and where there was no logistical support.[41] In addition, based on recent experience in Panama and with peacekeeping and humanitarian as-sistance operations, Foss thought that there ought to be a greater emphasis on LICs in the new manual. Before he could complete the revision, Foss left TRA-DOC.[42] Although in need of further development, the new army mission for the post–Cold War was in position by the fall of 1990. The focus on regional threats, then, was in place in army thinking prior to Desert Storm.[43]

After Desert Storm, the apparently unprecedented success of precision-guided munitions and airpower in that conflict called into question the efficacy and necessity of land power.[44] The army faced a challenge similar to the nuclear revolution in the 1950s. Army leaders argued, as they had in that earlier period, that only land forces could occupy territory, control populations, and protect resources.[45] In short, only land forces could decisively impose the will of the United States on enemies unwilling to give up their aims in the face of bombardment from air and sea.

General Sullivan succeeded General Vuono as army chief of staff.[46] Sullivan too appreciated the changed international environment the army faced, one he characterized as having moved from bipolarity to multipolarity, with "multiple centers of military, political, and economic power."[47] At TRADOC Sullivan replaced General Foss with General Frederick Franks and selected Colonel James R. McDonough to head the SAMS writing team for what would become *Operations 1993*.[48] Franks had been in the "combat developments planning group" under General Donn Starry during 1980–81. Franks had also led the VII Corps as part of the "left hook" against Saddam Hussein's forces on February 24–28, 1991.[49] Like DePuy and Starry before them, Sullivan and Franks and Vuono and Foss viewed doctrine as the engine that would guide change in the U.S. Army.[50] Sullivan recognized that the success of the Gulf War might lead to complacency and incremental change, like that predicted by the bureaucratic and military cultural perspectives. Such changes, Sullivan thought, would be woefully inadequate for the transformed post–Cold War environment. Sullivan pushed for additional changes. He would not do so alone.

Rather than compel change, Sullivan and company sought to establish a doctrinal consensus among the army's senior leadership. Between 1991 and 1992, he established the "Louisiana Maneuvers" process and Task Force, with himself as the head and Franks as his deputy and including all the most senior leaders in the army. The purpose of this "board of directors" was to get around the too slow bureaucratic process of innovation in the army.[51] Franks held numerous commander conferences to discuss what should go into the new doctrine and sent drafts of *Operations 1993* around to elicit comments from senior army leaders before settling on the final draft.[52]

According to the internal army consensus, the new mission would be global power projection. Military innovation scholars Farrell, Rynning, and Terriff agree that the need to transition to a power-projection army was the dominant driver of U.S. Army innovation in this period and that the change in the threat environment was a driving force.[53] Foss's rationale for this new mission still stood. In the absence of the Soviet threat and large numbers of forward-deployed troops, the army would have to prepare to deploy anywhere in the world on short notice to protect the interests, especially economic, of the United States.[54] Senior army leaders emphasized maintaining command of the global lines of communication.[55] This mission meant that the army required a strategic focus, rather than the operational and tactical focus of the 1970s and '80s. Army Chief Vuono argued that the army would need to prepare to conduct "opposed entry" into any region to protect U.S. interests.[56] As Jensen succinctly puts it, "The possibility of defending U.S. interests anywhere meant preparing for war everywhere."[57] In the post–Cold War, the military realists in the army shifted their focus away from addressing a dangerous state-based actor to preparing to protect and secure the distant interests that were the source of U.S. power. Jensen attributes this focus to "worst-case-scenario-bias."[58] However, it makes perfect sense from the military realist perspective to focus on securing distant interests in the absence of a major state-based threat. The new mission was front and center in *Operations 1993*: "Force projection replaces forward defense as a more likely employment of Army elements."[59] These elements would have to "rapidly alert, mobilize, deploy, and operate anywhere in the world."[60]

Strategic mobility would be essential to global power projection. Interestingly, this was the very kind of mobility that Army Chief of Staff Decker had rejected in the 1960s because of the need to address the Soviet threat in Europe. In the 1980s, Reagan meant the light infantry divisions to be a global rapid-reaction force, but the undermanned army co-opted them into the defense of Europe. In the past, the army focused on sending its reserves to Europe. After the Cold War, civilian leaders could ask it to send troops to any number of global flash points. However, the long time required to build up forces for the 1991 Gulf War showed the army was weak in the skill most vital to accomplishing its new mission, rapid deployment to trouble spots.[61] *Operations 1993* highlighted this lesson from the Gulf War.[62] In the years following the publication of *Operations 1993*, the extent of the changes this new mission would require became clear.

Conventional and Nuclear Forces in *Operations 1993* and *2001*
Operations 1993

Operations 1993 actually witnessed two core changes in army doctrine. First, as already mentioned, was the change in the main mission of the army's conventional forces from the defense of Europe to global power projection.[63] Second, nuclear weapons disappeared from army doctrine. Although the end of the Cold War left the United States an unrivaled superpower, senior army leaders and *Operations 1993* did not conclude that conventional military operations in the post–Cold War would be easy.[64] The interventions in regions of the world unsettled by the end of the Cold War that army leaders envisioned could see the army confronting third-world forces that had the "ability to fight at extended ranges with increased accuracy and lethality."[65] As *Operations 1976, 1982*, and *1986* had pointed out, the lethality, volume, and precision of modern conventional weapons were continually increasing. Indeed, drawing on the analysis of *Operations 1976*, Army Chief of Staff Sullivan and General Franks saw the 1973 October War as one of the milestones—placed squarely between World War II and the Gulf War—that marked this lethal trend.[66] Senior army leaders thought that the proliferation of these powerful conventional weapons, often provided by the Soviets to their proxies, would make it much more difficult for the United States to achieve rapid, decisive victories, like those in Panama and the Gulf War.[67] In power projection, the army had a difficult offensive mission. Nevertheless, the end of the Cold War led to a demand among Americans for defense cuts and a peace dividend. Therefore, the army would have to execute this new and difficult mission with significantly fewer resources. Despite these difficulties, army leaders believed civilian leaders would order the U.S. military to deploy globally.

The Clinton administration was changing and expanding the missions of the army but was also initiating a post–Gulf War "reduction in forces."[68] In the four years after Desert Storm, the U.S. government reduced army end strength from 760,000 to 495,000 and cut the defense budget by $50 billion in inflation-adjusted dollars from 1993 to 2000.[69] These cuts reduced the post–Cold War army by one corps and six divisions from its Cold War strength.[70] The United States cut army forces in Europe in half. This was the largest reduction in forces since the end of World War II.[71] As Army Chief of Staff Sullivan and *Operations 1993* understood, the army would have to do its part to apply force rapidly and win decisively with the least cost in personnel and matériel.[72]

The army's solution to this dilemma was to develop a doctrine that drew on the insights of AirLand Battle doctrine while abandoning those elements of Cold War doctrine that were ill-suited to the new missions and threat environment. Advances in conventional-weapons technology would assist in this doctrinal transition. The concepts introduced by AirLand Battle would heavily influence *Operations 93*.[73] The army sought the input of two of the key writers of *Operations 1982* and *1986*, Huba Wass de Czege and Donald Holder, to comment on drafts of *Operations 1993*. Their opinions were highly respected by General Franks, who had also worked with General Starry in the early '80s.[74] Despite this nod to the authors of AirLand Battle, the change in the army's core mission meant it had to abandon or modify significant portions of its Cold War doctrine. *Operations 1993* would not include the term *AirLand Battle*, for instance. According to senior army leaders, this was because AirLand Battle was concerned primarily with the defense of Europe by the army and air force. In November 1992, at the Senior Leader Warfighting Conference at Fort Leavenworth, participants agreed "doctrine had to transcend the former Air Force–Army set-piece of central Europe."[75] Post–Cold War operations, in contrast, would be more joint.[76] Thus, the conferees agreed that rather than designing doctrine primarily for a European contingency, the army would have to be capable of "full-dimensional operations"—meaning it had to be prepared for a major regional contingency, like the Gulf War, or peacekeeping operations in the developing world, or both. Therefore, some major revisions to the central AirLand Battle concepts were required.[77] While AirLand Battle introduced the "levels of war," it included only the operational and tactical levels and their interrelation. *Operations 1993* added the *strategic* level of war above the operational level. "At the strategic level of war," the new capstone manual stated, "a nation or group of nations uses national interests to determine their strategy to ensure an effective, responsive national power-projection capability."[78] AirLand Battle's peculiar link between the operational and tactical levels of war had to be broken, recast, and then joined to the higher strategic level. According to Franks, therefore, there were "gaping holes" in army doctrine that needed to be filled.[79]

Nevertheless, concepts from AirLand Battle were included in *Operations 1993*. For instance, the new manual included the tenets of AirLand Battle: initiative, agility, depth, and synchronization. However, this was not an attempt to preserve old doctrine and ideas for their own sake, because a number of officers and thinkers actually acknowledged AirLand Battle as the first step in the RMA. One of the fathers of RMA theorizing for U.S. forces, Admiral William Owens, acknowledged that the RMA actually began with the army in the 1970s and '80s and their development of AirLand Battle. Their use of sensors and new technology to "see and track events at greater distances and attack with longer-range precision weapons" led the navy and air force to begin experimenting with this technology.[80] "The result by the mid-1990s," Owen continued, "was the potential of a huge leap in U.S. military effectiveness and the transformation of U.S. military forces."[81] These army concepts also predated

Ullman and Wade's National Defense University study, *Shock and Awe: Achieving Rapid Dominance*, considered a seminal work in RMA theorizing.[82] AirLand Battle was the cutting edge of the RMA. This is surprising given that its critics consider the army the most traditional, that is, culturally determined, of all the U.S. military services. As will be shown in the next chapter, this mistaken view of the army dominated the thinking of Secretary of Defense Donald Rumsfeld. Although Rumsfeld realized that the transformation agenda that he pushed in the Pentagon did not originate with him, he did not recognize the role that army doctrine had played in the RMA.[83] The use of AirLand Battle principles in *Operations 1993*, therefore, was not simply an attempt to hold on to old doctrine. The concept of AirLand Battle was the leading edge of the RMA and had a legitimate place in its progression after the Cold War.

While preserving the four tenets of AirLand Battle, *Operations 1993* added a fifth: versatility. In his doctrinal guidance to Franks at TRADOC in July 1991, Sullivan emphasized that "versatility," along with deployability, was essential for "full-dimensional operations."[84] Versatility was required because the post–Cold War threat environment would be much more diverse than in the preceding era. Moreover, versatility was essential, as operations would likely include rapid transitions to noncombat tasks, such as refugee assistance.[85] This perspective on army missions constituted a major change in the focus of army doctrine. It was no longer just about the battlefield.[86] Other scholars have overlooked or dismissed these significant changes in doctrine.[87]

The integration of old and new doctrinal concept was evident in the manual's discussion of forced-entry operations and the need for increased jointness. A forced entry into hostile territory is among the most difficult military operations. However, it would be an essential part of power projection. What the army needed, according to its leaders, was a rapidly deployable force that could project power soon after a crisis erupted. Such a force could arrive before the opponent could consolidate their defensive position, making a forced entry even more difficult.[88] Successful forced entry would require close coordination among the army, air force, and navy.[89] The army was again not as jealous of its autonomy as theories of bureaucracy predict. Many of the conventional means necessary for "full-dimensional operations," such as precision-guided munitions, were only in the inventories of the U.S. Navy or U.S. Air Force. Yet they were central to the core army mission. Like AirLand Battle, the army recognized it could not accomplish its main mission without working jointly with the other services. The air force was so central to the army missions that the army lobbied Congress to provide funds to the air force to replace its

C-141 airlift fleet with the new C-17, this despite the extremely sparse military budgets of the period.[90]

Once in theater, this interservice cooperation would continue, as combat operations would involve detecting and attacking the enemy at "over-the-horizon" ranges, using deep attack to undermine the cohesion of the enemy force through its whole depth, and decisively engaging them through maneuver.[91] Advances in targeting technology, recently demonstrated in the Gulf War, would facilitate these operations.[92] New high-tech sensors, satellite surveillance technology, precision-guided weapons, and communications technology could integrate a military force and provide it with near real-time situational awareness. In *Operations 1993*, as in 1970s and '80s doctrine, the army curtailed organizational autonomy from the other services to accomplish its main mission and deal with critical threats.

The need to protect a lighter force far from home inspired army leaders to think seriously about the complex of technologies that made up the revolution in military affairs.[93] Army Chief of Staff Sullivan was one of the main proponents of the RMA as a means of executing the army's power-projection missions.[94] With the ubiquity of lethal conventional weapons came the requirement to disperse to avoid that lethality. Therefore, forces had to be smaller and more mobile to survive.[95] A smaller but integrated force could seek safety in superior mobility and dispersion, while calling on highly accurate conventional firepower from all the services. Through this mode of operations, Sullivan argued, "ever smaller units" were becoming capable of ever more "decisive effects."[96] Even a small Special Forces team, "in the right place, at the right time, and linked in with the right systems [had] the potential to produce, or at least contribute to, decisive results."[97] A highly deployable light force could also be survivable and lethal.[98]

The RMA also affected the army's interpretation of the principles of war. According to *Operations 1993*, the principles were the "bedrock of Army doctrine."[99] Nevertheless, the new doctrine reinterpreted some of the principles to fit the new doctrinal context. For instance, army commanders did not need to mass large numbers of troops to realize the principle of mass; in fact, such massing of troops was dangerous on a post–Cold War battlefield populated by lethal conventional weaponry. "Massing effects, rather than concentrating forces," could "enable a numerically inferior force" to achieve "decisive results, while limiting exposure to enemy fire."[100] The writers of *Operations 1993* saw this change in the principle of mass as significant and necessary.[101] The army did not simply see the RMA as a passing fad. The new doctrinal concepts it fostered required a reassessment even of the age-old principles of war. For the army to execute its main mission and operate globally, it had to rethink the "bedrock" of its doctrine. This is reminiscent of the doctrinal dilemmas presented by nuclear weapons and the army's attempts to deal with them. It is also reminiscent of the reinterpretation of the principles of war in AirLand Battle, where doctrine writers curtailed the principle of the offense to reflect the imbalance of capabilities.

However, advances in weapons and information technology had their limits.[102] The army assessment of these limits reflected the military realist perspective. These new technologies could not overcome the ever-present "friction" that accompanied the use of force. While some, such as military historian Williamson Murray, share this view,[103] others thought there was an "inverse relationship between friction and situational awareness."[104] According to Army Chief of Staff Sullivan, however, the vision of perfect situational awareness was a mirage.[105] After his retirement from the army, Sullivan would criticize the more radical interpretations of the RMA. These, Sullivan thought, were based on "the easy but erroneous conclusion that by . . . buying long-range precision weapons, we can avoid the ugly realities of conflict."[106] The *Operations* manual penned during Sullivan's tenure as chief of staff concurred. "Everything in war is very simple," *Operations 1993* noted, quoting Clausewitz, "but the simple thing is difficult."[107] War would still be a realm of uncertainty and great physical exertion. Imperfect information and the fog of war would still plague action in battle. Subordinates would still have to learn to act on their own initiative within the commander's intent.

Army attempts to bring a transformed force into being reinforced the limits of existing technology to make a transformed force a reality. In December 1991, TRADOC commander General Franks witnessed the potential of digitization in the M1A2 Abrams tank. Digitization would link all of the units in a division by digital circuits to produce shared situational awareness of the battlefield and the disposition of the whole force.[108] Franks envisioned a fully digitized army.[109] This vision lead to the Force XXI concept (networked battlefield systems and digitization), which the army promulgated in the same years as *Operations 1993*. Force XXI would leverage these integrative technologies to make a smaller conventional force more synchronized, lethal, and survivable.[110] This concept was tested and shown to be somewhat effective between 1992 and 1994. However, the testing of the Force XXI concept in Army XXI at the National Training Center showed that the technology had not yet caught up to the new combat concepts expressed in doctrine.[111] These concrete limits of RMA technology contributed to the evolutionary, rather than revolutionary, change in the army's force structure under Sullivan.[112] Although Chris Demchak sees Sullivan as prone to overconfidence in the RMA, she neglects Sullivan's substantial reservations about the idea of situational awareness.[113] Both Sullivan and *Operations 1993* argued that even in the age of the RMA, soldiers would still have to contend with the arduous physical conditions and radical uncertainty present in combat.[114] Senior leaders in the army were satisfied with an evolutionary approach because there was no peer competitor on the rise that could challenge the United States.[115]

Attempts to frame this period in bureaucratic or military cultural terms are problematic. Some have argued that army officers saw the Gulf War as a vindication of the universality of AirLand Battle. This confirmed their cultural and bureaucratic desire, the argument continues, not to abandon conventional Cold War doctrine and forces.[116] On the contrary, after the Gulf War, army officers, led by General Franks, who had commanded major ground forces there,[117] aggressively pushed to revise army doctrine away from the Cold War model. These revisions were necessary to address the new threats of the post–Cold War. These were the conclusions of a Gulf War "lessons-learned" conference convened by General Franks in March 1992. Present were the commanders of U.S. forces in Desert Storm and TRADOC representatives. The conferees thought that the next enemy would learn from Desert Storm and would be more effective at resisting the initial "forced entry into the theatre."[118] Therefore, although many thought the Gulf War demonstrated that the U.S. military was unrivaled and capable of imposing its will on anyone, senior army leaders were more skeptical of the lessons and U.S. indomitability. Despite the bureaucratic benefits of doctrinal continuity, Cold War doctrine would not suffice to address the most dangerous threats arising in its aftermath.

Culturally, when it came to conventional forces and the army's finest hour, *Operations 1993* actually distanced itself from the army's World War II tradition of conventional warfare. In the whole manual, except for one vignette from the Civil War, all of the historical examples of army operations were from the post–World War II period. The 1993 manual's use of more recent historical examples was intentional. As Romjue noted, "In the illustrations as elsewhere the doctrine writers and editors sought distance from an earlier strategic world."[119] Nor were examples limited to conventional warfare. While one-third of the historical examples came from the Gulf War, another third were from OOTW. It is worth emphasizing again that the authors of this manual had it vetted extensively through the army and approved by its most senior leaders. Thus, rather than using the lessons of the Gulf War to resurrect the army's finest hour or preserve Cold War doctrine, the doctrine writers, with the army's approval, sought to draw attention away from its finest hour to prepare its forces for the new threat environment.

Nor were the RMA technologies, put on display in the Gulf War, the main driver behind the post–Cold War army's doctrine. Senior leaders in the U.S. Army made power projection its new mission prior to the Gulf War. After the fall of the Soviet Union, senior army leaders focused on threats to U.S. global interests because they represented the most dangerous threat. RMA technologies would assist in making a very difficult new mission possible, but they did not determine that mission. New army doctrine incorporated these new technologies; it was not determined by them.

In conclusion, when it came to the operations of conventional forces, *Operations 1993* both introduced innovations and preserved elements of previous army doctrine. The army's new power-projection mission required a more versatile force with a strategic outlook rather than the tactical and operational focus of AirLand Battle doctrine. However, some of the tenets of that doctrine were still applicable to the army's new, and in some ways more difficult, post–Cold War mission. The decision to retain elements of AirLand Battle also made sense given that it was the leading edge of RMA theorizing.

Finally, what about the role of nuclear weapons? As shown in the previous chapters, from *Operations 1954* to *1986*, tactical nuclear weapons were central to U.S. Army doctrine. In NATO Europe, these were likely the only weapons capable of blunting a Soviet attack. With the dissolution of the Soviet Union and major reductions in Russian forces, tactical nuclear weapons ceased to play a vital role in army doctrine. In fact, the post–Cold War army no longer had tactical nuclear weapons as part of its "organic" force structure.[120] If needed, the army would rely on air force and navy nuclear capabilities.[121] The army no longer faced an enemy with dual-capable forces able to use tactical nuclear weapons with conventional maneuver forces to achieve a rapid, decisive victory.[122] With the fall of the Soviet Union, this grim threat disappeared. Therefore, the U.S. Army no longer required such a dual capability of its own.

Nuclear threats after the Cold War emanated from regional adversaries, weapons that *Operations 1993* dubbed "instruments of terror." Consequently, *Operations 1993* discussed nuclear weapons only in the context of army units protecting themselves from their effects.[123] Whereas Cold War manuals reserved entire chapters for nuclear weapons and their requirements for doctrine and organization, *Operations 1993* discussed them for only a single paragraph.[124] Gone were any references to how to employ tactical nuclear weapons with conventional maneuver forces.[125]

Offense and Defense in Operations 1993

During the 1990s, the central missions of the U.S. Army changed from one of fighting outnumbered in NATO Europe to global power projection to deal with regional crises and instability. Power projection is an offensive operation. Accordingly, the theory of victory at the core of army doctrine shifted from defensive to offensive. A clear sign of this change was the reintroduction of the principles of war into the body of the army's most important manual. In the 1960s, doctrine had given the principles a central place, a doctrinal custom since the 1920s. However, when it came to the application of the principles, these earlier manuals added significant caveats. As the defensive emphasis in doctrine increased, along with the imbalance of forces in Europe, army doctrine sidelined the principles of war, removing them altogether in *Operations 1976*. While the authors of *Operations 1982* and *1986* argued that they based doctrine soundly on the principles of war, they listed them in appendixes only. Instead, the last two manuals of the Cold War subsumed the principles into the "tenets" of AirLand Battle doctrine. Under this guise, the doctrine writers reinterpreted them to suit the defensive theory of victory at the core of doctrine. The death of the Soviet Union and the birth of the power-projection mission resurrected the principles of war.

Operations 1993 linked the return of the principles of war to the army's new mission. "Today's force-projection Army recognizes the following nine principles of war."[126] Returning to army tradition, *Operations 1993* listed the principles of war prior to any discussion of the tenets of operations or offense and defense. These principles of war were "the enduring bedrock of Army doctrine" and had been since 1921. The authors pass over in silence the demotion or absence of the principles in the 1960s, '70s, and '80s editions of *Operations*.[127]

The first principle of war is the objective, and the ultimate objective of war is to destroy the enemy's capabilities and his will to fight. Of most interest to the present analysis is the manual's treatment of the second principle of war, the principle of offense. First, the manual argued that traditional views of the offense were applicable to its new power-projection mission. "The fundamentals of the offense apply equally to entry operations as they do to more traditional offensive operations."[128] Offense enjoyed the initiative and with it freedom of action because the "side that retains the initiative through offensive action forces the enemy to react rather than act."[129] Repeating verbatim the traditional principle of the offense, *Operations 1993* maintained that if commanders adopt a defensive posture, they do so "only as a temporary expedient and must seek every opportunity to seize the initiative."[130]

When it came to offense and defense, however, *Operations 1993* did not completely break from the doctrinal insights of Cold War doctrine. For instance, while it used Desert Storm as an example of a successful offense, it used the Israeli defense of the Golan Heights in the 1973 October War as an example of a successful defense against a numerically superior foe.[131] *Operations 1993* continued to employ this key historical example from the '70s and '80s manuals. The 1993 manual also stated that the purpose of the defense was "to defeat an enemy attack."[132] While *Operations 1993* noted that offense was the "decisive form of war,"[133] defense could be stronger than the offense. This was because the defense still enjoyed the numerous advantages that the Cold War manuals had pointed out. The 1993 manual reiterated these advantages. The defender enjoyed better "cover and concealment, advance siting of weapons, shorter [lines of communication], and operations over familiar terrain among a friendly population."[134] Like AirLand Battle, the 1993 manual advocated organizing defenses in depth to exploit these defensive advantages to the fullest. It also advocated using deep attack in the service of that defense.[135]

The attacker, on the other hand, did not enjoy similar advantages because "tactical offensive operations often expose the attacker" to defensive fires.[136] In the post–Cold War, the accuracy and volume of these fires were more deadly than ever. Consequently, army commanders should avoid direct attacks into defenses because "such attacks are nearly always costly in lives and matériel. Commanders should undertake them only when no other approach will accomplish the mission."[137] To avoid the defenders' strengths, the commander should bypass dug-in defenders or attack in the flank, the object being to force the defenders out of their prepared position and to fight on ground not of their choosing. This describes exactly the "left hook" executed against Iraqi forces in Desert Storm.[138]

When discussing the initiative, *Operations 1993* also retained the view pioneered in Cold War doctrine that the defender could enjoy the initiative. He could do so by setting the "tempo" and "restrict[ing]" the attacker's options as much as possible. In short, the defender could force the attacker to react to the defensive plan rather than being at the mercy of the attacker's plans.[139] New RMA technology that enabled rapid mobility and reaction would augment defensive initiative.[140] In this way, the defender could enjoy the initiative and "turn the tables" on the attacker.[141]

There were also powerful echoes of Active Defense in the 1993 manual: "A successful defense consists of reactive and offensive elements existing together to deprive the enemy of the initiative. An effective defense is rarely passive. The defender resists and contains the enemy where he must but seeks every opportunity to conduct offensive operations such as local counterattacks."[142] As DePuy had noted, this use of counterattack was the "essence" of Active Defense. "Counterattacks," the 1993 manual went on, "can achieve greater effects than other attacks, given the same forces on both sides, because the defender can create more favorable conditions."[143] *Operations 1993* retained one of the central doctrinal insights of AirLand Battle and Active Defense. The counterattack was actually the most advantageous offensive maneuver because it first exploited the advantages of the defender and then attacked before the attacker could exploit those same advantages.

Operations 1993 also pointed out that defense was an essential mode of operations for the power-projection army. After the initial forced entry into the theater, the commanders would organize defensive operations to protect their foothold.[144] For this small expeditionary force to hold its tenuous position, deep attacks with precision weapons, as advocated by AirLand Battle, would be essential to disrupt and weaken the enemy counterattack.

Most interestingly, from a cultural perspective, when *Operations 1993* mentioned offensive operations from the army's finest hour in World War II, it chose examples where attacks did not go as planned or commanders pushed them further than was prudent. "Patton's rapid advance across France," the 1993 manual pointed out, was "bogged down for lack of supplies in Lorraine."[145] The Allies' pursuit of German forces in November 1944 ground to a halt at the Hürtgen Forest because of a failure to recognize that the pursuit had to be abandoned and replaced by the more careful "deliberate attack."[146]

This is all to show that, although the army recognized that its new mission had a strong offensive element, it did not promote the offense in a way that ignored the real problems that the advantages of the defense posed for the attacker. Simply because the army had returned to a more offensive theory of victory, it had not forgotten the advantages of the defense in a bureaucratic frenzy or a fit of World War II nostalgia. Preparing the defense of Europe had taught the army that a well-organized defender could frustrate a superior attacker. In the post–Cold War, circumstances were reversed. Rather than organizing a stalwart defense, the army had to devise an offensive doctrine to overcome a determined defender armed with lethal modern weapons. There was a recognition among the writers of the new doctrine that "offense and defense complemented one another," that "there was a flow between them."[147] "Often, elements of a defense are within every offense; within every defense, an offense."[148] This temperate view of offense and the army's finest hour is contrary to the expectations of military cultural theory, which expects U.S. Army culture to prefer offense and see defense as a temporary expedient. *Operations 1993* had not erased the Cold War doctrinal lessons regarding the power of the defense and incorporated them into its new power-projection mission where appropriate.

Operations 1993 initiated a core change in army doctrine from a defensive to a more offensive theory of victory. It returned the principles of war to their traditional place in army doctrine and with them the principle of offense. However, *Operations 1993* also drew on the doctrinal insights of the Cold War army regarding the power of the defense. For instance, it attributed initiative to the defender and pointed out the advantages of the defense, especially in the counterattack. Moreover, contrary to military cultural theory, this first post–Cold War manual used historical vignettes from the army's World War II finest hour to highlight the limits of sweeping attacks. Therefore, while *Operations 1993* recognized that its new mission required an offensive theory of victory, and changed doctrine accordingly, it did not forget the Cold War lessons learned from preparing a stubborn defense against a much stronger attacker. This is consistent with a military realist perspective that recognizes the power of the attack but appreciates the advantages of the defense.

Counterinsurgency and Operations 1993

While the army was honing its doctrinal ideas and developing and testing its Force XXI concept, civilian leaders were ordering them to engage in a force-projection operation to move troops into Bosnia.[149] After the Cold War, the army would need to prepare for war *and* operations other than war. For *Operations 1993*, OOTW included "peacekeeping, support for insurgencies and counterinsurgencies, noncombatant evacuation, and peace enforcement," among other missions. OOTW is then a stand-in for the third area of doctrine, known in other periods as COIN, stability operations, and LIC.[150] Army Chief of Staff Sullivan argued that preparing the army for OOTW could contribute to addressing threats to U.S. vital material interests. The global markets essential for U.S. prosperity were located in unstable areas where noncombat operations could assist in "setting the conditions under which economic interests [could] flourish."[151] As a practical step, Sullivan established the Peacekeeping Institute in the same year the army published *Operations 1993*.[152] As deputy commander of the CGSC, Sullivan had been one of the chief advocates of establishing two capstone manuals, one for combat operations and one for LICs. Sullivan's superiors had overruled this effort at the time.[153] As army chief of staff, Sullivan did not seek to revive the dual-manual proposal but worked to make OOTW a key part of *Operations 1993*. The end of the Cold War opened the door for Sullivan's push to make OOTW a focus in capstone doctrine.[154]

In doing so, Sullivan did not meet as much resistance as bureaucratic or cultural theorists would expect. In fact, many senior army leaders shared Sullivan's concerns and wanted OOTW included in the 1993 manual.[155] At a November 1992 commander conference organized by General Franks to discuss post–Cold War doctrine, the attendees agreed that OOTW deserved its own chapter in the first capstone manual of the post–Cold War.[156] When the completed draft of the manual went out to senior army commanders in September 1992, they applauded its treatment of OOTW. General Glenn K. Otis, who had taken over TRADOC after General Starry, called the draft of *Operations 1993* "a watershed for the Army."[157]

The real import of OOTW was clear throughout the pages of the 1993 manual. From the outset, the manual mentioned war and OOTW in the same breath, even in its definition of doctrine. Doctrine was "the statement of how America's Army, as part of a joint team, intends to conduct war and operations other than war."[158] *Operations 1993* invoked the historical traditions of the U.S. Army to support its emphasis on OOTW. It noted that throughout its history, the U.S. Army had participated in OOTW. These types of missions had been part of army operations since the frontier. In short, *Operations 1993* was arguing against Fitzgerald and others who argued that OOTW was not part of the army's "institutional identity."[159] This meant that the authors of *Field Manual 100-23, Peace Operations* were not, as Fitzgerald contends, exceptional outsiders in this period.[160] They were part of a broader movement within the post–Cold War army. Senior army leaders saw OOTW as a key component of their service's most important doctrinal manual.

The new manual's treatment of OOTW showed that its authors did not think that conventional-warfare solutions would produce victory in these kinds of conflicts.[161] The principles and tenets that guided operations in war were not necessarily transferable to OOTW. Principles of war, like the objective, were appropriate to OOTW, but more aggressive ones, such as the principle of offense, had to be tempered by commanders in an OOTW environment.[162] More important, the authors of the 1993 manual argued that OOTW had principles of their own that differed from and sometimes contradicted the principles of war. These principles were set out at a meeting of the principal doctrine writers at Fort A. P. Hill in July 1992. They included "the primacy of the political element, adaptability, legitimacy, perseverance, restricted use of force, and unity of effort with other, nonmilitary government agencies."[163] Later doctrine would designate these the "principles of stability operations." These principles were a mirror image of those at the heart of the classic COIN theorizing of the 1960s. Further echoing these ideas, *Operations 1993* pointed out the need to bolster local government "legitimacy" and follow the rules of engagement to "avoid excessive force" in OOTW.[164] COIN-like operations had not received a detailed treatment in an *Operations* manual since the 1962 and 1968 editions. The characterization of OOTW was very similar to the "Counterinsurgency" and "Stability Operations" sections of those 1960s manuals. Take the following passage, for example:

Immediate solutions to difficult problems may not be obvious or may jeopardize long-term objectives. . . . Certain military responses to civil disturbance may solve the immediate crisis but subvert the legitimacy of local authorities and cause further civil unrest. Humanitarian relief and nation assistance should not promote dependency on aid from outside sources. Quick, efficient action by US forces that resolves an immediate issue without considering the long-term consequences and goals may promote instability. *In operations other than war, victory comes more subtly than in war.* Disciplined forces, measured responses, and patience are essential to successful outcomes.[165]

This passage harks back to the subtle understanding of irregular operations present in 1960s army doctrine. The concept that immediate and violent reactions, often necessary in conventional combat operations, could be counterproductive was a central tenet of classic COIN theory, as expressed by thinkers such as David Galula.[166] However, Sullivan and others pointed out that OOTW could also involve intense combat operations.[167] The fighting in Mogadishu in October 1993 lent credence to this claim.[168] Such ideas proved prescient in light of later operations in Afghanistan and Iraq, where the army conducted OOTW operations in environments far less permissive than in the immediate post–Cold War.

Operations 1993 also argued that U.S. Army regular units could contribute to stability operations. "Army forces are extremely well-suited" to stability operations, the 1993 manual argued, because of their capacity to control populations and restore essential services after conflict.[169] Conventional combat skills would not suffice for army units in stability operations, but their capacity to further the principles of stability operations through civic actions would serve them well in OOTW.

In the past, observers accused the U.S. Army of assuming, motivated by bureaucratic or cultural imperatives, that the mind-set of conventionally trained soldiers was sufficient for COIN operations. As previous chapters, and now *Operations 1993*, show, there is strong evidence to the contrary. *Operations 1993* recognized that the principles that guided conventional war fighting were insufficient and sometimes dangerous in OOTW operations. Skeptics might point out that the OOTW chapter in *Operations 1993* was only 9 pages out of 173.[170] However, the authors of the manual mentioned OOTW and war in the same breath throughout. Therefore, the brevity of the OOTW chapter belies its importance to the whole of the manual and the army.

Civilian Strategy and Operations Other than War in Operations 1993

One might argue that civilian concerns with OOTW operations were actually the driving force behind their inclusion in *Operations 1993*. The Clinton Doctrine, much like Kennedy's early version of flexible response, argued that preparing for peripheral, unconventional conflicts—peacekeeping and humanitarian interventions in the 1990s—was just as important as preparing for major regional conflicts.[171] While Clinton sought to get the army to do more, he wanted it done with much less. In the 1990s, the Clinton administration consistently cut the size of the army budget. Simultaneously, army deployments to OOTW environments increased by 300 percent.[172] However, it would be an error to attribute the appearance of OOTW in *Operations 1993* to the Clinton administration's initiatives. As in previous cases, the timing of doctrinal change does not support this explanation. As early as the fall of 1990, senior army leaders recognized the need to include OOTW in the first capstone manual of the post–Cold War. Senior officers then solidified this view into consensus at the 1992 conference of commanders at Fort Leavenworth, where the participants agreed that OOTW would get its own chapter in the new manual.[173] All of this occurred before Clinton became president in January 1993. Moreover, as will be shown below, throughout the mid- to late 1990s, when the army was revising *Operations 1993*, senior army officers who reviewed drafts rejected attempts by some writing teams to downplay the importance of OOTW in the capstone manual.[174] By this time, the bloody end to the humanitarian intervention in Somalia had soured the Clinton administration on complex OOTW operations. After Somalia, Presidential Decision Directive 25 stated that the United States would use U.S. troops in these types of operations only after the warring parties had concluded a peace treaty and there was a defined clear exit strategy. This was consistent with the Powell-Weinberger Doctrine.[175] Thus, civilian strategy cannot account for the importance of OOTW in *Operations 1993* or its continued interest in OOTW in the revisions of that manual. Rather, senior army leaders assessed that the transformed threat environment required not only a transformed conventional fighting force but one capable of executing OOTW missions in the unsettled aftermath of the Cold War.

An Army for the Twenty-First Century: *Operations 2001*

The post–Cold War doctrinal process did not end with the publication of *Operations 1993*. During the 1990s and into the twenty-first century, the army revised its doctrine again and reevaluated its force structure in light of its new power-projection mission. Under the leadership of army chiefs of staff General Dennis J. Reimer[176] and then General Eric K. Shinseki,[177] the army continued to redefine itself for the post–Cold War world. As shown in the previous sections, however, these efforts at "transformation" had their origins in the early 1990s. The transformational concepts developed in Force XXI and Army XXI continued in the Army After Next (AAN) project and eventually took physical form in the First and Second Stryker Brigade Combat Teams. Because of their lightweight and networked technology, the army designed the SBCTs to be the globally deployable, but highly lethal, power-projection force of the future.

The army continued the close link between transformation and doctrinal development. When Reimer replaced Sullivan as army chief of staff in 1995, he ordered General William Hartzog, commander of TRADOC, to revise *Operations 1993* based on the Force XXI concept to enable the further transformation of the army for the twenty-first century.[178] Hartzog directed Lieutenant General Leonard D. Holder Jr. to form a writing team. Hartzog wanted to eliminate the distinction between war and operations other than war.[179] The initial draft unified war and OOTW through the concept of offense, defense, and stability and support operations (ODSS). The writers noted that some mix of all of these had been present in army missions in the 1980s and '90s. Moreover, as this work has argued, such a mix of conventional and unconventional warfare also characterized the army experience in Vietnam. More recently, the writing team and senior army officers pointed out, Desert Storm had also included a postconflict stability phase in Kuwait and policing the no-fly zone inside Iraq. The Holder draft used northern Iraq, Haiti, and Bosnia as historical vignettes.[180] Holder's team produced drafts of the new manual by the next year.

At the same time that the writing team began their work, the Clinton administration published National Security Strategy of the United States, 1996. The Holder writing team started with Army Chief Reimer's guidance and NS-SUS 1996 as guides.[181] Although this might seem like a close integration between civilian grand strategy and military doctrine, the Holder draft would not see the light of day. The manual would undergo two more revisions with new writing teams. Though the manual was in draft form by July 2000, the army would not publish its revision of Operations 1993 until June 2001, three writing teams later, five months after Clinton left office, and five years after the publication of NSSUS 1996.[182]

Holder retired in 1997, and Lieutenant General Montgomery C. Meigs replaced him at SAMS. Meigs did not approve of the 1997 draft because, he argued, it did not inspire intellectual debate or present an accurate picture of warfare in the twenty-first century.[183] In June 1998, Meigs released a new draft for review and received a very negative response from the army. Senior officers thought that the draft missed the mark. Operations was a "how to fight" manual and not "an intellectual exercise suited for the academic 'ivory tower.'"[184] In the summer of 1998, Hartzog retired and was replaced at TRADOC by General John Abrams. The army promoted Meigs to command U.S. Army Europe and put William M. (Mike) Steele in command at SAMS.

Steele agreed with the negative reviews of the Meigs draft and told the new writing team, led by Lieutenant Colonel Steve Rotkoff, to return to the 1997 "Holder version" and address the issues that its reviewers had brought up. Rather than attempting to merge war and OOTW, as the Holder version had done, the new draft echoed Operations 1993 by placing war and OOTW on a "spectrum of operations" that the army would confront in the twenty-first century. The army had to be prepared to execute "full spectrum operations."[185] However, some key concepts from the "Holder version" made their way into the new manual. Operations 2001 retained the categories of offense, defense, and stability and support operations, each with its own chapter. Steele cleared the drafts that the writing team produced before sending them to TRADOC in October 1999.[186] In May 2000, the army sent drafts to all army headquarters, other services, and some government agencies.[187] As with Operations 1993, the 2001 manual reiterated that the main mission of the U.S. Army was force projection as part of a joint military team.[188] This mission was not possible without the active participation of the other services. In recognition of this fact, the army changed the title of its capstone manual from *Field Manual 100-5* to *Field Manual 3-0* to reflect the numbering system of the joint-operations manuals.[189] Finally, in July 2000, Steele reached a consensus with senior army commanders and sent the draft to Army Chief of Staff Shinseki. However, Shinseki did not approve the manual until June 14, 2001. This approval came six months into the presidency of George W. Bush and just three months before the terrorist attacks of September 11, 2001.[190]

This delay was not due to Shinseki's lack of enthusiasm for the concepts underpinning the manual. Shinseki came into the position of chief of staff arguing that the army needed to make itself much more globally deployable. To accomplish this, the army would need to take full advantage of RMA technologies to make the force light enough to deploy globally but powerful enough to engage in combat once it arrived in the theater of operations.[191] The inability of the army to deploy rapidly to participate in campaigns such as the Kosovo War showed that the army was not progressing rapidly enough toward its goal of global deployability.[192] Shinseki called for an acceleration of army transformation in 1999 and pushed the army to field a transformed force earlier than it had previously anticipated.[193] In response, "the Army," according to one prominent group of military innovation scholars, "moved very quickly to realize Shinseki's vision."[194] The army achieved this rapid progress despite some internal parochial dissent and in the absence of any additional funds from government.[195]

Conventional and Nuclear Forces in Operations 2001

In June 2001, after its lengthy and circuitous revision process, *Operations 2001* replaced *Operations 1993*. Even more than *Operations 1993*, the 2001 manual was a doctrine designed to transform the U.S. Army and inform the training and operations of the transformed force. *Operations 2001* would bridge a doctrinal gap, as the army transitioned from the Cold War "heavy or legacy force," which was mostly mechanized, to an "interim force," both mechanized and "modernized."[196] This would be followed by an additional transition from the interim force to the "objective," that is, fully transformed, force by 2010. This transformed force would employ the Future Combat System,[197] "a joint, networked system of systems, based on a suite of vehicles, both manned and unmanned, linked through a tactical and operational Internet."[198] Among those vehicles would be the Future Combat Vehicle, which would replace the tank as the mainstay of the army.[199] Moreover, attitudes within the army toward heavy forces changed rapidly after Shinseki's initiative. In 2000, 56 percent of army officers surveyed thought heavy mechanized forces would be a mainstay of the U.S. Army in the twenty-first century. By 2002, that proportion had dropped to 18 percent.[200] Instead, according to 58 percent of army officers, their service was undergoing "a radical change in military technology, organization and doctrine."[201] The transformation agenda, initiated in the early to mid-1990s and reinvigorated by Shinseki, had penetrated the officer corps and had even undermined that cultural icon of the U.S. Army's finest hour, the main battle tank.

The army anticipated another doctrinal revision by 2007 to guide this final transition.[202] This more methodical transformation agenda likely resulted from the gap between the doctrinal concepts set out under Sullivan and the technology needed to execute those concepts, as demonstrated in the Army XXI exercises. The trend would continue into the Army After Next program begun in 1995. However, the central concepts driving this development were set out under Army Chief of Staff Sullivan in the early to mid-1990s.[203] Facilitation of power projection continued to be central to army thinking about future war. As Major General Robert Scales, leader of the AAN, argued, if "the Army is to remain relevant to the security needs of the nation we must begin now to accelerate the speed with which we project legitimate, powerful and balanced forces to threatened regions overseas."[204] Lighter lethal conventional forces for power projection remained the focus of army thinking approaching the new millennium.

Operations 2001 continued the doctrinal trends of its predecessor when it came to conventional forces. The post–Cold War army had become a "strategic force," with power projection as its central mission.[205] To execute this mission, the army would need to hone its "ability to get more lethal forces to contingencies faster and with a smaller logistical footprint."[206] *Operations 2001* also retained the spectrum of conflict to describe potential conflicts, a tradition going back at least to 1960s doctrine. Instead of "full-*dimensional* operations," *Operations 2001* stated that the army had to prepare for "full-*spectrum* operations." Despite the change in language, both terms meant that the army had to prepare to operate across the spectrum of conflict. At the low end of the conflict spectrum were military operations other than war. MOOTW replaced OOTW from *Operations 1993*. According to the 2001 manual, MOOTW could take place across the spectrum of conflict, though they were more prevalent at the lower end of the spectrum—more on this in the relevant section below.

The army published *Operations 2001* after it fielded its first transformed elements: the First and Second Stryker Brigade Combat Teams. Built around the Stryker combat vehicle, the SBCTs were ideal for power projection because of their lightweight and smaller size. However, because they also incorporated networked technologies, they would be more lethal than previous larger forces. According to General Shinseki, the transformed force exemplified by the lighter but more lethal SBCTs would be effective at engaging in conventional war and MOOTW, that is, peacekeeping and humanitarian assistance. A fully transformed army, Shinseki argued, would be dominant at "every point on the spectrum of operations."[207] The kinds of operations envisioned for the SBCTs were similar to those described by *Operations 1993*. "Situations would be developed out of contact, forces would maneuver to positions of advantage, enemy forces would be engaged beyond the range of their weapons and would be destroyed with precision fires."[208] Like its predecessor, *Operations 2001* ascribed to the tenets of AirLand Battle.

Moreover, *Operations '01* retained the focus on leveraging *joint* strategic, operational, and tactical capabilities to attack the enemy simultaneously throughout his depth. The army could not accomplish this without integrating air and naval assets closely into army operations. The first *Operations* manual of the twenty-first century also preserved the new interpretation of the principle of mass inaugurated by its predecessor, the massing of "effects" rather than forces.[209] Echoing the first post–Cold War manual, *Operations 2001* acknowledged that only through increased interservice cooperation could the army use RMA technology to address the new post–Cold War threat environment in the midst of major resource reductions.

Finally, as with *Operations 1993*, the 2001 manual discussed nuclear weapons only in the context of how to protect the army's conventional forces from these weapons, that is, "force protection." There was no discussion of how to integrate tactical nuclear weapons with conventional forces.[210] It was evident in both *Operations 1993* and *2001* that the dual nuclear-conventional capability that had been at the heart of army doctrine during the Cold War had vanished without a trace.

Therefore, when it came to conventional forces and operations, the changes introduced by *Operations 2001* were peripheral. These changes would contribute to the new power-projection mission that *Operations 1993* introduced into the core of army doctrine. The 2001 manual continued to exploit RMA technology and its necessary jointness to enable this mission. The nuclear mission, so central to Cold War army doctrine, disappeared. The first manual of the new millennium also preserved the new offensive theory of victory inaugurated by *Operations 1993*, as discussed in the next section.

Offense and Defense in Operations 2001

Operations 2001 stated that war is complex, but "war's essence was simple: win on the offense, initiate combat on Army terms, gain and retain the initiative, build momentum quickly, and win decisively."[211] *Operations 2001* kept the principles of war in the same central position as *Operations 1993*. Offense continued to be the "decisive form of warfare."[212] One of the manual's coauthors, Lieutenant Colonel Michael D. Burke, was blunt about the offensive nature of the manual: "This is a fundamentally offensive doctrine."[213] "Offensive operations," the 2001 manual stated, "aim at destroying or defeating an enemy. Their purpose is to impose US will on the enemy and achieve decisive victory."[214] *Operations 2001* used the distinction between operational- and tactical-level operations to categorize types of attack. Operational attacks sought to undermine enemy forces through direct and indirect attacks. Attacks at the tactical level consisted of battles that exploited the effects achieved by operational-level actions.[215] Defensive operations were temporary until the commander built up enough power to go on the attack.[216] The 2001 manual even retained the wording from *Operations 1993*, calling the principles of war "the enduring bedrock of Army doctrine" since the end of World War I.[217] Again, doctrine writers ignored the often problematic role of the principles of war in Cold War army doctrine. In this way, the doctrine writers oversimplify the U.S. Army's doctrinal history.

However, like the predecessors it overlooked, *Operations 2001* introduced a caveat to the application of the principles of war. The caveat was similar to those present in 1960s editions. *Operations 1993* had alluded to the limits of the principles in its use of World War II combat vignettes in which commanders took the principle of offense too far. "The principles of war," *Operations 2001* pointed out, were "not a checklist." Nor did they apply "in the same way to every situation."[218] This caveat primed its readers for the discussions of offense and defense that would follow. *Operations '01* argued that commanders often fought defensive operations in combination with offensive operations and not in sequence, as the principles of war implied. The 2001 manual then repeated innovations contrary to the principles of war that originated in the 1962 edition and carried through Cold War doctrine. Like *Operations 1993*, after listing the principles of war, the 2001 manual discussed the tenet of initiative. Like *Operations* manuals since 1962, *Operations 2001* argued that the defender could enjoy the initiative. He could do so by forcing the attacking force to respond to his defensive plan and by employing tactical counterattacks to destroy the attacking force and cause his attack to fail.[219] The defender could also mass the effects of combat power and shift forces and main effort more easily than the attacker because of the defender's shorter lines of communication.[220]

The 2001 manual also introduced a new name for defensive operations that caused an enemy attack to fail: "*decisive* defensive operations."[221] Although implied by previous doctrine, this was the first time army authors used the words *decisive* and *defense* together. Up to this point, offense had always been the "decisive form of warfare," as indeed the 2001 manual stated. Thus, *Operations 2001* gave its imprimatur to the concept of a "decisive defense," a concept consonant with ideas expressed in Active Defense and AirLand Battle.

Giving the defense a decisive role in the army's most important warfighting doctrine is contrary to the expectations of bureaucratic and military cultural theories. The dissolution of the Soviet Union represented an excellent opportunity for the army of the world's sole superpower to develop an offensive doctrine and leave behind the defensive insights of more desperate times. Instead, *Operations 2001* continued the trend in army doctrine, growing since Kennedy, of lauding the power of the defense. Moreover, the first capstone manual of the twenty-first century was not simply the opinion of a few isolated army officers. *Operations 2001* underwent extensive vetting. Only then did the army accept it as the manual that would take it into the new millennium.

Therefore, both post–Cold War manuals had an offensive theory of victory but held on to the Cold War appreciation of the power of the defense. Due to their appreciation of friction, these are the very insights military realists should retain. Even an offensive power-projection mission could not induce the army to forget its Cold War lessons about the power of defense. After all, once the lighter power-projection army arrived at any number of possible global hot spots, it would need to exploit the advantages of the defense to survive. Moreover, these doctrinal innovations were taking place at a time when civilian authorities were reducing the resources available to the army.

Counterinsurgency and Operations 2001

The revision of *Operations 1993* was a lengthy process with many fits and starts that did not produce a new version of *Operations* until 2001. The prominence of OOTW in the 1993 edition came under fire early in the process. General Hartzog, the new commander of TRADOC who had directed Holder to revise *Operations 1993*, instructed the writing team at SAMS to reconcile the debate between war and OOTW in the new manual. Hartzog instructed the writers to integrate the two concepts, and "OOTW" was not to appear in the update of *Operations 1993*. The subsequent Holder draft brought war and OOTW together in "offense, defense, stability, and support operations."[222] Meigs, the next leader of SAMS, did not approve of the Holder draft and sent its writers back to the drawing board. However, after review by the army at large, the army rejected Meigs's version as too academic. Meigs's replacement, Mike Steele, agreed that the Meigs draft was inappropriate and ordered the writing team to return to the Holder edition and fix its errors.

Operations 2001 replaced the term *OOTW* with *stability and support operations*. Somewhat confusingly, it then used the term *military operations other than war* to designate the environment in which stability and support operations would take place. These operations included "peace operations, foreign internal defense [the Kennedy era term for COIN], security assistance, humanitarian and civic assistance, support to insurgencies, counterdrug operations, combating terrorism, noncombatant evacuation, arms control, and show of force."[223] *Operations 2001* did not try to merge war and MOOTW but kept them separate and at either end of the "spectrum of operations." Borrowing the central concept from the Holder draft, four modes of operations—offense, defense, and stability and support operations—could occur simultaneously within the same conflict, though offense and defense dominated in war and stability and support operations in MOOTW.[224] Thus, ODSS operations spanned the entire spectrum of warfare. Interestingly, the unity of ODSS presaged the now popular concept of "hybrid warfare."[225] Like OOTW in *Operations 1993*, stability operations received their own chapter in *Operations 2001*.[226] Indeed, *Operations 2001* argued that "preparing for stability and support duties were equal priorities to war preparation."[227] The new manual argued that commanders could squander the success achieved through offensive operations through unsuccessful stability operations postconflict.[228] Thus, although offensive operations were the "first among equals," the army had to prepare for stability operations as much as it had to prepare for war.[229] Interestingly, President Kennedy instructed the army to make similar priorities, but at a time when the most dangerous threat emanated from Soviet forces in Europe. When that threat disappeared at the end of the Cold War, senior army leaders shared Kennedy's priorities.

The links between *Operations 1993* and *2001* make it clear that the 2001 manual does not mark the beginning of the post–Cold War U.S. Army's concern with stability operations. Some claim that *Operations 2001* was the progenitor of this concern.[230] However, a close reading of *Operations 1993* does not support this claim. This interpretation obscures the close link between the concern with OOTW and stability operations and the changed international threat environment. Military realism anticipates this link, but recent cultural interpretations of army doctrine in this period do not.

Like *Operations 1993*, the 2001 manual was not simply reflecting the idiosyncrasies of one TRADOC commander, as some argued was the case under DePuy in the '70s. The army vetted both post–Cold War manuals extensively throughout the institution. In the case of *Operations 2001*, while some officers objected to the inclusion of MOOTW in the army's war-fighting manual,[231] the majority of senior army officers approved.[232] As evidenced by *Operations 1962, 1968*, and now *1993*, the army's main war-fighting manual often dealt with its role in COIN-like operations.

Like the 1993 manual, to support its focus on stability operations, *Operations 2001* invoked U.S. Army history. The U.S. Army had been conducting operations similar to peacekeeping for its entire 225-year history.[233] Out of thirty-four historical vignettes used in the new manual, twenty-eight referred to U.S. Army operations. Of those twenty-eight, only eight referred to conventional military operations. *The other twenty vignettes were descriptions of different types of stability and support operations.*[234] The 2001 edition further sharpened the focus on stability operations. It did not simply graft a chapter on stability operations to existing doctrine. The operational implications of MOOTW permeated the whole manual. For instance, right in the heart of its discussion of the principles of war, *Operations 2001* described how commanders needed to modify those principles in a MOOTW environment. When discussing the principle of the objective, *Operations 2001* stated, "Military leaders cannot divorce objective from considerations of restraint and legitimacy, particularly in stability operations and support operations. The amount of force used to obtain the objective must be prudent and appropriate to strategic aims. The military objective must also sustain the willing acceptance of a lawfully constituted agency, group, or government by the population in the AO [area of operations]. Without restraint or legitimacy, support for military action deteriorates and the objective becomes unobtainable."[235] Like its 1990s predecessor, moreover, *Operations 2001* drew on the classic counterinsurgency principles of legitimacy and restraint. While *Operations*

1993 acknowledged that OOTW had its own "principles," however, it reserved discussion of them to the chapter on OOTW. *Operations 2001*, on the other hand, included them directly in the discussion of the principles of war from the very beginning of the manual.

In addition, in its discussion of the initiative, the 2001 manual described how the commander exercises initiative in stability operations: "In stability operations, initiative contributes to influence over factions. It establishes conditions conducive to political solutions and disrupts illegal activities. For instance, commanders may establish conditions in which belligerent factions can best achieve their interests by remaining peaceful. Other examples of exercising initiative include defusing complicated crises, recognizing and preempting inherent dangers before they occur, and resolving grievances before they ignite open hostilities."[236]

Here *Operations 2001* took a classic offensive tactical principle, initiative, central to army doctrine for decades, and adapted it to COIN-like operations. This is similar to how Cold War manuals attributed initiative to the defender and not just the attacker. *Operations 2001* did not employ the concept of the initiative to argue for an aggressive military solution to the problems of low-intensity conflict, as a military cultural perspective might expect. Instead, it reinterpreted the traditional principle of the initiative and adapted it to peaceful conflict resolution. In the end, both post–Cold War manuals pushed the army to take OOTW or stability operations seriously. These portions of the manuals even survived scrutiny by the wider leadership of the U.S. Army.

Civilian Strategy, Stability Operations, and Operations 2001

The prominence of MOOTW and stability operations in *Operations 2001* is especially surprising given the context. The civilian administration under which the army published the manual actively discouraged the U.S. military from paying attention to such missions.[237] The second Bush administration did not want the army to participate in stability operations such as peacekeeping and humanitarian assistance. However, Bush strongly supported the conventional, power-projection missions for major regional conflicts (MRCs).[238] Thus, as it entered the new millennium, the U.S. Army could expect robust civilian support for returning to its offensive, conventional-warfare roots. Instead, the army retained the emphasis on OOTW and stability operations that *Operations 1993* inaugurated. In fact, the writers of the 2001 edition expanded and integrated stability operations into the army's capstone manual. They did so despite a backlash among civilian leaders against the humanitarian missions of the Clinton era.

Conclusion
Competing Explanations and Conventional and Nuclear Missions in **Operations 1993 and 2001**

With the fall of the Soviet Union, U.S. Army doctrine lost the North Star by which it had navigated for four decades. In response, military realism argues, the U.S. Army should change the core of its doctrine. After the disappearance of the Soviet threat, and the absence of a great-power replacement, senior army officers should prioritize the protection of the vital material interests of the state that generate military capabilities. For the United States, separated from the rest of the world by two oceans, these interests include oil supplies and international lines of communication, and their protecting requires power projection. This should become the main mission of the U.S. Army. Nuclear weapons would be much less important in this new threat environment. Those weapons were part of the core of army doctrine during the Cold War because it was required to address the primary threat, a dual-capable, that is, nuclear-conventional, Soviet force in central Europe. Tactical nuclear weapons might have been the only means by which the army could slow a rapid attack on Europe by the Soviet's superior conventional forces. However, this threat disappeared with the end of the Cold War, and with it so too should the nuclear mission from army doctrine.

The army did indeed adopt global power projection as its main mission in the aftermath of the Cold War. Conventional forces would carry out this mission. The manuals did discuss how army forces might protect themselves from nuclear attack but not how to integrate such weapons into doctrine. The bureaucratic, military cultural, and military realist perspectives all predicted that the nuclear mission would disappear after the Cold War. However, in all previous cases dealt with here, organizational and cultural theories expected a downgrading of the nuclear mission or its assumption into traditional doctrine. Military realism, on the other hand, correctly predicted the opposite outcome. The case of the post–Cold War U.S. Army is the only one so far in which military realism predicted the end of the nuclear mission and the nuclear mission disappeared. When we place the progress of the nuclear mission in this cross-case comparative context, military realism outperforms the alternative explanations.

The power-projection army would gradually reduce its reliance on the heavy "legacy" forces so vital in the Cold War. It would replace them with lighter units tailored for rapid, global deployment. Better situational awareness and precision firepower would protect these lighter, and more vulnerable, forces. Senior army leaders based new doctrine on an assessment of the international threat environment and the dilemmas it presented. While civilian intervention in doctrine was limited, civilian decisions to slash military budgets after the Cold War presented additional obstacles to army innovation. In his examination of U.S. Army doctrine in this period, Jensen comes to the same conclusion: that doctrinal innovation in this period was "a fundamentally hierarchical phenomenon initiated and sustained by senior [U.S. Army] leaders."[239] However, while Jensen explains the mechanisms by which the army shepherds its new doctrinal concepts through the service, military realism provides the theoretical explanation for the doctrinal solutions it adopted in the post–Cold War. In the absence of a state-based threat, senior leaders in the army developed a doctrine, under extreme resource constraints, to address the next most dangerous threat, that to the vital material interests of the United States.

However, this new mode of operations would come at the cost of resources and organizational autonomy and is thus unexpected by theories focused on bureaucratic interests and cultural norms. The lighter, more lethal force that the RMA recommended required the army to reduce its reliance on the heavy mechanized forces developed for the Cold War. The army did not use doctrine to argue for the continued relevance of its traditional heavy forces. Rather, it used doctrine to address what it perceived as the major threat within the resource constraints of the period. Concerning organizational autonomy, the RMA necessitated increased "jointness." Without the participation of air force and navy platforms, army commanders could not execute their doctrine. Indeed, without the help of air- and sealift, the army could not be projected at all. Like Active Defense and AirLand Battle, senior army leaders built this abdication of organizational autonomy into doctrine. Its requirement for greater "jointness" also meant greater integration with the alien and competing cultures of the other services. Jensen's independent analysis of the same period concurs, arguing that "reform is possible in military organizations without external intervention, and it often transcends [the] parochial logic of service rivalry."[240] As military realism predicts, the army designed a doctrine that undermined organizational autonomy to provide itself with a credible doctrine.

Culturally, the new post–Cold War mission turned the traditional army on its head. Its emphasis on deployability required a rethinking of the traditional reliance on heavy mechanized units, artifacts of the army's World War II finest hour and Cold War doctrine. No matter how one rates the wisdom of the RMA, it did result in doctrinal changes inconsistent with army culture. Senior army leaders charged with protecting army culture spearheaded these countercultural changes.

In addition, the lessons the army drew from its most conventional post–Cold War conflict, the Gulf War, are more consistent with military realism than with the alternative explanations. Some have argued that the army interpreted the Gulf War as a repeat of its finest hour and a confirmation of the wisdom of AirLand Battle doctrine. This narrow perspective, they contend, stifled doctrinal innovation. On the contrary, General Franks, who had commanded army forces in the most offensive, conventional operations of that war, was one of the strongest advocates of major changes in army doctrine. He and other senior army leaders took a skeptical view of many of the lessons of the Gulf War.[241] In fact, historical examples in both post–Cold War manuals intentionally distanced the army from its finest hour and emphasized missions and modes of operations contrary to army culture.

Competing Explanations and Offense and Defense in Operations 1993 and 2001

Regarding offense and defense, military realism predicts a change from a defensive to an offensive theory of victory in army doctrine. Indeed, power projection necessarily involves developing an offensive capability. The army was no longer facing a known enemy in a predetermined theater of operations. However, military realism expects that available resources, the additional physical obstacles to projecting power over long distance, and the need to overcome the defender's advantages should temper the offensive theory of victory.

After the Cold War, the theory of victory at the core of U.S. Army doctrine did indeed move from defensive to offensive. Of course, here the outcome predictions of organizational theory, military culture, and military realism coincide again. However, this is the only case so far in which military realism has correctly predicted a return to an offensive theory of victory in army doctrine. In all of the other cases, the bureaucratic and military cultural perspectives mistakenly predicted such a return. As with the fate of the nuclear mission, when placed in the cross-case comparative context that this work provides, military realism outperforms the alternative explanations.

However, military realism also anticipates that a military realist appreciation of friction should temper the new offensive elements of doctrine. There is strong evidence that this did indeed happen. The writers of post–Cold War army doctrine retained the lessons from previous doctrine about the power of the defense. In fact, *Operations 2001* argued that there was such a thing as "decisive defense," a concept alien to army doctrine until the 1960s. Retaining these defensive lessons is contrary to bureaucratic interests and army culture but perfectly consistent with military realism. Although the army had a new offensive mission, army doctrine continued to emphasize the difficulties imposed on such a mission by the physical world. Projecting over vast distances would expose army forces to major strategic, operational, and tactical friction. In addition, the vulnerability of an expeditionary force meant that once in theater, it would have to exploit the advantages of the defense to secure a foothold. At the operational and tactical levels of war, *Operations '93* and *'01* recognized that opposed entries, essentially an attack against a prepared defensive position, were among the most difficult operations. The army knew how the defender could thwart even the most powerful attacker because it had prepared itself to do so for four decades in Europe. They moderated their new offensive theory of victory accordingly, pointing out the limits of RMA technology to overcome the ever-present friction and uncertainty of war. Although America was a power without peer in this period, the U.S. Army retained its Cold War doctrine's lessons about the power of defense and the limits of attack.

Competing Explanations and COIN-Like Missions in Operations 1993 and 2001

In the final key area of army doctrine, military realism argues that senior army leaders will appreciate the full spectrum of conflicts facing them in the aftermath of the Cold War to include unconventional threats. In general, however, unconventional threats, such as insurgencies, are less dangerous than the forces of great or regional powers. The peacekeeping experience of the army in the 1990s reinforced this view. Such operations were usually in permissive environments, where the belligerents were not targeting U.S. forces.[242] Nevertheless, due to the more permissive threat environment after the Cold War, COIN-like missions (operations other than war, in the parlance of the time) should receive more attention in army doctrine than previously.

For the U.S. Army, after the Soviet threat left the scene, preparing its conventional forces for their new power-projection mission did receive the lion's share of attention. As even some critics of the army in this period recognize, given that the consequences of failure in an OOTW were much less dire than failure in a major regional conflict, a focus on MRCs over OOTW, especially amid declining resources, was understandable.[243] Critics of the U.S. Army in this period often benefit from hindsight, looking back on the 1990s with the difficult insurgencies in Iraq and Afghanistan in mind. This is very similar to critics of army doctrine in the early 1960s, who look back armed with the knowledge that the army would soon be embroiled in an interminable counterinsurgency in Vietnam. In both cases, however, the choices that the army made regarding the balance between major conflicts and COIN-like operations made sense given the threat environment. As military realism predicts, the army chose to prioritize the protection of vital material interests from more dangerous regional threats.[244]

However, it would not be accurate to claim, as some do, that army leaders after the Cold War "dismiss the entire 'lower end' of the conflict spectrum as a distraction."[245] Though the power-projection mission was the priority, the army also reintroduced unconventional missions into its most important manual. Moreover, the majority of senior army leaders were in favor of this revival. Senior army leaders saw OOTW and stability operations increasing in the post–Cold War and wanted to prepare for them. In fact, contrary to military cultural perspectives, both manuals in this period argued that OOTW and stability operations were part of the proud historical tradition of the U.S. Army. In addition, although the post–Cold War manuals did not acknowledge it, COIN-like missions had been part of the army's "how to fight" manual throughout the 1960s. Moreover, in their discussions of OOTW and stability operations, *Operations 1993* and *2001* recognized that the principles of war used in conventional combat operations were insufficient for OOTW. They drew on concepts from classic COIN theories, such as the importance of legitimacy and restraint in the use of force. OOTW and stability operations did not simply receive their own chapter as a sop to their advocates. The manuals mentioned these unconventional operations in the same breath as traditional military operations, even more so in *Operations 2001*. Moreover, contrary to some analyses, army leaders recognized the limited utility of RMA technology in OOTW and stability operations.[246] Even more surprisingly, rather than using the lessons of the Gulf War to downplay the import of these missions, army doctrine used the postconflict phase of that war as an example of OOTW and stability operations for which the army had not been prepared.

Some might attribute the focus on OOTW and stability operations to civilian intervention and civilian realism. Clinton's concern with peacekeeping and the army's focus on OOTW and stability operations appear to line up. However, the timing does not support civilian realism. The army's vigorous interest in conflicts below the threshold of war began before Clinton assumed office.

In the case of the Bush II administration, the army's continued interest in low-intensity conflicts contradicted the turn of civilian leaders away from peacekeeping and nation building. In the case of unconventional missions, when the doctrinal priorities of civilians and the army aligned, civilian realism's timing was off. When priorities conflicted, the expectations of civilian realism went unfulfilled, even when they coincided with bureaucratic and military cultural preferences for avoiding unconventional war.

Civilian realism argues that military bureaucracies should capture the doctrinal process in cases where the balance of power does not inspire civilian intervention. Indeed, there is little evidence of extensive civilian intervention in this period.[247] However, the bureaucratic explanation does not fare well either in this case. OOTW and stability operations promised few resources because of their manpower- (as opposed to technology-) intensive nature. They undermine autonomy because they required close cooperation between the army and political actors on the ground. Doctrine acknowledged that OOTW placed army units in unique and complex politico-military environments that were not responsive to the application of the standard operating procedures of conventional warfare. Both post–Cold War manuals argued that political considerations such as government legitimacy were often the key to victory in such conflicts.

Across all three areas of post–Cold War U.S. Army doctrine, then, the evidence strongly supports the expectations of military realism. When confronted with a drastically different threat environment, the senior military realists in the U.S. Army moved to alter doctrine to prepare their force to deal with the new threats.[248] They did not revel in cultural nostalgia or argue for doctrinal business as usual to preserve bureaucratic imperatives. In all three areas of doctrine, there was evidence that the army reinterpreted its doctrinal concepts and even its history in order to prepare its forces to deal with the threat environment it confronted. Army doctrine reintroduced the principles of war but reinterpreted the principle of mass because lighter power-projection forces would have trouble massing in the traditional way. Recent and storied army history, from the frontier to the Gulf War, were enlisted to argue that OOTW operations were part of army traditions and were not out of place in its warfighting manual. These are just a few instances where writing teams reinterpreted doctrinal concepts and army history to better prepare the force for the uncertain threat environment.

In a number of instances, they overcame these parochial obstacles to begin building a force capable of navigating and fighting in this strange new world.

As we shall see, in hindsight, some of the doctrinal changes they made were ill-advised. Advisable or not, they are better explained by the military realist perspective than the alternatives.

6 TRANSFORMING UNDER FIRE

The Global War on Terror, Counterinsurgency, Iraq, and *Operations 2008*

THIS FINAL CASE study chapter seeks to address the puzzle that gave birth to this work. How did a U.S. Army that had rejected counterinsurgency during and after Vietnam come to embrace it as a solution to recent conflicts? While this chapter examines the capstone manual of this period, *Operations 2008*, it is impossible to tell its story without also telling the story of the highly publicized *Field Manual 3-24, Counterinsurgency*. Consequently, in addition to the usual structure, this chapter includes an extended discussion of the development of *Field Manual 3-24*, its relationship to ongoing operations, and, finally, the extent of its influence on *Operations 2008*. The chapter also briefly considers the decision to surge additional U.S. forces into Iraq to implement a new COIN strategy there.

In this final case, the behavior of the U.S. Army is more consistent with military realism than the other theoretical perspectives. For instance, regarding COIN doctrine, the U.S. Army did initially employ conventional warfare SOPs to fight the Iraqi insurgency, as organizational and cultural theories predict. However, senior army officers, both in the field and in the United States, soon recognized that they were facing an organized insurgency and needed to develop a *counter*insurgency plan. A new COIN doctrine would be an integral part of that plan. Its senior leaders worked to capture the lessons of Iraq in two COIN manuals, the first in 2004 and the second in 2006. In addition, the rebirth of COIN was not a temporary aberration. COIN theory and experience from Iraq and Afghanistan heavily influenced *Operations 2008*. Thus, contrary to the predictions of military cultural and bureaucratic theories, the U.S. Army developed a COIN doctrine and allowed it to permeate its most important doctrinal manual.

This case study also presents strong evidence against the contention that civilian leaders imposed COIN on army commanders. Interestingly, army officers began to consider COIN for its post-9/11 conflicts years before civilian authorities. In fact, the army started these COIN innovations while civilian authorities were pushing it to avoid nation building and focus instead on developing high-tech, conventional forces. Even though these civilian initiatives were in line with the supposed preferences of army culture and bureaucracy, the army developed a COIN doctrine and, more surprising still, made COIN a central part of its capstone doctrine.

This is not to say army doctrine in this period focused exclusively on COIN. *Operations 2008* kept many of the doctrinal concepts for conventional forces from previous doctrine. The main mission of the army continued to be power projection supported by new technologies, which would make the force light enough to project but strong enough to fight. The army underwent significant organizational changes in this period in an attempt to make this force a reality. However, these attempts met with serious setbacks that forced the army to reconsider its attempt to transform itself. There was also a recognition that conventional, offensive operations did not necessarily lead to decisive victory. To succeed, commanders had to unify offensive operations with defensive, stability, and civil-support operations. These ideas had been present in post–Cold War doctrine, but the post-9/11 experience of the army reinforced their wisdom. *Operations 2008* also incorporated the COIN lessons from Iraq and pointed out the limits of conventional forces and thinking in a COIN environment. The organization did not respond as the alternative theories expect in this case. Instead, consistent with military realism, the U.S. Army developed a doctrine to deal with a range of possible threats. Its doctrine was also responsive to changes in the threat environment brought about by the deteriorating situations in ongoing conflicts. Its doctrinal and organizational ideas were not perfect, by any means, but they were a response more to the threat environment than to cultural and bureaucratic preferences or civilian prodding.

We begin as before, by setting out the context in which doctrine was developed. The transformation agenda of Secretary of Defense Donald Rumsfeld shaped this context. In the midst of this transformation, the attacks of September 11, 2001, set America and its army on a course that led to the invasion of two countries and to two intractable counterinsurgencies. Each theoretical perspective has expectations about the behavior of the U.S. Army under these conditions. Some expect extensive changes in army doctrine, while others predict only minor alterations. As before, I assess the extent of doctrinal change and continuity across the three key areas of doctrine by comparing new doctrine, *Operations 2008*, to its predecessors *Operations 1993* and *2001*. The fact that the army published *Operations 2008* after almost ten years of conflict means that this case can also evaluate the effects of military operations on doctrine. The case study concludes with a summary of the performance of military realism and the alternative theoretical approaches.

Civilian Realism, Transformation, COIN, and Operations 2008

Civilian realism argues that civilian intervention is a key ingredient in military innovation. To ensure integration between military doctrine and their strategy, civilians should enlist the help of a military maverick whose professional expertise can impose innovation on an obstinate bureaucracy. In this case, there are two likely instances of civilian realism in action: Secretary of Defense Rumsfeld's "transformation" of the army and President Bush's shift to a COIN strategy in Iraq in 2006–7.

George W. Bush came into office with a different view of the U.S. military than his predecessor.[1] According to Bush and his advisers, the purpose of the U.S. military was winning the nation's wars, not engaging in humanitarian operations.[2] Nation building, peacekeeping, and humanitarian interventions were not jobs for the U.S. military.[3] Instead, by taking advantage of the U.S. edge in military technology to make itself lighter, more deployable, and more lethal, the U.S. military could become a global expeditionary force for winning wars quickly and decisively. This new force would leave a light footprint and avoid the ever-increasing commitments, or "mission creep," that led to indecisive quagmires. However, realizing this vision would require transforming the U.S. military, especially the U.S. Army.

Bush enlisted Donald Rumsfeld as defense secretary to implement this transformation agenda and to compel the U.S. defense bureaucracy to change. Rumsfeld personally intervened in the selection of three- and four-star officers and championed the ideas of advocates of the revolution in military affairs in the Pentagon.[4] The army, Rumsfeld contended, was a particularly tough nut to crack. He intervened to counter an army bureaucracy and culture that was wedded to Cold War weapons and doctrine and compelled it to become lighter and expeditionary through the RMA. Within three years of the 2001 terrorist attacks on the United States, the Bush administration tasked the military with two expeditionary wars using its new capabilities. Rumsfeld touted the rapid conventional victories in Afghanistan and Iraq as evidence that his transformation agenda had worked and that the RMA had proved itself in combat.[5] The transformation of the U.S. military had made it better able to execute the Global War on Terror.

Not satisfied with the efforts at transformation, Rumsfeld sought out a military maverick to help him transform the U.S. Army.[6] Rumsfeld framed his decision in civilian realist terms: "I recognized that the next [army] Chief would face significant internal resistance to the changes we needed to effect. I decided I wanted someone at the top of the Army who had the ability and the desire to jar the institution and transform it into the expeditionary force our country needed."[7] To this end, in August 2003, the Secretary brought General Peter J. Schoomaker out of retirement to be army chief of staff and lead the transformation of the army. Schoomaker's last army post had been as commander of U.S. Special Operations Command.[8] He was the first Special Forces officer to be army chief of staff.[9] Schoomaker was a former Delta Force commando, the army's elite counterterrorism force. He had been involved in the low-intensity conflicts in Central America in the 1980s. Schoomaker would prod the army bureaucracy and make the force more like the light and lethal Special Forces. With Rumsfeld's blessing, Schoomaker radically transformed the force structure of the army from the old division system to the smaller modular system of Brigade Combat Teams (BCTs),[10] a move Rumsfeld saw as revolutionary.[11]

This historical narrative seems to fit nicely with civilian realism. If so, the three key areas of doctrine should have the following character. Army doctrine should be highly offensive in order to carry out the expeditionary strategy of civilian leaders. It should abandon the heavy conventional forces that were part of the Cold War era. Finally, doctrine should focus on the operations of a lighter and more lethal transformed conventional force. These changes will lead to bureaucratic and cultural resistance, which civilian leaders and their military maverick will have to counter. Army doctrine should also remove its emphasis on operations other than war and stability operations, because these are contrary to a civilian strategy opposed to nation building.

However, Rumsfeld's transformation agenda was not the only case of civilian intervention in the U.S. Army in this period. As violence escalated in Iraq in 2006, a strategy review initiated by President Bush led to a new COIN strategy opposed by Rumsfeld and army commanders on the ground.[12] Bush replaced the civilian and military opponents of his new COIN strategy.[13] Bush selected a new secretary of defense, Robert Gates, and a new commanding general, David Petraeus. Bush compelled commanders in Iraq to change the strategic measure of effectiveness from killing and capturing insurgents and handing over security to the Iraqis to protecting the Iraqi population through a fully resourced COIN strategy. Bush used his authority and allies in the U.S. Army to overcome the military bureaucracy and its aversion to COIN. If COIN suddenly figures prominently in *Operations 2008*, we could attribute it to this civilian realist intervention.

Bureaucrats, Transformation, COIN, and Operations 2008

Military bureaucracies should prefer doctrines that focus on conventional warfare and offensive operations. This doctrinal arrangement ensures greater resources and autonomy and reduces uncertainty. If this logic is sound, we should observe the following in this case. The army should approve of the more offensive, conventional mission assigned to it by the Bush administration. Army bureaucrats should relish the opportunity to abandon nation building, which promises few resources. They should also use the lessons of the invasions of Afghanistan and Iraq as proof of the effectiveness of their offensive, conventional doctrine. However, these same bureaucrats should resist the extreme elements of Rumsfeld's transformation agenda because bureaucracy is opposed to major change. Indeed, Colin Jackson argues that army behavior during this period "represented the triumph of institutional preference [for conventional warfare] over experience and rational expectations."[14]

Regarding COIN, army bureaucrats should do all that they can to ensure that the worsening insurgency in Iraq does not lead to a major role for COIN, especially of the population security variety, in army doctrine. The army should continue to use the SOPs for conventional warfare, rather than adapt to a COIN campaign. Some contend this did indeed occur in Iraq, and use an analogy with Vietnam and the bureaucratic aversion to change to explain this case. As Thomas Ricks points out in his popular book *Fiasco: The American Military Adventure in Iraq*, "Militaries, like all big organizations, tend to do what they know how to do, rather than what they might need to do differently to address the situation they face. As French counterinsurgency expert Bernard Fall said in a 1964 speech to a U.S. military audience about flaws in the U.S. approach in Vietnam, 'Everybody likes to fight the war that he knows best; this is very obvious. But in Vietnam we fight a war that we don't "know best." The sooner this is realized the better it is going to be.'"[15] Indeed, during the early occupation of Iraq, under General Ricardo Sanchez, the army did apply the SOPs of conventional warfare to counter the growing insurgency. As in Vietnam, it relied on large unit sweeps to kill and capture as many insurgents as possible.[16]

If the bureaucratic logic is correct, the army should resist any attempts, internal or external in origin, to develop a COIN doctrine. If compelled to do so, army bureaucrats should work to ensure that COIN ideas do not spread from a subordinate manual, *Field Manual 3-24, Counterinsurgency*, to its main war-fighting manual, *Operations 2008*. This main manual should bear the hallmarks of bureaucratic preferences. It should have a highly offensive theory of victory based on the best traditions of conventional warfare. Nuclear weapons should continue to have a minor role in doctrine. Throughout this doctrinal process, army bureaucrats should hold the reins tightly and keep doctrine on a path consistent with bureaucratic imperatives.

The Guardians of Culture, Transformation, COIN, and Operations 2008

"Despite significant changes in both its domestic and international environment," argues one proponent of the military culture explanation, "U.S. Army culture in 2003 . . . was . . . remarkably similar to what it had been at the end of the Vietnam era."[17] Drawing on its proud cultural traditions, therefore, the U.S. Army in this period should design a doctrine focused on employing an offensive theory of victory to achieve decisive results in conventional warfare. Nuclear weapons, which were contrary to that culture from the beginning, should have a minor role in the most important doctrine, *Operations 2008*. Army culture should be grateful for the Bush administration's rejection of the peacekeeping and nation-building missions that were so contrary to its martial traditions. Like the rapid success of army units in the Gulf War, army leaders will use the precipitous and successful invasions of Afghanistan and Iraq as proof of the continued relevance of army culture. The army should be loath to abandon its heavy Cold War formations for the same reason it promoted them in the Cold War, because of their cultural affinity with its World War II finest hour. Senior leaders will resist Rumsfeld's transformation agenda when it threatens the traditions of the army. Army culture should also work to reduce the influence of COIN doctrine on its most important war-fighting manual, *Operations 2008*, even as the insurgency in Iraq raged. In Iraq U.S. Army culture should repeat the errors that it made in Vietnam. For instance, it should apply the SOPs for conventional, offensive warfare to combat the Iraqi insurgency. Cultural theorists have already argued that the army did just that.[18] The cultural guardians of the army, its senior leaders, should resist any attempts, internal or external, to develop a COIN doctrine and strategy for Iraq. However, if the army is compelled to do so, senior leaders will not codify such innovations by their inclusion in the *Operations* manual. Regarding the three key areas of doctrine, therefore, *Operations 2008* should conform to army culture and focus on decisive conventional operations guided by an offensive theory of victory. If COIN doctrines appear, the guardians of army culture—its senior officers—should ensure they are only a temporary aberration and not allow them to infect *Operations 2008*.

Military Realism, Transformation, COIN and Operations 2008

In the years following 9/11, military realism expects army doctrine to retain its power-projection mission and the requisite offensive theory of victory. Power projection and offensive operations were central to the army's two post-9/11 expeditionary wars. Other than discussions of force protection, army doctrine will pay little attention to nuclear weapons because they do not play a role in addressing the most dangerous threats of the period. However, army doctrine should continue to emphasize the limits that the physical world places on power projection and offensive operations. Doctrine writers should also preserve lessons about the power of the defense from Cold War doctrine.

Regarding COIN, such missions should continue to have an important place in doctrine due to the narrowing of the spectrum of international threats resulting from America's unrivaled power. The insurgencies in Iraq and Afghanistan should reinforce the import of stability operations in army doctrine introduced in *Operations 1993*. In ongoing military operations, military realism expects the army to alter doctrine and strategy if doing so is required to address a dangerous threat. Because the war in Iraq was waged in an area vital to the interests of the United States and its allies, senior army leaders should see failure there as particularly serious. If senior leaders are military realists, they should alter army doctrine to address that danger. Stability operations should also be included in *Operations 2008*, just as they were important elements of both post–Cold War editions. At the same time, however, the army should draw lessons from Iraq and Afghanistan for responding to major regional conflicts, the upper level of the spectrum of conflict in this period. The army should be able to undertake these adaptations without civilian intervention. In fact, senior army leaders may resist civilian masters if their demands contradict the requirements of the threat environment. Despite adaptations toward COIN, however, army leaders and *Operations 2008* should still prioritize major regional conflicts due to the greater costs of failure in such conflicts. In the end, military realism has the following expectations for the three key areas of doctrine in this case. Power projection will remain the main mission at the core of *Operations 2008*. Conventional forces with an offensive theory of victory will execute this mission. And Nuclear weapons will continue to have a minor role in doctrine. However, doctrine writers will also incorporate the lessons of Iraq and Afghanistan into the 2008 manual, even if that means making COIN an important part of the U.S. Army's most important war-fighting manual.

Rumsfeld and Army Transformation

It is reasonable to assume that aggressive civilian intervention drove the transformation of the U.S. Army's conventional forces during the second Bush administration. According to this narrative, Secretary of Defense Donald Rumsfeld prodded a hidebound army bureaucracy into abandoning its old ways of thinking and doing.[19] However, as will be shown below, although there was a coincidence between the new military strategies of the Bush administration and army force structure and doctrine, civilian intervention did not drive the process of doctrinal change. As in previous cases of army innovation, civilian leaders were taking up initiatives already present in army thinking and doctrine. Rumsfeld saw himself as an agent of change working to overthrow the bureaucratic and cultural prejudices of the army and transform it for the future. However, his interventions only accelerated changes that had been under way in the army since the end of the Cold War.

When President Bush came into office, his military strategy prioritized advanced conventional weapons[20] and downplayed peacekeeping and humanitarian assistance operations.[21] As Bush's influential national security adviser Condoleezza Rice put it, the purpose of the U.S. military was fighting and winning the nation's wars, not "escorting kids to kindergarten."[22] The administration and Secretary Rumsfeld[23] contended that the revolution in military affairs meant that the U.S. military could replace physical mass with information.[24] In the information age, for force to be overwhelming and decisive it did not require as much physical mass as in the past. Military forces could be both smaller and more lethal, enabling global deployment with a smaller footprint.[25] According to Rumsfeld, the main missions of these forces were rapid deployment to deter aggression and reassure allies and to do so before major conflict broke out. If deterrence failed, these forces would use their technological edge to win decisively. Such rapid and decisive deployment would avoid the "graduated response" policy that had led to greater and greater commitments in Vietnam but ultimate failure.[26] What Rumsfeld recommended was largely consistent with the Powell-Weinberger Doctrine. The father of that doctrine was Bush's secretary of state. After September 11, 2001, the Bush administration's military strategy would be put into practice through the Global War on Terrorism. Nine days after the attacks, President Bush addressed a joint session of Congress and set out the Bush Doctrine, which would eventually call for the rapid and decisive removal of enemy regimes by conventional forces.[27] Enacting the Bush Doctrine would give new urgency to the transformation of the U.S. military. The U.S. Army would play a major role in these efforts.[28]

Rumsfeld foresaw obstacles to his agenda in bureaucratic and cultural terms. "Change is hard," the secretary wrote in his memoir. "Large organizations especially favor practices they have already mastered, even if those practices, fashioned decades before, are outdated."[29] Rumsfeld knew that as secretary of defense under Bush he would have to "tangle with a bureaucracy" at Defense that was "entrenched and powerful" and "closely tied to the status quo."[30] In a September 10, 2001, speech, Rumsfeld portrayed the "Pentagon bureaucracy" as a "serious threat to the security of the United States of America."[31] As he wrote of his tenure as secretary of defense: "I steadily pushed each service to become more agile, more deployable, and better prepared to confront new, previously unanticipated threats."[32] These conclusions came from a number of internal Pentagon reviews, which then strongly influenced the 2001 Quadrennial Defense Review.[33] To push this agenda, Rumsfeld supported "unconventional thinkers" that could "move the institution,"[34] such as Andrew Marshall at the Office of Net Assessment, who coined the term *revolution in military affairs*.[35] Only in this way, Rumsfeld thought, could he enact the change that all large organizations fear.

Changing the U.S. Army for twenty-first-century warfare was particularly daunting.[36] Rumsfeld thought he needed renegades to change the army. According to the secretary, Schoomaker was to make the whole army look more like the Special Forces, light and lethal. For Rumsfeld, the performance of SF in Afghanistan was proof that they were the cutting edge of a transformed military and that the U.S. Army needed to follow their example.[37] In civilian realist terms, Rumsfeld had selected his maverick.

Rumsfeld's characterization of the challenge of transforming the U.S. Army is worth quoting and analyzing in full:

The Army faced the biggest challenges [in transforming]. It has a proud and storied history dating back to the Continental Army of 1775. Under such legendary generals as Grant and Sherman, it preserved the Union in a tough-fought civil war. Under Pershing and Eisenhower it liberated Europe in two world wars. The Army manned the front lines of the Cold War flashpoints, its heavy tanks and artillery acting as a deterrent against a Soviet ground advance in Central Europe. For decades the Army had been organized for large land battles between sovereign states, symbolized by the service's prized seventy-ton M-1 Abrams tank. The immediate challenges we confronted by 2001 though were not from massed enemy forces. By then our adversaries had learned that confronting the United States in a conventional war of massed force was a bad idea. As a result, America was unlikely to soon face the major land, sea, and air battles for which our military had organized, trained, and equipped over many decades. Instead, we needed a military that could quickly deploy in enough numbers to bring decisive lethality to bear, could leverage our country's technological advantages, such as precision, communications, and stealth, and—most important—could quickly adapt "to changing circumstances in a given conflict and prevail."[38]

This quotation nicely demonstrates two important points. First, Rumsfeld drew on organizational and military cultural theories to explain the absence of change in the army. Second, when seen in the doctrinal context of the previous chapter, the changes proposed by Rumsfeld actually originated with the very senior army leaders that he thought would be the greatest obstacles to change.

First, by invoking the "proud and storied history" of the army and the equipment that symbolized that history, like the M-1 tank, Rumsfeld implies that it was the army's attachment to its "finest hour" that kept it from adapting to the new threat environment.[39] As preceding chapters have shown, however, since the 1950s the army has actually undergone numerous important changes in the way that it prepares for war in terms of both doctrine and force structure. A number of these changes were contrary to its supposed bureaucratic interests and its cultural traditions. Rumsfeld's view of the army as culture bound caused him to overlook the recent post–Cold War adaptations the army had made in doctrine and force structure and underestimate its capacity for independent change and innovative thinking.

Second, examining the characteristics of the "new" capabilities and mindset that Rumsfeld wanted to instill in the army shows they were the very capabilities advocated by senior army leaders since the early 1990s. Rumsfeld himself admitted that the idea of "transformation" was not his and that the Pentagon was already pursuing it on his arrival.[40] However, he failed to note the role the U.S. Army had played in that prior pursuit. As a recent history of military transformation acknowledged, "The U.S. Army was an early adopter of the new technology and of the promise this held for the conduct of warfare."[41] President Bush insisted that Secretary Rumsfeld develop a "lethal, light, and mobile" military. However, this goal did not originate with civilian authorities.[42] What Bush described and what Rumsfeld sought to implement was a power-projection military exploiting the RMA.[43] As early as 1990, senior U.S. Army leaders advocated just such a force in *Operations 1993* and *2001*. The very idea that the military had to reconceptualize mass in the information age originated in the immediate post–Cold War army. Greater situational awareness could protect a lighter force designed for power projection, that is, information could substitute for mass. Army commanders would replace massed forces with the massed effects of precision guided weapons.[44] As chronicled in the previous chapter, for the remainder of the 1990s the army began to develop the units that would constitute a lighter and more lethal force, like the Stryker Brigade Combat Teams.

This is not to say that important changes were absent under Rumsfeld, but even these had originated in the army before he stepped onto the scene. Most notably, Secretary Rumsfeld oversaw the complete reformation of the U.S. Army force structure. A month after taking command of the army, Rumsfeld's military maverick, Schoomaker, ordered TRADOC to start the process of changing the army's force structure.[45] The building blocks of this new modular force would be brigades of thirty-nine hundred soldiers instead of divisions of ten to eighteen thousand.[46] Modular brigades would also be more deployable because their supporting elements were organic and they did not have to borrow them from a higher division.[47] The army completed this force-structure redesign in fifteen months and deployed the first modular force to Iraq at the end of this time. The realization that global deployments had stretched the army thin and that large numbers of army units would be needed in Iraq after 2004 accelerated the pace of change.[48]

Like previous senior army leaders, Schoomaker developed this new concept outside of the typical army bureaucracy for fear that it would slow the necessary changes. Importantly, the BCTs replaced the division as the most important building block of the army's fighting forces. From the cultural perspective, this is unexpected because the division was the culturally acceptable unit of organization in the U.S. Army, linked as it was to its finest hour.[49] Despite the threat jointness presented to organizational autonomy, modularity would increase it. Close coordination with the other services was crucial to a force projected into locales with limited logistics and lighter forces.[50]

Despite this correlation between Rumsfeld's initiative and the modular force, the army had long been contemplating designing tailored units. Recall that tailoring had been the driving force behind the ROAD redesign in the early 1960s. In the end, the army limited the tailoring concept because of the need to address the Soviet threat. However, with the end of the Cold War, the army embraced a global power-projection mission and with it a need to develop a force capable of being tailored to specific missions anywhere on the globe. The concept of modularity actually built on the thinking of Army Chief of Staff Sullivan, the intellectual driving force behind *Operations 1993*.[51] Between

1991 and 1993, Chief of Staff Sullivan and TRADOC commander Franks were developing doctrine and force structure to leverage the RMA and enable a light, lethal, and deployable force for power projection. In March 1994, Sullivan sought to twin doctrinal and structural change. As noted in the previous chapter, the Force XXI concept entailed the digitization of communications between combat units to increase situational awareness. Admittedly, however, exercises at the National Training Center demonstrated the limits of the concept. As *Operations 1993* noted, a transformed force would still be subject to the friction of warfare. Despite its limits, transformation continued, and the flip side of the Force XXI coin was a force-structure component. Force XXI sought to redesign army combat formations to give them the same combat power as current army units but increased deployability, that is, both lethal and light. Modularity was an outgrowth of this thinking.[52]

General Eric Shinseki became army chief of staff in 1999. However, Shinseki did not begin the restructuring of the force, as some claim.[53] Rather, he sought to accelerate the transformation of army force structure.[54] The result was the Stryker BCTs.[55] By the time Schoomaker succeeded Shinseki, the main elements of the modular force structure were in place.[56] The origin of these elements was the leadership of the post–Cold War army and the new threat environment they faced. Under Schoomaker's direction, the army overcame bureaucratic and cultural obstacles to organizational change.[57] Nevertheless, these changes were peripheral in the sense that they sought to enact the doctrinal concepts established by senior army leaders at the end of the Cold War. Modularity would enable to U.S. Army to become the light, lethal, global power-projection force that army leaders had wanted since the fall of the Soviet Union.

Like the ROAD concept, devised prior to Kennedy's election but for which the new president took credit, modularity was not a bolt from the blue. Like Kennedy and McNamara, Rumsfeld was pushing against an opening door. The army, its force structure and its doctrine, had been emphasizing light, lethal power projection long before the Bush administration came into office. The Bush Doctrine called on the army to do what it had been preparing to do since the end of the Cold War: global power projection as part of a joint U.S. military team.[58] A military maverick parachuted in by civilian authorities did not impose these changes on the army. Rumsfeld hastened changes that were already under way in the army prior to his ascendancy at the Pentagon.[59] On the other hand, this narrative is well within the expectations of military realism. Transformation in the U.S. Army was a process initiated internally to address the changed post–Cold War threat environment. That transformation entailed all the adaptations that the previous chapter showed were contrary to army culture and bureaucratic imperatives. Given the threat environment and resource constraints of the post–Cold War, transformation represented a plausible doctrinal means of protecting the global material interests of the United States.

Civilian and Military Influence on the Road to a Counterinsurgency Doctrine

The deteriorating situation in Iraq between 2004 and 2006 led to the development of a new COIN doctrine for the army and a new COIN strategy for stabilizing the country. The original military plan for Iraq called for army forces to leave Iraq by September 2003. However, between June 2003 and January 2005, Iraq was engulfed by a complex insurgency and escalating sectarian violence verging on civil war.[60] In the early part of the occupation, army units used cordon and sweep operations to kill or capture as many insurgents as possible.[61] For instance, Austin Long, a cultural theorist, points to the operations of the Fourth Infantry Division in Iraq between 2003 and 2004. Commanded by Major General Raymond Odierno, the division used conventional warfare SOPs such as harassment and interdiction fires against suspected insurgent positions.[62] Despite such efforts, in December 2004 and February 2005, President Bush received two briefings that argued the insurgency in Iraq was worsening. Both briefers were army officers, Colonel Derek Harvey,[63] an intelligence officer, and General Gary Luck (retired). Bush had sent Luck to Iraq to analyze progress there. Both Harvey and Luck stated that the insurgency was worsening. Luck added that Iraqi security forces were seriously underdeveloped.[64]

Concerns about the progress of the occupation, however, were not limited to a few low-ranking and retired army officers. In August 2003, Army Chief of Staff Schoomaker visited Iraq on a fact-finding mission. He was impressed with the progress that General David Petraeus was making in Mosul through classic COIN techniques.[65] Petraeus combined operations to kill or capture insurgents with population protection and control to erode the insurgents' support base.[66] Petraeus also received permission to limit the scope of de-Baathification in Mosul so that former Baath Party members could retain their positions and participate in reconstruction. He also helped organize local elections.[67] In Mosul, unlike in the rest of Iraq, violence declined. Upon his return to the United States, Schoomaker kept these lessons and Petraeus in mind.

By November 2003, U.S. Central Command (CENTCOM) commander John Abizaid tried to convince Secretary Rumsfeld that U.S. forces in Iraq were facing a "classic guerrilla-type campaign," an insurgency.[68] Rumsfeld was not convinced. A full two years later, in November 2005, Rumsfeld was still reluctant to call the enemy in Iraq an insurgency.[69] Moreover, when Secretary of State Rice suggested that U.S. forces would be directly involved in the "hold, build" phase of a "clear, hold, build" strategy for Iraq, Rumsfeld countered that the Iraqis, and not U.S. forces, "are clearing . . . holding . . . and building. They're going to be the ones doing the reconstruction in that country."[70] Rumsfeld was expressing the distaste for "nation building" that the Bush administration, including Rice, had shown from its inception. The civic action so central to COIN based on population security was exactly what the Bush Doctrine did not want the U.S. Army to engage in.

In December 2003, Lieutenant Colonel H. R. McMaster, working at CENTCOM, wrote a report for General Abizaid recommending that the army be vocal about the fact that it now faced an insurgency in Iraq and needed to develop a counterinsurgency strategy. The language of McMaster's report was reminiscent of classic COIN strategy and of Walt Rostow's modernization theory. "Military operations alone cannot defeat an insurgency," McMaster wrote, "because only economic development and political action can address most sources of disaffection." To rely on conventional military means alone would lead to the alienation of the population and "reduce the amount of intelligence available to US and Iraqi security forces, and strengthen rather than weaken the enemy."[71] Multinational Force Iraq (MNF-I), McMaster continued, needed to "enhance [the] political legitimacy" of the Iraqi government and restrain "troop behavior and firepower."[72] This recommendation is especially interesting coming from McMaster, who was a tank commander in the battle of 73 Easting, the most celebrated tank engagement of the Gulf War. McMaster, an exemplar of army culture, was advocating COIN based on population security, an idea supposedly anathema to army culture. Abizaid had tried to get Rumsfeld to accept that the United States faced an insurgency in Iraq without success. Soon, however, McMaster would have an opportunity to put his COIN ideas into practice.

In February 2005, after his stint at CENTCOM, Colonel McMaster took command in Tal Afar, Iraq. As Petraeus had done in Mosul, McMaster demonstrated during his command that COIN based on securing the population could work to reduce insurgent violence.[73] He replaced local political leaders and moved his units out among the population, establishing thirty combat outposts in the city.[74] McMaster's guiding principle was population control. He surrounded Tal Afar with an earthen berm and built camps outside of the berm for civilians displaced by the inevitable violence. Then his units cleared the city and defeated the insurgents with "superior numbers and firepower."[75]

This was contrary to the plan of the U.S. commander of MNF-I, General George Casey, who advocated patrolling from large bases and handing over security to the Iraqis.[76] However, Casey recognized McMaster's accomplishment and visited him in Tal Afar, a rare honor Casey paid to only a few commanders before he departed. Casey told McMaster that his departure from the commanding general's plan for Iraq had been noted and that McMaster should be more willing "to take no for an answer" from superiors. In the same meeting, however, Casey told McMaster that he thought the younger officer had a better sense of the complex nature of the war in Iraq than almost any other commander there.[77] While Casey recognized McMaster's success, he also appreciated its limits. Tal Afar was a city of two hundred thousand people where there was one U.S. soldier for every twenty-two Iraqis. Given the number of U.S. troops in Iraq at the time, it would have been impossible to execute a similar strategy in Baghdad, for instance.[78]

Moreover, this was not the first time Casey had considered COIN in the context of Iraq. In May 2004, he met with Army Chief Schoomaker, who had been to Iraq the year before and was impressed with Petraeus's COIN operations in Mosul. Casey had just been appointed the new commander of MNF-I. Schoomaker gave Casey a copy of John Nagl's *Learning to Eat Soup with a Knife: Counterinsurgency Lessons from Malaya and Vietnam*. Schoomaker told Casey, as Fred Kaplan recounts, "that he'd been handing [Nagl's book] out to all the four-star generals, that it offered the clearest analysis he'd read of how to think about counterinsurgency."[79] Both Casey and Schoomaker had experience in unconventional conflicts in their careers. Both had served in Bosnia. Schoomaker saw those operations and those he witnessed in Mosul as the face of future warfare. Casey agreed but doubted the efficacy of a major U.S. role in such conflicts. He saw Bosnia as an example of how U.S. intervention could draw out a conflict by breeding dependence in the indigenous actors, undermining those ultimately responsible for the long-term success of the missions.[80]

Casey and Schoomaker agreed that the United States faced an insurgency in Iraq. When Casey arrived in Baghdad on July 1, 2004, one of his first questions was "Where is my counterinsurgency plan?" When his question was greeted with silence, Casey asked for a "counterinsurgency expert."[81] On August 5, 2005, Colonel William Hix joined Casey's command as his COIN expert. Hix was a Special Forces officer who had advised COIN forces in the Philippines and peacekeepers in the Sinai.[82] Casey ordered Colonel Hix to conduct a study of the conduct of the war from the perspective of COIN, which he did with the help of Kalev Sepp, another Special Forces officer (retired), who had advised COIN forces in El Salvador in the 1980s.[83] Sepp, who as discussed below had commented on the 2004 interim COIN manual, wrote a piece titled "Successful and Unsuccessful Counterinsurgency Practices." Casey approved of the piece and allowed *Military Review* to publish it to spread the word about COIN in the army more broadly.[84] In September 2005, Hix and Sepp concluded that most units in Iraq were ineffective: 20 percent were employing COIN best practices, 60 percent were "struggling," and the final 20 percent were employing the SOPs for conventional warfare to combat the insurgency. Some commanders were judging progress by "body count."[85] Even units that were implementing COIN, however, did not have enough troops to clear and hold areas. Hix and Sepp argued that Casey needed ten thousand more troops to conduct civic-action missions in Iraq to improve local services and governance, as General Creighton Abrams had done with some success at the end of Vietnam. Hix and Sepp advocated an integrated politico-military COIN strategy under Casey's direction.[86] Casey sent the Hix and Sepp report to Rumsfeld.

Despite this negative appraisal of U.S. operations in Iraq, Casey and Abizaid continued to think that the best strategy for Iraq was to hand over security responsibility to the Iraqis as quickly as possible.[87] Both thought that the presence of U.S. troops in Iraq was the cause of the insurgency and that more U.S. troops would worsen the situation by raising the specter of permanent occupation. Once the occupying forces left, the generals thought, the insurgency would wither.[88] Accordingly, when Rumsfeld asked Abizaid if he needed more troops in 2004, Abizaid replied on July 13, 2004, that "the forces in theatre are adequate to perform the current tasks."[89] In his campaign plan for Iraq, Casey joined COIN language with the operational concepts articulated in *Operations 1993* and *2001*. MNF-I would conduct "full-spectrum counter-insurgency operations to isolate and neutralize the enemy."[90] The campaign plan invoked classic COIN concepts, such as "enhancing the legitimacy" of the Iraqi government.[91] Its legitimacy, Casey thought, depended on successful elections, the securing of which represented the other priority in Casey's plan.[92] Instead of population security, then, the key missions were handing security responsibilities over to Iraqi security forces and securing three key votes.[93] Rumsfeld concurred with the generals and thought that Vietnam had shown, as Casey had observed in Bosnia, that too much assistance bred dependence in U.S. allies.[94] Rumsfeld was determined not to see this mistake repeated in Iraq. Therefore, he continually advocated "taking the hand off of the bicycle seat" and allowing the Iraqis to lead the fight against the insurgency and reconstruct their country.[95] As Rumsfeld wrote of Iraq and Afghanistan in his 2011 memoir, "They are not our broken societies to fix."[96]

Some have criticized General Casey for not advocating COIN concepts enough during his tenure in Iraq.[97] However, General Stanley McChrystal, a COIN expert who worked closely with Casey in this period, argues, "Casey had been beating the drum to do counterinsurgency . . . and do it well."[98] Casey did not reject the idea of preparing the U.S. Army in Iraq for COIN, even if he did think additional troops were unadvisable. In November 2005, Casey established a COIN academy in Iraq called the Hix Academy, after his Special Forces COIN expert.[99] Casey made attendance at the academy mandatory for all commanders rotating into Iraq.[100] This one-week intensive course advocated the mentoring of Iraqi units and the use of measured force in order to avoid alienating the Iraqi populace. The academy distilled these COIN principles into a counterinsurgency handbook, which it distributed to all its students.[101] The purpose of the school was to counter the exclusively conventional training army units were receiving prior to deployment to Iraq, a problem highlighted in the Hix-Sepp study. "Because the Army won't change itself," Casey had said, "I am going to change it here in Iraq."[102] Casey could implement this change without asking permission from his civilian superiors in Washington. It was also consistent with Schoomaker's vision of a COIN strategy for Iraq that he had conveyed to Casey just prior to Casey assuming command over MNF-I.

Schoomaker also declared his support for COIN doctrine in a more public forum when the army chief of staff wrote a new foreword to John Nagl's *Learning to Eat Soup with a Knife*, the same book he gave Casey as a parting gift. The subject of the monograph was how militaries learn effective COIN practices.[103] The language in the foreword was a hybrid of Rumsfeld's "transformation" agenda and COIN. For instance, when discussing the British COIN success in Malaya, which was the positive counterpoint to the U.S. Army's flawed performance in Vietnam, Schoomaker wrote, "The armies of these two great nations were challenged to *transform* to meet the demands of a different kind of war than the one they had planned for."[104] However, "The British Army was more successful in *transforming* itself largely because it was a more effective 'learning organization' than the U.S. Army."[105] Schoomaker pointed out that the U.S. Army at the time of writing was capturing lessons from the theaters in Iraq and Afghanistan and was using those lessons to "transform" army "organization and culture." This kind of transformation was necessary because in Iraq the rapid decisive operations envisioned by *Operations 1993* and *2001* had given way to a protracted and violent insurgency for which doctrine had not prepared the army. During Vietnam, Schoomaker wrote, army culture "overpowered innovative ideas from within the Army and from outside it." Schoomaker would send General Petraeus to Fort Leavenworth to use his Iraq experience to shape a COIN manual to ensure that the army would not stifle innovative ideas from *within* this time. In a reference to Petraeus's recent assignment and new COIN doctrine, Schoomaker noted, "Officers with recent combat experience are now teaching in our Army schools, ensuring that our education programs and doctrine stay relevant to the current operational environment."[106] Schoomaker was determined to make the army adapt to COIN in Iraq and co-opted the language of "transformation" to do so. Finally, John Nagl himself became part of the writing team that would design COIN doctrine and help the army learn to eat soup with a knife.

Therefore, contrary to the logic of civilian realism, the military maverick that Rumsfeld handpicked to direct his transformation agenda in the army was working at cross-purposes with the secretary of defense. Rumsfeld's negative reaction to the language of insurgency and "clear, hold, build," at this time showed that he was still hostile to a COIN-type mission for the army. This discontinuity between the views of the Secretary and his military maverick stemmed from the fact that Rumsfeld misunderstood Schoomaker's views on future warfare. For instance, while both Rumsfeld and Schoomaker thought the rest of the army should look more like the Special Forces, they had different ideas of what that meant. Rumsfeld had put Schoomaker in place to make a lighter, more lethal army that could win decisively through conventional means and withdraw rapidly to avoid nation building. Rumsfeld increased Special Forces funding by 107 percent, doubled the number of recruits, and secured better equipment. He saw them as having an important "reconnaissance and direct-action role," and he shifted emphasis away from more traditional Special Forces tasks, such as "training foreign militaries" in counterinsurgency. According to Rumsfeld, "This freed up special operators for more upper-tier tasks—reconnaissance and direct-action missions."[107]

Schoomaker, on the other hand, thought that soldiers in the post–Cold War had to be "'warrior diplomats,' ready for combat *and* nation-building."[108] For Schoomaker, this versatility was the hallmark of the Special Forces. Schoomaker did not share Rumsfeld's animosity toward nation building or the use of Special Forces in that role. Moreover, Schoomaker's view was not a minority view in the army. As shown in the previous chapter, after the Cold War most senior leaders in the army reserved an important place for operations other than war and stability operations in army doctrine. The short, decisive campaign in Iraq envisioned by Rumsfeld's transformation agenda had given way to a protracted and bloody insurgency. In Schoomaker's view, the army had "to transform to meet the demands of a different kind of war than the one [it] had planned for." Schoomaker pressed the army to transform to meet this challenge despite Rumsfeld's resistance. *Operations 1993* and *2001* had laid some of the groundwork for accomplishing this goal. Like Kennedy and his military maverick, General Maxwell Taylor, the civilian leader who selected the military officer to represent their innovation did not fully understand their maverick's views of warfare. The result was a military doctrine more consistent with the views of the mavericks, and the institutional army, than their civilian sponsors'.

It is clear that Secretary Rumsfeld did not impose COIN on the U.S. Army. Nor did the commander in chief. On March 20, 2006, in a speech to the City Club of Cleveland, President Bush described U.S. strategy in Iraq as "clear, hold, and build." Bush delivered the speech the month after the bombing of the al-Askaria mosque in the Iraqi city of Samara. This attack on one of the holiest sites in Shia Islam ignited sectarian violence. By the time of the speech, the violence had escalated considerably.[109] The central part of the speech was a detailed discussion of H. R. McMaster's success in Tal Afar. However, Bush described this new strategy in terms consistent with Rumsfeld and Casey's handover plan, arguing that it focused on building up Iraqi security forces. U.S. and Iraqi forces would clear an area of insurgents, and then *Iraqi* units would be left behind to hold and build.[110] Bush's concept of "clear, hold, build" did not represent a new strategy. Nor did it accurately reflect what occurred in Tal Afar, where the role of U.S. forces extended to the hold-and-build phase of the operation. In short, the new strategy of "clear, hold, build," was the old strategy by another name.

Despite the rising violence, civilian leaders and their theater commanders remained wedded to the strategy of transfer.[111] After Bush's speech, Casey launched Operations Together Forward I and II in Baghdad in July and August 2006, respectively. In both operations, U.S. forces cleared an area, and then Iraqi forces held and built. Both operations failed to stamp out the violence in the Iraqi capital. By that fall, sectarian attacks in Baghdad had increased by 40 percent.[112]

As of March 2006, then, Bush still held to the strategy adopted by Rumsfeld and his military commanders. Moreover, this strategy was consistent with the original disinclination of the Bush administration with nation building.

Indeed, Rice still agreed with the broad thrust of the handover strategy in June 2006, when she suggested that U.S. forces pull out of Iraqi cities and not be drawn into a sectarian civil war. On December 7, 2006, Rice was still advocating that U.S. troops pull back to their bases and intervene only in the event of a "massacre."[113] Sectarian violence was an issue that only the Iraqis could solve.[114]

In his memoir, Bush argued that the Samara bombing and the rising sectarian violence made him start to doubt the efficacy of the "handover strategy."[115] However, those doubts were not evident in his public pronouncements a month after the bombing when the extent of the sectarian violence was becoming evident.[116] Even by May and June 2006, Bush was not yet advocating a COIN strategy based on population security as he would later. He would not advocate such a strategy until December 2006, the same month that the army published the final draft of the COIN manual.[117] Luckily for Bush, for years prior to his Cleveland speech, the army had been fashioning a COIN doctrine based on population security for implementation in Iraq, largely under the nose of the secretary of defense.

The Doctrinal Process: The Making of *Field Manual 3-24*

The publication of *Field Manual 3-24, Counterinsurgency* in December 2006 has received much attention. However, this was not the first COIN manual the army published after the invasion of Iraq. In fact, in October 2004, one year and seven months after the invasion, the Combined Arms Center (CAC) at Fort Leavenworth published *Field Manual (Interim) 3-07.22, Counterinsurgency*. However, the process that led to its publication began nine months earlier, in February 2004,[118] when McMaster was beginning his command in Tel Afar. The initiative for the new manual began with General William Scott Wallace, the new commander of the CAC, which included the Command and General Staff College. Wallace thought the army focused training too much on conventional warfare and was determined to use the CAC and army schools to distill the lessons of ongoing operations. Wallace had participated in the Force XXI exercises and used insights gleaned from them in his command of U.S. Army troops in the 2003 invasion. However, by 2004 the army was no longer engaged in major combat operations there, but in stability operations.[119]

From the beginning, the insights of classic COIN principles guided army COIN doctrine in the aftermath of the Iraq invasion. Wallace enlisted Colonel Clinton Anker III and Lieutenant Colonel Jan Horvath to produce the 2004 interim manual to fill the gap between army training and stability operations in Iraq.[120] These two officers enlisted Thomas Marks, an expert in COIN, to write the first chapter. Marks had taught for twenty years at the Joint Special Operations University and advised governments from Colombia to India on COIN.[121] The new interim manual defined COIN as "protracted politico-military struggle designed to weaken government control and legitimacy while increasing insurgent control." "The support of the people," the manual continued, "is the center of gravity."[122] Subject matter experts within the army wrote the remaining chapters. Horvath also sent a draft to Kalev Sepp, who was teaching at the Naval Postgraduate School before going to Iraq to help William Hix with Casey's COIN study. Sepp and his students, some of whom had recently served in Iraq, criticized the manual for its lack of emphasis on using cultural divisions to play insurgent groups and tribes off one another. Horvath agreed with the criticisms and inserted some revisions that dealt with these concerns.[123]

In the end, Horvath thought the army rushed the manual to publication without resolving its faults. General Wallace agreed. However, the soldiers and marines in the field were demanding a doctrine to combat insurgencies. As Conrad Crane later said of COIN doctrine in this period, "This is not a doctrine that is being jammed down people's throats, this is doctrine that they are demanding."[124] Wallace also thought the manual would send a clear message that the army was facing an *insurgency* in Iraq and needed a *counterinsurgency* strategy there.[125]

In September 2005, the same month the idea for the "Hix Academy" was taking shape; the army made General David Petraeus commander of CAC. Petraeus was sent to Leavenworth on the orders of Army Chief Schoomaker. In October 2005, before departing for Leavenworth, Petraeus met Schoomaker at the Pentagon. Schoomaker told him that he planned to send Petraeus back to Iraq as commander to replace Casey. Schoomaker informed Petraeus that the CAC at Leavenworth had put together a COIN manual that needed revision. Schoomaker wanted Petraeus to make the manual his top priority and use it to influence the curriculum at Leavenworth. Schoomaker told Petraeus, "Go out there and shake up the Army, Dave!"[126]

Contrary to the expectations of civilian realist, bureaucratic, and cultural theories, the first steps on the road to a new COIN doctrine for the U.S. Army began within the army itself.[127] Wallace's efforts at the CAC were the first step in a doctrinal process that General David Petraeus, with the support of the Army Chief Schoomaker, would guide through the army doctrinal system. The result would be a COIN manual that drew on the tenets of classic COIN theorists and prioritized population security. Unbeknownst to General Casey, therefore, the army at home *was* trying to change, and it was doing so through doctrine and with the help of Rumsfeld's military maverick.

Armed with Army Chief Schoomaker's blessing, General Petraeus made the rewriting of the COIN manual his top priority upon arrival at Fort Leavenworth.[128] Hoping to follow Schoomaker's command to "shake up the Army," Petraeus "wanted his counterinsurgency doctrine to have the same impact as AirLand Battle."[129] He used the pages of *Military Review* to publish papers on the COIN lessons learned in Iraq and Afghanistan.[130] Along with Marine Lieutenant General James Mattis, Petraeus established the Army/Marine Corps Counterinsurgency Center at Leavenworth.[131] Both Petraeus and Mattis commanded units in Iraq, led their service's training and doctrine commands, and then returned to command in Iraq. Petraeus asked Dr. Conrad Crane, a history professor at the Army War College, to lead the writing team for the new manual.[132] He also enlisted Eliot Cohen, of the Johns Hopkins School of Advanced International Studies, and John Nagl to assist in crafting the manual. Continuing the close relationship with the marines on COIN, one army and one Marine Corps writer teamed up to draft each chapter. Crane then made revisions of the drafts before submitting them to Petraeus for review.[133] *Field Manual 3-24* was a joint army and Marine Corps manual. Consistent with the expectations of military realism, but contrary to organizational and military culture theories, senior army leaders again sacrificed organizational autonomy to develop doctrine suitable to the threat environment. In this way, Petraeus's COIN manual was similar in process to AirLand Battle, which entailed extensive interservice cooperation. After two months of work, Crane's writing team had prepared a draft manual.[134]

The revision under Petraeus borrowed "liberally" from the work of David Kilcullen, a noted Australian COIN expert.[135] His "Twenty-Eight Articles: Fundamentals of Company-Level Counterinsurgency" was reprinted in *Military Review* in the summer of 2006.[136] Prior to its reprinting in *Military Review*, Petraeus sent the "28 Articles" around the army via e-mail to assist commanders in Iraq and Afghanistan.[137] In 2007, when Petraeus was made commander of MNF-I, he brought Kilcullen to Baghdad to be his main COIN adviser. The 28 Articles argued against making killing and capturing insurgents the focus of COIN strategy. Commanders should engage insurgents, the Articles contended, only when they "got in the way." By focusing on the population, military forces could force the insurgents to react to their COIN plan and gain the initiative.[138] This conception of the initiative in COIN was a lesson Kilcullen learned from army officers like Lieutenant Colonel Chris Cavoli. Cavoli was battalion commander I-32 Infantry in Kunar Province in Afghanistan from 2005 to 2006. He wrote of this means of gaining the initiative: "This seeming 'defensive' orientation . . . is actually a great way to steal the initiative from the enemy. . . . [P]ersistent presence [that is, among the population], correctly done, can force the enemy to come to you on your terms—this is true initiative." When insurgents did respond, U.S. forces defeated them with their superior firepower.[139] Kilcullen made this the most important and final article: "Whatever else you do, keep the initiative." As Cavoli advocated, initiative did not always entail attacking. Rather, the counterinsurgent possessed the initiative when the insurgents were reacting to the COIN plan. Conversely, the counterinsurgent does not enjoy the initiative if he is reacting to the insurgents' plan by fighting an "enemy-centric" kill/capture COIN campaign.[140] Thus, although protecting the population appears defensive, it retains the initiative because it forces the enemy to fight on the COIN force's terms.

Like the Cold War U.S. Army, the army in this period reinterpreted one of its most cherished concepts, initiative, to devise a doctrine that could address the threats it faced. This is especially important to note because traditionally army officers argued that only offensive actions seized the initiative. Offensive operations appeal to both army bureaucrats and cultural guardians, so such a reinterpretation of the initiative is unexpected from these perspectives. Not so for military realism, which expects just such doctrinal flexibility in the face of a changing threat environment.

The draft manual also drew heavily on the work of David Galula, a French officer who fought insurgencies in Indochina and Algeria. Although written in 1964, his work *Counterinsurgency Warfare* seemed to speak directly to the problems confronting the army in Iraq. Galula argued that the "reflexes and decisions" of the conventionally trained soldier were counterproductive in COIN. As Casey and Wallace observed in Iraq, Galula argued that conventionally trained troops were ill equipped for COIN. For instance, not firing back with all available means when fired upon is a grave error in conventional warfare, Galula observed, but a best practice in COIN. In COIN, "the rule is to apply the minimum of fire." Galula also advised that encouraging soldiers to gauge their success by their ability to "kill or capture the largest number of enemies . . . may well be disastrous in counterinsurgency warfare."[141] Conventional soldiers must also overcome their distaste for politics because "in counterinsurgency warfare, the soldier's job is to help win the support of the population, and in so doing, he has to engage in practical politics." In October

2006, a special COIN issue of *Military Review* singled out Galula's observations and primed the army for the publication of *Field Manual 3-24* two months later.[142]

Petraeus made sure that the drafting of the new manual received extensive public attention. In February 2006, Fort Leavenworth and the Carr Center for Human Rights at Harvard, directed by Sarah Sewall, cosponsored a conference at Leavenworth to discuss a draft of the new manual. Present at the conference were academics, public intellectuals, journalists, congressional staffers, and military historians.[143] Six months after briefing Casey on the worrying COIN trends in Iraq, Kalev Sepp was at the conference.[144] David Kilcullen was also present, though news of the Samara bombing forced him to leave early for Baghdad.[145] By the date of the conference, the central aspects of the manual were already in place. Petraeus said later that the purpose of the conference was to "convince 95 percent of the rational thinkers" about the content of the manual.[146] There was no intention of drastically changing its content based on the input of the participants. Rather, this gathering would make the participants advocates of the COIN manual in the public square. Thomas Marks, author of the first chapter of the 2004 interim COIN manual, best expressed the role of the conference in the doctrinal process. "This cake was already baked," Marks remarked. "We were the icing."[147]

After minor revisions based on the February conference, the draft manual had to go through the approval process by the different commands in the army. These commands had the authority to stop the presses if they disapproved of the manual's content. During this process, Petraeus, like Generals Starry and Franks, sought consensus. As he said, "Inclusion is generally the appropriate course of action."[148] Nevertheless, the Army Intelligence Center at Fort Huachuca threatened to send the drafters of the manual back to the drawing board. Upon hearing this, Chief of Staff Schoomaker made it clear to Petraeus that this was out of the question. The manual was already behind schedule, and the army needed it to fight the wars in Iraq and Afghanistan. In the end, the army settled the dispute, and the manual went forward with only minor revisions.[149]

While it is true that the doctrinal process was partly unconventional, it was largely an internal army process. For instance, the role that outside intellectuals played in the shaping of the manual has been overstated.[150] Long argues that *Field Manual 3-24* was heavily influenced by "academics." However, as support he cites an article authored by Eliot Cohen, Conrad Crane, Jon Horvath, and John Nagl, only the first of which is a conventional academic.[151] The other three were present or former army officers, often with doctorates to be fair. Horvath was a chief author of the 2004 interim COIN manual. Not surprisingly, then, as Long notes, "the basic substance remain[ed] similar."[152] The impetus to revise the manual came from within the army, and from the very top, Army Chief of Staff Schoomaker. The 2006 Leavenworth conference brought some intellectuals from outside of the military on board, but they did not drive or hinder the process. Like the impetus for change, the main obstacles to the publication of the manual were within the army. Senior officers overcame these internal disputes to address the threat environment they confronted. They did so even when the doctrine to be adopted, COIN, was contrary to the army's supposed parochial interests and civilian strategy and initiatives.

It is important to comment here on the role of General Petraeus in the doctrinal process. A number of commentators who have written on the development of the 2006 COIN manual overlook the 2004 manual. Moreover, they portray General Petraeus as a voice crying out in a bureaucratic wilderness. In short, Petraeus is often portrayed as a military maverick who overcame the bureaucratic and cultural inclinations of the institutional army to develop the COIN manual.[153] Based on the broader context provided above, the evidence does not support this portrayal. General Petraeus had the support of the chief of staff of the army and other senior officers such as General Wallace, who saw the development of the COIN manual as a top priority for the army. Throughout his career, Petraeus had often supported the initiatives and views of the institutional army. Recall, for instance, his 1980s article that argued that the COIN forces of the 1980s, LIDs, be used as a force multiplier for the nuclear-conventional defense of Europe, a position advocated by General DePuy.[154] Others have pointed to Petraeus's central role in the writing of the manual as unique.[155] However, as previous chapters have shown, senior army officers have often taken a very central role in the development of doctrine. While Thomas Ricks might be right that manuals are sometimes "written by two tired majors laboring in a basement somewhere in Fort Leavenworth," senior army leaders, such as DePuy, Starry, Sullivan, Franks, and Schoomaker, were the intellectual fathers of what those tired majors wrote. These senior leaders approved what they wrote and thought sound doctrine was vital to the army.[156] This contradicts the view that *Field Manual 3-24* was a bottom-up innovation that bypassed a sluggish army institution.[157] General Petraeus was only one link in the chain of doctrinal innovation. While it does not provide as compelling a narrative as a renegade general bucking the system, this more modest assessment seems more consistent with the evidence.

Content of Field Manual 3-24, Counterinsurgency

To determine the degree of influence of *Field Manual 3-24* on *Operations 2008* it is necessary to summarize its content in brief. According to the new COIN manual, the centerpiece of any COIN campaign was the securing of the population. The goal of a COIN campaign was legitimacy. Both the insurgents and the counterinsurgents were struggling for recognition by the people of their legitimate authority. COIN campaigns without such a focus would fail. All successful COIN campaigns accomplish five goals: restore government legitimacy, control one area, retain population centers, expand control, and employ information operations to influence the population and discredit the insurgency.[158]

The manual emphasized that conventional military forces had to turn away from their SOPs and adapt to the specific circumstances of the COIN environment.[159] Conventional military operations alone could not prevail. A combination of civilian and military activities was required.[160] The focus was on the population's needs: political, economic, and social programs were primary. Therefore, a COIN campaign had to include building indigenous security forces, essential services, improving governance, and economic development.[161] However, as Peter Mansoor, Petraeus's executive officer during the surge and now professor of military history at Ohio State University, noted, there could also be "plenty of killing."[162] Although much emphasis is placed on the "hearts-and-minds" aspect of COIN, "in the end," Mansoor observed, "*control* of the population is far more important than winning its hearts and minds, for effective control of the people isolates the insurgents from their support base."[163] Despite the violent aspects of COIN, *Field Manual 3-24* stressed that the majority of activities in COIN were nonmilitary in nature.

The manual reinterpreted concepts associated with traditional conventional operations to suit the COIN environment. For instance, it argued that if military forces remained in their compounds and out of contact with the populace, they had ceded the *initiative* to the enemy.[164] The goal, as Kilcullen argued, was to seize the initiative by working among the population and forcing the enemy to react to the COIN plan. Here a classic concept of conventional war fighting, initiative, was adapted to COIN operations. This conceptual move was also important because the traditional view of initiative, requiring offensive operations against the enemy, would lead to the aggressive use of conventional firepower. In its discussion of leadership and ethics in COIN, the manual emphasizes repeatedly that the indiscriminate use of force is counterproductive. While the use of firepower can increase security, the collateral damage it causes alienates the population and aids insurgent recruiting by making the COIN force appear illegitimate.[165]

The longest chapter in the manual was on intelligence. The manual advocated that commanders get to know the people as well as the insurgents. The protection of the population would be the key to gaining the intelligence necessary to find the insurgents hiding in their midst.[166] Intelligence about the tribal and social networks in which the counterinsurgent will be operating was key. Units should gather this intelligence prior to deployment. Knowing the sociocultural aspects of the population enables the counterinsurgent to influence the population and bolster the legitimacy of the host-nation government.

Developing host-nation security forces was also a key task according to the manual.[167] These forces would be responsible for the long-term security of the populace. It was important that the counterinsurgent force avoid "mirror imaging," that is, making the indigenous security forces look like the U.S. Army, for instance. Rather, local forces must be tailored to local conditions. The primary host-nation force in COIN is the police. In the end, only viable host-nation security forces could win the fight against the insurgents. Outside actors could only assist.[168]

In its content, the manual reflected the principles of COIN theorizing based on population security. These ideas had their roots in the COIN theorists of the 1960s. The COIN manual echoed many of the COIN ideas that appeared in 1960s *Operations* manuals. It also included a number of insights garnered from recent COIN experience in Iraq and Afghanistan. Foremost among these was a new understanding of the concept of initiative. This new COIN manual and its authors would play an important role in the development of a new strategy for Iraq.

The Surge Decision and Military Threat Assessment

Senior army leaders did not oppose developing a COIN doctrine or implementing it in Iraq. In fact, the army chief of staff, General Schoomaker, led a campaign within the army to capture the COIN lessons of Iraq and Afghanistan, shape them into doctrine, and then have them implemented there. However, this did not mean that senior army leaders were in favor of the surge of U.S. troops into Iraq in 2007. General Schoomaker pointed out that the five Brigade Combat Teams that were needed to carry out the surge represented the U.S. strategic reserve and that to send them would endanger the United States by leaving it unprepared for any other contingency.[169]

Schoomaker was not in favor of increasing U.S. troop presence in Iraq but did think that a transition to a COIN campaign there was desirable. On December 13, 2006, Chairman of the Joint Chiefs of Staff Peter Pace presented the Chiefs' advice on Iraq strategy to President Bush. Pace argued that the United States should transition to a COIN strategy in Iraq and to an advisory role. Michael Vickers, formerly of the Special Forces, had already presented this view to President Bush in May and June 2006.[170] Pace thought the transition made sense, even if it meant doing so, as Vickers had put it, "while the insurgency is still raging."[171] It was unnecessary to use the U.S. strategic reserve to defeat the Iraqi insurgency because the United States could accomplish this goal through a long-term COIN strategy.[172] In addition, without a strategic reserve the United States would be vulnerable to other more dangerous threats. In the same meeting, Schoomaker said, "I am concerned about our lack of capacity to deal with any other threats in the world. Building forces takes time. Investing all our eggs in Iraq is a big risk."[173] In another meeting, Schoomaker advised, "We need to look at our strategic depth for handling other threats."[174] Moreover, like Vickers, Schoomaker doubted that a surge of U.S. troops into Iraq would "transform the situation."[175] In the December 13, 2006, meeting with the Joint Chiefs and President Bush, Schoomaker stated directly that he disagreed with the president's decision to surge additional troops into Iraq.[176] Nevertheless, President Bush argued that his priority was to win the war in Iraq and that he would not hold back a surge to deal with hypothetical threats.[177] Cheney, who was also present, thought that Schoomaker was the most persuasive advocate of the JCS's views in the meeting, but he dismissed the JCS's advice because the institutional interests of their services motivated them and they were not in the "war-fighting business" anymore.[178] In essence, Cheney was using a bureaucratic argument to dismiss the Joint Chiefs' advice on the surge.

All this is to show that it was possible for Schoomaker to be in favor of developing a COIN doctrine for the army and for Iraq, while also being opposed to a surge of U.S. troops to carry out that COIN strategy. Such a surge endangered the ability of the United States to respond to other possible crises, for which its strategic reserve would be required. While this may not represent the best strategic reasoning under the circumstances, it is consistent with the military realist perspective. Senior army leaders were in favor of dealing with the range of threats in the international system. Making the army capable of fighting an effective COIN campaign in Iraq was an essential part of addressing the contemporary threat environment. Therefore, the army overcame cultural, bureaucratic, and civilian obstacles and designed a COIN doctrine based on population security. However, Schoomaker was opposed to sending five BCTs to Iraq because this would exhaust the U.S. strategic reserve, making it incapable of dealing with more dangerous threats. This assessment of the limits of U.S. forces was not a gambit to avoid an unconventional COIN campaign, as alternative theories would argue, but was based on a broader assessment of the limits of U.S. capabilities. This became clear in the months and years that followed. After Robert Gates became secretary of defense and as the situation in Afghanistan deteriorated, commanders there began asking for additional troops. Gates learned that the army was indeed unable to provide them due to the surge in Iraq.[179] Schoomaker's opposition to the surge was not because it would employ a COIN strategy, which he advocated early on, but because it would make the army incapable of responding to other threats.

A number of analysts have written on the effectiveness of the surge in reducing violence in Iraq. Was it the surge or the "Anbar Awakening" that brought down the violence?[180] This debate will continue. However, the above analysis shows that the COIN doctrine that those additional U.S. troops employed was not the result of civilian intervention in the army. On the contrary, the army began developing COIN doctrine for Iraq as early as 2004, when civilian officials were still wedded to a strategy of handover and refused to call the violence an insurgency. If COIN doctrine did play a central role in the decline of violence in Iraq,[181] it was not due to the intervention of civilian leaders in their military bureaucracies. On November 28, 2005, two months after Petraeus had taken command at Fort Leavenworth, the Department of Defense issued Directive 3000.05, which directed that "stability operations" were to be made a core mission of the U.S. military.[182] Some point to this directive to explain subsequent changes in the army.[183] As already shown above, however, the army's interest in COIN and stability operations predated the Department of Defense's directive. In fact, since the 1990s, army doctrine had been focusing more and more on stability operations. Next, we assess whether that COIN doctrine would influence the army beyond the battlefield.

Development and Content of *Operations 2008*

While this section examines the three key areas of the 2008 *Operations* manual, there is a particular focus on the treatment of COIN therein. Because it is contrary to parochial interests, army bureaucrats and cultural guardians should resist attempts to institutionalize COIN doctrine in their main war-fighting manual. Military realism, on the other hand, sees such a codification as consistent with the increased import of stability operations inaugurated in post–Cold War army doctrine. The eventual insurgencies in Afghanistan and Iraq would seem to confirm the wisdom of including such unconventional conflicts in the *Operations* manual. *Field Manual 3-0, Operations 2008* captured important lessons from the army's COIN experience in Iraq and Afghanistan and made COIN a major component of army keystone doctrine.

The process of developing a replacement for *Operations 2001* began with a series of concept papers sent out by the army for comment prior to the 2005 Defense Department Directive 3000.05. After overseeing the writing of the interim COIN manual at the CAC, General Wallace took command of TRADOC. Subsequently, on the orders of Wallace, Lieutenant General William B. Caldwell IV established a writing team headed by Lieutenant Colonel Steve Leonard.[184] Despite this early start, the new manual was not published until February 28, 2008, because the COIN manual had taken doctrinal priority. *Operations 2008* called itself "a revolutionary departure from past doctrine." However, this was an overstatement. As Kretchik points out, the manual was *both* revolutionary and evolutionary.[185] This dual character is clear from General Wallace's description of the manual in its foreword: "[Operations 2008] describes an operational concept where commanders employ offensive, defensive, and stability or civil support operations simultaneously as part of an interdependent joint force to seize, retain, and exploit the initiative, accepting prudent risk to create opportunities to achieve decisive results . . . this edition will take us into the 21st century urban battlefields among the people without losing our capabilities to dominate the higher conventional end of the spectrum of conflict."[186]

Comparing this description of army doctrine with *Operations 1993* and *2001*, it is evident that the 2008 manual was not a revolution in army doctrine. For instance, *Operations 1993* implied the combination of offense, defense, and stability and support operations, and the acronym *ODSS* originated in *Operations 2001*, which the army published prior to 9/11. Moreover, as made clear throughout this work, Wallace's emphasis on the joint character of army missions and the initiative were also central to the earlier manuals. Nevertheless, *Operations 2008* was the culmination of the doctrinal initiatives begun in *Operations 1993* and *2001*. This is not to say the manual did not have revolutionary elements. Specifically, the influence of the new COIN manual was evident throughout the new edition.[187] For instance, Wallace's mention of "battlefields among the people" is a recognition of the COIN experience in Afghanistan and Iraq. However, in keeping with a military realist perspective, the same passage keeps the "higher conventional end of the spectrum of conflict" in view.

Conventional and Nuclear Forces in Operations 2008

Like its post–Cold War predecessors, the 2008 edition did not integrate nuclear weapons into the doctrine for its conventional forces, but focused on force protection. *Operations 2008* was concerned only with how best to protect army forces from nuclear attack. Reflecting its post-9/11 context, the manual discussed the danger of nuclear proliferation to terrorist groups and the army role in the aftermath of a nuclear terrorist attack on the United States.[188] Otherwise, the 2008 manual followed the lead of the two previous manuals and barely mentioned nuclear weapons.

The main mission of the U.S. Army's conventional forces remained power projection as part of a joint U.S. military team.[189] However, what such operations would look like had changed. *Operations 2008* argued that rapid, decisive operations, "however desirable, are the exception."[190] When missions require the holding of terrain and control of populations, as in Afghanistan and Iraq, there was also a requirement for sustaining "protracted" campaigns.[191] In an obvious reference to those two campaigns, the 2008 manual noted, "Winning battles and engagements is important but alone may not be decisive. Shaping civil conditions (in concert with civilian organizations, civil authorities, and multinational forces) is just as important to campaign success." In 2008 the army needed to unify its combat and noncombat, or lethal and nonlethal, capabilities even more. "In many joint operations," the manual continued, "stability or civil support are often more important than the offense and defense."[192]

As drastic as it might seem, this assessment of the army's mission was not revolutionary. *Operations 1993* and *2001* sought to prepare army units for situations other than conventional combat operations. They included chapters on stability operations and gave them their own set of guiding principles. The traditional principles of war, among them the offense, were ill-suited to these types of operations and might be counterproductive. Instead, both the 1993 and 2001 manuals argued, principles of restraint in firepower and legitimacy were more important to success in stability operations. The 2008 manual did recognize its lineage. "Full spectrum operations—simultaneous offensive, defensive, and stability or civil support operations—is the primary theme of this manual. This continues a major shift in Army doctrine that began with FM 3-0 (2001)." The writers of *Operations 2008* also recognized that this was a progression from *Operations 1993*. However, the new edition argued, "Stability and civil support operations cannot be something that the Army conducts in 'other than war' operations."[193] Though this implicit criticism of OOTW in *Operations 1993* does not accurately represent the content of that earlier manual. The 1993 manual argued that stability operations could occur at all levels of the spectrum of conflict but were most prominent in OOTW. As that first post–Cold War manual pointed out, OOTW operations in the Gulf War followed close behind the conventional phase of that war. Nor did *Operations 1993* think that these operations were someone else's responsibility. It argued that army units were "extremely well-suited" in "skills and staying power" to provide "humanitarian assistance and support the social needs of the civilian population," "utilities and other civil affairs."[194] Therefore, although *Operations 2008* more clearly unified combat and stability operations, the writers of the earlier post–Cold War manuals recognized the need for this unity. It appears that the authors of the 2008 manual thought their concept of the army's mission was more revolutionary than it was.

In terms of conventional combat, *Operations 2008* held on to the central concepts expressed in *Operations 1993* and *2001*. It argued that army forces must be prepared for "full spectrum operations."[195] Commanders succeeded in these operations by employing combined arms enhanced by advanced communications, battlefield intelligence, and precision-strike capabilities. To make such operations possible, however, the army had to work hand in glove with the other services, where much of the precision strike capability resided. In addition, *Operations 2008* kept the novel interpretation of the principle of mass introduced by *Operations 1993*, arguing that decisive results could be achieved through the massing of the "*effects*" of "combat power," rather than the massing of forces.[196] Commanders massed effects most successfully when actions were "synchronized" to deliver the most shock in the enemy, resulting in his disintegration.[197] Both post–Cold War manuals preserved the concept of synchronization at the tactical and operational level that originated in Air-Land Battle doctrine. *Operations 2008* retained this concept and, like AirLand Battle, advocated synchronization of attacks through the whole depth of the enemy to produce incapacitation.[198] The new lighter modular force would facilitate these types of operations. The manual included a thirteen-page appendix explaining the new force structure.[199]

Operations 2008 also drew important combat lessons from recent operations in Iraq, including those during the surge. There is a tendency to emphasize the hearts-and-minds aspect of COIN in Iraq and downplay the role played by conventional weapons and forces. However, during the surge in 2007, more U.S. forces were killed in action than in any other year of the war, 961 in total. At the same time, U.S. Army regular units and Special Forces killed more insurgents in 2007, at least 7,400, than in any previous year.[200] This was because, in addition to securing the population, MNF-I had gone on the offensive against insurgents and militias. Far from focusing exclusively on hearts and minds and nation-building, COIN operations during the surge were highly offensive and leveraged the conventional firepower of the U.S. military. For instance, in the battle for Basra, drones identified Jaish al-Mahdi positions and then destroyed them with standoff missiles.[201] Operations in Iraq were actually a combination of limited conventional engagements, supported by some RMA technologies, and stability operations. These operations were in effect a mix of ODSS, and *Operations 2008* reflected their lessons.

The contention here, however, is not that in Iraq the U.S. Army fielded its transformed force and that this force was successful against insurgents. Army commanders engaged in the fighting in Iraq lamented their lack of situational awareness, an essential component of transformation.[202] While the army in Iraq was fighting, the army at home was learning that the technologies needed to actualize the vision of a fully transformed force were likely out of reach, both in terms of cost effectiveness and technological feasibility.[203] In 2009 the multiple problems with the Manned Ground Vehicle as part of the Future Combat System led Secretary of Defense Gates to cancel the MGV, the heart of the lighter power-projection army.[204] Moreover, the vulnerability of light vehicles, like the Stryker armored vehicle, to rocket-propelled grenades and improvised explosive devices demonstrated the limits of lighter forces in combat zones.[205] The army in Iraq and at home was coming to grips with the fact that replacing mass with information may not be possible. The army had overcome and bypassed significant bureaucratic and cultural obstacles to change its doctrine and organization. The army's drive to make its forces globally deployable in service of its new post–Cold War missions had introduced vulnerabilities into that force. In this case, the military realist drive to change the army to address the most dangerous threats had significant negative effects on ongoing military operations. The army would try to address these issues in future doctrine. However, this realization had not sunk in by the time the army penned *Operations 2008*.

In general, therefore, when it came to conventional and nuclear forces, *Operations 2008* did not represent a core change in army doctrine. Nuclear weapons continued to play a minor role. The disappearance of the Soviet threat and its overwhelming capacity to escalate the use of force eliminated the need to integrate conventional and tactical nuclear forces. The result in all three post–Cold War manuals, including the 2008 edition, was a focus on conventional over nuclear forces.

Despite significant continuity, however, *Operations 2008* did place increased emphasis on the need for conventional forces to prepare to transition from combat operations to stability operations. If commanders could master this transition, they could avoid unstable postconflict situations like Iraq and Afghanistan—although experience in both of those theaters also showed that in stability operations where the level of violence was high, conventional forces and weapons could play an important role. Drawing on the experience of the battle of Mogadishu, *Operations 1993* and *2001* had pointed out that stability operations could often involve high levels of violence. Nowhere was this more evident than in postinvasion Afghanistan and Iraq. U.S. Army conventional forces would continue to leverage America's technological edge in conventional weapons as part of a joint U.S. military team. They would do so through concepts such as initiative, synchronization, and attack through the whole depth of the enemy. After 2008, as I point out in the concluding chapter, the vocabulary would change from Full-Spectrum Operations to Unified Land Operations (ULO), but the actual content of those concepts was very similar. The continuity between immediate post–Cold War doctrine and the doctrine that emerged after a decade of fighting in Iraq and Afghanistan is in part a testament to the prescience of senior army leaders in assessing the complex character of the threats after the Cold War. Immediate post–Cold War doctrine was not infallible, but it laid a doctrinal foundation on which the army could build.

Offense versus Defensive in Operations 2008

In the aftermath of 9/11, the U.S. Army had engaged in two wars involving offensive power projection, the main mission it had identified for itself after the Cold War. However, contrary to the expectations of bureaucracy and military culture, *Operations 2008* did not focus on the rapid success of these offensive operations. If anything, it focused on their limits. The central theme of *Operations 2008* was the unity of offense, defense, and stability and support operations. In its preface, *Operations 2008* emphasized that chapter 3, "Full Spectrum Operations," was "the most important chapter in the book."[206] This chapter set out the unity of ODSS. In order to underline the unification of ODSS operations, the authors of *Operations 2008* made a number of structural changes to the manual. Despite significant continuity with its post–Cold War predecessors, *Operations 2008* reverted to the practice of placing the principles of war in an appendix, rather than at the very beginning of the manual. The appendix also included the three additional principles for stability operations from the 1993 and 2001 editions: perseverance, legitimacy, and restraint.[207] This made sense, given that the principles of war tended to characterize military operations as only a mix of offense and defense, while the central theme of the 2008 manual was the unification of offense, defense, *and* stability and support operations. Nor did *Operations 2008* include separate chapters for offense, defense, and stability operations, a significant departure from previous manuals. Instead, the writers discussed all three together as part of the "continuum" of Full-Spectrum Operations.[208] These two structural changes would help unify ODSS in the manual and in army thinking about operations. Therefore, although the unification of ODSS originated in *Operations 2001*, *Operations 2008* made this unity much more explicit in army doctrine.

Despite these structural changes, *Operations 2008* included a now familiar assessment of the offense. Offense was "the decisive element of full spectrum operations." Offense was the most direct means of seizing the initiative because it compelled "the enemy to react." The pressure of continuous offensive operations could cause a "cycle of deterioration" that disintegrated the coherence of the enemy force. The manual used the invasion of Iraq in 2003 as an example of this concept in action.[209] However, *Operations 2008* argued that attacking was not the only way to gain the initiative. Commanders could seize the initiative in offense, defense, and stability operations so long as the enemy was reacting to the commander's plan, rather than vice versa. "Initiative gives all operations the spirit, if not the form, of the offense. It originates in the principle of the offensive. The principle of the offensive is not just about attacking."[210] This practice of discussing the initiative in offense, defense, and stability operations was not new. AirLand Battle too discussed of the "spirit of the offense" while emphasizing the limits of offensive operations. *Operations 2008* was very explicit about its departure from traditional views of the offense. Highlighting the unity of ODSS, *Operations 2008* noted that commanders could use offensive operations to create "a secure environment for stability operations."[211] MNF-I offensives during the surge, such as Phantom Thunder, were prime examples of this synergy between offensive action and stability operations. Offensive actions represented the "clear" phase of "clear, hold, build."

However, the 2008 manual also preserved the expanded purposes of the defense established by Cold War army manuals. Defensive operations were not, as the principles of war claimed, just a temporary expedient. Commanders could use defensive operations to "defeat attacks, destroying as much of the attacking enemy as possible." Well-planned defensive operations could also set favorable conditions for a decisive counterattack, as the attacking force lost its momentum and became vulnerable.[212] The transition to counterattack was necessary because "defeating an enemy at any level sooner or later requires shifting to the offense."[213] Focusing again on the unity of ODSS, commanders could use defensive operations to "establish a shield behind which stability operations can progress."[214] This was the "hold" phase of "clear, hold, build." The forming of combat outposts throughout Baghdad during the surge was a concrete example of this combination of defensive and stability operations. In this case, army units would select a building within a Baghdad neighborhood, occupy it, and then hold the building against insurgent counterattacks. Once established in this defensive position, the army unit and its Iraqi counterpart would begin COIN operations in the area, engaging in saturation patrolling, local intelligence gathering, and civic action.[215] Mansoor saw this relationship play out on the ground in Iraq. "Counterinsurgency warfare," Mansoor wrote, in a quote he could have taken directly from the pages of *Operations 2008*, "is a mixture of offensive, defensive, and stability operations."[216] *Operations 2008* constantly reinforced the unity of offense, defense, and stability operations, a unity army commanders were coming to appreciate through ongoing COIN operations.

Both *Operations 1993* and *2001* sought to make stability operations a key part of army doctrine. *Operations 2008* continued and was the culmination of this doctrinal trend. Here it was even more explicit than its predecessors. "In many joint operations," *Operations 2008* stated, "stability or civil support are often more important than the offense and defense."[217] Decisive operations often required a combination of offensive and stability operations. COIN campaigns "usually combine offensive and stability tasks to achieve decisive results."[218] In short, the "clear" and "hold" phases would be irrelevant without the "build" phase provided by stability and civil support operations. The more violent character of stability operations in Iraq and Afghanistan, after rapid conventional victories, highlighted this interplay between combat and stability operations.

Through its structure and discussions of offense and defense, *Operations 2008* argued that army commanders had to unify offensive, defensive, and stability operations to achieve truly decisive results. Recent experience reinforced the limits of offense and the need to unify ODSS. The U.S. military had rapidly defeated the Iraqi state in 2003 but was then embroiled in a protracted counterinsurgency campaign. However, these recent experiences were not the root cause of the doctrinal drive to unify ODSS. As shown in the previous chapter, in the uncertain post–Cold War threat environment, senior army leaders recognized that stability operations would be part of their organization's future. The bloody postconflict phases in Afghanistan and Iraq, despite the initial success of rapid, offensive operations, reinforced the import of stability operations to accomplishing the U.S. Army's missions. The structure and content of *Operations 2008* made more explicit the necessary unity of ODSS, but the push toward this unity began after the Cold War. Senior army officers drove this doctrinal innovation in response to an uncertain threat environment. What is more, this innovation is contrary to the supposed bureaucratic benefits of offensive doctrine and the U.S. Army's cultural focus on decisive offensive operations.

COIN Doctrine and Forces in Operations 2008

As should be clear already, *Operations 2008* referred often to insurgency and counterinsurgency. The 2008 manual included *eighty* references to "insurgency," "insurgent," "counterinsurgency," or "counterinsurgent," as opposed to only fifteen and thirty in *Operations 1993* and *2001*, respectively. The term *insurgency* even appeared in the spectrum of conflict. The low end of the spectrum of conflict was "stable peace," which could escalate into "unstable peace," which itself could escalate further to "insurgency," and violence peaked in "general war."[219] On the spectrum of conflict, insurgency replaced what *Operations 1993* and *2001* had termed *operations other than war* and *military operations other than war*, respectively. As the analysis below shows, these many references to insurgency and COIN were not just for public consumption, but reflected an increased focus on COIN in army doctrine and recent operational experience.

Operations 2008 drew heavily on the experience of COIN in Iraq and Afghanistan and the insights of the interim COIN manual and *Field Manual 3-24*. This should hardly be surprising given that General Wallace was in charge of TRADOC while it developed the new *Operations* manual. Wallace had been in command of CAC when he ordered the writing of the interim COIN manual before the arrival of Petraeus and well before the public ferment over COIN had begun. As mentioned previously, Wallace was inspired to promulgate a COIN manual by the incompatibility between army conventional training and stability operations in Iraq. While Petraeus did much to make COIN acceptable inside and outside of the army, Wallace ensured it made its way into the army's most important doctrine.

Operations 1993 and *2001* had used the terms *OOTW* and *stability operations* to designate a broad range of missions, from peacekeeping and humanitarian assistance to counterdrug operations. In *Operations 2008*, however, *stability operations* were synonymous with *COIN*. There were five tasks in stability operations: civil security, civil control, restoring essential services, support of local governance, and support of economic development.[220] This description of stability operations and these five tasks represent the job description of the counterinsurgent, according to classic COIN theorists and *Field Manual 3-24*. Stability operations occurred simultaneously with offensive and defensive operations and were not simply what happened after combat operations.[221] In these operations, nonlethal means were as important as lethal means.[222] Moreover, force misused could be dangerous. "Commanders at every level emphasize that in stability operations, violence not precisely applied is counterproductive."[223] The new manual also emphasized the importance of interagency cooperation.[224] The army had to operate effectively with civilian organizations because it was fighting in the midst of civilian populations.

The clearest example of the influence of *Field Manual 3-24, Counterinsurgency* was the discussion of initiative in stability operations. "In stability and civil support operations," the 2008 manual noted, "initiative is about improving civil conditions and applying combat power to prevent the situation from deteriorating." Commanders can seize the initiative through programs that "ensure effective governance," "promote social well-being," and "improve public safety." "Stability operations must maintain the initiative by pursing objectives that resolve the causes of instability." Moreover, these operations could not "succeed if they only react to enemy initiatives."[225] "An enemy insurgent," *Operations 2008* continued, "cannot allow stability efforts to succeed without serious consequences and must react." By making the population and its needs the focus of operations, rather than the enemy, the commander forces the insurgent enemy to react and thereby gains the initiative.[226] This is exactly the same conception of the initiative in COIN as expressed by Lieutenant Colonel Cavoli in Kunar Province, by Kilcullen in his "Twenty-Eight Articles," by *Field Manual 3-24*, and subsequently by General Petraeus in his COIN Guidance to MNF-I during the Surge.[227]

As important as COIN was in the new manual, this was a natural progression from *Operations 1993* and *2001*. These two post–Cold War manuals had introduced the principles of stability operations because, according to senior army leaders, applying the principles of war was not suitable in stability operations. The principles of stability operations were perseverance, legitimacy, and restraint. Recall that Casey's COIN academy, McMaster's COIN plan, the 2004 interim COIN manual, and *Field Manual 3-24* all argued that COIN was a battle for "legitimacy." *Operations 2008* retained these principles, stating that "perseverance, legitimacy, and restraint are vital considerations in stability and civil support operations."[228] The manual also listed the principles of stability operations in the same appendix as the principles of war. Again, *Operations 2008* was expanding upon concepts originally developed in *Operations 1993* and *2001*. However, it brought to these concepts the concrete COIN experience from Iraq and Afghanistan. The violence of these operations reinforced the need for close integration between combat and stability operations.

Operations 2008 also argued that regular army units had to become proficient in COIN operations. The first manual of the post–Cold War had also appreciated this reality. *Operations 1993* argued, "Army forces are extremely well-suited" to stability operations because of their capacity to control populations and restore essential services after conflict.[229] *Operations 2008* argued that not only *could* the army train its units for such operations, but it *should*. With proper training, conventional soldiers were capable of conducting stability and civil-support operations.[230] Army doctrine did not dismiss COIN capabilities as a lesser-included case covered by conventional training, a prejudice its critics accused it of in Vietnam and after. As *Operations 2008* noted, although training for combat operations developed some characteristics necessary "to address the ambiguities and complexities inherent" in stability operations, "operational experience demonstrates that forces trained exclusively for offensive and defensive tasks are not as proficient at stability tasks as those trained specifically for stability." This deficiency in army training led General Wallace to commission the 2004 interim COIN manual and led General Casey to establish the Hix COIN Academy in Iraq. Regular forces require dedicated stability operations and COIN training to be effective. However, *Operations 2008* did argue that units deployed in protracted stability operations needed "intensive training to regain proficiency in . . . combat operations."[231] The new manual argued that there was an incompatibility between being prepared for COIN and being prepared for major combat operations. COIN experts like Galula had long recognized this incompatibility. However, the army could address this issue with proper training.

Operations 2008 made the COIN mission a priority for the army. Its unification of ODSS through both its structure and content made this clear. However, this increased focus on stability operations and COIN was not a revelation. Rather, *Operations 2008* was continuing a trend established by *Operations 1993*, expanded in *Operations 2001*, and made most explicit in its own pages. In short, as Rosen wrote of peacetime innovations in British air defense before World War II, these two post–Cold War manuals "laid a sound intellectual foundation"[232] on which later army doctrine and operations built. As Brigadier General David Fastabend, who wrote parts of *Operations 2001*, nicely summarized, "In 1993, we introduced military operations other than war, and then we introduced the idea of full-spectrum operations. From '97 to 2001, we introduced the ideas that operations are a seamless combination of offense, defense, stability and support."[233] *Operations 2008* drew on the lessons of Iraq and Afghanistan and the insights of COIN doctrine to reinforce this doctrinal trajectory.

Conclusion

Even after the surprise attacks of September 11, 2001, the United States remained an unrivaled international superpower. In the absence of a superpower rival, military realism expects senior military leaders to focus on protecting the vital material interests of the state, the source of its material strength. As army leaders recognized at the end of the Cold War, for the United States protecting such interests required power projection. In the years following 9/11, power projection would remain the mission at the core of army doctrine and civilian leaders would call on the army to execute two expeditionary wars. However, after initial, rapid success, both war zones festered into protracted insurgencies. The progress of these two conflicts exposed weaknesses in the army's post–Cold War doctrine. At the same time, however, these conflicts highlighted the wisdom of other doctrinal initiatives sparked by the end of the Cold War.

This period also witnessed a civilian initiative to transform the conventional forces of the U.S. Army to facilitate the military strategy of the new administration. George W. Bush came into the presidency with a different view of the U.S. military from his predecessor.[234] He brought Donald Rumsfeld into the Pentagon to transform the US military to enable this new strategy. In the subsequent wars in Afghanistan and the early phase of the Iraq War, Rumsfeld's transformation agenda was tested in combat and, according to the secretary of defense, passed with flying colors.[235] However, the development of army doctrine in the previous and present chapters shows that the transformation agenda, which Rumsfeld was supposedly imposing on the army, was of the army's own design. Since the early 1990s, army leadership had recognized that the post–Cold War mission would be power projection and leveraging technological advancements would be a key part of accomplishing this mission. Many of Rumsfeld's initiatives were in process when he arrived at the Pentagon. Much like Kennedy and McNamara, the innovations Rumsfeld adopted as his own actually originated within the army. After the Cold War, the U.S. Army was developing a mode of operations that recognized the irrelevance of its heavy Cold War forces and the cultural finest hour they represented. This early embrace of transformation is also surprising from a bureaucratic perspective. Army bureaucrats should have favored continuity with Cold War doctrine and organization instead of the major changes required by transformation. The army also continued to undermine its own bureaucratic autonomy. It asserted that it could not accomplish its main mission without the assistance of the other services. Autonomy was not as paramount as a bureaucratic perspective might anticipate. In addition, contrary to civilian realism, Rumsfeld's military maverick, General Schoomaker, and other senior army officers worked to prepare the army for the very nation-building mission that the secretary abhorred.

Innovation here is not surprising for military realism, however. Transformation was a response by military realists in the army to a new post–Cold War threat environment, where such a mission was essential to protecting U.S. vital material interests around the globe. Army doctrine and organization were ill-suited to this new setting and senior army leaders sought to change them accordingly. It might be the case, as some have argued, that transformation was an ill-conceived doctrinal innovation. Nevertheless, it did represent a major change in army doctrine driven by a major change in the threat environment. Ill-conceived or not, the timing and character of the innovation are unexpected by alternative explanations but anticipated by the logic of military realism.

The character of the conflicts in Iraq and Afghanistan also helped innovation toward COIN. Within the war zones themselves, military realists in the army did not confront a multifaceted enemy as they had faced in Vietnam. There were no large, conventionally trained enemy formations waiting in the wings to swoop down and destroy the army's efforts at nation building. Thus, within the theater of operations, there was no more dangerous threat than the low-level insurgency for military realists to latch onto.

As military realism predicts, at the end of the Cold War U.S. Army doctrine shifted to an offensive, power-projection mission to protect vital material interests, like oil and economic lines of communication. This led to an increased emphasis on regional conflicts and stability operations to secure areas where instability threatened U.S. interests. In terms of material power, little had changed after 9/11. Despite the Global War on Terror, no major power had risen to threaten the preeminent position of the United States. However, the relatively benign stability operations of the 1990s gave way to very violent COIN operations in Afghanistan and Iraq. However, "the ground truth of combat operations [in Iraq]" also taught the army that its plans for a lighter future force, in which information would replace mass, were highly problematic.[236] Nevertheless, whether we consider army transformation a success or failure, it represented a major change in army doctrine and organization in response to the threat environment and the limited resources available to the army for responding to that environment. Moreover, many of the changes required were contrary to the bureaucratic affinity for the status quo and the traditions of U.S. Army culture. Operations after 9/11 demonstrated that successful expeditionary warfare required effective stability operations to succeed.[237] Stability operations and counterinsurgency had to be part of a doctrine for protecting the vital material interests of the United States. At the same time, however, General Schoomaker opposed the surge into Iraq, not because it would employ a COIN strategy, which he had championed, but because it undermined the capacity of the army to deal with more dangerous threats should they arise. Subsequently, the army did not simply treat operations in Iraq as a sideshow, but incorporated these lessons into its most important war-fighting manual, *Operations 2008*. Furthermore, as briefly discussed in the conclusion, the army expanded on and preserved many of these unexpected doctrinal innovations in updates and changes to its doctrine after its withdrawal from Iraq in 2011.

CONCLUSION

THIS BOOK WAS born from a puzzle. Why did the U.S. Army, which had said "never again" to counterinsurgency doctrine after Vietnam, come to embrace it in recent conflicts? To solve this particular puzzle, I set out to answer a more general question: What causes military organizations to change or preserve their doctrine? Answering this question is important because change and continuity in military doctrine can increase or decrease the likelihood of international conflict and affect the quality of civil-military relations and the allocation of precious national resources. Regarding international conflict, for instance, other states can interpret doctrines with a highly offensive theory of victory as a sign of hostile intentions. This can exacerbate the security dilemma and turn crises into wars. On the other hand, a state can signal its benign intentions and dampen international hostility through a clearly defensive theory of victory. This reasoning assumes, of course, a spiral model of war. A deterrence model would argue that a defensive doctrine signals weakness and can provoke adventurism on the part of aggressive states.[1] However, the merits of either view have not been central to this work. In either case, the offensive or defensive character of military doctrine is a significant variable, underlining the importance of military doctrine from both perspectives.

Military doctrines can also undermine civil-military relations when they contradict changes in civilian strategy and foreign policy. For instance, the retention of a highly offensive doctrine by the military can undercut a civilian foreign policy meant to foster international cooperation and mutual trust. In addition, if military doctrines are simply bureaucratic tools for securing more resources and not a genuine means to national security, then they waste limited national resources and undermine civilian attempts to balance security and other national interests. Such conflicts between military doctrine and foreign policy can lead to distrust between civilian and military leaders. This distrust can isolate civilian leaders from their military advisers. These are but a few reasons for taking military doctrines seriously as a variable in international and civil-military relations.

I presented military realism as a new theory for explaining doctrinal continuity and innovation. Military realism argues that explaining why doctrine changes or persists requires an understanding of how military officers view force, war, and threats. According to military realism, the preparation for and participation in conflict produces a two-part military realist mindset in military officers. First, military realists appreciate that the use of force to impose one's will on the unwilling produces an escalatory interaction. The use of force has an escalatory logic that is only partially under the control of the belligerents. Second, military realists appreciate that the physical world and its friction always hinder the use of force. When assessing threats, military officers emphasize the relative balance of material capabilities and the doctrines of potential adversaries. Senior officers design their doctrines to deal with the range of threats but prioritize the most dangerous. Typically, the most dangerous threat is the presence of a powerful state, or group of states, that can use force to threaten the vital material interests and even survival of the state. In the absence of such a threat, and in keeping with the emphasis on material factors and friction, doctrine focuses on threats to physical access to the vital material interests of the state, the sources of its material power. Military realism also anticipates whether the theory of victory at the core of doctrine will be offensive or defensive. According to a military realist view of war, appealing to the logic of force through offensive action is the surest means of defeating an opponent in war. All else being equal, therefore, military officers prefer an offensive theory of victory at the core of their doctrine. However, the perennial physical limits on the use of force mean that attack will be physically more difficult than defense and that defensive actions have certain inherent advantages over offensive ones. Consequently, the attacker needs greater numbers to overcome the defender, as the three-to-one rule has long recognized. Therefore, military realism anticipates that when faced with a materially superior opponent, military officers should design a doctrine with a defensive theory of victory. A defensive theory of victory can offset material disadvantages by exploiting friction and the inherent advantages of the defense. Moreover, even when the threat environment is more permissive, due to the absence of threatening states, military realists will still emphasize the limits that the friction of geography places on the deployment of military forces. Of special concern will be the advantages geography provides to the defender and the obstacles it presents to the attacker.

Regarding doctrinal change, military realism argues that senior military officers should change the core of existing doctrine if it does not address the most dangerous threats. For instance, contrary to a bureaucratic perspective, military officers should transition from an offensive to a defensive theory of victory when faced with a much more powerful adversary. In addition, military realism argues that senior officers should design doctrines that contradict cultural traditions, organizational autonomy, and the desire for resources, when doing so is necessary to address critical threats. Despite the bureaucratic aversion to uncertainty, military realists will even initiate revolutionary changes in doctrine if demanded by the threat environment. Further, in opposition to the predictions of civilian realism, senior military officers can undertake these doctrinal changes in the absence of prodding by civilian leaders. However, when civilian doctrinal initiatives coincide with those spearheaded by senior military officers, they can accelerate those doctrinal changes with their added authority and resources.

Subsequently, the work sought to test the predictions of military realism against the bureaucratic, military culture, and civilian realist alternatives through the development of U.S. Army doctrine from 1960 to 2008. The U.S. Army represents an unlikely case for military realism to succeed because the alternative theories appear to explain its doctrinal behavior so well. The U.S. Army's strong bureaucracy, long-standing cultural traditions, and subordination to civilian authority made it an easy case for the organizational, military cultural, and civilian realist theories. Thus, military realism fought on ground carefully selected to advantage the alternative theories. Given these adverse conditions, the strong showing of military realism in the case studies indicates that it represents an important rival explanation of military innovation.

These consecutive case studies allowed for the long-term evaluation of the degree of doctrinal change and continuity. In this way, doctrine was placed in a broader context, revealing the process by which changes occurred, the actors that drove them, and the most salient environmental factors. Repeatedly in the case studies that followed, this framework for evaluating the competing theories bore fruit. When seen in an extended doctrinal context, doctrinal changes previously considered revolutionary proved to be part of a gradual process of change motivated by gradual changes in the threat environment. For instance, broader historical context reveals that *Operations 1976*, Active Defense, was an evolutionary rather than revolutionary doctrinal change. The defensive theory of victory at its heart was the product of a worsening balance of forces between the United States and the USSR. In the final chapter, *Operations 2008* was placed in the broader context of post–Cold War army doctrine, and it became clear that the emphasis on stability operations and unconventional missions was not a bolt from the blue inspired by the wars in Afghanistan and Iraq. Nor did civilian intervention, in the form of Department of Defense Directive 3000.05 prioritizing stability operations, drive doctrinal innovation. Rather, senior army leaders recognized the import of stability operations in the post–Cold War threat environment of the early 1990s. The more violent post-9/11 stability operations revealed the need to adapt doctrine in important ways, but they were not the spark for including stability operations in army doctrine. The disappearance of the Soviet threat and the subsequent preeminence of U.S. power provided that spark. In the absence of a state-based threat, senior leaders in the U.S. Army focused on projecting power to protect U.S. vital material interests threatened by regional powers and instability. Below, I briefly summarize the findings of this work across the three key areas of doctrine and the process that drove doctrinal change and continuity. I then show how we can use the analysis in this book to shed light on more recent doctrinal developments in the U.S. Army. I follow this with a discussion of the theoretical implications of the findings and the final section addresses the policy implications of military realism.

U.S. Army Doctrine, 1960–2008
Conventional versus Nuclear Weapons in U.S.
Army Doctrine: Doctrinal Outcomes

Bureaucratic and military cultural explanations imply that closely integrating nuclear weapons into U.S. Army doctrine would undermine the army's culture and bureaucratic interests. From the cultural perspective, preparing for the use of tactical nuclear weapons would not allow the army to use doctrine to replay its World War II finest hour, attacking across Europe with conventional forces. Army culture, therefore, should have resisted the close integration of conventional and nuclear forces. If civilian authorities foil such resistance, for instance, the army will graft nuclear weapons onto doctrinal routines grounded in its cultural essence and the finest hour that birthed it, resulting in only peripheral doctrinal innovation. Bureaucratically, military organizations seek to increase their autonomy and resources and reduce uncertainty. Its logic implies that U.S. Army doctrine should avoid a heavy nuclear focus for three reasons. First, developing a doctrine that relies heavily on nuclear weapons provides fewer resources than conventional doctrines. Second, even if senior army leaders could simply add resources for nuclear warfare to conventional possessions, the tight civilian control of nuclear weapons in the United States would undermine organizational autonomy. The army would not be in control of a major part of its weapons. This problem would be especially acute if the army closely integrated the operations of conventional and nuclear forces. Finally, designing a doctrine that closely integrated nuclear and conventional forces would generate major uncertainty because the U.S. Army had never fought on a nuclear battlefield. Civilian realism provides an additional reason. It argues that civilian strategy should determine the role of nuclear weapons in U.S. Army doctrine. If civilian strategy emphasized nuclear over conventional weapons, or vice versa, U.S. Army doctrine should be made to reflect that emphasis. Alternatively, military realism argues that if closely integrating nuclear weapons and conventional forces is required to address the most dangerous threats, the U.S. Army should overcome bureaucratic, military culture, and civilian objections to such doctrinal innovations.

From 1960 to 1991, the most dangerous threat to the physical security and vital material interests of the United States was the combined conventional and nuclear capabilities of the Soviet Union. Consistent with military realism, addressing this threat was the main mission at the core of U.S. Army doctrine for this whole period. According to senior army leaders, a Soviet invasion of Europe constituted the greatest threat to the security and interests of the United States. In addition to major conventional capabilities in the European theater, Soviet forces were equipped with tactical nuclear weapons. Due to the imbalance in conventional forces, which only worsened as the Cold War went on, senior army officers argued battlefield nuclear weapons would likely be necessary to stop a Soviet assault on Europe. *Operations 1962, 1968, 1976, 1982,* and *1986* all made battlefield nuclear weapons a major part of army doctrine. In this period, army doctrine very closely integrated its conventional and nuclear forces. For instance, rather than emphasizing conventional concepts like the massing of forces, army doctrine continually advocated dispersion and the use of helicopters to move forces around the battlefield. Senior officers continually warned their colleagues and subordinates against allowing nostalgia for the army's World War II finest hour to hinder innovative thinking about doctrine for future war. This nuclear revolution in army doctrine runs contrary to the expectations of bureaucratic and military culture perspectives.

Nuclear weapons did not drop out of army doctrine until *Operations 1993* and were largely absent from *Operations 2001* and *2008*. The 1993 edition was the first *Operations* manual written after the fall of the Soviet Union. As military realism predicts, when the primary threat for which the army designed nuclear doctrine disappeared, the nuclear emphasis in army doctrine disappeared with it. Military realism correctly predicted the variation in conditions that precipitated the variation in nuclear doctrine.

Conventional versus Nuclear Weapons in U.S. Army Doctrine: Doctrinal Process

The process by which the U.S. Army integrated nuclear weapons into its warfighting doctrine also supports military realism. Bureaucratic and military culture theories imply that senior military officers should guide doctrinal development. Senior military bureaucrats should design doctrines that increase organizational resources and autonomy while reducing uncertainty. Senior guardians of U.S. Army culture should keep the doctrinal process within the boundaries set by cultural norms. A nuclear revolution in doctrine is contrary to the interests of both groups. Nevertheless, from 1960 to 1986, senior army officers were the driving force behind making nuclear weapons central to its main war-fighting manual, *Operations*. They did so because, despite bureaucratic and cultural friction, they saw tactical nuclear weapons as a vital means of countering the superior capabilities of the Soviets in Europe.

The evidence also contradicts the doctrinal process envisioned by civilian realism. For instance, President Kennedy enlisted a military maverick, General Maxwell Taylor, to try to reduce the nuclear emphasis in army doctrine and force structure. Instead, General Taylor actively opposed his civilian patrons when it came to nuclear weapons. Taylor continually advocated for making tactical nuclear weapons a key part of flexible response. Military realism best explained even the behavior of this military maverick. Taylor thought that just because civilian leaders considered the use of battlefield nuclear weapons unthinkable did not mean that armies would not use them. According to Taylor, the logic of force and the relative balance of material capabilities meant that the United States had to prepare for the use of battlefield nuclear weapons. Although the Kennedy case follows the civilian realist process closely, beginning with a new civilian strategy, flexible response, the doctrinal process and outcome contradict it and corroborate military realism.

Offensive versus Defensive Theories of Victory in U.S. Army Doctrine: Doctrinal Outcomes

Both bureaucratic and military cultural perspectives contend that the U.S. Army should prefer offensive theories of victory at the core of its doctrine. Bureaucratically, offensive doctrines are preferred because they provide more resources, autonomy, and certainty than defensive doctrines; because their complexity shields them from civilian meddling; and because offense imposes SOPs on the enemy, while defense waits and reacts to an attack. From the military cultural standpoint, the norms of the U.S. Army promote the offense. The army's finest hour was in the offense, attacking into German-held territory to end World War II. The U.S. Army should prefer offensive doctrines that reinforce its cultural norms.

While bureaucratic and cultural perspectives predict doctrinal continuity when it comes to offense and defense, civilian and military realism argue for variation under certain conditions. According to civilian realism, the imperatives of civilian strategy should dictate the offensive or defensive orientation of U.S. Army doctrine. Military realism, on the other hand, concurs with bureaucratic theory that military organizations should prefer offensive theories of victory. However, they prefer the offense not because it secures more resources, but because it is the surest path to victory. Attacking destroys the material capabilities of the enemy, occupies his territory to stop continued resistance, and ends wars. However, unlike the bureaucratic and cultural viewpoint, military realism argues that the U.S. Army should adopt a defensive doctrine when confronted with a physically superior threat. This is because while the escalatory logic of force recommends an offensive doctrine, the limits that the physical world place on the use of force, that is, friction, mean that the attacker requires material superiority over the defender. The power of the defense means that an outnumbered defender can hold off a numerically superior attacker. Under these conditions, doctrine should highlight the advantages of the defender and even reinterpret time-honored doctrinal principles into a defensive theory of victory. Therefore, according to military realism, when confronted with a physically superior foe, the U.S. Army should develop a defensive doctrine to offset disadvantages in material capabilities.

From 1960 to 2008, variation in the offensive and defensive orientation of U.S. Army doctrine conformed best to the predictions of military realism. Starting with *Operations 1962*, army doctrine began to downplay the dominance of the offense and to promote the power of the defense. Doctrine reinterpreted key concepts like the initiative and enlisted them in the promotion of defensive operations. The defense was no longer a temporary expedient until offense was possible, as the principles of war had urged, but a means of seizing the initiative and destroying the enemy. This defensive emphasis persisted into *Operations 1968* and was most prevalent in *Operations 1976*. The 1960s manuals added a number of caveats to the principles of war and the highly defensive 1976 edition removed the principles of war from *Operations* altogether. The 1980s manuals brought back the principles, but relegated them to an appendix. This shift in army doctrine coincided with decreases in U.S. capabilities vis-à-vis the Soviets in the European theater. For instance, the highly defensive nature of *Operations 1976* coincided with the shift in the army to an all-volunteer force, which cut the size of the U.S. Army in half. At the same time, the Soviets were expanding and modernizing their conventional forces.

Contrary to civilian realism, this defensive theory of victory persisted into the Reagan administration, which had abandoned détente and promoted a more aggressive Cold War strategy. AirLand Battle doctrine, published under Reagan as *Operations 1982* and *1986*, and considered highly offensive by some scholars, actually continued the defensive emphasis of *Operations 1976*. AirLand Battle did argue for deep strikes against Soviet second-echelon forces by army artillery and the air force. However, these were not a prelude to a major counteroffensive but were essential to enable an Active Defense. Even under AirLand Battle, the theory of victory at the core of army doctrine remained defensive.

As military realism predicts, the shift from a defensive to an offensive theory of victory in U.S. Army doctrine occurred after the fall of the Soviet Union. In the absence of an overwhelming threat to replace the USSR, the United States became the sole superpower in the international system. As a result, U.S. Army doctrine shifted from a defensive doctrine designed to address the Soviet threat in Europe to an offensive, power-projection doctrine designed to secure the vital material interests of the state. *Operations 1993*, the first army doctrine published after the fall of the Soviet Union, resurrected the principles of war from the appendixes of army doctrine and placed them at the center of the 1993 *Operations* manual. Organizational and military cultural theories continually predicted that U.S. Army doctrine would be offensive. However, army doctrine contradicted this expectation until *Operations 1993*. Only military realism correctly predicted the conditions under which the U.S. Army would vary the offensive or defensive character of its theory of victory.

Offensive versus Defensive Theories of Victory in U.S. Army Doctrine: Doctrinal Process

As noted already, alternative explanations argue that army bureaucrats and cultural guardians should guide doctrinal development to ensure that it served bureaucratic preferences or cultural norms. In the case of the U.S. Army, both bureaucratic and cultural perspectives expect senior army officers to advocate from an offensive theory of victory at the core of doctrine.

On the contrary, from 1960 to 1986, in the face of a powerful Soviet threat, senior army officers promoted a defensive theory of victory in doctrine. As military realism predicts, senior army leaders increased the defensive emphasis in doctrine as the imbalance of capabilities increased. In a particularly striking example from the cultural perspective, General William E. DePuy, an actual participant in the army's World War II finest hour, was the strongest advocate for a defensive doctrine to address the Soviet threat. He rejected a draft of the *Operations* manual based on the principles of war and argued against those who thought his doctrine too defensive. In addition, contrary to the process predictions of civilian realism, these variations in the theory of victory did not result from changes in civilian strategies supported by military mavericks.

In sum, when it came to offense versus defense in army doctrine, the process of doctrinal development conformed best to the predictions of military realism. Senior army leaders changed the offensive or defensive orientation of army doctrine in response to the relative balance of material capabilities in the threat environment. These same leaders overcame what should have been insurmountable bureaucratic and cultural opposition to these doctrinal initiatives.

Counterinsurgency in U.S. Army Doctrine: Doctrinal Outcomes

On the subject of the role of counterinsurgency missions in army doctrine, bureaucratic and cultural expectations agree. Both imply that the U.S. Army, from 1960 to 2008, should at most relegate COIN missions to the appendix of *Operations* manuals. COIN, especially of the population security variety, does not serve the bureaucratic thirst for resources, autonomy, and certainty. First, because they are defensive and rely on infantry rather than expensive platforms, such as tanks and artillery pieces, COIN missions do not promise many additional resources. Second, COIN doctrines based on securing the population undermine autonomy because they require a unified civil-military strategy to be successful. Finally, COIN missions produce major uncertainty because they are defensive and the SOPs of offensive, conventional warfare are often ineffective, at best, and counterproductive, at worst, in COIN operations. Commanders cannot graft the routines of conventional warfare onto COIN campaigns. The culture of the U.S. Army, influenced by its World War II finest hour, favors offensive, conventional doctrines. COIN, on the other hand, awakens cultural memories of the U.S. Army's darkest hour, Vietnam. COIN based on population security is also very defensive, contrary to an army culture that favors attack. Therefore, for both bureaucratic and cultural reasons, the army should not make COIN a major part of its *Operations* manuals.

On the contrary, civilian and military realism argue that these bureaucratic and cultural obstacles can be overcome. For civilian realism, if civilian strategy requires that the U.S. Army make COIN a major part of its doctrine, then the organization will be compelled to change. Civilian leaders can use military mavericks to help bring this about. On the other hand, military realism argues that military organizations can make COIN an important part of their doctrine under the right conditions. According to military realism, doctrine should prepare for the range of threats in the international system, but prioritize the most dangerous. In general, insurgencies do not represent dangerous threats to the state and its vital material interests. Therefore, in the presence of a grave threat of overwhelming force, COIN missions should have a minor role in U.S. Army doctrine. However, in the absence of such threats, COIN missions should begin to have a larger role in army doctrine, especially if insurgencies threaten vital material interests. As threats to the physical security of the state recede, lesser threats should receive more attention in doctrine, despite bureaucratic and cultural preferences to the contrary.

From 1960 to 1991, in the presence of a perilous threat embodied in the Soviet Union, COIN missions had only a minor role in U.S. Army *Operations* manuals. In fact, doctrine co-opted forces designated as COIN specialists, like Special Forces and the light infantry divisions, into the mission of resisting the Soviets in Europe. In addition, as the Soviet threat increased in material terms, the COIN mission gradually disappeared from the *Operations* manuals. This relegation of COIN was not the result of an army that did not understand COIN or was blind to its importance because of bureaucratic or cultural prejudice. The U.S. Army of the 1960s understood COIN and recognized its power to topple states. COIN appeared regularly in the pages of *Military Review*. The chapters devoted to COIN missions in both *Operations 1962* and *1968* showed a clear understanding of classic COIN theory on the part of the army. Nevertheless, insurgencies were not as dangerous as Soviet forces threatening Europe. Therefore, the army gave COIN a lesser role in doctrine than conventional and nuclear missions that addressed the main danger. This minor role for the COIN mission in army doctrine was not the result of the Vietnam War but actually began before and persisted through that conflict and into the late 1970s and 1980s. This contradicts the common narrative that the U.S. Army's rejection of COIN was the result of failure in Vietnam.

When the threat from the Soviet Union disappeared in 1991, and the United States became the sole superpower, the U.S. Army gave COIN-like missions a more prominent role in *Operations* manuals. In the early 1990s, senior army officers were arguing for the inclusion of "stability operations" in the first post–Cold War *Operations* manual, a term used to describe COIN operations beginning in *Operations 1968*. Throughout the 1990s, the army was engaged in continual stability operations in the form of peacekeeping and humanitarian assistance deployments. The import of stability operations persisted into *Operations 2001*. In a departure from both the army's supposed fetish for the offense and its aversion to COIN, the 2001 manual actually argued for the unification of offense, defense, and stability and support operations. With the rise of the insurgencies in Iraq and Afghanistan, the emphasis on stability operations in general and COIN in particular greatly increased in army doctrine. The army developed two COIN manuals, one in 2004 and another in 2006. Importantly, COIN and stability operations were central components of *Operations 2008*, the U.S. Army's first post-9/11 keystone doctrine. The 2008 manual continued to push for the unity of ODSS and argued that operations were unlikely to be decisive without proper stability operations. This was a major departure from the principles of war, for which offensive operations were the primary means of reaching a decision. Nonetheless, seen in the broader context of post–Cold War army doctrine, the development of the two COIN manuals and the heavy COIN emphasis in *Operations 2008* are less drastic than some have portrayed. We should not attribute COIN's larger role in army doctrine solely to the wars in Afghanistan and Iraq. Those operational experiences did increase the emphasis on stability operations, but *Operations 1993* and the end of the Cold War inaugurated a focus on such operations. The import of stability and COIN operations in U.S. Army doctrine represent an adaptation to a threat environment not characterized by a major existential threat, like the Soviet Union. Thus, the U.S. Army had an acute sensitivity to the new realities of the post–Cold War threat environment and demonstrated a doctrinal prescience unexpected by bureaucratic and cultural perspectives.

Counterinsurgency in U.S. Army Doctrine: Doctrinal Process

According to these perspectives, army bureaucrats and cultural guardians should keep doctrinal change within the bounds set by either bureaucratic preferences or cultural norms. Both perspectives expect senior U.S. Army officers to resist any attempt to make COIN a major part of army doctrine, especially its main war-fighting manual, *Operations*. Conversely, civilian realism argues that if COIN is a major component of civilian strategy, then with the help of a military maverick, civilians will compel their military organizations to make COIN a major component of doctrine. According to the logic of this process, changes in civilian strategy should precede their required doctrinal changes. On the other hand, military realism argues that senior military officers can make COIN missions an important part of doctrine in the absence of a more dangerous threat. These officers can implement this change without civilian intervention. In fact, under these conditions, senior officers can give a high priority to such missions even when civilians hold other priorities. Clearly, such expectations are contrary to the institutional opposition to COIN anticipated by bureaucratic and cultural viewpoints.

Many scholars have argued that in the early 1960s, Kennedy pushed the army to embrace the COIN mission. However, the intensity of the Kennedy COIN initiative has been overstated. After some prodding, the army complied, and Kennedy was satisfied with the peripheral doctrinal changes the army made. The evidence does not support the argument that Kennedy pushed the army to make COIN a priority as well, as previously thought. Moreover, army officers like Chief of Staff Decker understood that the COIN mission was important, though it was secondary to addressing the Soviet threat to Europe. Therefore, this classic case of civilian intervention in army doctrine in the name of COIN has been overblown. Analysts of this case often view it with the benefit of hindsight and outside of the context of the broader Cold War threat environment. When placed in this broader context, the limited role of the COIN mission in army doctrine by senior army officers makes sense. As the Soviet threat increased through the 1960s and '70s—through a combination of U.S. cuts to its European forces, the escalation of the Vietnam War, and the expansion and modernization of Soviet conventional forces—the COIN mission receded further into the doctrinal background. As military realism predicts, the relegation of the COIN mission would continue until the danger from the Soviet threat abated.

Not long after the fall of the Soviet Union, senior U.S. Army officers, like Generals Sullivan and Franks, argued that stability operations needed to have a more prominent place in the new post–Cold War *Operations* manual. Moreover, based on a number of high-level army conferences in the early 1990s that discussed future doctrine, this was a consensus view among senior army officers. The result was a stability operations chapter and the inclusion of new principles for stability operations in *Operations 1993*. The prominence of stability operations persisted into *Operations 2001*. This persistence is surprising from all three alternative viewpoints, because the incoming Bush administration's strategy emphasized decisive conventional operations and disdained "nation-building" missions. Army bureaucrats and cultural guardians should have jumped at the chance to put the unconventional missions of the 1990s behind them. Instead, the U.S. Army continued to include stability operations in its doctrine. In fact, the army expanded the role of such missions by arguing for the unification of offense, defense, and stability and support operations.

Even as the insurgency in Iraq escalated, President Bush and Secretary of Defense Rumsfeld discouraged the army from adopting a COIN strategy to address the rising violence. Despite the civilian distaste for COIN, senior army officers worked to develop a COIN manual for use in Iraq and Afghanistan. The commander of the Combined Arms Center, General Wallace, began work on an interim COIN manual in February 2004. In Iraq General George Casey established a COIN academy with the help of his Special Forces advisers. Army Chief of Staff Schoomaker was also pushing the army to think hard about COIN. He made the importance of COIN clear to General Casey just before he took command in Iraq and sent General Petraeus to Fort Leavenworth to revise the 2004 interim COIN manual before he replaced Casey in Iraq.

Some have argued that civilian intervention with the help of a few maverick army officers compelled the army to adapt to COIN in Iraq. However, the evidence does not support this narrative. The U.S. Army began to prepare for COIN in Iraq while the Bush administration was still reluctant to call the violence there insurgency. In fact, the military maverick that Donald Rumsfeld enlisted to push Bush's defense agenda—including its aversion to nation building—Army Chief of Staff Schoomaker, helped spearhead the development of a COIN doctrine in the army.

Even more surprisingly, the U.S. Army incorporated the COIN mission into the next edition of it most important doctrine, *Operations 2008*. However, as already noted, the inclusion of stability operations did not originate in this most recent manual or solely because of army experience in Iraq and Afghanistan. Stability operations began to reappear in army doctrine in the first post–Cold War manual, *Operations 1993*. In short, post–Cold War army doctrine built the intellectual foundation for the army's rediscovery of COIN and the inclusion of COIN in *Operations 2008*. Iraq and Afghanistan sharpened rather than initiated the focus on stability operations. Consistent with the expectations of military realism, this focus on the lower end of the spectrum of conflict occurred in the absence of a major threat to U.S. security. Moreover, the fact that this change occurred in the U.S. Army, a very unlikely adaptation according to the alternative theories, further strengthens the case for military realism as an explanation of doctrinal innovation.

Military Operations and Military Doctrine

Between 1960 and 2008, the U.S. Army was most heavily engaged in four military conflicts: the Vietnam War, the Gulf War, and the wars in Afghanistan and Iraq. Bureaucratic and military culture theories imply that the U.S. Army will draw lessons from conflicts that reinforce doctrines that satisfy bureaucratic and cultural desires. Therefore, the U.S. Army should have drawn lessons from military operations that highlight the wisdom of conventional, offensive military doctrine. Military realism, on the other hand, argues that senior army officers should focus on the lessons learned from military operations that would make the organization more effective at addressing the immediate threat environment. Organizational learning should not be limited to conventional, offensive doctrines, and, under certain conditions, lessons from COIN operations can play a prominent role in U.S. Army doctrine.

Scholars of military innovation often criticize the U.S. Army for not learning the right lessons from the Vietnam War. However, they base this argument on a narrow view of the conduct of that war. It assumes that the main enemy the army faced in Vietnam was a low-level guerrilla force and that the army should have adopted a classic COIN strategy in response. As the chapter on Vietnam in this work shows, however, the enemy in Vietnam also included major main-force enemy units employing conventional tactics and sometimes seeking battles of annihilation. Recent historical scholarship shows that these forces were not a figment of the U.S. Army's conventional-warfare imagination. They were real, and their ability to escalate the use of force often undermined the COIN efforts that the U.S. Army made in Vietnam. In addition, the army fought in Vietnam in a broader Cold War context in which failure in Vietnam did not represent the main threat. Consequently, the doctrine of this period, Operations 1968, continued to focus on the Soviet threat, which became graver still in the late 1960s.

Moreover, this work shows that the U.S. Army did appreciate the threat of insurgency in this period and understood the proper response to it in classic COIN terms. Insurgent movements threatened the allies and interests of the United States and were capable of conquest. However, when the army hit the ground in Vietnam, it did not confront a classic insurgency, but met a mix of heavy conventional fighting and low-level insurgent violence for which classic COIN doctrine was ill-suited. Within the theater of war, the military realist perspective led army commanders to focus on the main-force threat, even when that threat receded in some phases of the war. Here military realist inclinations may have hindered adaptive military strategy. Despite its struggles in Vietnam, the army's concern with COIN did make an appearance in *Operations 1968*, which included an important chapter on COIN operations, coining the term "stability operations." A number of scholars of military innovation employ an incomplete appraisal of the U.S. Army in Vietnam to support their theories. The more complete story presented here, and placed in its broader Cold War context, is more consistent with the expectations of military realism than the alternatives. Although this case also shows how the military realist perspective can skew strategy within a theater of operations.

Almost two decades after the fall of Saigon, military innovation theorists employing bureaucratic and cultural variables argue the U.S. Army used the lessons of the 1991 Gulf War to reinforce parochial doctrine. They argue that the U.S. Army saw the rapid and decisive ground operations as a vindication of its conventional doctrine, a cultural artifact designed to fight the Soviets. Army bureaucrats and cultural guardians argued that the war proved the continued relevance of such doctrine, even after the fall of the USSR. Here, however, I have presented significant evidence to the contrary. In the early 1990s, senior army officers, including General Franks, who had led a major part of the Gulf War ground assault, were arguing that the army needed to replace its heavy Cold War formations. The army needed lighter forces to accomplish its new power projection mission. The difficulties the army experienced in getting its heavy forces to Iraq reinforced this reality. Instead of using the Gulf War to reinforce conventional doctrine, *Operations 1993* used the postconflict phase of that war to highlight the importance of stability operations. Moreover, the post–Cold War *Operations* manuals included numerous references to stability and peacekeeping operations and championed a new set of principles of stability operations. In general, the historical vignettes used in the post–Cold War manuals tended to distance army doctrine from its World War II finest hour. These manuals and senior army officers argued that future missions would not resemble its finest hour. Senior army officers took a military realist view of the post–Cold War threat environment. They sought to design doctrine to protect the vital material interests of the United States through power projection and stability operations. They were able to look past the army's cultural traditions and design a doctrine to address the range of threats that had come to the fore since the fall of the Soviet Union.

Bureaucratic and cultural perspectives have similar expectations for the lessons U.S. Army doctrine would draw from Afghanistan and Iraq. The army should use the rapid conventional invasions of those two countries as proof of the continued relevance of offensive operations by conventional force. They should not highlight the lessons of the subsequent COIN campaigns in doctrine, especially not in the keystone *Operations* manual. Conversely, given the threat environment and the intense level of violence in these COIN campaigns, military realism expects the army experience in Iraq and Afghanistan to increase the emphasis in doctrine on stability operations, which began with the fall of the Soviet Union.

A close examination of *Operations 2008* shows that the U.S. Army drew lessons from the campaigns in Afghanistan and Iraq contrary to bureaucratic and cultural expectations. For instance, *Operations 2008* pointed out that in both conflicts, the rapid, decisive wars envisioned by *Operations 1993* and *2001* and the Bush administration did not take place. Postconflict stability operations, the 2008 manual argued, were essential to preserve the success of initial combat operations. To secure victory, army doctrine had to unify offense, defense, and stability and support operations, as the 2001 manual had pointed out. In short, contrary to the expectations of a bureaucratic or cultural outlook, the U.S. Army's most important manual was arguing that proficiency in stability operations was essential to accomplish its main mission. This outcome is consistent with the military realist perspective, which helps solve the puzzle that launched this investigation. Army experience in Iraq and Afghanistan increased the focus on stability operations initiated by *Operations 1993* at the end of the Cold War. The absence of a threat comparable to the Soviet Union allowed the post–Cold War U.S. Army to focus more on the lower end of the spectrum of conflict. Despite the attacks of September 11, 2001, this threat environment persisted up to and beyond the invasions of Afghanistan and Iraq.

The military realist perspective on U.S. Army doctrine from Vietnam to the Iraq War provides an answer to the main puzzle that inspired this work: Why did an army with such a seemingly powerful aversion to COIN during and after Vietnam come to embrace it as a solution to its most recent wars? First, the lower priority the U.S. Army gave to the COIN mission in its main doctrine in the 1960s, '70s, and '80s had more to do with the threat environment, and the complex situation the army encountered in Vietnam, than the trauma of defeat or its bureaucratic and cultural preferences. When the U.S. Army took up COIN again, beginning in 2004, it had already begun to make unconventional missions, such as stability operations, a key part of its most important doctrine, the *Operations* manuals. The disappearance of the Soviet threat and the preeminence of American power facilitated this doctrinal innovation. Recent conflicts in Iraq and Afghanistan brutally highlighted the importance of such missions for army doctrine, but those conflicts were not the cause of this realization. Military realists in the U.S. Army gave unconventional threats an important role in doctrine when the threat environment permitted.

Military Realism and U.S. Army Doctrine since 2008

Military realism and the findings in this book can also shed light on more recent doctrinal developments in the U.S. Army. Below, I do not provide a complete case study of recent army doctrine. Missing from the following analysis, for instance, is a detailed account of the doctrinal process. Therefore, its conclusions are preliminary. Nevertheless, since *Operations 2008*, the changes and continuities in army doctrine appear highly consistent with the expectations of military realism and problematic for some of the alternative explanations.

In the lead-up to and following the army's withdrawal from Iraq, its senior leaders shifted doctrine from COIN to dealing with the more dangerous threats emerging in the second decade of the twenty-first century. Thus, as military realism expects, changes in the threat environment drove doctrinal change. Those doctrinal changes appear more responsive to the requirements of military realism than to assumed bureaucratic and cultural objectives. For instance, recent army doctrine did not, as these parochial theories expect, witness a return to a highly offensive theory of victory and the sweeping aside of COIN doctrine and lessons. Although recent army doctrine emphasizes the importance of preparing for large-scale combat operations, it also preserves and refines some of the most important lessons from a decade of COIN experience. Army doctrine did so even when these doctrinal elements contravened bureaucratic interests and cultural norms. For instance, recent army doctrine preserves the unity of offense, defense, and stability operations, curtailing the parochial preference for the offense. It also points to the necessity of increasing interservice and -agency jointness and unity, intentionally reducing organizational autonomy.

In 2010 the army published Change 1 to *Operations 2008*. However, this revision took place in the midst of a larger initiative to reorder all army doctrine. In 2009 the army established *Doctrine 2015*, a process of "doctrine reengineering" begun by the Combined Arms Center to reduce the size and number of doctrinal manuals.[2] Senior army leaders were concerned that doctrinal manuals were too lengthy and that their central concepts were buried within that unwieldy bulk. *Doctrine 2015* reorganized manuals hierarchically with Army Doctrine Publications (ADPs) at the top, followed by Army Doctrine Reference Publications (ADRPs), then Field Manuals, and finally Army Techniques Publications.[3] At the top of the doctrinal pyramid were the intentionally brief ADP series of manuals that set out the fundamentals and principles of army doctrine. ADRPs were lengthier and provided a more detailed interpretation of the fundamentals and principles expressed in the ADPs. As Clinton Ancker and Michael Scully of the Combined Arms Doctrine Directorate put it, ADP 3-0 and ADRP 3-0 "provide direction for how the Army will operate in the future" through fundamentals and principles.[4] ADRP 3-0 "provides the foundational understanding," Ancker and Scully continued, "so everyone in the Army can interpret the fundamentals and principles [set out in ADP 3-0] the same way."[5] Together, ADP 3-0 and ADRP 3-0 represented the key operational manuals. In terms of doctrinal process, draft ADPs undergo conferencing through a Council of Colonels and then a General Officer Review Board for issues not resolved by the colonels.[6] Depending on the ADP, the TRADOC commander or the army chief of staff makes the final decision. After undergoing this process, therefore, "the doctrine found in the ADPs represents the consensus of Army leaders."[7] Importantly, under this new construct, the *Operations* field manual no longer represented capstone doctrine. The new field manuals would speak only to army tactics and procedures in a specific area within the broader doctrinal framework established by ADPs and ADRPs.[8]

In accordance with *Doctrine 2015, Army Doctrine Publication 3-0, Unified Land Operations* (ADP 3-0) quickly followed Change 1 to *Operations 2008* and set out the doctrinal fundamentals and principles that would guide subordinate army doctrine.[9] As was often the case in the past, senior army leaders watched doctrinal development closely. Although it was published during Army Chief of Staff General Raymond Odierno's tenure, General Martin Dempsey, Odierno's predecessor in that position and previously commander of TRADOC, "was actively involved in the development of ADP 3-0."[10] The import of the manual was clear to senior army leaders, as it was "a template for the development of all other ADPs under *Doctrine 2015*."[11] Following Change 1 to *Operations 2008*, army doctrine writers had begun another revision of the *Operations* field manual. However, *Doctrine 2015* transformed this revision into *Army Doctrine Reference Publication 3-0, Operations* (ADRP 3-0), which the army published in 2016.[12]

Within the army the new doctrine was seen as an essential response to a changing threat environment. In *Foreign Affairs* in the summer of 2012, Chief of Staff Odierno described his service as an "army in time of transition." Odierno recognized the importance of the experience gained in a decade's worth of COIN operations. However, he argued that the army had to shift its focus away from the Middle East and toward the Asia Pacific and place less emphasis on COIN operations and more on preparing for regional conflicts "worldwide." Odierno was especially concerned about the emergence of hybrid warfare and its use by powerful nation-states. Hybrid warfare was an "environment with both regular military and irregular paramilitary or civilian adversaries, with the potential for terrorism, criminality, and other complications."[13] In 2014, in an effective use of hybrid warfare, the Russians combined numerous military, paramilitary, criminal, and civilian actors to take control of Crimea. However, by placing such "hybrid threats" at the center of the threat environment confronting the army, ADP 3-0 was not breaking new ground. General Odierno was echoing the concerns of the commanders of TRADOC from 2008 to 2014, General Martin Dempsey and then General Robert Cone, who saw hybrid threats as the biggest challenge facing the army.[14] One could argue that even earlier, the unity of offense, defense, and stability operations in the first post–Cold War army doctrine, *Operations 1993* and *2001*, anticipated such a hybrid conflict environment.[15]

Here General Odierno demonstrated a significant amount of mental flexibility, not allowing his extensive COIN experience in Iraq to blind him to the realities of the broader threat environment and the doctrinal changes it demanded. As he noted, the army must manage its transition "from a force focused on counterinsurgency, counterterrorism, and advising and assisting to . . . actively prepar[ing] to effectively conduct a fuller range of potential missions."[16] Like DePuy and his World War II experience, General Odierno was able to look beyond his own combat experience and appreciate the need for change. Again, military officers may not be condemned to continually fight the last war.

As in the past, the army had to do all this in a period of shrinking budgets and manpower.[17] The post–Cold War peace dividend had cut army budgets. During Odierno's tenure, budgets shrank due to sequestration and the reduction of funding for the Global War on Terror. In 2012 its most senior officer thought the U.S. Army faced a very similar threat environment to the one confronting it immediately after the Cold War, but with the addition of a rising and increasingly assertive China. As in the 1990s, the army had to be prepared to deploy globally to deter and, if necessary fight, regional conflicts, all while the U.S. government reduced its available resources. While stability operations remained a key component of doctrine, the army could not neglect preparing for combat operations against powerful regional adversaries.[18]

This refocusing on more dangerous threats persisted among senior army leaders after Odierno's retirement. However, subsequent forgers of army doctrine thought Odierno had not gone far enough. In 2016 Army Chief of Staff General Mark Milley directed TRADOC to write an operations manual "for prevailing in large-scale ground combat against enemies whose military capabilities, in regional contexts, rivaled" those of the United States.[19] The doctrinal establishment responded, and the following year Lieutenant General Michael Lundy and Colonel Richard Creed introduced the new edition of field manual *Operations* in the pages of *Military Review*. At the time, Lundy was the commanding general of the Combined Arms Center and the commandant of the Command and General Staff College, and Creed was the director of the Combined Arms Doctrine Directorate. As in the past, then, the close link between army doctrine and the CGSC persisted. The year 2017 also saw the publication of a new ADP 3-0 manual to replace the 2011 edition published under Odierno.

In their piece Lundy and Creed pointed to Russia's "physically aggressive behavior" and China's "maritime claims in the South China Sea" as changes in the international threat environment that demanded a revision of the army's doctrine for large-scale combat operations.[20] General David Perkins, commanding general of TRADOC, added "continuing challenges in the Middle East" to the list of threats.[21] General Perkins argued that existing army doctrine focused on "low-intensity hybrid fights" that the army might face in the near future, but it did not appreciate the perils of large-scale combat operations against near-peer or peer threats.[22] If the army did not change its doctrine, Perkins warned, it could be confronted by a shock comparable to that faced by the American Expeditionary Force in World War I, when Pershing's concept of "open warfare" met the bloody realities of trench warfare on the western front. Perkins argued that the army must recognize that the wars of the future will not be like those fought in Iraq and Afghanistan. Moreover, army adaptations to fight those wars had some negative consequences. Lundy and Creed agreed, arguing that continual COIN deployments "created a view of ground combat incongruent with the realities of fighting large-scale combat against a peer threat."[23] "Our army and our doctrine," they continued, "became optimized for limited contingency operations that primarily focused on operations where counterinsurgency and stability tasks made up the bulk of what both units and headquarter were expected to do."[24] Moreover, Perkins argued that while the army was developing and implementing COIN doctrine in Iraq and Afghanistan, its peer and near-peer competitors "were investing heavily in modernizing their capabilities to degrade and defeat the advantages U.S. forces had enjoyed since the end of the Cold War."[25] Most concerning were the antiaccess and area-denial capabilities Russia, China, and Iran were devising to restrict the U.S. ability to enter areas vital to its national interests, such as the Strait of Hormuz and the South China Sea. The increases in Russian capabilities, for instance, were not a figment of the army's cultural imagination. In his recent book, *The Future of Land Warfare*, Michael O'Hanlon of the Brookings Institution, notes the extent of Russian military modernization initiatives beginning in 2008.[26] According to Lundy and Creed, the army's "tactical doctrine for large-scale combat operations was inadequate."[27] The more dangerous threat of a peer or near-peer competitor engaging in large-scale combat operations required a change in army doctrine.[28] Interestingly, theories of military innovation based on bureaucratic or cultural parochialism did not anticipate the very changes in army doctrine that these army officers considered to have gone too far.

This apparent shift away from COIN and stability operations in army doctrine was largely consistent with civilian national security strategy under President Obama, as civilian realism would expect. The 2012 Defense Strategic Guidance and the 2014 Quadrennial Defense Review both demanded a reduction in emphasis on stability operations. In 2012, that Defense Strategic Guidance noted that "U.S. forces will no longer be sized to conduct large-scale, prolonged stability operations."[29] President Obama reiterated this in a speech to U.S. troops in 2014, saying, "The time of deploying large ground forces with big military footprints to engage in nation-building overseas, that's coming to an end."[30] President Obama's step away from stability operations made sense, given his ire when his senior military leaders worked to "box in" the president on a COIN strategy for Afghanistan.[31] The irony is that President Obama was staking out a strategic position held by his much-maligned predecessor George W. Bush, who initially rejected nation building for U.S. forces, what National Security Adviser Rice had likened to "escorting kids to kindergarten."[32] Thus, a stark departure from COIN in army doctrine also appears consistent with civilian realism. However, it is impossible in this brief treatment of recent army doctrine to test the process predictions of civilian and military realism, the area where their divergence would become most clear. I would point to the development of the two Department of Defense documents cited above as a key starting point for any future evaluations of military and civilian realism in this period.

Upon closer examination, however, these most recent doctrinal innovations appear more evolutionary than revolutionary when compared to doctrine under Odierno and his predecessors. The emphasis on more dangerous regional threats was consistent with Dempsey' and Odierno's focus on regional adversaries and on the higher end of the spectrum of conflict. Appreciating this evolutionary process, Perkins saw Dempsey and Odierno's ADP 3-0, 2011, as the first step in a doctrinal progression that "reintroduced . . . previously discarded elements" of doctrine related to major combat operations.[33] ADP 3-0, 2011, recaptured these "elements" in its two "core competencies" of the army, set out in Unified Land Operations: combined arms maneuver (CAM) and wide-area security (WAS), both of which are discussed below. ADRP 3-0 set out these two doctrinal task in more detail.[34] So this doctrinal shift was already under way in army doctrine and culminated in *Operations 2017*, which provided a "single, up-to-date, unifying doctrinal manual focused on large-unit tactics for use against contemporary threats." The new manual was "benchmarked against the most potent adversary capabilities and methods that have proliferated worldwide."[35] *Operations 2017* introduced the concept of Multi-Domain Battle to provide the army with a doctrinal concept for large-scale combat operations. Multi-Domain Battle "captures the idea that military success depends upon capabilities in the air, cyberspace, land, maritime, and space domains and in the electromagnetic spectrum" and "guides closer coordination and integration of capabilities than ever before."[36] Still, Multi-Domain Battle did not supersede Unified Land Operations. In fact, in 2017 the army also promulgated a new ADP 3-0, and in its foreword General Perkins reiterated that Unified Land Operations remained the army's contribution to unified action, meaning action by joint forces.[37] *Operations 2017* was largely consistent with ADP 3-0, and the concept of Unified Land Operations remained the army's "foundational operational concept." The authors of *Operations 2017* acknowledged this link between their manual and higher doctrine, arguing that to fully understand *Operations 2017*, readers must become familiar with the discussion of offense and defense in *ADRP 3-90, Offense and Defense* and stability operations in *ADRP 3-07, Stability.*[38] "Together with ADP 3-0 and ADRP 3-0," the preface of *Operations 2017* stated, "this manual provides a foundation for how Army forces conduct prompt and sustained large-scale combat operations . . . against a peer threat." More specifically—and in a clear reference to the threat posed by China, Russia, and Iran—*Operations 2017* focused on "the roles of echelons, initiative, and maneuver against enemies employing anti-access and area denial operational approaches to gain and exploit positions of relative advantage."[39] Consistent with the reengineering of doctrine precipitated by *Doctrine 2015*, *Operations 2017* "augmented" ADP 3-0 and ADRP 3-0 by setting out the "fundamentals, tactics, and techniques focused on fighting and winning large-scale combat operations."[40] The *Operations* manual had become a subordinate tactical manual and no longer represented the capstone doctrine of the U.S. Army.

Army doctrine from 2011 to 2017, then, appears highly consistent with military realism. It was a response to the drawdown of the army's recent COIN missions and the rise of more dangerous regional threats. However, as we will see below, though the army was walking away from its intense involvement in COIN missions, it was looking over its shoulder and embedding its COIN experience in new doctrine.

That these doctrinal changes were an evolutionary response to a changing threat environment seems borne out by an examination of our three key areas of doctrine. In terms of nuclear weapons, these new manuals continue the post–Cold War focus on protecting army units from attack by weapons of mass destruction, rather than the use of such weapons by army forces.[41] It is possible that this might change in the years to come if the Trump administration follows through with its proposal to field smaller nuclear weapons.[42] Conceivably, the dilemmas of the nuclear battlefield could again confront the U.S. Army. For now, however, there have not been major changes to army doctrine with regard to nuclear weapons.

When it comes to COIN and the mix of offense and defense, doctrinal continuity is also evident, though one has to look for it. The shift away from COIN in recent manuals is obvious and coincided with the U.S. drawdown in Iraq. U.S. troops were in the final stages of withdrawing from Iraq when the army published Change 1, a withdrawal completed by the time it published its first ADP 3-0. As early as Change 1 to *Operations 2008*, published in 2010, army doctrine dropped "insurgency" from its prominent position as part of the spectrum of warfare, where *Operations 2008* had placed it. Instead, Change 1 listed COIN as one of a number of forms of "irregular warfare." In this category it was joined by "foreign internal defense, support to insurgency, combatting terrorism, and unconventional warfare."[43] Under *Doctrine 2015*, the army categorized *Field Manual 3-24, Counterinsurgency* of recent fame, as a manual that described "types of operations/activities." In the same category were highly specialized manuals like *Personnel Recovery* and *Airspace Control*.[44] ADP 3-0, 2011 and 2017, went a step further, however. The words *insurgency* or *counterinsurgency* did not appear at all in ADP 3-0, 2011 or 2017.

However, it is clear that the army did not forget about COIN after the draw-down in Iraq. In 2014 the army published an update of *Field Manual 3-24, Counterinsurgency*, titled *Insurgencies and Countering Insurgencies*.[45] The new manual retained the broad characterization of COIN operations and best practices expressed by its predecessor. For example, cultural considerations, the new manual argued, were central to the entire process of devising a path to victory in COIN.[46] Concurring with its predecessor and the principles of stability operations from *Operations 1993*, the new manual stated flatly that "legitimacy is the main objective" in COIN campaigns.[47] However, whereas the previous manual provided a more abstract, conceptual framework for think-ing about COIN, the revised edition sought to assist soldiers and marines with running a COIN campaign on a day-to-day, tactical basis.[48] This was consis-tent with the new doctrinal function of field manuals: setting out the tactics and procedures in a specific doctrinal area. The update sought to capture many of the lessons from COIN operations in Iraq and Afghanistan. Army and Ma-rine Corps experience in these wars showed that COIN operations take place in diverse environments and under different conditions. There is no one-size-fits-all COIN strategy or tactic. For instance, army units will not always be the "primary [COIN] force" and must appreciate the "indirect methods of countering insurgencies."[49] Echoes of recent experience were everywhere in statements such as the following: "U.S. forces must never assume they will be welcomed by a local population. They may even be viewed as occupiers."[50]

Although the update to the COIN manual is important, there is insuffi-cient space in this concluding section to systematically evaluate this revision. Moreover, the primary focus here has been the influence of COIN on the ar-my's most important manuals. It is in these higher manuals—here ADPs and ADRPs—that army bureaucrats and cultural guardians should excise COIN from army doctrine. These parochial forces should not allow the lessons of COIN operations that contradict their preferences to shape the pinnacle of doctrine. Therefore, rather than engage in a detailed discussion of the updates to the COIN manual, the discussion below seeks to isolate the influence of COIN, or lack thereof, on higher manuals.

Even if COIN appears absent from recent doctrine, the signs of its influence are everywhere. For instance, Change 1 to *Operations 2008* defined irregular warfare as "a violent struggle among state and nonstate actors for legitimacy and influence over a population."[51] Although ADP 3-0, 2011 and 2017, did not mention "insurgency" or COIN, ADRP 3-0, 2016, did. Recall that the purpose of ADRPs was to provide the doctrinal detail missing from the higher ADP manual. ADRP 3-0, 2016, dealt with insurgency and reiterated some of the central tenets of *Field Manual 3-24*. It recognized, for instance, that combating insurgency required the support of the population among whom army forces were fighting. "Cultural understanding," ADRP 3-0 continued, was key when dealing with these populations and local security forces.[52] "Security force assistance" to local forces was a key component of "foreign internal defense," which was defined as "participation by civilian and military agencies of a government in any of the action programs taken by another government or other designated organization to free and protect its society from subversion, lawlessness, insurgency, terrorism, and other threats to its security (JP 3-22)."[53] These definitions clearly encompassed the understanding of COIN set out in *FM 3-24, Counterinsurgency* and *Operations 2008*. So, despite some signs of a growing institutional amnesia, there is strong evidence that the army had not forgotten the lessons of a decade of COIN operations. The emphasis on legitimacy in the eyes of the population also links it to the principles of stability operations articulated in early post–Cold War doctrine. Recently, in fact, the army codified these principles across both army and joint doctrine. More on this below.

In the realm of offense and defense, the new doctrine also retained the unity of offense, defense, and stability and support operations. *Operations 2008* and its 2010 update unified them under Full-Spectrum Operations and ADP 3-0, 2011, and ADRP 3-0, 2016, kept them together under the new concept of Unified Land Operations. ADP 3-0 did change the phrase "civil support operations" to "defense support of civil authorities," but the terms had largely identical definitions.[54] The first editions of ADP 3-0 and ADRP 3-0 discussed the unity of offense, defense, and stability operations in their definition of *decisive action*. "Decisive Action," they both argued, included "offense, defense, stability and DSCA [defense support of civil authorities]."[55] In addition, under *Doctrine 2015*, three manuals near the top of the doctrinal pyramid dealt with "Decisive Action": *Offensive and Defensive Operations, Recon, Security and Enabling Operations*, and *Stability Operations*.[56] ADP 3-0, 2017, the most recent update of the ADP 3-0 class of army manuals, also described offense, defense, stability, and DSCA as potentially "decisive actions."[57] Note the term *decisive* used in the context of all four types of actions. Traditionally, the army reserved this descriptor for offensive actions alone. Recent army doctrine recognized that offensive operations could not in themselves be decisive unless defensive and stability and support operations consolidate gains and provide security, hence the inclusion of defense and stability operations among its list of "decisive actions."

The unity of offense, defense, and stability was also evident when the first editions of ADP 3-0 and ADRP 3-0 set out the army's two "core competencies": combined arms maneuver and wide-area security. CAM was defined as "the use of combat power in *unified action* to defeat enemy ground forces; to seize, occupy, and defend land areas; and to achieve physical, temporal, and psychological advantages over the enemy to seize and exploit the initiative."[58] WAS entailed "the application of the elements of combat power in *unified action* to protect populations, forces, infrastructure, and activities; to deny the enemy positions of advantage; and to consolidate gains in order to retain the initiative."[59] ADP 3-0, 2011, went on to say that "offensive, defensive, and stability operations each requires a combination of combined arms maneuver and wide area security; neither core competency is adequate in isolation."[60] Its successor, ADP 3-0, 2016, retained this unity of offense, defense, and stability operations.[61] The limits of solely offensive operations were a key lesson learned from the U.S. Army's recent wars. From the parochial perspective, army bureaucrats and cultural guardians should have resisted learning this lesson. Instead, they embedded it in their most important doctrine.

Even in *Operations 2017*, a manual setting out tactics for large-scale combat operations, post–Cold War army doctrine and COIN experience left their mark. *Operations 2017* also listed offense, defense, stability, and DSCA as "Decisive Actions."[62] Even in "large-scale ground combat," the 2017 manual stated, "Army forces combine offensive, defensive, and stability tasks to seize, retain, and exploit the initiative in order to shape OEs [operational environments]." The unity of offense, defense, and stability operations, which characterized the Full-Spectrum Operations of *Operations 2001* and COIN operations in *Operations 2008* was alive and well in Unified Land Operations. Peter Mansoor and *Operations 2008*'s characterization of "counterinsurgency warfare [as] a mixture of offensive, defensive, and stability operations" still applied in these more recent manuals, even if they made fewer explicit references to COIN.[63] ADP 3-0, 2011, correctly noted that this unity of modes of operation predated *Operations 2008* and were not solely the result of the last decade of combat experience.[64] They originated in *Operations 2001*, published prior to the 9/11 terrorist attacks, and were refined in recent wars and the resulting doctrine.

Operations 2017 also placed heavy emphasis on the consolidation of gains, which clearly had its origin in recent experience. Indeed, the manual characterized the proper consolidation of gains made through offensive operations as a preventive medicine against an enemy transition to resistance using insurgency. Again, doctrine appears to keep on board many of the key lessons learned from Iraq and Afghanistan. However, *Operations 2017* places them in the context of large-scale combat operations against a regional threat with peer or near-peer capabilities. In this context, consolidation operations are responsible for ensuring that rear areas do not become areas of operations for insurgents once the main fighting force has captured that terrain. Units involved in consolidation operations "initially conduct offensive, defensive, and minimal stability tasks necessary to defeat bypassed forces, control key terrain and facilities, and secure population centers."[65] In this way, commanders will not permit the enemy to "reconstitute new forms of resistance to protract the conflict and undo our initial battlefield gains."[66] Note that these requirements for success are in a manual focused on large-scale combat operations, where army culture and its aversion to unconventional lessons should be most in evidence. The reality appears quite different.

More recently, ADP 3-0, 2017, exhibits the influence of the army's COIN experience. It also puts a premium on consolidation operations.[67] According to this current ADP 3-0, army forces consolidate gains "by executing area security and stability tasks" after large-scale combat operations. However, these operations can "occur across the range of military operations," whether they be offensive, defensive, or stability.[68] The current ADP argues that "understanding the human context that enables the enemy's will, which includes culture, economics, and history, is as important as understanding the enemy's military capabilities." "Commanders cannot presume," ADP 3-0, 2017, continued, "that superior military capability alone generates the desired effects on the enemy."[69] Like the COIN manuals the army developed for its recent wars, the 2017 edition of ADP 3-0 stressed the importance of understanding the cultural context in which one is fighting.

It is important to note, however, that both *Operations 2017* and ADP 3-0, 2017, stress that army forces should be responsible for "minimum" stability tasks. Although army doctrine drew important lessons from its recent COIN experience, the rise of more dangerous threats and disillusion among civilian leaders with COIN likely tempered the influence of recent experience. The army's enthusiasm for COIN was also dampened by the apparently deleterious effects of protracted COIN operations on skills requisite for large-scale combat. There was an incompatibility between training for combat operations and training for COIN or stability operations. In fact, General Wallace's observation of the discordance between combat training and the requirements of COIN during the campaign in Iraq triggered the development of the first COIN manual. And COIN experts have long appreciated the incompatibility of conventional military training and effective counterinsurgency operations. The often-unappreciated conclusion being that forces that immerse themselves in a COIN environment let their conventional warfare skills atrophy. ADRP 3-0, 2016, recognized that troops trained in conventional combat operations were ill-suited to stability operations and vice versa: "Operational experience demonstrates that forces trained exclusively for offensive and defensive tasks are not as proficient at stability tasks as those trained specifically for stability tasks. For maximum effectiveness, tasks for stability and defense support of civil authorities require dedicated training, similar to training for offensive and defensive tasks. Likewise, forces involved in protracted stability or defense support of civil authorities tasks require intensive training to regain proficiency in offensive or defensive tasks before engaging in large-scale combat operations."[70]

Similarly, ADP 3-0, 2017, advocated "specific, dedicated training on offensive, defensive, and stability or defense support of civil authorities (DSCA) tasks."[71] *Operations 2008* also pointed to the same issue and argued that it could be resolved through dedicated training rather than refocusing on combat operations.[72] To be clear, in 2016 the army was not claiming that preparing for combat operations prepared its soldiers for the complex environments in which they would fight, where stability operations would be essential to success.[73] Although recent manuals recognize that training for stability operations could dull skills necessary for effective combat operations, and vice versa, the response was not, as the bureaucratic and cultural perspective might expect, to discontinue training for stability operations in favor of more lucrative and culturally approved combat operations. The army recognized that this was not an either-or choice. Recent operational experience had shown that stability operations could be accompanied by intense offensive and defensive combat operations, hence their unity; the two could not be compartmentalized with combat operations given preferential treatment. Despite a recognition that prolonged exposure to COIN operations could dull combat skills, the army did not push the lessons and requirements of COIN aside.

The publication of ADRP 3-0 in 2016, the year after General Odierno's retirement, also saw the return of principles of war, but in an important new form. *Operations 2008* and Change 1 had set out the principles of war in an appendix.[74] Instead, ADRP 3-0 introduced the "principles of joint operations," earlier set out in joint doctrine.[75] However, these principles were not new to the army. They were a combination of the principles of war: objective, offensive, mass, maneuver, economy of force, unity of command, security, surprise, simplicity, and the principles of stability operations, that is, restraint, perseverance, and legitimacy.[76] The army first introduced the principles of stability operations more than two decades earlier, in *Operations 1993*. Even earlier, General Harold K. Johnson had championed the term *stability operations* during the Vietnam War, and it had its doctrinal roots in *Operations 1962* and *1968*. More than fifty years later, ADRP 3-0 argued that commanders applied these principles of joint operations in their "operational approach," which consisted of applying "defeat mechanisms" and "stability mechanisms." Defeat mechanisms include offensive and defensive combat operations, while "stability mechanisms" include "stability tasks that establish and maintain security and facilitate consolidating gains in an area of operations."[77] Although the nomenclature is different, ADRP 3-0 was clearly setting out the combination of offense, defense, and stability and support operations that characterized its doctrinal predecessors. This combination of defeat and stability mechanisms reflected again one of the main lessons of the army's recent wars: combat operations are decisive only when stability operations consolidate the gains those operations achieve.

ADP 3-90, Offense and Defense also set out these principles of joint operations.[78] ADP 3-90 emphasized that the principles were "not a checklist, and their degree of application varies with the situation. Blind adherence to these principles does not guarantee success."[79] ADP 3-0, 2017, also included the principles of joint operations and warned against this checklist mentality.[80] Although *Operations 2017* did not mention the principles of stability operations directly, it remarked on the importance of "legitimacy, ideas, and popular perceptions," perseverance or "will," and the "support of domestic audiences" in achieving "relative advantages" over one's opponent.[81] Acknowledging rather than erasing its recent COIN experience, recent army doctrine gave equal standing to the principles of stability operations and its traditional principles of war.

Most important for the present study, the return of the principles of war meant the return of the principle of offense. However, ADRP 3-0, 2016, was not reviving a traditional view of the offense. It defined the principle of offense as follows: "Seize, retain, and exploit the initiative."[82] However, like its doctrinal predecessors, ADRP 3-0 promoted a broader conception of the initiative, in which a commander could seize and retain the initiative in offensive, defensive, or stability operations. As the manual puts it in one place: "Momentum comes from retaining the initiative and executing high-tempo operations that overwhelm enemy resistance. . . . Commanders maintain momentum by anticipating and transitioning rapidly between any combination of offensive, defensive, stability, or defense support of civil authorities tasks."[83] Based on the definition of offense in the principles of joint operations, offensive, defensive, and stability operations could all be "offensive" because they can seize, retain, and exploit the initiative and are "tasks of decisive action."[84] This echoed *Operations 2008*, which noted: "Initiative gives all operations the spirit, if not the form, of the offense. It originates in the principle of the offensive. *The principle of the offensive is not just about attacking.*"[85]

Doctrinal continuity surrounding the concept of initiative is also evident in the rise of the concept of "mission command" in recent army doctrine. Change 1 to *Operations 2008* argued that the army had not paid enough attention to the complexities of command in a full-spectrum environment, where transitions between offense, defense, and stability operations were a daily if not hourly occurrence. According to General Robert Cone, commander of TRADOC from 2011 to 2014, army leaders in the field struggled to adapt to this complex threat environment.[86] In an attempt to resolve this issue, Change 1 introduced the concept of "mission command" to the *Operations* manual.[87] Mission command operated through mission orders, where commanders tell their subordinates what their intent or goal is but do not tell their subordinate how to achieve that goal. In Change 1, ADP 3-0, ADRP 3-0, and *Operations 2017*, "mission command" is intimately linked to initiative. The purpose of mission command, Change 1 contended, was to "enable disciplined initiative within the commander's intent to empower agile and adaptive leaders in the conduct of full spectrum operations."[88] *Operations 2017* cited General Patton in support of the concept: "Never tell people how to do things," Patton advised. "Tell them what to do and they will surprise you with their ingenuity."[89] Echoing its doctrinal predecessors, *Operations 2017* stated that "the philosophy of mission command guides commanders, staffs, and subordinates in their approach to operations."[90]

Like Change 1 to *Operations 2008*, ADRP 3-0, 2016, used the concept of "*disciplined* initiative."[91] The use of the modifier *disciplined* looks to signal the retention of the understanding of initiative expressed in previous manuals like *Operations 1976* and *Operations 2008*. The 1976 manual argued that the commander could enjoy the initiative in the defense and the 2008 edition that they could enjoy the initiative in stability operations. A commander had the initiative so long as the enemy was being compelled to respond to the commander's plan, whether it be in an offensive, defensive, or stability operation, though any plan would likely involve a mixture of all three. Commanders and their subordinates were not to interpret the initiative as being reserved solely to the offensive. In conflicts fought among civilian populations, *un*disciplined initiative could lead to unnecessary civilian casualties, undermining legitimacy, security, and the consolidation of gains. In the language of Unified Land Operations, the unreflective use of offensive combined arms maneuver could undermine wide-area security operations aimed at consolidation of gains. When discussing the offense, *ADP 3-90, Offense and Defense*, which *Operations 2017* deferred to on this topic, argued that tactical leaders must engage in "offensive tasks" within the limits of "the higher commander's intent," that is, the superior commander's intent must *discipline* the offensive initiative of subordinates. *Operations 2017* too implies that initiative need not be limited to the offense. It argues that consolidation operations need to be thought of "as a form of exploitation and pursuit" of the enemy. This newest manual appears to recommend that commanders impart an offensive spirit and type of initiative to these consolidation operations, which are often a combination of offense, defense, and stability operations. Clearly drawing on experiences from Iraq and Afghanistan, the purpose of this broadly conceived concept of initiative is "to avoid giving enemies the time to reorganize for a different kind of fight."[92] So despite its focus on combat, *Operations 2017* adheres to the conceptualization of initiative advocated by its doctrinal predecessors and higher doctrine. This higher doctrine in the form of ADP 3-0, 2017, also espouses "mission command" and "disciplined initiative."[93] Nowhere does the newest ADP 3-0 argue that only the attacker enjoys the initiative. Instead, it argues that a commander is able to "seize, retain, and exploit the initiative" when they force "the enemy to respond to friendly action."[94] These friendly actions can take the form of offensive, defensive, and stability operations. Army doctrine after 2008 retained an understanding of initiative that reached beyond offensive operations. This is surprising given that bureaucratic interests and U.S. Army cultural norms should promote a predominantly offensive understanding of this key doctrinal concept.

Operations 2017 did, however, have separate chapters on offense and defense, unlike *Operations 2008* or Change 1, which treated offense, defense, and stability operations together. *Operations 2017* argued that here it was being consistent with higher doctrine in the form of *ADP 3-90, Offense and Defense*. But ADP 3-90 explicitly stated that as part of "the art of tactics" commanders "must understand how to train and employ forces simultaneously conducting offensive, defensive, and stability or [DSCA] tasks."[95] Only after preserving the unity of offense, defense, and stability operations in this way did ADP 3-90 go on to discuss offense and defense in isolation. ADP 3-90 argued that in tactics, that is, in an engagement between opposing military forces, offense was the decisive form of fighting and that commanders could achieve decisive results therein only by transitioning to the offense. Nevertheless, like previous army doctrine, ADP 3-90 simultaneously preserved an appreciation for the unique powers of the defense. It argued that defense was the stronger form of fighting. The defender could succeed with fewer forces and could take advantage of opportunities to prepare the terrain to provide tactical benefits. Finally, as Active Defense and AirLand Battle had pointed out, the defender was especially powerful when transitioning to the counterattack before the attacker had an opportunity to consolidate their gains and transition to the defense. The commander could use these defensive advantages to defeat an attack by a numerically superior enemy. Commanders could employ local defensive counterattacks to "defeat, destroy, or neutralize" isolated enemy units and capabilities.[96] *Operations 2017* also appreciated the power of the defense in relation to stability operations, arguing that one purpose of the defense was not only to prepare for the offense but to prepare for "stability tasks." It cited ADRP 3-0 in support.[97] Recent army doctrine preserved the lessons about the power of the defense codified by its Cold War predecessors. It had learned the limits of the offense firsthand after its rapid conventional victories in Afghanistan and Iraq were indecisive.

Recent doctrine also witnessed important and unexpected changes in the vocabulary of war. Interestingly, in Change 1 *mission command* replaced the term *command and control*, and in ADP 3-0 and ADRP 3-0 *mission command* replaced *battle command* and *operational environment* replaced *battlespace*.[98] Although these might seem like minor changes, such shifts in language emphasize that army commanders were not concerned solely with combat. When one examines the definitions of *battlespace* and *operational environment* closely, though, they are virtually identical. This change in language was not just window dressing. It acknowledged earlier doctrinal changes to the idea of the battlespace. *Operations 2008* was at pains to point out that battle was not the only thing that happened in the battlespace.[99] After all, in the battlespace, offense, defense, and stability operations were intermixed, and stability operations included numerous noncombat responsibilities. Army units were part of a "joint, interagency, intergovernmental, and multinational" team, with responsibilities beyond the battlefield.[100] In 2017 the new edition of ADP 3-0 preserved this change in combat nomenclature and this broader understanding of the army's role.[101] Within their "operational environment," army commanders "defeat enemy forces, control terrain, secure populations, and preserve joint force freedom of action."[102]

These were not the only surprising changes in combat vernacular since 2008, however. According to Army Chief of Staff Odierno, the "central idea" of the first ADP 3-0 was Unified Land Operation. In ULO "Army units seize, retain, and exploit the initiative," Odierno wrote, "to gain and maintain a position of relative advantage in sustained land operations to create conditions for favorable conflict resolution."[103] In this central idea we see the influence of ADP 3-0's immediate doctrinal predecessor, recent army experience, and the trend away from doctrinal vocabulary focused on battle. Commanders gain the "initiative" in "land operations" not "offensive combat operations." Neither is the goal "victory in battle" but "conflict resolution." This trend away from battle-centric language is also in evidence in the newest edition of ADP 3-0, which sits atop the doctrinal pyramid and has doctrinal supremacy over *Field Manual 3-0, Operations 2017*. ADP 3-0, 2017, argues that as part of seizing, retaining, and exploiting the initiative, combined arms—traditionally focused on combat—can be used both "destructively," in offensive and defensive operations, and "constructively," in stability operations.[104] In addition, ADP 3-0, 2017, defined *combat power* as "the total means of destructive, *constructive*, and information capabilities that a military unit or formation can apply at a given time."[105] Army commanders apply this combat power "through simultaneous offensive, defensive, [and] stability . . . tasks."[106] Even the most battle-centric concepts in recent army doctrine appreciated its roles beyond the battlefield. The replacement of terms like *battle command* and *battlespace* with *mission command* and *operational environment*, among others, represent a move away from a view of war centered on combat, which is supposed to characterize U.S. Army culture. But these changes in the way the U.S. Army talks about war are not revolutionary, but rather drive home the doctrinal realities established by previous manuals.

Over the past decade, the U.S. Army has also continued and broadened the doctrinal trend of focusing on the need for jointness. Army Chief of Staff Raymond Odierno emphasized "that success requires fully integrating Army operations with the efforts of joint, interagency, and multinational partners."[107] From December 2006 to February 2008, Odierno experienced this need for unity of effort firsthand as commander of Multi-National Corps-Iraq under General Petraeus during the surge. Again, however, this call for unity was not significantly different from *Operations 2008*, which argued that interservice, -agency, and -governmental cooperation were essential for long-term mission success.[108] ADP 3-0 recognized, as DePuy and Starry did when setting out Active Defense and AirLand Battle, that the army "cannot operate effectively without [the] support" of the other services because it "depends on its joint partners for capabilities that do not reside within the Army."[109] In fact, although Full-Spectrum Operations and Unified Land Operations were very similar, General Odierno and doctrine writers preferred the language of *Unified* Land Operations (ULO) because it was more consistent with joint U.S. military doctrine known as "Unified Action."[110] ULO explained how the army contributed to the joint force.[111] Subsequent doctrine publications made the same point. *ADP 3-90, Offense and Defense* emphasized that the army was part of an "interdependent joint force" that relies on other services' capabilities to "maximize the complementary and reinforcing effects of both."[112] In 2016 ADRP 3-0, fleshing out the concept of ULO, reiterated this need for unity.[113] *Operations 2017* also points to the importance of unified operations because the army performs its roles as part of a joint force, often in a multinational context. Like ADP 3-0, 2011, *Operations 2017* pointed out its consonance with the doctrine of the joint force, *JP 3-0, Joint Operations*.[114] Finally, ADP 3-0, 2017, argued that because the army was an "expeditionary" force, its operations "are dependent upon joint air and maritime support."[115] Discussing the army's news doctrinal framework, Multi-Domain Battle, in *Military Review*, the commander of TRADOC, General Perkins, argued that this new doctrinal concept hinged on extensive unity across services and agencies. "The Army's dominance on land," wrote Perkins, "has become dependent, if not contingent, on access to the air, cyber, and space domains." Perkins argued that the army could not allow "domain-based parochial positions" to undermine doctrinal innovation. Since early in the process, and building on their doctrinal collaboration on *Field Manual 3-24, Counterinsurgency*, the U.S. Marine Corps had been helping the army refine Multi-Domain Battle. The U.S. Air Force has also worked with the army to hone the concept.[116] As previous chapters show, however, such calls for more jointness and unity were not new. Previous doctrine already established the doctrinal imperative of unity across services and agencies. As Ancker and Scully point out in their discussion of ADP 3-0, 2011, "Unified land operations is a natural extension of doctrine that has advised the Army for many years."[117] As with Active Defense and post–Cold War doctrine, the army was calling for this unity during a period of shrinking defense budgets.[118] Continuing its contravention of bureaucratic and cultural expectations, more recent army doctrine recognizes that narrow parochialism is not an option amid drastically diminished resources. Like previous doctrinal periods, it was the threat environment and the dearth of available resources that drove this need for unity. In the second decade of the twenty-first century, the army could not confront insurgency, hybrid threats, or near-peer adversaries in regional contexts isolated from other services, nonmilitary agencies, or local political and security partners. To have a plausible chance of addressing these dangerous threats, army doctrine advocated unity over autonomy.

After 2008 it appeared at first that the U.S. Army was eliminating COIN from its doctrine at the earliest opportunity. The drawdowns in Iraq and Afghanistan were bringing an end to a COIN doctrine that army bureaucrats disliked and from which army culture instinctively recoiled. It seemed that U.S. Army preferences for conventional, offensive warfare were rearing their parochial heads again after a brief hiatus. The preceding chapters show, however, that often these bureaucratic and cultural perspectives have a difficult time explaining the doctrinal behavior of the U.S. Army, an organization they often claim to explain well. Moreover, recent doctrinal changes appear to be as much a result of changes in the threat environment as the resurrection of parochialism. As the army left Iraq and formidable regional powers such as Russia and China began to flex their muscles, it reduced the emphasis on COIN in its most important doctrine and sought to adapt to these emerging and, in the military realist view, more dangerous threats. Despite this shift, a closer examination of recent doctrine reveals that army bureaucrats and cultural guardians did not turn away from the lessons of more than a decade of COIN warfare. Nor did they revive an exclusively offensive theory of victory. Instead, army doctrine continued to argue for the unity of offense, defense, and stability operations as essential to decisive results.[119] Those who had a hand in the recent doctrine anticipated and rejected a parochial interpretation of it.[120] They argue, for instance, that *Operations 2017* deals with the actual threat environment the army is facing today and at the same time recognizes that there are "linkages" between the army's COIN experience and large-scale combat operations.[121] True, the new manuals largely excised the term *COIN*, but the doctrinal fingerprints of a decade of COIN warfare are everywhere. The Obama administration's disillusionment with COIN might have played a role in this excision. Although General Odierno retired the year before the army published ADRP 3-0, army doctrine captured many of the lessons from a decade of war that the general so badly wanted to preserve. This makes sense because the hybrid threats the army faces today share many of the characteristics of the complex threat environments it faced in Iraq and Afghanistan.[122] It does not appear that army doctrine treated its experience in recent wars as an aberration to be swept aside in favor of culturally approved modes of fighting. On the contrary, it institutionalized the lessons of this experience while adapting doctrine to an evolving threat environment.[123] As General Perkins, TRADOC commander, put it in his foreword to ADP 3-0, 2017: "In this edition, we retain lessons of the past but also look to a future where large-scale ground combat against peer threats is a distinct possibility."[124] The above analysis of recent doctrine shows that this was not simply a doctrinal facade.

Moreover, since 2008 there is good evidence that parochialism did not dominate the doctrinal process. The consistent drive for more and more jointness and unity in army doctrine is problematic for bureaucratic and cultural explanations. This initiative is, however, consistent with military realism. As the case-study chapters have shown, the army consistently sacrificed its autonomy to develop doctrines that could plausibly address the most dangerous threats it faced. The most recent permutations of army doctrine are no exception. At the top of the doctrinal pyramid, ADP 3-0 placed major emphasis on jointness and interbureaucratic and -governmental cooperation as part of *Unified* Land Operations. The inclusion of organizations outside of other military services represented an even greater threat to bureaucratic autonomy and predictability. Nevertheless, the U.S. Army has determined that this unity is necessary to produce a doctrine that could plausibly address the most dangerous threats in a time of declining resources. Multi-Domain Battle, the army's most recent doctrinal innovation, will be impossible to implement without cooperation and integration with other services and government agencies. The military realist need to develop a doctrine responsive to the threat environment appears to have trumped bureaucratic and cultural preferences once again. I must acknowledge, however, that the above analysis is insufficient to evaluate the role of civilian realists in recent doctrinal processes. I leave this and other tasks to future researchers and make some additional recommendations for them below.

Military Realism: Implications for Theory

Although additional research is no doubt required, the success of military realism in the unlikely case of the U.S. Army has a number of implications for theorizing about military organizations and innovation. For instance, a thirst for resources, autonomy, and certainty is not always the main motivation of military organizations. Nor do they always develop offensive doctrines to serve these purposes. Neither are military cultures necessarily insurmountable obstacles to doctrinal innovation. In addition, military organizations are not necessarily averse to change and do not always require outside intervention to change their doctrines. Moreover, military organizations are not always using international threats to justify bureaucratic and cultural desires. Changes in the threat environment can actually lead to real changes in doctrine that sacrifice organizational autonomy and contradict cultural traditions. Military organizations can sacrifice these parochial goals to develop a plausible doctrine for addressing critical threats. Additionally, civilian interventions in doctrine are often more consistent with initiatives already at work within their military institutions.

Instead, military realism argues that under certain conditions, military organizations will develop defensive rather than offensive doctrines. Moreover, they will do so independently of civilian intervention. In fact, in some of the cases examined here, the U.S. Army developed defensive doctrines when civilian leaders expressed a desire for a more aggressive approach. For instance, the army preserved its defensive doctrine despite a more aggressive Reagan strategy, and *Operations 2001* retained the new post–Cold War emphasis on stability operations despite Bush administration calls to concentrate on war fighting instead of nation building. Theoretically, this contradicts the bureaucratic and cultural contention that militaries and their officers are inherently aggressive and prefer offensive doctrines. The new analysis presented here dovetails nicely with the findings of Richard Betts, who has shown that when it came to the use of force during the Cold War, civilian officials were often more aggressive than their military subordinates.[125] In his doctoral dissertation, David Petraeus, later General Petraeus, showed that this trend continued into the late 1970s and '80s.[126]

Rather than constantly designing doctrines that called for more resources to fuel its bureaucracy, no matter the threat environment, the army often designed its keystone doctrines to adapt to the resource constraints placed on them by civilian leaders. These resource constraints led to doctrinal innovations that contradicted bureaucratic interests. For instance, cuts to the size of the army through the 1960s and '70s led to the development of the Active Defense and AirLand Battle doctrines. These doctrines undermined army autonomy by making close cooperation with the U.S. Air Force a precondition for the successful completion of the army's main mission. Consistent with a military realist outlook, the army sacrificed its organizational autonomy in order to develop a doctrine that could plausibly address the main threat. In the army's most recent doctrine, the emphasis on jointness and unity across services and agencies during a period of resource constraints continues this unexpected trend.

The U.S. Army also developed doctrinal innovations contrary to its cultural essence, like the adoption a defensive theory of victory and stability operations. Explaining U.S. Army doctrine from 1960 to 2008 should have been easy for bureaucratic and cultural theories. Indeed, a number of works on military innovation have already used these theories to explain the US Army at different points during these five decades. Despite the favorable conditions enjoyed by these alternative approaches, however, the findings presented here have told a different story.

Finally, changes in strategy often failed to change U.S. Army doctrine in the ways envisioned by civilians or civilian realism. Even when civilians enlisted military mavericks to impose doctrinal changes, those mavericks often behaved more like military realists. Civilian doctrinal initiatives accelerated changes already under way, but they did not determine their character. Instead, the threat assessments of senior military officers, based on the logic and limits of force, determined the degree of doctrinal change. These results in cases where civilians actively intervened undercut the explanatory power of civilian realism. On the other hand, the fact that military realism successfully explained the difficult case of U.S. Army doctrine is strong evidence in favor of its theoretical foundations.

The Need for Further Research

All books have their limits. This one is no different. Although there were good reasons to focus the testing of military realism on one military over time, there are also numerous paths not taken. Because I seek to answer a puzzle arising between the Vietnam and Iraq Wars, this bracketed time frame makes sense. However, the army has revised its doctrine since 2008. I provided only a preliminary examination of those doctrinal changes above. This initial examination says too little about the doctrinal process and timing of recent manuals, which proved so essential to the evaluation of theories in the case-study chapters. The present study indicates avenues for future research. For instance, in terms of civilian realism, recent army doctrine appears highly responsive to the Obama Administration's pivot to Asia. These changes in civilian strategy may have had a powerful influence on the development of army doctrine. At the same time, however, the preservation of major elements of stability operations appears to contravene the Obama administrations opposition to stability operations in the 2012 Defense Strategic Guidance.[127] More recently, senior army leaders, and their doctrinal ideas focusing on peer competitors, may have influenced the Trump administration's recent strategic shift toward "great-power competition."[128] This would make sense given the prominence of retired military officers in Trump's early cabinet. Interestingly, H. R. McMaster, until recently Trump's national security adviser, was a powerful advocate of COIN in the U.S. Army during the fighting in Iraq. However, during his tenure in the Trump administration, the new U.S. National Security and Defense Strategies shifted focus away from COIN operations to threats arising from great-power competition. This change in focus mirrors that which has taken place in U.S. Army doctrine since 2008. Such a shift in focus is perfectly consistent with a military realist perspective that seeks to address the gravest threats. However, while military realists in the army sought to bring more balance to the force, they did not forget the lessons of recent wars. The departure of McMaster and Secretary of Defense Mattis, more recently, might be in protest against a Trump administration that appears to be turning its back on the lessons of more than a decade of counterinsurgency war.

In terms of broader research, the next step would be to place military realism in a more traditionally comparative context. Scholars need to evaluate military realism in other historical contexts, other countries, other regime types, and especially other military organizations. Many questions remain unanswered. For instance, because military realism has friction as one of its central concepts, will it have less explanatory power in military forces less acquainted with the friction of ground combat, such as navies, air forces, and cyber forces? Does the lesser role of friction in the operations of such forces mean that they will be more optimistic about their potential missions and the efficacy of offensive doctrines? Elsewhere I provide a partial answer to this question by showing that U.S. Army lessons about the power of the defense have purchase even in the cyber realm.[129] The question remains: Does military realism decrease the further one gets from the requirements of ground combat? This work must leave these questions unanswered.

Military Realism: Implications for Policy and Strategy

Some might object to this section given that this book analyzed only one military organization over time. However, the U.S. Army, with its powerful bureaucracy, strong culture, and tradition of civilian subordination, was an easy case for the competing theories and a very difficult case for military realism. The new theory passed a difficult test and should be considered as an alternative explanation of military innovation. Consequently, it is reasonable to examine its potential policy implications. Even if the reader is unwilling to grant this concession, and limits the policy implications to the United States, they are nonetheless important. The United States remains one of the most important actors in international affairs, so even these more limited policy implications warrant attention.

At the beginning of this study, I argued that understanding change and continuity in military doctrine was important for at least three reasons. First, offensive military doctrines can exacerbate international conflict by leading to apprehension among other states, increased security dilemmas, crisis escalation, and even wars. Conversely, doctrines with a clearly defensive theory of victory could dampen international hostility by signaling benign intentions. Second, military doctrines can waste limited national resources if they serve bureaucratic desires for funds rather than responding to real threats to national security and appreciating that government resources are finite. Finally, military doctrines could contradict foreign policy. For instance, if a military preserves its offensive doctrine when civilian foreign policy seeks to signal benign intent, then doctrine undermines the credibility of this signal. Such crossed signals can undermine civil-military relations by breeding distrust.

Regarding aggressive theories of victory, with their destabilizing international effects, under certain conditions the U.S. Army voluntarily developed defensive doctrines. The army did as *Operations 1962* advised and "deliberately undertook the defensive."[130] Therefore, militaries can voluntarily develop the defensive doctrines that can mitigate international tensions and support a pacific foreign policy. They can do so even when civilian leaders are demanding a more aggressive approach. In such cases, military doctrine could reduce the international alarm caused by aggressive foreign policy initiated by civilian authorities. Therefore, making military realists a central part of policy making and strategy may be less dangerous than bureaucratic and cultural theorists fear.

In addition, the case studies here show that U.S. Army doctrine often adapted to the resource constraints put on the army by civilian leaders, rather than using doctrine as a tool to push for more resources. Limited resources led to defensive theories of victory and important doctrinal innovations like Active Defense, AirLand Battle, and Unified Land Operations. Necessity does indeed appear to be the mother of invention. One way civilians might inspire innovation, including shifts to defensive theories of victory—with all their apparent benefits—is to reduce the resources available to a military organization. However, inspiring innovation in this way can be a double-edged sword. In the 1960s, as civilian leaders reduced U.S. Army resources while Soviet capabilities increased, the army adopted a more and more defensive theory of victory.

However, this imbalance of capabilities also led to a doctrine that more closely integrated conventional and nuclear forces. If one ascribes to the spiral model of the causes of war, the defensive doctrine might have reduced international tensions, but the highly integrated nuclear-conventional doctrine made escalation from limited to nuclear war more likely.

In addition, defensive doctrines might not produce the international results we expect. If, for instance, one thinks deterrence failure, rather than conflict spirals, is the main cause of war, passive defensive doctrines might embolden revisionist states. President Donald Trump labeled himself a believer in the deterrence model of the causes of war in his 2018 State of the Union address, stating, "We know that weakness is the surest path to conflict, and unmatched power is the surest means of our defense." In the same address, President Trump asked for an end to defense sequestration.[131] We should consider both the positive and the negative consequences of constraining resources as a policy tool and how our theories of war, implicit or explicit, affect policy choices and blind us to alternative viewpoints.

Reducing available resources also appears to have played a role in less successful innovations. In the post–Cold War, the army developed highly innovative doctrinal concepts that attempted to reconcile a new and difficult power projection mission with major budget cuts. The result was a doctrine so ahead of its time that many of its technological components were untested. In this case, the U.S. Army proved too innovative and spearheaded problematic innovations, such as the Future Combat System. A highly constrained budget environment can lead to innovation, but not all innovations are good ideas. Civilian leaders should keep this in mind too when contemplating major cuts to the resources of their militaries, whether to inspire innovation or for other reasons. In the age of sequestration, resource constraints could again prove to be a driver of innovation. However, using the drastic curtailing of resources to drive innovation in military organizations is not without its risks. The unattainable revolution in military affairs pursued by the U.S. Army was in part a response to the resource constraints of the 1990s. The campaigns in Iraq and Afghanistan exposed the chinks in this revolutionary armor. Resource constraints in the second decade of the twenty-first century could also foster flawed innovations.

The other theories of organizational and military innovation have had important effects on civil-military relations. The belief that military officers are just bureaucrats in uniform has had a real impact on policy. For instance, both Presidents Kennedy and Nixon distrusted the military because they thought it motivated by narrow bureaucratic interests. Both isolated themselves from traditional military advisers in the national security structure and used bureaucratic arguments to discount military advice. More recently, the Obama administration viewed high-level military advice with suspicion when it did not conform to its policy goals.[132] The Trump administration seemed more inclined to accept military advice, appointing former Marine Corps Generals James Mattis as secretary of defense and John Kelly as White House chief of staff and Lieutenant General H. R. McMaster as national security adviser. However, at the time of writing, all three have departed the Trump administration. The fact that military officers inhabited chief positions in the cabinet worried many observers. But I would argue that their absence is more worrying. As military realism argues, the experience of and preparing for conflict inculcates in military officers an appreciation of the underlying logic of force and its limits. They also appreciate the fact that the use of force brings about an interaction that is only partially under the control of each belligerent, even when one of those belligerents is the sole superpower. Military realists are cautious about the efficacy of force. If civilian officials see their military subordinates as military realists, rather than bureaucrats or cultural guardians, and evaluate their advice accordingly, their foreign policies and strategy could benefit from this caution. Today, fewer and fewer civilian leaders have military experience. More than ever, fractured civil-military relations could lead to the ill-considered use of force. Problematic understandings of the motives of military representatives can widen this civil-military gap. A military realist perspective, on the other hand, can help to preserve a strong civil-military link when we most need it. The Trump administration appears to have served that vital link, and the consequences could be dire.

This does not mean that civil-military relations will be harmonic if a military realist view is adopted. As this work has shown, civilians and military leaders will often disagree about what threats the military needs to prepare for. These disagreements will continue. Moreover, military doctrine will at times contradict civilian strategy. However, this contradiction will not be due solely to bureaucratic or cultural motives, but contrary assessments of the threat environment. Civil-military friction will continue, but understanding this friction in light of military realism will bring new clarity to its causes, solutions, and benefits.

NOTES

Introduction

1. Colin L. Powell, *My American Journey*, 149.

2. Conrad C. Crane, "Avoiding Vietnam: The U.S. Army's Response to Defeat in South East Asia," 2, http://www.strategicstudiesinstitute.army.mil/pdffiles/pub58.pdf; Robert M. Cassidy, *Counterinsurgency and the Global War on Terror: Military Culture and Irregular War*, 97.

3. Andrew F. Krepinevich, *The Army and Vietnam*; Douglas S. Blaufarb, *The Counterinsurgency Era: U.S. Doctrine and Performance, 1950 to the Present*, 288.

4. Austin Long, *The Soul of Armies: Counterinsurgency Doctrine and Military Culture in the US and UK*; David Fitzgerald, *Learning to Forget: U.S. Army Counterinsurgency Doctrine and Practice from Vietnam to Iraq*; Cassidy, *Counterinsurgency*; Carl H. Builder, *The Masks of War: American Military Style in Strategy and Analysis*; John A. Nagl, *Learning to Eat Soup with a Knife: Counterinsurgency Lessons from Malaya and Vietnam*.

5. Unknown army general in Vietnam quoted in Brian M. Jenkins, *The Unchangeable War*, 3, http://www.rand.org/content/dam/rand/pubs/research_memoranda/2006/RM6278-2.pdf.

6. Lewis Sorely, *A Better War: The Unexamined Victories and Final Tragedy of America's Last Years in Vietnam*; Krepinevich, *The Army and Vietnam*.

7. Peter D. Feaver, "The Right to Be Right: Civil-Military Relations and the Iraq Surge Decision."

8. Thomas E. Ricks, *Fiasco: The American Military Adventure in Iraq, 2003 to 2005*, 168–72; Peter R. Mansoor, *Surge: My Journey with General David Petraeus and the Remaking of the Iraq War*. Michael Desch makes this point briefly but forcefully in his correspondence with Peter Feaver and Richard K. Betts. Betts, Desch, and Feaver, "Correspondence: Civilians, Soldiers, and the Iraq Surge Decision."

9. Desch points this out in his response to Peter Feaver. Betts, Desch, and Feaver, "Correspondence."

10. Thomas E. Ricks, *The Gamble: General David Petraeus and the American Military Adventure in Iraq, 2006–2008*.

11. Robert M. Gates, "A House Divided," chap. 10 in *Duty: Memoirs of a Secretary at War*.

12. Stephen Peter Rosen, *Winning the Next War: Innovation and the Modern Military*, 38. The shift in the strategic measure of effectiveness from killing and capturing insurgents to securing the population in the midst of a war is particularly problematic for Stephen Peter Rosen's theory of military innovation, which argues that such changes should not occur.

13. John Keegan, *The Face of Battle: A Study of Agincourt, Waterloo, and the Somme*, 175.

14. Walter E. Kretchik, *U.S. Army Doctrine: From the American Revolution to the War on Terror*, 2, 5.

15. Samuel P. Huntington, *The Soldier and the State: The Theory and Politics of Civil-Military Relations*, 63.

16. Carl von Clausewitz, *On War*, trans. Michael Howard and Peter Paret, 149.

17. Clausewitz, *On War*, trans. Howard and Paret, 100–113.

18. Williamson Murray, *Military Adaptation in War: With Fear of Change*, chap. 4.

19. Some have argued that doctrine is not important to militaries and that the conduct of operations is determined on a more ad hoc basis. Janne E. Nolan, *Guardians of the Arsenal: The Politics of Nuclear Strategy*; Peter D. Feaver, *Guarding the Guardians: Civilian Control of Nuclear Weapons in the United States*.

20. "Change of doctrine cannot be entirely ignored, for adopting a new doctrine can result in substantial changes in the practices and structures of a military organization." Harald Hoiback, "What Is Doctrine?," 892. Military doctrine guides training, and "armies fight the way that they train." John A. Lynn, *Battle: A History of Combat and Culture*, 306. See also Murray, *Military Adaptation in War*.

21. Robert Jervis, "Cooperation under the Security Dilemma." As an example, Kimberly Martin Zisk shows that U.S. and NATO war-fighting doctrines were watched closely by Soviet political and military leaders and led to Soviet concerns over the alliance's intentions. Zisk, *Engaging the Enemy: Organizational Theory and Soviet Military Innovation, 1955–1991*.

22. The following texts all point to this important aspect of military doctrines. Jervis, "Cooperation," 186–213; Charles L. Glaser, "The Security Dilemma Revisited"; Andrew Kydd, "Sheep in Sheep's Clothing: Why Security Seekers Do Not Fight One Another"; Barry R. Posen, *The Sources of Military Doctrine: France, Britain, and Germany between the World Wars*; Posen, *Inadvertent Escalation: Conventional War and Nuclear Risks*, 16–24; Jack Snyder, *The Ideology of the Offensive: Military Decision Making and the Disasters of 1914*; Jeffrey W. Legro, *Cooperation under Fire: Anglo-German Restraint during World War II*; Elizabeth Kier, *Imagining War: French and British Military Doctrine between the Wars*; Isabel V. Hull, *Absolute Destruction: Military Culture and the Practices of War in Imperial Germany*; John J. Mearsheimer, *Conventional Deterrence*.

23. My thanks to Dr. David Clinton of Baylor's Political Science Department for pointing out that the deterrence model also needs to be taken into consideration when discussing the consequences of doctrine.

24. Jack S. Levy and William R. Thompson, *Causes of War*, 29–31.

25. Donald Kagan, *On the Origins of War and the Preservation of Peace*, 415–17.

26. Posen, *Sources of Military Doctrine*, 24–29; Posen, *Inadvertent Escalation*; Snyder, *Ideology of the Offensive*; Stephen Van Evera, *Causes of War: Power and the Roots of Conflict*, 194–98; Zisk, *Engaging the Enemy*.

27. Snyder, *Ideology of the Offensive*.

28. Michael C. Desch, "Civil-Militarism: The Civilian Origins of the New American Militarism," 579; Desch, "Explaining the Gap: Vietnam, the Republicanization of the South, and the End of the Mass Army," 303; William T. Bianco and Jamie Markham, "Vanishing Veterans: The Decline of Military Experience in Congress."

29. Theorists of bureaucracy argue that this is one of the central motivations of military organizations. Snyder, *Ideology of the Offensive*; Graham Allison and Philip Zelikow, *Essence of Decision: Explaining the Cuban Missile Crisis*.

30. Clausewitz, *On War*, trans. Howard and Paret, 78, 80, 86–87, 119–21. In his discussion of the "military mind," Samuel Huntington illuminated many of the tendencies of the military realist. However, Huntington did not trace the origins of these tendencies to the logic and limits of force as the present work does. Huntington, *Soldier and the State*, 59–79.

31. For instance, a recent assessment of the military profession argued that the "six elements paramount in shaping the character of military officers" could be applied to any large organization. Sam C. Sarkesian, John Allen Williams, and Stephen J. Cimbala, *US National Security: Policymakers, Processes and Politics*, 167.

32. Thucydides, *The Landmark Thucydides: A Comprehensive Guide to the Peloponnesian War*, 352.

33. Margaret MacMillan, *The War That Ended Peace: The Road to 1914*, esp. chap. 11, "Thinking about War." See also Michael Howard, "Men against Fire: Expectations of War in 1914."

34. Stephen Biddle points out that if an officer of 1914 were transported to the battlefield of 1918, he would not have recognized the modern combat system that his fellow officers, only four years later, were using. Biddle, *Military Power: Explaining Victory and Defeat in Modern Battle*, 78–107.

35. Fitzgerald, *Learning to Forget*.

36. Patrick Porter, "Good Anthropology, Bad History: The Cultural Turn in Studying War." See also Porter, *Military Orientalism: Eastern War through Western Eyes*.

37. Porter, "Good Anthropology," 54–55.

38. A careful reader will no doubt observe the similarities between military realism and certain aspects of Stephen Peter Rosen and Elizabeth Kier's explanations of military innovation. There are, however, important differences that I address in the next chapter. Rosen, *Winning the Next War*; Kier, *Imagining War*.

39. Gregory A. Daddis, *Westmoreland's War: Reassessing American Strategy in Vietnam*; Ingo Trauschweizer, *The Cold War U.S. Army: Building Deterrence for Limited War*.

40. Examples of Vietnam focused analysis are Nagl, *Soup with a Knife*; and Krepinevich, *The Army and Vietnam*.

41. Long, *Soul of Armies*; Fitzgerald, *Learning to Forget*; Nagl, *Soup with a Knife*; Krepinevich, *The Army and Vietnam*; Chad C. Serena, *A Revolution in Military*

Adaptation: The U.S. Army in the Iraq War, 6; Cassidy, *Counterinsurgency*, chap. 5. See also Builder, *Masks of War*; Adrian R. Lewis, *The American Culture of War: The History of U.S. Military Force from World War II to Operation Iraqi Freedom*; Sarkesian, Williams, and Cimbala, *US National Security*, 167–70; and Russell F. Weigley, *The American Way of War: A History of United States Military Strategy and Policy*.

42. Williamson Murray provides an account of the development of *blitzkrieg* doctrine that includes the crucial post–World War I years. Murray, *Military Adaptation in War*, 119–52.

43. Posen attributes German doctrinal innovation to Hitler's intervention in the German Army. Posen, *Sources of Military Doctrine*, 69.

44. Cassidy, *Counterinsurgency*; Builder, *Masks of War*; Long, *Soul of Armies*; Fitzgerald, *Learning to Forget*.

45. Alastair Iain Johnston, "Thinking about Strategic Culture"; John Shy, "The American Military Experience: History and Learning," 210; Gil-li Vardi, "The Enigma of German Operational Theory: The Evolution of Military Thought in Germany, 1919–1938," 8–9.

46. On the importance of looking at the process of change rather than simply outcomes, see Alexander L. George and Andrew Bennett, *Case Studies and Theory Development in the Social Sciences*, 20–22, 151–53, 157–58, 161, 176–77, 186; and John Gerring, *Case Study Research: Principles and Practices*, 70–71.

47. Stephen M. Walt, "The Relationship between Theory and Policy in International Relations."

48. United States, *Operations: Field Manual 100-5*, for the years 1976, 1982, and 1986.

49. *Operations 1986* is only examined briefly because it was nearly identical to *Operations 1982*.

50. John Lewis Gaddis, "Grand Strategy in the Second Term," 2.

51. David H. Ucko, *The New Counterinsurgency Era: Transforming the U.S. Military for Modern Wars*.

1. Military Realism: A New Perspective on Military Innovation

1. This definition of doctrine is most consistent with that provided by Long in *Soul of Armies*, 20–21. It should be clear from this definition of military doctrine that I do not intend to include the Nixon Doctrine or the Bush Doctrine in my definition of military doctrine, for instance. These are more properly understood as expressions of civilian strategy. These "doctrines" may play an important role in the formation of military doctrine, but they do not constitute military doctrines as I define them here. However, as will become clear below, these expressions of civilian strategy are essential for understanding the causal relationship between the threat assessments of civilian authorities, their military subordinates, and their effect on doctrine.

2. I borrow the dual-level nomenclature for doctrinal change from Rynning, but the conceptualization differs because his definition of military doctrine refers to what I would call grand strategy. Sten Rynning, *Changing Military Doctrine: Presidents and*

Military Power in Fifth Republic France, 1958–2000. I also borrow from James Q. Wilson, who argues that significant innovation requires the redefinition of an organization's mission and its central task. In the context of doctrine, I would characterize such changes as changes in the doctrinal core. Wilson further states more minor changes involve, for example, technological advancements that make organizations better at what they *already* do. I characterize such changes as peripheral. J. Q. Wilson, *Bureaucracy: What Governments Do and Why They Do It*, 222. Benjamin Jensen also draws on Wilson in this way. However, he makes a distinction between formal an informal doctrine that I do not assess in these pages. Like Jensen, I focus on "service-level formal doctrine." Jensen, *Forging the Sword: Doctrinal Change in the U.S. Army*, 4. Luttwak provides a good example of core and peripheral differences between operational doctrines in his examination of blitzkrieg and defense-in-depth doctrines. Edward N. Luttwak, "The Operational Level of War."

3. See Anthony Beevor, *The Second World War*, 441; Bernard Brodie, *Strategy in the Missile Age*, 116, 131–38. Strategic bombing theory had its origin in the work of Giulio Douhet in *The Command of the Air* (1921, republished in *Roots of Strategy*, bk. 4 [Mechanicsburg, PA: Stackpole, 1999]). See also Alexander W. Vacca, "Military Culture and Cyber Security," 162.

4. Allan R. Millet, "Patterns of Military Innovation in the Interwar Period," 331; Murray, *Military Adaptation in War*, chaps. 5–6; Rosen, *Winning the Next War*, chap. 6.

5. Rynning, *Changing Military Doctrine*, 5–7; Rosen, *Winning the Next War*, 60.

6. Murray, *Military Adaptation in War*, 246.

7. Biddle, *Military Power*; Murray, *Military Adaptation in War*; Gary Sheffield, *The Chief: Douglas Haig and the British Army*.

8. We associate body counts with Vietnam, but in fact it was first used in Korea after that war slid into a bitter stalemate. Scott Sigmund Gartner and Marissa Edson Myers, "Body Counts and 'Success' in the Vietnam and Korean Wars."

9. Clausewitz, *On War*, trans. Howard and Paret, 77.

10. Clausewitz, *On War*, trans. Howard and Paret, 75. Although this understanding of violence had its origin in Clausewitz, it has been mirrored in important ways in René Girard's work, especially in *The One by Whom Scandal Comes*, trans. M. B. DeBevoise (East Lansing: Michigan State University Press, 2014).

11. Clausewitz, *On War*, trans. Howard and Paret, 119–21.

12. Clausewitz, *On War*, trans. Howard and Paret, 78, 80, 86–7, 119–21. It might be the case that the less contact that a military organization has with friction, the more optimistic it will be regarding the efficacy of force. Thus, among modern military organizations, air forces and navies would be more optimistic about the prospects for force to be effective than land armies.

13. Clausewitz, *On War*, trans. Howard and Paret.

14. Clausewitz, *On War*, trans. Howard and Paret, 78, 80, 86–87.

15. Clausewitz, *On War*, trans. Howard and Paret, 86–87.

16. Note that this interpretation of Clausewitz shows the lack of understanding of Basil Liddel Hart when he criticized Clausewitz in the following terms: "Clausewitz's principle of force without limit and without calculation of cost fits, and is only fit for,

a hate-maddened mob. It is the negation of statesmanship—and of intelligent strategy, which seeks to serve the ends of policy." In his criticism of Clausewitz, Hart accuses Clausewitz of the very conception of war that Clausewitz was adamantly arguing against, the logic of force divorced from friction and politics. Hart quoted in Hew Strachan, *Clausewitz's "On War": A Biography*, 16.

17. Clausewitz, *On War*, trans. Howard and Paret, 99.

18. Clausewitz, *On War*, trans. Howard and Paret, 77.

19. Jack Snyder, "Civil-Military Relations and the Cult of the Offensive, 1914 and 1984," 118–19.

20. Cicero, *Cicero to Cassius*, Rome, early October, 44 BC, http://www.attalus.org /translate/cassius.html.

21. Clausewitz, *On War*, trans. Graham, xxxiii.

22. Clausewitz, *On War*, trans. Graham, 71–73; Clausewitz, *On War*, trans. Howard and Paret, 113–14.

23. Clausewitz, *On War*, trans. Howard and Paret, 119.

24. Military officers are often less aggressive than their civilian counterparts. Richard K. Betts, *Soldiers, Statesmen and Cold War Crises*, 5; Huntington, *Soldier and the State*, 68–69. German generals opposed Hitler's plans of attack for France and Poland because of the power of the defense and friction. He replaced them with "men who were entirely his creatures." Kagan, *Origins of War*, 383, 391. See also Beevor, *The Second World War*, 41; Harold C. Deutsche, *Hitler and His Generals: The Hidden Crisis, January–June 1938*; Franz Halder, *The Halder War Diary, 1939–1942*; and Eliot A. Cohen, *Supreme Command: Soldiers, Statesmen, and Leadership in Wartime*, 17–59.

25. Stanley McChrystal interview in *Manhunt: The Inside Story of the Hunt for Bin Laden*.

26. Robert M. Gates, *From the Shadows: The Ultimate Insider's Story of Five Presidents and How They Won the Cold War*, 275 (emphasis added).

27. Betts, *Soldiers, Statesmen, and Cold War Crises*.

28. Betts, *Soldiers, Statesmen and Cold War Crises*, 122.

29. Dick Cheney, *In My Time: A Personal and Political Memoir*, 188, 203.

30. Beevor, *The Second World War*, 93–94.

31. Kagan, *Origins of War*, 383, 391. See also Beevor, *The Second World War*, 41; Deutsche, *Hitler and His Generals*; and Halder, *The Halder War Diary*.

32. Field Marshal Lord Alanbrooke, *War Diaries, 1939–1945*, 590; Beevor, *The Second World War*; Cohen, *Supreme Command*, 17–59.

33. Brodie, *Strategy in the Missile Age*, 174.

34. Huntington, *Soldier and the State*, 59–79.

35. Betts, *Soldiers, Statesmen and Cold War Crises*, 5. Although Betts points out this aspect of military thinking on the use of force, military realism explains its origin (25).

36. Powell quoted in Sarkesian, Williams, and Cimbala, *US National Security*, 154–55.

37. Huntington, *Soldier and the State*, 66–67.

38. Betts points out the emphasis on material capabilities, but military realism explains its origin. Betts, *Soldiers, Statesmen and Cold War Crises*, 5, 25.

39. For a more comprehensive discussion of theories of victory, see Jensen, *Forging the Sword*, 16–17. For instance, Rosen defines theories of victory more broadly than this work. Rosen, "Thinking about Military Innovation," chap. 1 in *Winning the Next War*.

40. Barry Posen divides doctrines into offensive, defensive, and deterrent doctrines. I use only offensive or defensive because deterrent doctrines often have a defensive theory of victory at their core to be used if deterrence fails.

41. Elizabeth Kier is an important exception here, and her cultural argument for defensive theories of victory will be addressed below. Kier, *Imagining War*.

42. Clausewitz, *On War*, trans. Howard and Paret, bk. 6, chap. 1, 358, 360–61.

43. See Clausewitz, *On War*, trans. Howard and Paret, bk. 6; and John J. Mearsheimer, "Assessing the Conventional Balance: The 3:1 Rule and Its Critics."

44. Clausewitz argued that defense was the stronger form of warfare for reasons that he sets out in book 6 of *On War*, trans. Howard and Paret. For a more recent treatment of the relationship between attack and defense, see B. A. Friedman, "The Offense, the Defense, and the Initiative," chap. 13 in *On Tactics: A Theory of Victory in Battle*. For a strategic perspective from the Cold War, see Mearsheimer, "Assessing the Conventional Balance."

45. Biddle, *Military Power*; Stephen D. Biddle, "Afghanistan and the Future of Warfare."

46. A defensive doctrine will often call for local, tactical counterattacks but not a strategic offensive.

47. Clausewitz, *On War*, trans. Howard and Paret, 357.

48. Kier, *Imagining War*.

49. Posen, *Sources of Military Doctrine*, 82–85; Kier, *Imagining War*, 77.

50. Fitzgerald, *Learning to Forget*, 15.

51. Colonel Victor W. Hobson Jr. and Colonel Oliver G. Kinney, "Keeping Pace with the Future: Development of Doctrine at USA CGSC."

52. I am grateful to an anonymous reviewer for pointing out this fact.

53. Long, *Soul of Armies*, 29–30; Fitzgerald, *Learning to Forget*, 6; Hobson and Kinney, "Keeping Pace."

54. Kretchik, *U.S. Army Doctrine*, 178.

55. Brian McAllister Linn, *Elvis' Army: Cold War GIs and the Atomic Battlefield*, 97.

56. Fitzgerald, *Learning to Forget*, 6.

57. Snyder, *Ideology of the Offensive*; Deborah D. Avant, *Political Institutions and Military Change: Lessons from Peripheral Wars*; Hull, *Absolute Destruction*; Gerhard Ritter, *The Schlieffen Plan*; L. C. F. Turner, "The Significance of the Schlieffen Plan"; Adam Grissom, "The Future of Military Innovation Studies," 909.

58. Grissom, "Future of Military Innovation Studies," 906.

59. Posen, *Sources of Military Doctrine*, 49–50, 174–75; Posen, *Inadvertent Escalation*, 16–17.

60. A number of scholars have argued instead that domestic politics and political culture cause civilian interventions or shape military cultural responses to changes in military policy. Kier, *Imagining War*, 10–14; Avant, *Political Institutions and Military*

Change, 5, 12. Gaddis and Dallek enumerate the domestic political roots of flexible response. See John Lewis Gaddis, *Strategies of Containment: A Critical Appraisal of American National Security Policy during the Cold War*; and Robert Dallek, *Camelot's Court: Inside the Kennedy White House*. Others also challenge the maverick mechanism. Rosen, *Winning the Next War*, 11–21; Barry Watts and Williamson Murray, "Military Innovation in Peacetime," 410.

61. Rosen and Kier show the limits of mavericks within military organizations. Rosen, *Winning the Next War*, 11–18; Kier, *Imagining War*, 13.

62. Although military realism argues against Kier's cultural perspective, here I concur with Kier's criticism of civilian realism and its neglect of the domestic political forces that shape civilian decision making on strategy and military policy. Kier, *Imagining War*, 11.

63. Rosen, *Winning the Next War*, 10–13. Arguing from a military cultural perspective, Elizabeth Kier concurs with the idea that mavericks have limited influence within the military. Kier, *Imagining War*, 13.

64. Desch, "Explaining the Gap," 303; Bianco and Markham, "Vanishing Veterans."

65. Rosen and Kier show the limits of mavericks within military organizations. Rosen, *Winning the Next War*, 11–18; Kier, *Imagining War*, 13.

66. Rosen, *Winning the Next War*, 21.

67. Rosen, *Winning the Next War*, 20, 57.

68. Rosen also discusses theories of victory but not primarily their offensive or defensive character. Rosen, *Winning the Next War*, 20.

69. Rosen, *Winning the Next War*, 7, 20.

70. Rosen, *Winning the Next War*, 7.

71. Rosen, *Winning the Next War*, 21–22.

72. Rosen, *Winning the Next War*, 20.

73. Rosen, *Winning the Next War*, 14–18.

74. Rosen, *Winning the Next War*, 27.

75. "A redefinition of the strategic measure of effectiveness tells the organization what and how it should be learning from wartime experiences. Until such a redefinition takes place, a wartime military organization will learn from its experiences in terms of existing measures." Rosen, *Winning the Next War*, 35.

76. Rosen, *Winning the Next War*, 27, 30, 34–35.

77. Rosen, *Winning the Next War*, 38.

78. Rosen, *Winning the Next War*, 7, 101–5.

79. See Karl W. Deutsch, "On Theory and Research in Innovation," in *Innovation in the Public Sector*, edited by Richard L. Merritt and Anna J. Merritt (Beverly Hills, CA: Sage, 1985), cited in Rosen, *Winning the Next War*, 2.

80. Jay M. Shafritz, J. Steven Ott, and Yong Suk Jang, eds., *Classics of Organization Theory*, 5; J. Q. Wilson, *Bureaucracy*, 375; Morton H. Halperin and Priscilla A. Clapp, *Bureaucratic Politics and Foreign Policy*, 51–54.

81. Anthony Downs, *Inside Bureaucracy*, 198–200. Posen ably sets out the implications of bureaucratic theories for military doctrine. Posen, *Sources of Military Doctrine*, 41–59.

82. Posen, *Sources of Military Doctrine*; Snyder, *Ideology of the Offensive*.

83. Gaddis, *Strategies of Containment*, 169; Brian McAllister Linn, *The Echo of Battle: The Army's Way of War*, 152–53, 164–65; Linn, *Elvis' Army*, 86.

84. J. Q. Wilson, *Bureaucracy*, 179–80; Halperin and Clapp, *Bureaucratic Politics and Foreign Policy*, 51–54.

85. Gaddis, *Strategies of Containment*, 213–14.

86. Interservice rivalry theories of bureaucratic motivation would make such an argument. See, for instance, Harvey M. Sapolsky, *Polaris System Development: Bureaucratic and Pragmatic Success in Government*. I am grateful to an anonymous reviewer for pointing out this possible objection.

87. My thanks to an anonymous reviewer for pointing out this potential alternative explanation.

88. Cited in Kier, *Imagining War*, 15.

89. Posen, *Sources of Military Doctrine*, 44, 47–50; Snyder, *Ideology of the Offensive*, 24, 29, 30; Van Evera, *Causes of War*; Allison and Zelikow, *Essence of Decision*, 143–44, 151.

90. J. Q. Wilson, *Bureaucracy*, 222–23; David Galula, *Counterinsurgency Warfare: Theory and Practice*, 70–86; Morris Janowitz, *The Professional Soldier: A Social and Political Portrait*.

91. I am not the first to point out the weaknesses in the bureaucratic explanation of the behavior of military officers. For more on this, see Robert J. Art, "Bureaucratic Politics and American Foreign Policy: A Critique"; Stephen D. Krasner, "Are Bureaucracy Important? (or Allison Wonderland)"; and Edward Rhodes, "Do Bureaucratic Politics Matter? Some Disconfirming Findings from the Case of the U.S. Navy."

92. Peter J. Katzenstein and Nobuo Okawara, "Japan's National Security: Structures, Norms, and Policies," 116–17; Thomas U. Berger, "From Sword to Chrysanthemum: Japan's Culture of Anti-militarism," 142; Jeffrey W. Legro, "Military Culture and Inadvertent Escalation in World War II," 139.

93. Ann Swidler, "Culture in Action: Symbols and Strategies," 273; Theo Farrell, "World Culture and the Irish Army, 1922–1942," 73; J. Q. Wilson, *Bureaucracy*, 92–93, 105.

94. Johnston, "Thinking about Strategic Culture," 45; Vardi, "Enigma of German Operational Theory," 7, 9; Lynn, *Battle*, 124–25; Legro, "Military Culture," 115–16, 142; Stephen Peter Rosen, "Military Effectiveness: Why Society Matters," 13; John S. Duffield et al., "Isms and Schisms: Culturalism versus Realism in Security Studies," 164.

95. Long, *Soul of Armies*, 26. For accounts of innovation rooted in "finest hours," see Nagl, *Soup with a Knife*, 215–16; J. Q. Wilson, *Bureaucracy*, 107; and Krepinevich, *The Army and Vietnam*, 4–7. The diversity among cultural explanations is summarized nicely in Grissom, "Future of Military Innovation Studies," 916–19.

96. Cassidy, *Counterinsurgency*; Builder, *Masks of War*; Long, *Soul of Armies*; Fitzgerald, *Learning to Forget*.

97. Cassidy, *Counterinsurgency*, 108, 110–11.

98. Whether one argues the army's foundational war was World War II or the American Civil War, the predictions are largely the same: the army likes large-scale

conventional operations that use offense to attrite the enemy and is not interested in COIN because its foundational war was a total war. Long, *Soul of Armies*, 34; Cassidy, *Counterinsurgency*, 100, 113; Builder, *Masks of War*, 132; J. Q. Wilson, *Bureaucracy*, 96; Shy, "American Military Experience," 207; Martin van Creveld, *The Culture of War*, 359–61.

99. Long, *Soul of Armies*, 44–45.

100. Cassidy, *Counterinsurgency*, 122; Builder, *Masks of War*; Long, *Soul of Armies*.

101. Long, *Soul of Armies*, 34.

102. Kier, *Imagining War*.

103. Kier, *Imagining War*, 5, 18–21.

104. Kier, *Imagining War*, 2, 4, 12–13, 26.

105. Kier, *Imagining War*, 26, 28.

106. Kier, *Imagining War*, 5.

107. Kier, *Imagining War*, 2, 4, 12–13, 26.

108. Kier, *Imagining War*, 12.

109. Trauschweizer, *Cold War U.S. Army*, 163; Nagl, *Soup with a Knife*; Builder, *Masks of War*.

2. Flexible Response, the Nuclear Battlefield, and Counterinsurgency: Kennedy and Army Doctrine in the 1960s

1. The irony is, of course, that President Kennedy suffered from multiple degenerative medical ailments, worst of all Addison's disease. However, he managed to keep this truth from coming out and damaging his youthful image and his political aspirations. Robert Dallek, *Camelot's Court: Inside the Kennedy White House*, 11, 56–57, 79.

2. Gaddis, *Strategies of Containment*, 201.

3. Gaddis, *Strategies of Containment*, 214.

4. Gaddis, *Strategies of Containment*, 204–5.

5. Trauschweizer, *Cold War U.S. Army*, 123.

6. Gaddis, *Strategies of Containment*, 207.

7. Gaddis, *Strategies of Containment*, 206; Dallek, *Camelot's Court*, 67.

8. Gaddis, *Strategies of Containment*, 202.

9. Gaddis, *Strategies of Containment*, 208.

10. Gaddis, *Strategies of Containment*, 211.

11. Shafritz, Ott, and Jang, *Classics of Organization Theory*, 5; J. Q. Wilson, *Bureaucracy*, 375; Morton H. Halperin and Priscilla A. Clapp, *Bureaucratic Politics and Foreign Policy*, 51–54.

12. A. J. Bacevich, *The Pentomic Era: The U.S. Army between Korea and Vietnam*, 119–27. See also Thomas E. Ricks, *The Generals: American Military Command from World War II to Today*, 203–14.

13. Bacevich, *Pentomic Era*.

14. Thomas C. Schelling, *Arms and Influence*, 18–26; Shafritz, Ott, and Jang, *Classics of Organization Theory*, 5; J. Q. Wilson, *Bureaucracy*, 375.

15. Posen, *Sources of Military Doctrine*, 44, 47–50; Snyder, *Ideology of the Offensive*, 24, 29.

16. *Operations 1954* was updated in 1956 and '58 but only to incorporate the new pentomic division design. Jensen, *Forging the Sword*, 7.

17. J. Q. Wilson, *Bureaucracy*, 179–80; Halperin and Clapp, *Bureaucratic Politics and Foreign Policy*, 51–54.

18. J. Q. Wilson, *Bureaucracy*, 213–14.

19. Interservice rivalry theories of bureaucratic motivation would make such an argument. See, for instance, Sapolsky, *Polaris System Development*. I am grateful to an anonymous reviewer for pointing out this possible objection.

20. My thanks to an anonymous reviewer for pointing out this potential alternative explanation.

21. J. Q. Wilson, *Bureaucracy*, 222–23; Galula, *Counterinsurgency Warfare*, 31–32, 70–86. Janowitz argues that soldiers are biased against "constabulary" roles. Janowitz, *Professional Soldier*.

22. Galula, *Counterinsurgency Warfare*, 32.

23. Paul Dixon, "'Hearts and Minds'? British Counterinsurgency from Malaya to Iraq."

24. For disagreements on the origins of the army's finest hour, see Builder, *Masks of War*, 132; and Long, *Soul of Armies*, 34.

25. Nagl, *Soup with a Knife*, 215–16; J. Q. Wilson, *Bureaucracy*, 107.

26. Krepinevich, *The Army and Vietnam*, 4–7.

27. Krepinevich, *The Army and Vietnam*, 4–7; Nagl, *Soup with a Knife*.

28. Johnston, "Thinking about Strategic Culture," 45; Vardi, "Enigma of German Operational Theory," 7, 9; Lynn, *Battle*, 124–25; Legro, "Military Culture," 115–16, 142; Rosen, "Military Effectiveness," 13; Duffield et al., "Isms and Schisms," 164.

29. Bacevich, *Pentomic Era*, 131–32, quoting S. L. A. Marshall, "Arms in Wonderland," *Army* 7 (June 1957): 19.

30. Long, *Soul of Armies*, 44–45.

31. Nagl, *Soup with a Knife*, 215–16; J. Q. Wilson, *Bureaucracy*, 107.

32. Krepinevich, *The Army and Vietnam*; Nagl, *Soup with a Knife*.

33. Posen, *Sources of Military Doctrine*, 49–50, 174–75; Posen, *Inadvertent Escalation*, 16–17.

34. A number of scholars have argued instead that domestic politics and political culture cause civilian interventions or shape military cultural responses to changes in military policy. Kier, *Imagining War*, 10–14; Avant, *Political Institutions and Military Change*, 5, 12. Gaddis and Dallek enumerate the domestic political roots of flexible response. Gaddis, *Strategies of Containment*; Dallek, *Camelot's Court*. Others also challenge the maverick mechanism. Rosen, *Winning the Next War*, 11–21; Watts and Murray, "Military Innovation in Peacetime," 410.

35. Gaddis, *Strategies of Containment*, 215–16.

36. Massive retaliation fell out of favor with a number of senior officials not long after it was announced. Marc Trachtenberg, "Strategic Thought in America, 1952–1966,"

330–31. Eisenhower admitted in 1955 that massive retaliation could not stop communists' "political and military nibbling." Nevertheless, Kennedy sought to correct perceived weaknesses of massive retaliation. Gaddis, *Strategies of Containment*, 176, 202, 214.

37. Quoted in Karl F. Inderfurth and Lock K. Johnson, eds., *Fateful Decisions: Inside the National Security Council*, 63.

38. Dallek, *Camelot's Court*, 162.

39. According to civilian realism, civilian leaders use military mavericks to intervene in their militaries to integrate doctrine with their grand strategy. These handpicked military officers help impose doctrinal change on a resistant military bureaucracy. Posen, *Sources of Military Doctrine*, 49–50, 54, 59, 74–78, 174–75; Posen, *Inadvertent Escalation*, 16–17. Posen's maverick mechanism has been challenged by a number of other studies. Rosen, *Winning the Next War*, 11–18. See also Watts and Murray, "Military Innovation in Peacetime," 410.

40. Dallek, *Camelot's Court*, 184.

41. See Nagl, *Soup with a Knife*; Long, *Soul of Armies*, 106–7.

42. Dallek, *Camelot's Court*.

43. Brodie, *Strategy in the Missile Age*.

44. Prelinger Archives, San Francisco, https://www.youtube.com/watch?v=ZWS MoE3A5DI.

45. Gaddis, *Strategies of Containment*, 198.

46. Dallek, *Camelot's Court*, 86–90.

47. Dallek, *Camelot's Court*, 75.

48. Robert F. Kennedy, *Robert Kennedy in His Own Words: The Unpublished Recollections of the Kennedy Years*, 13, 246–48; H. R. McMaster, *Dereliction of Duty: Johnson, McNamara, the Joint Chiefs of Staff, and the Lies That Led to Vietnam*, 4–5, 6–8, 18–19, 26–28. Secretary of the Army Elvis Stahr noted this belief among Kennedy and his officials. They did not trust the military and thought high-ranking military officers were unintelligent. Stahr, *Oral History*, 16, 45, 70.

49. This was from a conversation with Rusk and Bundy. Kennedy continued: "And I know that you get all this sort of virility over at the Pentagon and you get a lot of Arleigh Burkes [chief of naval operations]: admirable, nice figure, without any brains." Dallek, *Camelot's Court*, 257.

50. Dallek, *Camelot's Court*, 156.

51. Kennedy also shuffled his chief military advisers and manipulated the officer promotion process. Betts, *Soldiers, Statesmen and Cold War Crises*, 65–66; McMaster, *Dereliction of Duty*, 22, 31, 43.

52. Kennedy read Taylor's memoir and wrote him to express his agreement with its ideas. John M. Taylor, *General Maxwell Taylor: The Sword and the Pen*, 8; Maxwell D. Taylor, *The Uncertain Trumpet*, 130–64.

53. Dallek, *Camelot's Court*, 157.

54. R. Kennedy, *In His Own Words*, 255–56. Taylor's influence "made opposition to his views futile." McMaster, *Dereliction of Duty*, 23. See, for example, his assessment

of General Norstad's force requirements for the Berlin crisis. Memo for the President from Taylor, October 3, 1961, POF, box 103, subjects: NATO—Norstad Meetings, JFK Library.

55. Marc Trachtenberg, *A Constructed Peace: The Making of the European Settlement, 1945–1963*, 286; Gaddis, *Strategies of Containment*, 214. Kennedy wanted NATO to increase its conventional "capabilities." Trauschweizer, *Cold War U.S. Army*, 123.

56. Gaddis, *Strategies of Containment*, 198–99.

57. Dallek, *Camelot's Court*, 19, 26.

58. Marc Trachtenberg points out that massive retaliation fell out of favor with a number of senior officials not long after it was announced. Trachtenberg, "Strategic Thought in America," 330–31.

59. Quoted in Trauschweizer, *Cold War U.S. Army*, 122 (emphasis added).

60. Memo for the President, May 10, 1961, "Appraisal of Capabilities of Conventional Forces," NSF, box 273, JFK Library, 2 (hereafter "Appraisal of Capabilities" memo); Alain C. Enthoven and K. Wayne Smith, *How Much Is Enough? Shaping the Defense Program, 1961–1969*, chap. 4; Trauschweizer, *Cold War U.S. Army*, 127–32; "National Security Action Memorandum Number 109: U.S. Policy on Military Actions in a Berlin Conflict," October 23, 1961, Digital Archive, JFK Library.

61. The overestimation of Soviet strength was conceived of "low in the bureaucratic hierarchy and carried up to the highest policy levels" in order to elicit "more forces and higher budgets." Enthoven and Smith, *How Much Is Enough?*, 158–60.

62. Gaddis, *Strategies of Containment*, 215.

63. *Foreign Relations of the United States* (hereafter *FRUS*), '61–'63, vol. 8, doc. 93, BNSP draft, June 22, 1962, 315. No document outlined flexible response, but Gaddis argues that the BNSP is "the most comprehensive guide to what the administration . . . was trying to do in world affairs." Gaddis, *Strategies of Containment*, 199. See also Trachtenberg, *Constructed Peace*, 298; and Francis J. Gavin, "Myths of Flexible Response: United States Strategy in Europe during the 1960s," 849–50, 855.

64. *FRUS*, '61–'63, vol. 8, doc. 93, BNSP draft, June 22, 1962.

65. The Advisory Council for the Democratic National Committee, which included Dean Acheson and Paul Nitze, argued for increasing conventional forces but not tactical nuclear weapons. Trauschweizer, *Cold War U.S. Army*, 121.

66. Quoted in Lewis Sorley, *Honorable Warrior: General Harold K. Johnson and the Ethics of Command*, 137. See also Trachtenberg, *Constructed Peace*, 288.

67. Gavin, "Myths of Flexible Response," 858.

68. "Appraisal of Capabilities" memo, 2–3; Trauschweizer, *Cold War U.S. Army*, 116–17.

69. John F. Kennedy, *Public Papers of the Presidents of the United States: John F. Kennedy, 1961*, 401.

70. Andrew J. Birtle, *U.S. Army Counterinsurgency and Contingency Operations Doctrine, 1942–1976*, 226.

71. George H. Decker, *Oral History*, U.S. Army Military History Institute, Carlisle, PA (hereafter MHI), sec. 3, 49–50. General Norstad agreed. Trauschweizer, *Cold War U.S. Army*, 129.

72. General Freeman thought NATO forces would have to use nuclear weapons after only a few *hours*. Based on a May 1961 exercise, General Clarke and General Smith (of the Tactical Air Command) argued that battlefield nuclear weapons were necessary for a forward defense of Europe. Trauschweizer, *Cold War U.S. Army*, 122, 125; Gavin, "Myths of Flexible Response," 857.

73. Colonel S. Kozlov, "Soviet Military Art and Science"; Raymond L. Garthoff, "Soviet Doctrine on the Decisive Factors in Modern War"; anonymous American officer, "Offensive Doctrines of the Soviet Army," *Military Review* (September 1962); Lieutenant Colonel Truman R. Boman, "Current Soviet Tactics."

74. Enthoven, *How Much Is Enough?*, 149–50, 152.

75. Enthoven, *How Much Is Enough?*, 149–50, 152.

76. Henry Kissinger, *Nuclear Weapons and Foreign Policy*; Raymond Aron, *On War*.

77. Kretchik, *U.S. Army Doctrine*, 178–79.

78. Decker, *Oral History*, sec. 4, 21, MHI; Sorley, *Honorable Warrior*, 130–31; Kretchik, *U.S. Army Doctrine*, 175–78; John B. Wilson, *Maneuver and Firepower: The Evolution of Divisions and Separate Brigades*, 291–93; Stahr, *Oral History*, 112.

79. J. B. Wilson, *Maneuver and Firepower*, 293.

80. Richard W. Kedzior, *Evolution and Endurance: The U.S. Army Division in the Twentieth Century*, 29–30; Bacevich, *Pentomic Era*; Long, *Soul of Armies*, 58.

81. Hobson and Kinney, "Keeping Pace," 10.

82. Major D. F. Wharry (British Artillery), "Atomic Weapons and the Principles of War," 109.

83. Taylor quoted in Linn, *Elvis' Army*, 87.

84. Linn, *Elvis' Army*, 87–89.

85. Department of the Army, Office of Chief of Staff, General C. D. Eddleman to Commanding General, USCONARC, Fort Monroe, VA, "Subject: Reorganization of Infantry and Armored Divisions and Creation of a Mechanized Division," December 16, 1960 (hereafter ROAD letter); J. B. Wilson, *Maneuver and Firepower*, 297; "Appraisal of Capabilities" memo, 65.

86. Decker, *Oral History*, Sec. 4, 20, MHI.

87. Trauschweizer, *Cold War U.S. Army*, 163–64; *Operations 1962*, 35, 73; Hamilton H. Howze, *A Cavalryman's Story: Memoirs of a Twentieth-Century Army General*, 235–36; J. B. Wilson, *Maneuver and Firepower*, 314.

88. *Operations 1962*, 99. When asked if there was a connection between the army aviation and Vietnam, Army Chief of Staff Decker said, "No . . . this was something I wanted for the Army, not only in Vietnam, but in Europe." Decker, *Oral History*, sec. 4, 44–45. See also Trauschweizer, *Cold War U.S. Army*, 165.

89. Linn, *Elvis' Army*; Bacevich, *Pentomic Era*.

90. George H. Decker, "Address to the World-Wide Combat Arms Conference II," CGSC, June 25, 1962, 15–16.

91. Theo Farrell, Sten Rynning, and Terry Terriff, *Transforming Military Power since the Cold War: Britain, France, and the United States, 1991–2012*, 41.

92. J. B. Wilson, *Maneuver and Firepower*, 298, 306–7; Trauschweizer, *Cold War U.S. Army*, 115–16.

93. George H. Decker, "Doctrine: The Cement That Binds," 60.

94. Hobson and Kinney, "Keeping Pace," 18.

95. Harold K. Johnson, *Oral History*, 23; Sorley, *Honorable Warrior*, 129–30.

96. One might argue that the use of nuclear weapons against Japan and its subsequent surrender provide a decisive counter to this argument. However, recent histories of the Japanese decision to surrender show that the threat of a Soviet land invasion from Manchuria was the most important variable in the Japanese calculus. Tsuyoshi Hasegawa, *Racing the Enemy: Stalin, Truman, and the Surrender of Japan*.

97. *Operations 1962*, 13 (emphasis added).

98. "Readiness for the Little War," 17.

99. Clive D. Eddleman, "The Concept of Warfare in 1967," speech before the Canadian National Defense College, Kingston, Ontario, March 21, 1957, Office of the Deputy Chief of Military Operations, Records of the Army Staff, Record Group 319, box 1, National Archives and Records Administration (NARA), College Park, MD.

100. Eddleman, "Concept of Warfare," 18.

101. *Operations 1962*, 4–5, 9, 30–31, 34, 35, 60; Major Robert A. Doughty, *The Evolution of U.S. Army Tactical Doctrine, 1946–76*, 24.

102. *Operations 1962*, 8–9, 61.

103. Hobson and Kinney, "Keeping Pace," 15–16.

104. Russell F. Weigley, *The American Way of War: A History of United States Military Strategy and Policy*; Long, *Soul of Armies*, 34.

105. Major Nels A. Parson Jr. (Artillery, Office of the Deputy Chief of Staff for Operations), "The Confederates Talk on Nuclear Warfare"; Brigadier General Lynn D. Smith (United States Army), "Gettysburg + 100." All data gathered by the author. Available on request.

106. Hobson and Kinney, "Keeping Pace," 15–16.

107. Linn, *Elvis' Army*, 97.

108. Data on *Military Review* gathered by the author from the complete online archive at the Combined Arms Research Library, Leavenworth, KS, http://cgsc.con tentdm.oclc.org/cdm/search/collection/p124201coll1/searchterm/english!1965/field/ editio!date/mode/all!all/.

109. "Appraisal of Capabilities" memo, 64–65.

110. "Appraisal of Capabilities" memo, 115.

111. Biddle, *Military Power*, 29.

112. J. B. Wilson, *Maneuver and Firepower*, 303.

113. Decker, *Oral History*, Sec. 4, 21–22.

114. Trauschweizer, *Cold War U.S. Army*, 143.

115. *FRUS*, '61–'63, vol. 8, doc. 104, "Taylor (Military Representative to the President) to President Kennedy, August 23, 1962; doc. 80, "Ltr. Taylor to Rostow," April 23, 1962; doc. 80, Taylor to Rostow on March 26, 1962, BNSP draft, April 23, 1962. The army had been developing such forces "since 1953." Trauschweizer, *Cold War U.S. Army*, 120–23.

116. Trachtenberg, *Constructed Peace*, 290–93.

117. *FRUS*, '61–'63, vol. 8. doc. 86, "Memo, McNamara to CJCS Lemnitzer," May 23, 1962.

118. Johnson discussed nuclear doctrine with the army deputy chief, Lieutenant General Barksdale Hamlett, who said Chief of Staff Decker agreed. Johnson to Hamlett, March 26, 1962, Harold K. Johnson Papers, MHI; J. B. Wilson, *Maneuver and Firepower*, 298, 306–7.

119. Sorley, *Honorable Warrior*, 136–37.

120. Trauschweizer, *Cold War U.S. Army*, 143, 171; Gavin, "Myths of Flexible Response."

121. Gavin, "Myths of Flexible Response," 858.

122. See War Department Training Regulation 10-5 (1921); John I. Alger, *The Quest for Victory: The History of the Principles of War*; and *Operations 1962*, 46.

123. *Operations 1954*, 113; *Operations 1962*, 46–48.

124. Trauschweizer, *Cold War U.S. Army*, 163.

125. *Operations 1954*, 113.

126. Kretchik, *U.S. Army Doctrine*, 182.

127. *Operations 1954*, 73 (emphasis added).

128. *Operations 1962*, 73–74 (emphasis added).

129. *Operations 1962*, 74 (emphasis added).

130. Doughty, *Army Tactical Doctrine*, 23–25.

131. Doughty, *Army Tactical Doctrine*, 74.

132. *Operations 1962*, 74 (emphasis added).

133. Lieutenant Colonel Mitchel Goldenthal (Corps of Engineers Faculty, USA CGSC), "Corps in the Mobile Defense," 14.

134. Goldenthal, "Corps in the Mobile Defense," 15.

135. Goldenthal, "Corps in the Mobile Defense," 16.

136. Goldenthal, "Corps in the Mobile Defense," 21.

137. Goldenthal, "Corps in the Mobile Defense," 20.

138. Committee on Appropriations, 86th Congress, *Department of Defense Appropriations for 1960*, 1391–93.

139. Gaddis, *Strategies of Containment*, 201.

140. Dallek, *Camelot's Court*, 152.

141. Dallek, *Camelot's Court*, 253.

142. Dallek, *Camelot's Court*, 119, 239.

143. Serhiy Kudelia, "Choosing Violence in Irregular Wars: The Case of Anti-Soviet Insurgency in Western Ukraine," 161.

144. "Summary of President Kennedy's Remarks to the 496th Meeting of the National Security Council," January 18, 1962, *FRUS*, vol. 8, doc. 69, 239–40.

145. Birtle, *U.S. Army Counterinsurgency*, 223.

146. W. W. Rostow, *The Stages of Economic Growth: A Non-communist Manifesto*; Dallek, *Camelot's Court*, 91.

147. Rostow, *Stages of Economic Growth*; Dallek, *Camelot's Court*, 91; Gaddis, *Strategies of Containment*, 207.

148. BNSP draft, June 22, 1962; *FRUS*, vol. 8, doc. 93, 321. For instance, indigenous police programs were an important part of this "preventive medicine." "Memo from NSA Bundy to Taylor," February 14, 1962, *FRUS*, vol. 8, doc. 71, 248; "Memo from the Interagency Committee on Police Assistance Programs to Kennedy," July 20, 1962, *FRUS*, vol. 8, doc. 99. See also Gaddis, *Strategies of Containment*, 216.

149. *FRUS*, '61–'63, vol. 8, doc. 93, 321, BNSP draft, June 22, 1962; doc. 71, 248, "Memo from NSA Bundy to Taylor," February 14, 1962; Birtle, *U.S. Army Counterinsurgency*, 223, 238; Gaddis, *Strategies of Containment*, 216.

150. *FRUS*, '61–'63, vol. 8, doc. 91, NSAM 131, "Training Objectives for Counterinsurgency," March 13, 1962; NSAM 162, "Subject: Development of U.S. and Indigenous Police, Paramilitary and Military Resources," June 19, 1962, Digital Archive, JFK Library.

151. *FRUS*, '61–'63, vol. 8, doc. 69, 239–40, "Summary of President Kennedy's Remarks to the 496th Meeting of the National Security Council," January 18, 1962.

152. Gaddis, *Strategies of Containment*, 216, 244; *FRUS*, '61–'63, vol. 8, doc. 65, 231–32, NSAM 119, Bundy to Rusk and McNamara, "Subject: Civic Action," December 18, 1961.

153. Members included Robert F. Kennedy, McGeorge Bundy, Lyman Lemnitzer, Deputy Secretary of Defense Roswell Gilpatrick, Deputy Undersecretary of State U. Alexis Johnson, chiefs of USAID and USIA, and the director of the CIA, John McCone. *FRUS*, '61–'63, vol. 8, doc. 68, NSAM 124, "Establishment of the Special Group (Counter-Insurgency)," January 18, 1962.

154. *FRUS*, '61–'63, vol. 8, doc. 67, 235–36; Kennedy to McNamara, January 11, 1962.

155. Long, *Soul of Armies*, 107.

156. Nagl, *Soup with a Knife*; Krepinevich, *The Army in Vietnam*; Max Boot, *The Savage Wars of Peace: Small Wars and the Rise of American Power*; Cassidy, *Counterinsurgency*, 116. For a response to these "if only" arguments, see Daddis, *Westmoreland's War*, 116.

157. Nagl, *Soup with a Knife*; Krepinevich, *The Army in Vietnam*; Boot, *Savage Wars of Peace*; Cassidy, *Counterinsurgency*, 116.

158. Krepinevich, *The Army in Vietnam*, 30–32; Rosen, *Winning the Next War*, 101.

159. Stahr, *Oral History*, 32–34.

160. "Memorandum of Conference with the President," February 6, 1961, National Security Files, C. V. Clifton, box 345, JFK Library.

161. *FRUS*, '61–63', vol. 8, doc. 18, "Memorandum of Conference with President Kennedy," February 23, 1961; Kretchik, *US Army Doctrine*, 99. The administration was not opposed to this rationale, approving a May 1961 budget request to expand SF in Europe because they would "enhance capability of capitalizing on resistance potential in Satellite countries." "Appraisal of Capabilities" memo, 26; *Operations 1962*, 50, 56, 127, 130–31, 133.

162. *FRUS*, '61–'63', vol. 8, doc. 67, 235–36; Kennedy to McNamara, January 11, 1962.

163. Birtle, *U.S. Army Counterinsurgency*, 276.

164. *FRUS*, '61–'63, vol. 8, doc. 74; memo, Parrott to Kennedy, "Subject: Activities of the Special Group (Counterinsurgency)," March 22, 1962.

165. Birtle, *U.S. Army Counterinsurgency*, 227–28, 277–78.

166. Krepinevich, *The Army and Vietnam*, 31.

167. Birtle, *U.S. Army Counterinsurgency*, 237, 257–58, 268.

168. For examples, see Rosen, *Winning the Next War*, 11; Avant, *Political Institutions and Military Change*; and Long, *Soul of Armies*, 106–7, 109.

169. Trauschweizer, *Cold War U.S. Army*, 174; Birtle, *U.S. Army Counterinsurgency*, 227.

170. Long, *Soul of Armies*, 109; Krepinevich, *The Army and Vietnam*, 37, 43–44; Kretchik, *U.S. Army Doctrine*, 185.

171. Trauschweizer, *Cold War U.S. Army*, 167n34; Birtle, *U.S. Army Counterinsurgency*, 225.

172. Birtle, *U.S. Army Counterinsurgency*, 225; memo, Decker to Kennedy, February 15, 1961, subject: "Army Role in Guerrilla and Anti-guerrilla Operations," Record Group 335, box 385, Secretary of the Army, NARA; Decker, *Oral History*, 9.

173. Boyd L. Dastrup, *The U.S. Army Command and General Staff College: A Centennial History*, 111; "Cold War Activities of the United States Army, 1 Jan. 1961 to 26 Jan. 1962," NSF, box 269, folder "Army," JFK Library, 1-1.

174. *Operations 1962*, 7, 12.

175. *Operations 1954*, 171–73.

176. *Operations 1962*, 7, 127–54.

177. *Operations 1962*, 139.

178. "National Security Action Memorandum 119, Bundy to Rusk and McNamara, Subject: Civic Action," December 18, 1961, *FRUS*, vol. 8, doc. 65, 231–32.

179. Mao Zedong, *On Guerrilla Warfare*, 50, 55, 60.

180. Galula, *Counterinsurgency Warfare*, 80.

181. "In countries threatened by external aggression, local forces should participate in civic action projects which do not materially impair performance of the primary military mission." *FRUS*, '61–'63, vol. 8, doc. 65, 231–22. See also NSAM 119, Bundy to Rusk and McNamara, "Subject: Civic Action," December 18, 1961.

182. See especially chap. 1 of Daddis, *Westmoreland's War*.

183. "Readiness for the Little War," 18.

184. "Readiness for the Little War," 20.

185. "Readiness for the Little War," 15.

186. Data collected by the author, available on request.

187. Birtle, *U.S. Army Counterinsurgency*, 234.

188. Quoted in Birtle, *U.S. Army Counterinsurgency*, 234–35.

189. Birtle, *U.S. Army Counterinsurgency*, 239.

190. My thanks to an anonymous reviewer for pointing out this possible objection.

191. Trauschweizer, *Cold War U.S. Army*, 174.

192. Dallek, *Camelot's Court*, 19.

193. Hobson and Kinney, "Keeping Pace," 10.

3. Army Doctrine in the Shadow of Vietnam: *Operations 1968*

1. David H. Petraeus, "The American Military and the Lessons of Vietnam: A Study of Military Influence and the Use of Force in the Post-Vietnam Era," 101–3.

2. Krepinevich, *The Army and Vietnam*; Nagl, *Soup with a Knife*.

3. Krepinevich, *The Army and Vietnam*, 4–7; Williamson Murray, "Thinking about Revolutions in Military Affairs," 76. Wilson also employs this historical example. J. Q. Wilson, *Bureaucracy*, 44, 164.

4. Nagl, *Soup with a Knife*; Builder, *Masks of War*, 130; Cassidy, *Counterinsurgency*, 99.

5. Part of this logic is borrowed from Barry Posen's *Sources of Military Doctrine*. However, Posen does not discuss the implications of cultural factors in situations where civilians are preoccupied with other matters.

6. Thomas Alan Schwartz, *Johnson and Europe: In the Shadow of Vietnam*, 75.

7. McMaster, *Dereliction of Duty*, 48, 54.

8. Michael R. Beschloss, ed., *Taking Charge: The Johnson White House Tapes, 1963–1964*, 209.

9. However, as early as July 1964, in a conversation with his trusted friend Texas governor John Connally, Johnson lamented, "Every man in my Cabinet's a Kennedy man. . . . I haven't been able to change 'em and I don't have the personnel if I *could* change 'em. They didn't go to San Marcos Teachers College. . . . It's just agony." Beschloss, *Taking Charge*, 470.

10. Johnson quoted in Doris Kearns, *Lyndon Johnson and the American Dream*, 252.

11. Betts, *Soldiers, Statesmen, Cold War Crises*, 131–32.

12. Maxwell D. Taylor, *Swords and Plowshares: A Memoir*, 381–92.

13. Taylor dedicated the entire content of this chapter to decisions about Vietnam. Taylor, *Swords and Plowshares*, 381.

14. Cassidy, *Counterinsurgency*, 120.

15. McMaster, *Dereliction of Duty*, 32; Birtle, *U.S. Army Counterinsurgency*, 315.

16. Birtle, *U.S. Army Counterinsurgency*, 323.

17. McMaster, *Dereliction of Duty*, 58.

18. Birtle, *U.S. Army Counterinsurgency*, 364–65.

19. Lewis Sorley, *Westmoreland: The General Who Lost Vietnam*, 208–9.

20. Taylor, *Swords and Plowshares*, 381.

21. Sorley, *Westmoreland*, 208–9; McMaster, *Dereliction of Duty*, 94.

22. McMaster, *Dereliction of Duty*, 29–30, 62–63.

23. Civilian authorities often selected these targets from much larger lists of targets suggested by the JCS. McMaster, *Dereliction of Duty*, 93, 96, 128; Betts, *Soldiers, Statesmen, and Cold War Crises*, 27–28.

24. The limited use of force would also preserve Johnson's Great Society initiatives. Schwartz, *Johnson and Europe*, 236; McMaster, *Dereliction of Duty*, 62–63, 73, 76, 130.

25. William E. DePuy, "Lecture of Opportunity—'Vietnam,'" in *The Selected Papers of Gen. William E. DePuy*, 53; Gregory A. Daddis, *No Sure Victory: Measuring U.S. Army Effectiveness and Progress in the Vietnam War*, 133–35.

26. Daddis, *Westmoreland's War*, 88–89.

27. Daddis, *Westmoreland's War*, 89. Fewer North Vietnamese units were involved. Dale Andrade, "Westmoreland Was Right: Learning the Wrong Lesson from the Vietnam War," 164.

28. Andrade, "Westmoreland Was Right," 145–81.

29. Daddis, *Westmoreland's War*, 89.

30. Fitzgerald, *Learning to Forget*, 30.

31. "April 6, 1968—1:30 p.m. Presidents Meeting with Gen. William C. Westmoreland," Tom Johnson Notes, box 3, LBJ Library, 2, 7; William C. Westmoreland, *A Soldier Reports*, 405; Birtle, *U.S. Army Counterinsurgency*, 325. See also Taylor, *Swords and Plowshares*, 383.

32. Taylor, *Swords and Plowshares*, 387; Robert Dallek, *Flawed Giant: Lyndon Johnson and His Times, 1961-1975*, 511–12; Westmoreland, *A Soldier Reports*, 382.

33. Leslie H. Gelb and Richard K. Betts, *The Irony of Vietnam: The System Worked*, 333–34.

34. Bruce Palmer, *The 25-Year War: America's Military Role in Vietnam*, 87.

35. DePuy was working on the Joint Staff at the time. William E. DePuy, *Changing an Army: An Oral History of General William E. DePuy*, 170.

36. Schwartz, *Johnson and Europe*, 202; Dallek, *Flawed Giant*, 511–13.

37. Schwartz, *Johnson and Europe*, 75.

38. Schwartz, *Johnson and Europe*, 48–49.

39. "Cabinet Meeting," August 23, 1968, *FRUS*, vol. 17, doc. 85; Gavin, "Myths of Flexible Response," 866–67. However, for McNamara and Johnson, resolving the balance-of-payments issue was more important than maintaining the ability to employ a flexible response in Europe.

40. Gavin, "Myths of Flexible Response," 865–66; Schwartz, *Johnson and Europe*, 115–16.

41. Trauschweizer, *Cold War U.S. Army*, 185.

42. The JCS told Defense Secretary Clifford that they were willing to remove one hundred thousand troops but that any additional reductions would lead them to recommend complete withdrawal of U.S. forces from Europe. Nevertheless, Clifford thought further withdrawals were possible. Schwartz, *Johnson and Europe*, 123, 215.

43. "Notes of the President's Meeting with the Tuesday Luncheon Group, 25 June 1968," Tom Johnson Notes, LBJ Library, 4.

44. Schwartz, *Johnson and Europe*, 14–15, 86–87, 137–38, 151–52; Gavin, "Myths of Flexible Response," 869–70. Johnson and his advisers justified the continued presence of U.S. troops in Europe as a means of keeping the Germans from "develop[ing] neuroses that can be catastrophic for all of us. They did it before and they can do it again. . . . A neurotic disaffected Germany could be like a loose ship's cannon in a high sea," Ball said on September 21, 1966. Gavin, "Myths of Flexible Response," 870. See also Schwartz for Johnson's fear that West Germany might "go off the reservation." Schwartz, *Johnson and Europe*, 39–40, 43, 112.

45. Schwartz, *Johnson and Europe*, 17–19.

46. "Cabinet Room Meeting," July 29, 1968, *FRUS*, vol. 17, doc. 75.

47. Schwartz, *Johnson and Europe*, 17.

48. Kretchik, *U.S. Army Doctrine*, 190.

49. Birtle, *U.S. Army Counterinsurgency*, 226.

50. Birtle, *U.S. Army Counterinsurgency*, 226.

51. Trauschweizer, *Cold War U.S. Army*, 145, 180–82.

52. Enthoven and Smith, *How Much Is Enough?*, 149–51; W. S. Bennett et al., "Correspondence," 776.

53. Recently released records of the Warsaw Pact states show that the estimates of Soviet forces in Europe in the late 1960s and 1970s were far more accurate than those of the 1950s. These estimates "more accurately represented actual threats." Trauschweizer, *Cold War U.S. Army*, 183.

54. Trauschweizer, *Cold War U.S. Army*, 145, 180–82.

55. Trauschweizer, *Cold War U.S. Army*, 187.

56. The JCS argued that restoring U.S. combat power in Europe would take eighteen months. Trauschweizer, *Cold War U.S. Army*, 181, 186–87.

57. Trauschweizer, *Cold War U.S. Army*, 187.

58. Bruce Palmer, *Oral History*, 416.

59. Betts, *Soldiers, Statesmen, and Cold War Crises*, 87–88.

60. Dubcek was elected in January 1968 and began significant reforms, including increased freedom of the press. Schwartz, *Johnson and Europe*, 213.

61. "Moscow's unwillingness to allow any challenge to the ruling Communist Party, the so-called Brezhnev doctrine, underlined the limitations to the vision of building bridges to Eastern Europe." Schwartz, *Johnson and Europe*, 216. See also "Cabinet Room Meeting on Czech Crisis," August 23, 1968, *FRUS*, vol. 17, doc. 85.

62. "Cabinet Meeting," August 23, 1968, *FRUS*, vol. 17, doc. 85.

63. Rusk notes that NATO forces might have to be repositioned to prevent this in a meeting with House leaders. In the same meeting, the president lists these countries as possible targets. "Notes on President's Meeting with House Leadership on Monday, 9 September 1968," Tom Johnson Notes, LBJ Library, 2, 4.

64. Schwartz, *Johnson and Europe*, 216. Walt Rostow stated, "The Soviets will not move militarily against them, I don't think." Secretary Rusk stated, in the same July 1968 meeting, that "the real crisis has subsided." "Notes of the President's Meeting with the Tuesday Luncheon Group, 24 July 1968," Tom Johnson Notes, LBJ Library, 2–3. Ten days before the invasion, CIA director Helms was arguing that the situation had "eased." "Notes on Briefing Former Vice President Nixon and Governor Agnew," August 10, 1968, Tom Johnson Notes, LBJ Library, 1.

65. "Notes on Cabinet Meeting," August 22, 1968, Tom Johnson Notes, LBJ Library, 2.

66. "Notes of Emergency Meeting of the National Security Council," August 20, 1968, *FRUS*, vol. 17, doc. 81.

67. "Notes on Cabinet Meeting," August 22, 1968, Tom Johnson Notes, LBJ Library, 2; Schwartz, *Johnson and Vietnam*, 218. This may have been a reference to de Gaulle's claim that the Cold War was over in Europe and that the United States should leave. Schwartz, *Johnson and Vietnam*, 99–100.

68. "Cabinet Meeting," August 23, 1968, *FRUS*, vol. 17, doc. 85.

69. Lyman L. Lemnitzer, *Oral History*, 24.

70. Lemnitzer, *Oral History*, 10–11.

71. Lemnitzer, *Oral History*, 10–11.

72. "Summary Notes of the 590th Meeting of the National Security Council," September 4, 1968, *FRUS*, vol. 13, doc. 324.

73. "Notes on President's Meeting with House Leadership on Monday, 9 September 1968," Tom Johnson Notes, LBJ Library, 5; Trauschweizer, *Cold War U.S. Army*, 187.

74. There were 250,000 Soviet troops in Czechoslovakia. On paper NATO had 620,000, but their readiness was poor. The United States made up 300,000 of those troops. "Notes of Emergency Meeting of the National Security Council," August 20, 1968, *FRUS*, vol. 17, doc. 81.

75. Schwartz, *Johnson and Europe*, 219; Elsey Notes, September 21, 1968, LBJ Library.

76. Johnson thought that a strong U.S. reaction would not be "in Czech interests or ours." "Notes on Cabinet Meeting," August 22, 1968, Tom Johnson Notes, LBJ Library, 2.

77. Johnson thought before the United States made any declarations, they should find out "what kind of money, marbles, and chalk the NATO states are prepared to put in to counter the Soviet threat." "Summary Notes of the 590th Meeting of the National Security Council," September 4, 1968, *FRUS*, vol. 13, doc. 324. Subsequently, Johnson told the West German leader Kiesinger that it was vital that the Czech crisis be used to strengthen NATO. In response, Kiesinger increased the German military budget and the readiness of its forces. The Czech crisis also took the steam out of the Symington Amendment. Schwartz, *Johnson and Europe*, 219. According to Clifford, "Domestically, the crisis has ended the threat of passage by the Senate of the Symington Amendment. Senator Mansfield no longer is urging a major reduction in the level of U.S. forces in Europe." "Summary Notes of the 590th Meeting of the National Security Council," September 4, 1968, *FRUS*, vol. 13, doc. 324.

78. The JCS were "violently opposed" to talks in the aftermath of the invasion, and Secretary Clifford agreed. The timing of the overtures to the Soviets would give "tacit approval" to the invasion. Elsey Notes, September 11, 1968, 121, LBJ Library. In stark contrast, the British supported Johnson in his pursuit of détente after the Czech crisis. Schwartz, *Johnson and Europe*, 220.

79. "Notes on President's Meeting with House Leadership on Monday, 9 September 1968," Tom Johnson Notes, LBJ Library, 2.

80. Some argue it was a tragedy that Johnson was unsuccessful in his attempts to achieve a summit with the Soviets because nuclear weapons increased in the following years. Schwartz, *Johnson and Europe*, 220.

81. Kretchik, *U.S. Army Doctrine*, 190.

82. Trauschweizer, *Cold War U.S. Army*, 179. Note, however, that the minor changes in word choice and grammar constitute proof that the manual was revised and that the retention of much of the previous manual met with the approval of the army.

83. Trauschweizer, *Cold War U.S. Army*, 185. The German commander of Allied Forces, Central Europe, thought that selective use of tactical nuclear weapons would be required to hold off the Soviets. However, he doubted that political authorization

would come in time. Trauschweizer, *Cold War U.S. Army*, 186; Gavin, "Myths of Flexible Response," 871.

84. *Operations of Army Forces in the Field*, 1968, 6-4. The number before the dash represents the chapter number and the number after the dash represents the page within the chapter: 5-1, therefore, means the first page of chapter 5. See also Kretchik, *U.S. Army Doctrine*, 192.

85. *Operations 1962*, 59; *Operations of Army Forces in the Field*, 1968, 6-1.

86. *Operations of Army Forces in the Field*, 1968, 6-4; Kretchik, *U.S. Army Doctrine*, 192.

87. Trauschweizer, *Cold War U.S. Army*, 183–84.

88. For example, like *Operations '62*, *Operations '68* argues that the use of nuclear weapons provides the field commander with a major increase in "combat power." *Operations 1962*, 59; *Operations of Army Forces in the Field*, 1968, 6-1.

89. Dispersion "minimize[s] presentation of targets remunerative to nuclear weapons attack." *Operations 1962*, 59; *Operations of Army Forces in the Field*, 1968, 6-1 to 6-2. Quote is identical in both manuals. "In the nuclear environment," *Operations '62* and *Operations '68* state, "combat forces must be highly mobile to reduce vulnerability, facilitate control of extended areas of responsibility, provide mutual support, maintain freedom of action, and exploit the effects of nuclear fires." *Operations 1962*, 60; *Operations of Army Forces in the Field*, 1968, 6-2.

90. For example, "More than 5 rad per day, or 75 rad in a 30-day period, should be considered unacceptable." *Operations of Army Forces in the Field*, 1968, 6-3.

91. *Operations of Army Forces in the Field*, 1968, 5-1. Pagination in *Operations '68* is slightly different from *Operations '62*.

92. *Operations of Army Forces in the Field*, 1968, 6-13.

93. *Operations of Army Forces in the Field*, 1968, 6-13.

94. Trauschweizer, *Cold War U.S. Army*, 179–80.

95. *Operations of Army Forces in the Field*, 1968, 6-14 to 6-15.

96. "This has been criticized in the wake of military defeat in Vietnam, but it was nevertheless prudent. In the Cold War, the specter of nuclear war in Europe was much more threatening than defeat in a peripheral war." Trauschweizer, *Cold War U.S. Army*, 162.

97. Trauschweizer, *Cold War U.S. Army*, 162.

98. *Operations 1962*, 7, 127–54.

99. My thanks to Joshua Boucher of Baylor University's Political Science Department for his help compiling this data.

100. Daddis, *Westmoreland's War*, 1–35.

101. General Arthur S. Collins, commander of I Field Force Vietnam, quoted in Fitzgerald, *Learning to Forget*, 25–26.

102. Andrade, "Westmoreland Was Right," 149.

103. Daddis, *Westmoreland's War*, 84.

104. Andrade, "Westmoreland Was Right," 151.

105. Andrade, "Westmoreland Was Right," 153.

106. Andrade, "Westmoreland Was Right," 154.

107. Daddis, *Westmoreland's War*, 105.

108. Mao, *On Guerrilla Warfare*, 50, 55.

109. Mao, *On Guerrilla Warfare*, 62.

110. Andrade, "Westmoreland Was Right."

111. Quoted in Daddis, *Westmoreland's War*, 83.

112. Lewis Sorley, *A Better War: The Unexamined Victories and Final Tragedy of America's Last Years in Vietnam*, 20.

113. Johnson quoted in Birtle, *U.S. Army Counterinsurgency*, 371. For instances of the PROVN study being used to criticize Westmoreland and the army in Vietnam, see Krepinevich, *The Army and Vietnam*, 181–82; and Ricks, *Generals*, 264.

114. Daddis, *Westmoreland's War*, 83.

115. Birtle, *U.S. Army Counterinsurgency*, 371.

116. Daddis, *Westmoreland's War*, 117–19.

117. Daddis, *Westmoreland's War*, 120.

118. See table on 156.

119. Daddis, *Westmoreland's War*, xxi.

120. Daddis, *Westmoreland's War*, 126.

121. Daddis, *Westmoreland's War*, 112.

122. Daddis, *Westmoreland's War*, 113–14.

123. Long, *Soul of Armies*, 112–13.

124. Long, *Soul of Armies*, 118.

125. Boot, *Savage Wars of Peace*; Long, *Soul of Armies*, 120–27.

126. Michael E. Peterson, *The Combined Action Platoons: The U.S. Marines' Other War in Vietnam*.

127. Long, *Soul of Armies*, 124. Long is careful to point out the conventional nature of the PAVN enemy to explain the Marines' shift away from COIN, but not when the army did the same (125–27).

128. Long, *Soul of Armies*, 139.

129. Daddis, *Westmoreland's War*, 173.

130. Daddis, *Westmoreland's War*, 172.

131. Long, *Soul of Armies*, 127.

132. Fitzgerald points out that Abrams also prioritized the fight against main-force enemy units, contrary to Lewis Sorley's contention that COIN was Abrams's highest priority. Fitzgerald, *Learning to Forget*, 26–29. See also Sorley, *Better War*.

133. Andrade, "Westmoreland Was Right."

134. Andrade, "Westmoreland Was Right," 164–65.

135. Betts sums up the common view when he points out that the American military perceived that they were not allowed to win in Vietnam by amateur civilians who tied their hands "and that they were then left with the responsibility when they indeed failed to win." Betts, *Soldiers, Statesmen, and Cold War Crises*, 11.

136. Sorley, *Westmoreland*, 209–10.

137. Palmer, *Oral History*, 413.

138. Sorley, *Westmoreland*, 208.

139. Daddis, *Westmoreland's War*, 116.

140. According to Westmoreland, "appreciable numbers" of helicopters were not available until 1969, after he had left Vietnam. This slow procurement rate was due to "parochial views relative to service roles and missions." Westmoreland, *A Soldier Reports*, 415.

141. Westmoreland, *A Soldier Reports*, 414–15.

142. Trauschweizer points out that the assumption that tanks would be of no use in Vietnam was based on journalistic accounts of French fighting in Vietnam rather than on a close examination of French after-action reporting. Trauschweizer, *Cold War U.S. Army*, 175. An army study in 1966 showed that armored and mechanized units could be very useful in Vietnam. This study led Westmoreland to request more armored and mechanized units. Eventually, the army deployed twelve tank and mechanized battalions to Vietnam. Trauschweizer, *Cold War U.S. Army*, 176; Westmoreland, *A Soldier Reports*, 415; Kretchik, *U.S. Army Doctrine*, 188; Birtle, *U.S. Army Counterinsurgency*, 384.

143. Westmoreland pointed out, "As the memory of those who did the job in Vietnam fades, the Army and the Air Force must work closely together to maintain and refine the techniques" of tactical air support. Westmoreland, *A Soldier Reports*, 415, 418.

144. "Better security with less expenditure of manpower and thus economy of force." Westmoreland, *A Soldier Reports*, 418.

145. Westmoreland, *A Soldier Reports*, 418.

146. Westmoreland, *A Soldier Reports*, 418.

147. Trauschweizer, *Cold War U.S. Army*, 178–79.

148. "I was the commandant of the U.S. Army Command and General Staff College when General William Westmoreland asked me to prepare this monograph." John H. Hay, preface to *Vietnam Studies: Tactical and Material Innovations*, http://www.histo ry.army.mil/books/Vietnam/tactical/. "I have decided on John Hays [sic] for Leavenworth. With his combat experience, he's a good man for that job." FONECON between General Woolnough, CONARC, and Westmoreland, July 23, 1968, Westmoreland Papers, box 28, folder 8, MHI.

149. Westmoreland, *A Soldier Reports*, 418.

150. Westmoreland, *A Soldier Reports*, 418.

151. Westmoreland, *A Soldier Reports*, 373.

152. *Operations of Army Forces in the Field*, 1968, 8-1 to 8-4; Kretchik, *U.S. Army Doctrine*, 192.

153. *Operations of Army Forces in the Field*, 1968, 8-1.

154. Trauschweizer, *Cold War U.S. Army*, 178–79. Airmobile operations had their share of problems in Vietnam. They were present in too few numbers, they were loud, they were vulnerable to adverse weather conditions and to ground fire, they required landing zones, and their vulnerability to ground fire made it difficult to move troops engaged in a fight. However, according to Birtle, helicopters remained "the single best method available to the Army to compel a reluctant enemy to accept battle." Birtle, *U.S. Army Counterinsurgency*, 378. Despite all of these shortcomings, the army still considered helicopters to be a viable source of battlefield mobility.

155. *Operations* 1962, 136–54.

156. Trauschweizer points this out but neglects to acknowledge that much of the elements of this section were placed in the new section on stability operations. Trauschweizer, *Cold War U.S. Army*, 179; *Operations of Army Forces in the Field*, 1968, 12-1.

157. *Operations of Army Forces in the Field*, 1968, 12-1.

158. *Operations of Army Forces in the Field*, 1968, 13-1.

159. *Operations of Army Forces in the Field*, 1968, 13-1 to 13-9.

160. Birtle, *U.S. Army Counterinsurgency*, 250.

161. Long, *Soul of Armies*, 115; Sorley, *Honorable Warrior*; Rosen, *Winning the Next War*, 101–5.

162. Birtle, *U.S. Army Counterinsurgency*, 223, 238.

163. Stability operations were those in which army personnel would assist "U.S. efforts to aid friendly nations in preventing and combating insurgency." *Operations of Army Forces in the Field*, 1968, 13-1 to 13-3.

164. *Operations of Army Forces in the Field*, 1968, 1-4. "Establishing a peaceful climate for permitting modernization, military assistance and operations are directed to strengthening the host country's military capabilities, to include the invigoration of its regular and paramilitary forces and, in some instances, the civil police organization." *Operations of Army Forces in the Field*, 1968, 13-2.

165. *Operations of Army Forces in the Field*, 1968, 13-1 to 13-2.

166. Fitzgerald, *Learning to Forget*, 54.

167. Long, *Soul of Armies*, 128.

168. Lemnitzer, *Oral History*, 31–32.

169. Andrade, "Westmoreland Was Right."

4. From Active Defense to AirLand Battle: The Cold War Doctrine of the '70s and '80s

1. Fitzgerald, *Learning to Forget*, 50.

2. Gaddis, *Strategies of Containment*, 282.

3. Francis J. Gavin, *Nuclear Statecraft: History and Strategy in America's Atomic Age*, 108. "Great powers always looked out for their own national interests, [Nixon] told his White House staff just after the announcement that he was to visit China, 'or else they're played for suckers by those powers that do.'" Margaret MacMillan, *Nixon and Mao: The Week That Changed the World*, 9, 48–49.

4. Kenneth Waltz, *Theory of International Politics*, 203.

5. Gaddis, *Strategies of Containment*, 273. Donald Rumsfeld, chairman of Ford's transition team, later his chief of staff (1974) and then his secretary of defense (1975), points out that Ford leaned heavily toward continuity in foreign policy with the Nixon administration. Ford signaled this by making Kissinger secretary of state and national security adviser. Donald Rumsfeld, *Known and Unknown: A Memoir*, 167, 174–75. Cheney notes that Ford did not want foreign policy suggestions from the transition team and that he would keep Kissinger on as secretary of state. Cheney, *In My Time*, 68.

6. Gaddis, *Strategies of Containment*, 296. As Gaddis points out, the drawdown of U.S. troops in Vietnam was the clearest expression of the Nixon doctrine.

7. Jensen, *Forging the Sword*, 29.

8. MacMillan, *Nixon and Mao*, 6, 164, 203.

9. Terry Terriff, *The Nixon Administration and the Making of US Nuclear Strategy*, 18–19.

10. Most recently, Jensen argued that such a shift in focus guided army doctrine. Jensen, *Forging the Sword*, 30. See also Kretchik, *U.S. Army Doctrine*, 193–94.

11. The Nixon Doctrine "required that strategic planners shift their attention from Asia to NATO Europe, with a '1/2 war' glance at the Middle East, especially the security of Israel and the access routes to Persian Gulf oil." Paul H. Herbert, *Deciding What Has to Be Done: General William E. DePuy and the 1976 Edition of "FM 100-5 Operations,"* 5; Richard M. Nixon, "Address to the Nation on Vietnam," May 14, 1969; Nixon, "A Redefining of the United States Role in the World"; Kretchik, *U.S. Army Doctrine*, 193; Betts, *Soldiers, Statesmen, and Cold War Crises*, 76.

12. "The Nixon Doctrine can help remove the need for similar American ground combat involvement in future Asian wars, an important objective of our new strategy." Melvin Laird, testimony to Senate Armed Services Committee, quoted in Richard Lock-Pullan, "'An Inward Looking Time': The United States Army, 1973-1976," 485. See also Gaddis, *Strategies of Containment*, 296.

13. Gaddis, *Strategies of Containment*, 349–51.

14. Barry R. Posen and Stephen Van Evera, "Defense Policy and the Reagan Administration: Departure from Containment," 5.

15. Posen and Van Evera, "Defense Policy and the Reagan Administration."

16. The army was cut from 1.6 million to 800,000. DePuy, *Changing an Army*, 174.

17. "Each armed force under Laird retained control over the definition of its critical tasks." J. Q. Wilson, *Bureaucracy*, 179–80. Laird returned the selection boards for flag officers to their pre-Kennedy arrangement, whereby the services had control over the decisions. Betts, *Soldiers, Statesmen, Cold War Crises*, 8, 65.

18. MacMillan, *Nixon and Mao*, 60. See also Gaddis, *Strategies of Containment*, 299; MacMillan, *Nixon and Mao*, 49, 54; and Robert Dallek, *Nixon and Kissinger: Partners in Power*, 84–85.

19. William Burr, ed., *The Kissinger Transcripts: The Top Secret Talks with Beijing and Moscow*, 305.

20. Henry Kissinger, *Years of Upheaval*, 593; Kissinger, *The White House Years*, 398.

21. The threat to Europe promised a role for all branches of the army and a share of the budget. J. Q. Wilson, *Bureaucracy*, 222–23. Kretchik argues that DePuy used doctrine to draw more money from Congress. Kretchik, *U.S. Army Doctrine*, 196.

22. Gaddis, *Strategies of Containment*, 349–51.

23. Posen and Van Evera, "Defense Policy," 5.

24. Gaddis, *Strategies of Containment*, 353.

25. Colin Jackson, "From Conservatism to Revolutionary Intoxication: The U.S. Army and the Second Interwar Period," 44; Cassidy, *Counterinsurgency*, 100, 119. See also Lock-Pullan, "Inward Looking Time," 486; Herbert, *Deciding What Has to Be Done*, 6, 9; and Ucko, *New Counterinsurgency Era*, 29–30.

26. Betts, *Soldiers, Statesmen, and Cold War Crises*, 83; Craig M. Cameron, "The US Military's 'Two-Front War,' 1963–1988," 30; Lock-Pullan, "'Inward Looking Time,'" 483–84, 486; Jackson, "From Conservatism to Revolutionary Intoxication," 44; Herbert, *Deciding What Has to Be Done*, 6, 9; Ucko, *New Counterinsurgency Era*, 29–30; Ricks, *Generals*, 335.

27. Herbert, *Deciding What Has to Be Done*, 9; L. D. Holder, "Development of Army Doctrine, 1975 to 1985," 50; *Operations 1976*, 1–2.

28. Lock-Pullan, "'Inward Looking Time,'" 488.

29. The defense of Europe provided the army with an "operational goal" that reinforced its organizational culture. J. Q. Wilson, *Bureaucracy*, 35–36; Fitzgerald, *Learning to Forget*, 45.

30. J. Q. Wilson, *Bureaucracy*, 219.

31. Gaddis, *Strategies of Containment*, 349.

32. Ucko, *New Counterinsurgency Era*, 45.

33. Kretchik, *U.S. Army Doctrine*, 194.

34. Herbert, *Deciding What Has to Be Done*, 25.

35. *Operations* was the first manual revised, and "all others in some way or other, are related to, or derived from FM 100-5." DePuy, *Changing an Army*, 188. See also Kretchik, *U.S. Army Doctrine*, 198; and Herbert, *Deciding What Has to Be Done*, 49.

36. Ricks, *Generals*, 244.

37. "We tried to orient [doctrine] towards Europe, which is the principal and directed mission of the Army." DePuy, *Changing an Army*, 187. See also Herbert, *Deciding What Has to Be Done*, 18.

38. Jensen, *Forging the Sword*, 29.

39. Lock-Pullan, "'Inward Looking Time,'" 487; Kretchik, *U.S. Army Doctrine*, 193; Herbert, *Deciding What Has to Be Done*, 5.

40. "For almost eight years prior to 1973, we had concentrated on the war in Vietnam to the exclusion of modernization and doctrinal and organizational development." Donn A. Starry, *Press On! Selected Works of General Donn A. Starry*, 611–12.

41. Gaddis, *Strategies of Containment*, 318.

42. Defense expenditures as a proportion of GDP went from 8.1 percent in 1970 to 4.9 percent in 1977. When adjusted for inflation, U.S. defense expenditures declined by 4.9 percent per year. Soviet expenditures in the same period were between 11 and 13 percent during the same period and showed annual increases of 3 percent when adjusted for inflation. In the same period, Congress cut defense budget requests by $6 billion and increased nondefense budget requests by $4.7 billion. Gaddis, *Strategies of Containment*, 318–19. In the 1971–72 fiscal year, DePuy had witnessed the cancellation of the Cheyenne attack helicopter and the MBT70 main battle tanks. The army considered both systems to be critical to its modernization. Herbert, *Deciding What Has to Be Done*, 27.

43. In a 1975 correspondence in *Foreign Affairs*, Enthoven admitted that "the Soviets have been increasing their armed forces while we have been reducing ours." However, he did not point out that this condition originated in 1967. Bennett et al., "Correspondence," 776.

44. DePuy, *Changing an Army*, 191.

45. DePuy, *Changing an Army*, 191. Inspired by this mismatch with the Soviets, Army Chief of Staff Abrams increased army divisions from thirteen to sixteen. However, because resources were tight, Abrams had to guarantee that he could do so without increasing the size of the army. Abrams also watched the doctrinal process closely and was kept abreast of the doctrinal developments by DePuy and approved them. Herbert, *Deciding What Has to Be Done*, 25, 75.

46. John J. Mearsheimer, "Maneuver, Mobile Defense, and the NATO Central Front," 112–15.

47. Lock-Pullan, "'Inward Looking Time,'" 486.

48. Herbert acknowledges this but still insists, incorrectly I think, that the Soviet threat was greatest in 1973. Herbert, *Deciding What Has to Be Done*, 5–6.

49. Starry: "Almost without exception it validated everything we thought we had discovered in the studies we had done. . . . Everything that happened out there validated, almost without exception, what we thought the future battlefield was going to look like." Starry, *Press On!*, 1110. See also DePuy, *Changing an Army*, 190–91; and Herbert, *Deciding What Has to Be Done*, 29, 33–36.

50. *Operations 1976*, 2-1 to 2-2; Herbert, *Deciding What Has to Be Done*, 31.

51. *Operations 1976*, 2-2.

52. *Operations 1976*, 2-7 to 2-9.

53. Jensen, *Forging the Sword*, 33; Herbert, *Deciding What Has to Be Done*, 30.

54. Jensen, *Forging the Sword*, 33.

55. Herbert, *Deciding What Has to Be Done*, 30.

56. Jensen, *Forging the Sword*, 35.

57. *Operations 1976*, 2-18 to 2-19.

58. Starry, *Press On!*, 273.

59. Herbert, *Deciding What Has to Be Done*, 16. DePuy consciously modeled army training on the Israeli system. DePuy, *Changing an Army*, 187.

60. DePuy, *Changing an Army*, 193.

61. Jensen, *Forging the Sword*, 33.

62. Jensen, *Forging the Sword*, 32–33.

63. DePuy, *Changing an Army*, 191. See also Herbert, *Deciding What Has to Be Done*, 9, 29–30; Starry, *Press On!*, 273; and Lock-Pullan, "'Inward Looking Time.'"

64. *Operations 1976*, 12-13; Herbert, *Deciding What Has to Be Done*, 26–27.

65. *Operations 1976*, 1-1; Kretchik, *U.S. Army Doctrine*, 198; Herbert, *Deciding What Has to Be Done*, 7.

66. Herbert, *Deciding What Has to Be Done*, 26, 35.

67. "The Army's need to prepare for battle overrides every other aspect of unit missions." *Operations 1976*, 1-5.

68. Herbert, *Deciding What Has to Be Done*, 85, 86–87, 92–93.

69. Kretchik, *U.S. Army Doctrine*, 197.

70. "Traditionally the Army had always taught the superiority of offensive maneuvers." J. Q. Wilson, *Bureaucracy*, 219. See also Holder, "Development of Army Doctrine," 50–51.

71. Herbert, *Deciding What Has to Be Done*, 35, 96–97; Kretchik, *U.S. Army Doctrine*, 201–2.

72. Kretchik, *U.S. Army Doctrine*, 202.

73. Herbert, *Deciding What Has to Be Done*, 42–43, 75; Kretchik, *U.S. Army Doctrine*, 202.

74. Starry, *Press On!*, 1123–25; John L. Romjue, *From Active Defense to AirLand Battle: The Development of Army Doctrine, 1973–1982*, 23.

75. Jensen, *Forging the Sword*, 57.

76. Jensen, *Forging the Sword*, 61.

77. Jensen, *Forging the Sword*, 62.

78. Jensen, *Forging the Sword*, 58–59.

79. Jensen, *Forging the Sword*, 61.

80. Herbert, *Deciding What Has to Be Done*, 95–96. Herbert argues of *Operations '82*: "Army published an entirely new manual that not only addressed all the points of criticism that had emerged but took a wholly different approach to warfare" (98). "The writers of the 1982 manual set out to describe 'how soldiers, not systems, fight and win'" (101).

81. John Whiteclay Chambers II, *The Oxford Companion to American Military History*, 234.

82. Starry, *Press On!*, 1128, 1158, 1160.

83. Fitzgerald, *Learning to Forget*, 44; Jensen, *Forging the Sword*, 60–61.

84. *Operations 1976*, 4-9 to 4-10; Herbert, *Deciding What Has to Be Done*, 46.

85. *Operations 1976*, 3-6, 5-12, 4-9.

86. *Operations 1976*, 3-6, 3-3, 4-10 to 4-11, 5-2, 5-7, 5-10; DePuy, *Changing an Army*, 191; Jensen, *Forging the Sword*, 40–41.

87. The combined arms team was made up of infantry, field artillery, tanks, attack helicopters, air force aircraft, engineers, air defenses, and electronic warfare units. *Operations 1976*, 1-4, 3-10, 4-7; Kretchik, *U.S. Army Doctrine*, 199; Herbert, *Deciding What Has to Be Done*, 45–46.

88. Ricks, *Generals*, 344–48.

89. Herbert, *Deciding What Has to Be Done*, 6.

90. Herbert, *Deciding What Has to Be Done*, 1, 33.

91. Herbert, *Deciding What Has to Be Done*, 35.

92. Like ROAD, *Operations '76* also espoused tailoring. "The basic building block in mounted defensive warfare is the cross-reinforced tank or mechanized company team or battalion task force." *Operations 1976*, 3-9. See also Herbert, *Deciding What Has to Be Done*, 34; and Kretchik, *U.S. Army Doctrine*, 198.

93. Herbert, *Deciding What Has to Be Done*, 49.

94. *Panzergrenadier* units were in APCs and accompanied tanks and participated in tank battles. Herbert, *Deciding What Has to Be Done*, 63.

95. In the spring of 1974, after a visit to Europe, Starry wrote to DePuy to express his admiration for the German *panzergrenadier* concept, and DePuy was convinced. Herbert, *Deciding What Has to Be Done*, 49, 62, 64–65.

96. Herbert, *Deciding What Has to Be Done*, 62–63.

97. *Operations 1976*, 2-10; Herbert, *Deciding What Has to Be Done*, 36.

98. Herbert, *Deciding What Has to Be Done*, 43.

99. Herbert, *Deciding What Has to Be Done*, 8; Jensen, *Forging the Sword*, 51.

100. Starry, *Press On!*, 1161.

101. Herbert, *Deciding What Has to Be Done*, 70; Kretchik, *U.S. Army Doctrine*, 200.

102. *Operations 1976*, 8-4.

103. Herbert, *Deciding What Has to Be Done*, 7.

104. *Operations 1976*, 8-4. DePuy and TRADOC retained the primary role of the helicopter established by Howze and others in the 1950s and '60s as a "tank-killing" instrument. *Operations* 1976, 2-21; Herbert, *Deciding What Has to Be Done*, 46. According to *Operations '76*, helicopters would move troops and equipment rapidly around the battlefield with ten to twenty times the mobility of ground units. *Operations 1976*, 2-30, 4-8, 5-5.

105. Jensen, *Forging the Sword*, 36.

106. *Operations 1976*, 3-7 to 3-8; Herbert, *Deciding What Has to Be Done*, 14–15, 31, 88.

107. *Operations 1976*, 8-1.

108. DePuy to General Dixon, November 20, 1975, quoted in Herbert, *Deciding What Has to Be Done*, 69.

109. Jensen, *Forging the Sword*, 36–37.

110. For the Soviets, "a high rate of advance reduces the danger of troop destruction by enemy nuclear strikes." *Operations 1976*, 2-32.

111. "Warsaw Pact doctrine anticipates use of nuclear weapons in the future war, but teaches preparedness to fight without them. For both conditions, it emphasizes heavy concentrations of armor." *Operations 1976*, 2-2.

112. *Operations 1976*, 11-3.

113. *Operations 1976*, 11-4.

114. *Operations 1976*, 11-4; Herbert, *Deciding What Has to Be Done*, 91–92.

115. *Operations 1976*, 13-6.

116. *Operations 1976*, 2-28, 10-5 to 10-6.

117. *Operations 1976*, 10-2.

118. *Operations 1976*, 2-28.

119. *Operations 1976*, 2-29.

120. Nuclear weapons could "negate the enemy's offensive advantage and deny him his objective." *Operations 1976*, 3-4, 10-1, 10-9.

121. *Operations 1976*, 10-8.

122. *Operations 1976*, 2-10, 11-4.

123. Kretchik, *U.S. Army Doctrine*, 198–99; *Operations 1976*, 2-32, 5-3.

124. *Operations 1976*, 2-10 to 2-11, 2-30.

125. *Operations 1976*, 10-2.

126. In 1975 DePuy brought the tactical nuclear weapons community into the doctrinal discussion. This community pointed out that the United States, thanks to the buildup initiated under Kennedy and Johnson, had a major advantage over the Soviets in tactical nuclear weapons. Herbert, *Deciding What Has to Be Done*, 90.

127. Herbert, *Deciding What Has to Be Done*, 90–91.

128. Instead, tactical nuclear doctrine was set out in its own manual, *Field Manual 100-5-1, Conventional-Nuclear Operations*. The dual nuclear-conventional aspect of the title shows that dual capability and the integration of conventional and nuclear forces were still central to army doctrine and organization. Moreover, TRADOC included *Field Manual 100-5-1* as one of only three "CAPSTONE" "'how to fight' manuals," further pointing out the key role of nuclear weapons at the highest levels of army doctrine. *Operations 1976*, 3-1, app. B, "'How to Fight' Manuals," B-1.

129. Interestingly, although he mentions the pentomic reorganization, Herbert does not even mention ROAD and *Operations '62* in his discussion of organizational changes that led to doctrinal changes. Herbert, *Deciding What Has to Be Done*, 7.

130. Herbert, *Deciding What Has to Be Done*, 7.

131. Jensen, *Forging the Sword*, 34.

132. National Security Decision Directive (NSDD) 75, "U.S. Relations with the Soviet Union," January 17, 1983, http://www.fas.org/irp/offdocs/nsdd/nsdd-075.htm; Gaddis, *Strategies of Containment*, 355.

133. Reagan was returning to "symmetrical" containment. Gaddis, *Strategies of Containment*, 354.

134. NSDD 32, "US National Security Strategy," May 20, 1982, http://www.fas.org/irp/offdocs/nsdd/nsdd-32.pdf; Starry, *Press On!*, 1130. In the 1980s the Soviets were exporting more tanks than the United States had built over an extended period while still modernizing and increasing the size of their tank forces. Starry, *Press On!*, 1155–56.

135. Quoted in James Graham Wilson, "How Grand Was Reagan's Strategy, 1976–1984?," 778–79.

136. Caspar W. Weinberger, *Annual Report to the Congress: Fiscal Year 1983*, I-3; NSDD 13, "Nuclear Weapons Employment Policy," October 19, 1981, http://www.fas.org/irp/offdocs/nsdd/nsdd-13.htm.

137. Starry, *Press On!*, 1127, 1147.

138. *Operations 1982*, 16-1 to 16-4.

139. Starry, *Press On!*, 1128.

140. *Operations '82* was rife with references to Soviet doctrine. See, for instance, *Operations 1982*, 4-4 to 4-5.

141. Starry, *Press On!*, 1130.

142. Starry, *Press On!*, 1155–56.

143. Starry, *Press On!*, 1148.

144. "In the 1976 edition of FM 100-5, we really did a reasonable job of describing doctrine for the close-in battle. . . . I wrote most of the defense and offense parts of that 1976 manual, and I knew something was missing—what to do about the follow-on echelons." Starry, *Press On!*, 1110, 1125. See also Holder, "Development of Army Doctrine," 51.

145. Starry notes that there are four echelons of Soviet forces in Europe, and NATO would have to fight at least three of them. "We're not going to succeed against the first

of those echelons . . . unless we can prevent the follow-on echelon from loading up the frontline battle." Starry, *Press On!*, 1129.

146. Starry, *Press On!*, 1110–11.

147. Starry, *Press On!*, 1147; Jensen, *Forging the Sword*, 47.

148. *Operations 1982*, 7-12.

149. *Operations 1982*, 7-11, 11-7.

150. Starry, *Press On!*, 1130.

151. Romjue, *From Active Defense to AirLand Battle*, 40.

152. The air force, through commander of Tactical Air Command Robert Creech, overcame bureaucratic resistance to deepen ties with the army. Starry, *Press On!*, 1148.

153. Jensen, *Forging the Sword*, 76.

154. Depth and synchronization were the key. "The battle in depth should delay, disrupt, or destroy the enemy's uncommitted forces and isolate his committed forces so that they may be destroyed. The deep battle is closely linked with the close-in fight." *Operations 1982*, 2-2, 7-13.

155. Starry, *Press On!*, 1125.

156. Starry, *Press On!*, 1129.

157. *Operations 1982*, 9-10.

158. Message to Lieutenant General E. C. Meyer, deputy chief of staff for operations, December 28, 1978, in Starry, *Press On!*, 731–32; *Operations 1982*, 7-12.

159. "This selective targeting allows friendly units in contact to defeat engaged enemy forces by conventional means." *Operations 1982*, 7-12, 7-15.

160. *Operations 1982*, 7-2.

161. *Operations 1982*, 2-9, 7-8 to 7-9, 7-10, 11-12.

162. Starry, "Subject: Integrated Operations," July 7, 1980, TRADOC; Romjue, *From Active Defense to AirLand Battle*, 96–97.

163. *Operations 1982*, 2-3, 7-3.

164. Jensen, *Forging the Sword*, 72.

165. *Operations 1982*, 4-1, 17-4.

166. Jensen, *Forging the Sword*, 84.

167. Kretchik, *U.S. Army Doctrine*, 196–97.

168. Jensen, *Forging the Sword*, 26.

169. Jensen, *Forging the Sword*, 46.

170. See, for example, *Operations 1976*, 3-4 to 3-6.

171. *Operations 1976*, 3-4 to 3-5; Jensen, *Forging the Sword*, 38–39; Herbert, *Deciding What Has to Be Done*, 8.

172. For a discussion of the three-to-one rule, see Mearsheimer, "Maneuver, Mobile Defense, and the NATO Central Front," 112–13; and Mearsheimer, "Assessing the Conventional Balance." Interestingly, Mearsheimer cites *Operations '76* in his 1981 piece but does not note that the 1976 manual argued that the attacker actually requires a *six-to-one* advantage against modern weapons, thus pointing out the extreme difficulty of attack on a modern battlefield and attributing more power to the defense than even the three-to-one rule. *Operations 1976*, 3-4 to 3-5.

173. Jensen, *Forging the Sword*, 37.

174. "The success of the defense will ultimately depend greatly on how well the companies, platoons, tank crews, and squads exploit all the *built-in* advantages of the defender." *Operations 1976*, 3-3, 5-7 (emphasis added).

175. Jensen, *Forging the Sword*, 46.

176. Starry, *Press On!*, 611.

177. Starry, *Press On!*, 611–13.

178. Starry, *Press On!*, 1111; Herbert, *Deciding What Has to Be Done*, 56–58.

179. Herbert, *Deciding What Has to Be Done*, 59.

180. Herbert, *Deciding What Has to Be Done*, 78.

181. *Operations 1976*, 4-10 to 4-11.

182. *Operations 1976*, 5-1.

183. The "defense must be elastic—must absorb the shock—slow the attack—weaken it—and then destroy it." *Operations 1976*, 5-6 (emphasis added). Public intellectuals in the 1980s acknowledge that tactical counterattack was a major part of an active defense. Mearsheimer, "Maneuver, Mobile Defense, and the NATO Central Front," 104–22, 105–6.

184. Herbert, *Deciding What Has to Be Done*, 82–83, 97; *Operations 1976*, 4-1 to 4-2, 5-7. Such maneuvers surrender the "innate advantages of the defender." *Operations 1976*, 5-14.

185. *Operations 1976*, 5-2, 5-7.

186. DePuy, *Changing an Army*, 192.

187. Quoted in Jensen, *Forging the Sword*, 52.

188. Kretchik, *U.S. Army Doctrine*, 199.

189. *Operations 1976*, 3-3, 5-7.

190. Haig to DePuy, September 10, 1976, quoted in Herbert, *Deciding What Has to Be Done*, 96–97; Kretchik, *U.S. Army Doctrine*, 201.

191. DePuy, *Changing an Army*, 192.

192. Jensen, *Forging the Sword*, 42.

193. *Operations 1962*, 75-77.

194. Mearsheimer, "Maneuver, Mobile Defense, and the NATO Central Front," 118–19. See also Christopher N. Donnelly, "Tactical Problems Facing the Soviet Army: Recent Debates in the Soviet Military Press" and "Soviet Tactics for Overcoming NATO Anti-tank Defenses."

195. *Operations 1976*, 4-9 to 4-10; Herbert, *Deciding What Has to Be Done*, 46.

196. *Operations 1976*, 3-6, 4-10 to 4-11, 5-10; DePuy, *Changing an Army*, 191. Taking advantage of terrain as a means of fighting outnumbered was central to the doctrine. *Operations 1976*, 3-3, 5-7. Active Defense avoided many of the pitfalls of a mobile defense, as pointed out by Mearsheimer years later. Mearsheimer, "Maneuver, Mobile Defense, and the NATO Central Front," 112–13.

197. "The combination of all these advantages repeated in each set of positions in depth supported by field artillery, close air support and attack helicopters, should easily inflict very high losses on an attacking enemy." *Operations 1976*, 5-7. DePuy stated directly, "We want to emulate the Germans." Like *Operations '76*, the West Germans'

HDv. 100/100 had a highly defensive orientation. Herbert, *Deciding What Has to Be Done*, 65–66, 88.

198. *Operations 1976*, 5-3, 5-13.

199. "Attack helicopters, should easily inflict very high losses on an attacking enemy." *Operations 1976*, 5-7.

200. DePuy, *Changing an Army*, 192.

201. *Operations 1976*, chap. 6.

202. *Operations 1976*, 6-2.

203. DePuy, *Changing an Army*, 192. Just when the enemy has concentrated to destroy the defender, "the delay force leaves, and the enemy must repeat the time-consuming process at the next delay position." *Operations 1976*, 6-3.

204. *Operations 1976*, 14-15. "The defender has the advantage in the use of built-up areas." *Operations 1976*, 13-10 to 13-16, 14-15.

205. Kretchik, *U.S. Army Doctrine*, 200.

206. Fitzgerald, *Learning to Forget*, 49.

207. *Operations 1962*, 74 (emphasis added).

208. *Operations 1976*, 6-2 to 6-3 (emphasis in the original).

209. *Operations 1976*, 11-11.

210. Sometimes these ratios were as high as fifty to one, which DePuy attributed to the superior training of Israeli over Arab tank crews. Herbert, *Deciding What Has to Be Done*, 80. DePuy argued that you could actually "get more combat effectiveness by increasing the performance of the unit than you ever could by putting new weapons in it." DePuy, *Changing an Army*, 190.

211. DePuy, *Changing an Army*, 193.

212. *Operations 1976*, 5-1.

213. *Operations 1976*, 3-6.

214. Herbert, *Deciding What Has to Be Done*, 13–15.

215. Herbert, *Deciding What Has to Be Done*, 9.

216. DePuy, *Changing an Army*, 188.

217. Gaddis, *Strategies of Containment*, 350–51, 356.

218. Posen and Van Evera, "Defense Policy."

219. Snyder, "Civil-Military Relations."

220. Benjamin Jensen provides a nice summary of the efforts that DePuy and his team took to promote *Operations 1976* around the army. Jensen, *Forging the Sword*, 50–53.

221. Herbert, *Deciding What Has to Be Done*, 98; Kretchik, *U.S. Army Doctrine*, 202–3.

222. Herbert, *Deciding What Has to Be Done*, 95–96.

223. DePuy, *Changing an Army*, 192.

224. *Operations 1976*, 5-2, 5-7.

225. Starry, *Press On!*, 1110, 1125.

226. Starry, "Modern Armor Battle II: The Defense," 39–44; Jensen, *Forging the Sword*, 42–52.

227. David L. Tamminen, "How to Defend Outnumbered and Win."

228. Jensen, *Forging the Sword*, 55.

229. William S. Lind, "Some Doctrinal Questions for the United States Army"; Edward N. Luttwak, "The American Style of Warfare and the Military Balance."

230. Mearsheimer, "Maneuver, Mobile Defense, and the NATO Central Front," 120.

231. Richard Lock-Pullan, "Civilian Ideas and Military Innovation: Manoeuvre Warfare and Organisational Change in the U.S. Army."

232. Starry, *Press On!*, 1128 (see also 1125–26). However, many of these criticisms, like William Lind's insistence that the army adopt "maneuver warfare" rather than attrition warfare, were flawed. As John Mearsheimer pointed out in 1981, "A close examination of the prescribed maneuver-oriented defense, however, reveals a fundamentally flawed idea." Mearsheimer, "Maneuver, Mobile Defense, and the NATO Central Front," 107. The concept of maneuver warfare was too vague to base a strategy on and involved major risks against an enemy employing blitzkrieg-like tactics such as the Soviets. Mearsheimer, "Maneuver, Mobile Defense, and the NATO Central Front," 105–12.

233. *Operations 1982*, 2-2.

234. Starry, *Press On*, 611.

235. Holder, "Development of Army Doctrine," 51.

236. *Operations 1982*, 2-1.

237. *Operations 1982*, 2-1.

238. *Operations 1982*, 2-6 to 2-10.

239. *Operations 1982*, 8-1.

240. *Operations 1976*, 4-11 to 4-12.

241. *Operations 1982*, 9-16 to 9-20.

242. *Operations 1982*, 8-1, 8-8, 9-9.

243. *Operations 1976*, 3-3, 3-6, 4-10 to 4-11, 5-7, 5-10; DePuy, *Changing an Army*, 191.

244. *Operations 1982*, 3-4 to 3-8, 10-3.

245. *Operations 1982*, 10-1.

246. *Operations 1982*, 10-1.

247. *Operations 1982*, 10-1.

248. *Operations 1982*, 12-8.

249. Starry, *Press On!*, 1129.

250. "Initiative, the ability to set the terms of battle by action, is the greatest advantage in war. Whether US forces are attacking or defending, they must seize and preserve the initiative to hasten the enemy's defeat and to prevent his recovery." *Operations 1982*, 7-2, 10-4, 12-1 to 12-3, 12-7.

251. *Operations 1982*, 11-1.

252. John Keegan, *A History of Warfare*.

253. Starry, *Press On!*, 1112.

254. Starry, *Press On!*, 1110, 1125.

255. Starry, *Press On!*, 1110, 1125.

256. *Operations 1982*, 11-4 to 11-5.

257. The operational level of war "is concerned with the actions of large units—field armies and army groups—in determining and implementing military measures to gain strategic goals in a theatre of war. They must decide not only how they will fight but also when, where and whether they will fight and what use they will make of tactical successes." Holder, "Development of Army Doctrine," 52; *Operations 1982*, 2-3.

258. Jensen argues that AirLand Battle's introduction of the operational level of war constituted a new "theory of victory." Jensen, *Forging the Sword*, 77, 79. However, here I define a theory of victory by its offensive or defensive character. Based on this definition, AirLand Battle does not constitute a new theory of victory because the actions prescribed at the operational level of war were meant to make a defensive theory of victory possible, not enable an offensive one.

259. *Operations 1982*, 11-3; Starry, *Press On!*, 1129.

260. *Operations 1982*, 11-1.

261. *Operations 1982*, 11-4 to 11-5.

262. *Operations 1982*, 11-2 to 11-4.

263. *Operations 1982*, 10-4.

264. Jensen, *Forging the Sword*, 77.

265. Jensen, *Forging the Sword*, 79.

266. *Operations 1982*, 7-2.

267. The main means of deep attack would be battlefield air interdiction, long-range artillery, attack helicopters, Special Forces, Ranger units, and airmobile and airborne units. *Operations 1982*, 7-15 to 7-17, 9-10.

268. Fitzgerald, *Learning to Forget*, 45.

269. "The Nixon Doctrine can help remove the need for similar American ground combat involvement in future Asian wars, an important objective of our new strategy." Melvin Laird, testimony to Senate Armed Services Committee, quoted in Lock-Pullan, "'Inward Looking Time,'" 485. See also Fitzgerald, *Learning to Forget*, 37; and Gaddis, *Strategies of Containment*, 302.

270. Lock-Pullan, "'Inward Looking Time,'" 486.

271. *Operations 1976*, 1-5.

272. *Operations 1976*, app. B, B-3.

273. Fitzgerald, *Learning to Forget*, 46–48.

274. Fitzgerald, *Learning to Forget*, 47.

275. Fitzgerald, *Learning to Forget*, 47.

276. However, Fitzgerald is right to point out that some in the army did have a powerful negative response to COIN after Vietnam. At Fort Bragg in the 1970s, for instance, the staff was ordered to throw out their material on COIN. Fitzgerald, *Learning to Forget*, 47. This response may have been because army leaders did not feel they had been well served by COIN ideas in Vietnam. The conflicts described in this literature did not prepare the army for the mix of unconventional and heavy conventional engagements they encountered in Vietnam. This is, of course, speculation because we do not know why an unidentified senior leader ordered the material thrown out.

277. Gian Gentile, *Wrong Turn: America's Deadly Embrace of Counterinsurgency*; Douglas Porch, *Counterinsurgency: Exposing the Myths of the New Way of War*.

278. DePuy quoted in Fitzgerald, *Forgetting the Past*, 46.

279. Gaddis, *Strategies of Containment*, 355; Chester Pach, "The Reagan Doctrine: Principle, Pragmatism, and Policy"; Ucko, *New Counterinsurgency Era*, 31–33.

280. NSDD 82, "US Policy Initiatives to Improve Prospects for Victory in El Salvador," February 24, 1983, http://www.fas.org/irp/offdocs/nsdd/nsdd-082.htm.

281. Weinberger's congressional testimony quoted in Ucko, *New Counterinsurgency Era*, 33.

282. In addition, in 1987, the U.S. government established Special Operations Command (SOCOM), making SF part of the unified command level. Ucko, *New Counterinsurgency Era*, 37.

283. Petraeus, "Lessons of Vietnam," 211–14, 218–19.

284. Fitzgerald, *Learning to Forget*, 63.

285. Fitzgerald, *Learning to Forget*, 61–62; Ucko, *New Counterinsurgency Era*, 39.

286. National Security Strategy of the United States, 1987, quoted in Fitzgerald, *Learning to Forget*, 69.

287. Ucko, *New Counterinsurgency Era*, 42.

288. Gates, "1983: The Most Dangerous Year" and "The War in Washington, 1983: Shultz against the Field," chaps. 14–15 in *From the Shadows*, 258–77, 278–92; George P. Shultz, "Tension and Tragedy in Lebanon," chap. 15 in *Turmoil and Triumph: My Years as Secretary of State*, 220–34; Rumsfeld, "Lessons in Terror," pt. 1 in *Known and Unknown*, 1–34; Caspar W. Weinberger, "Lebanon," chap. 5 in *Fighting for Peace: Seven Critical Years in the Pentagon*, 135–74; Weinberger, *In the Arena: A Memoir of the 20th Century*, 308–13; Petraeus, "Lessons of Vietnam," 178–79, 190–97.

289. Ucko, *New Counterinsurgency Era*, 32.

290. "Special Forces can disrupt the enemy's ability to prosecute the main battle by conducting either unconventional warfare or unilateral operations deep in his rear areas." *Operations 1982*, 7-23, 7-13.

291. Guerrillas are also used for escape and evasion, subversion, and sabotage. *Operations 1982*, 7-23.

292. *Operations 1982*, 7-23 to 7-24, 16-1.

293. Betts, *Soldiers, Statesmen, and Cold War Crises*, 133. A recent work on U.S. Army adaptation in Iraq echoes this incomplete view of SF. Serena, *Revolution in Military Adaptation*, 63.

294. Fitzgerald, *Learning to Forget*, 81.

295. Fitzgerald, *Learning to Forget*, 63–66.

296. Meyer quoted in Fitzgerald, *Learning to Forget*, 63.

297. Jensen, *Forging the Sword*, 66.

298. Colonel Cecil B. Currey quoted in Fitzgerald, *Learning to Forget*, 75.

299. Galvin speech quoted in Fitzgerald, *Learning to Forget*, 72.

300. Fitzgerald, *Learning to Forget*, 78–79.

301. Fitzgerald, *Learning to Forget*, 78.

302. "Reagan Favors Developing New Light Divisions in '85," *Army Times*, February 6, 1984, 10; Michael J. Mazaar, *Light Forces and the Future of U.S. Military Strategy*, 167.

303. Timothy A. Wray, *The Army's Light Infantry Divisions: An Analysis of Advocacy and Opposition.*

304. Although doctrine mentioned LICs, the majority of U.S. training was for mid- to high-intensity conflict. Kretchik, *U.S. Army Doctrine*, 215.

305. Fitzgerald, *Learning to Forget*, 72.

306. Mazaar, *Light Forces*, 165.

307. *Operations 1982*, 17-6.

308. William E. DePuy, "The Light Infantry: Indispensable Element of a Balanced Force."

309. David H. Petraeus, "Light Infantry in Europe: Strategic Flexibility and Conventional Deterrence"; Huba Wass de Czege, *NATO Interim Report: Employment Concepts for Light Infantry in Europe.*

310. Peter N. Kafkalas, "The Light Infantry Divisions and Low-Intensity Conflict: Are They Losing Sight of Each Other?"; Kevin D. Stringer, "Light Infantry Divisions: Cold War Chimera."

311. Fitzgerald, *Learning to Forget*, 82–83.

312. Raymond R. Drummond, *Light Infantry: A Tactical Deep Battle Asset for Central Europe.*

313. Starry, *Press On!*, 1157.

314. Holder, "Development of Army Doctrine," 52.

315. Mazaar, *Light Forces*, 169; Ucko, *New Counterinsurgency Era*, 35, 41.

316. Ucko, *New Counterinsurgency Era*, 41–42. Interestingly, the U.S. Marines, often touted as experts in COIN-type operations, also based their doctrine in this period on highly deployable light-armored units for countering a heavily armored force, that is, the Soviets or their allies.

317. DePuy was a manager and lamented that prior to its reorganization, CONARC "was a decade behind in management techniques." DePuy, *Changing an Army*, 177. See also Ricks, *Generals*, 335–53.

318. Herbert, *Deciding What Has to Be Done*, 73.

5. The Power-Projection Army: Doctrine in the Post– Cold War Era until the Eve of September 11

1. Farrell, Rynning, and Terriff, *Transforming Military Power*, 16.

2. John L. Romjue, *American Army Doctrine for the Post–Cold War*, 79.

3. For the 2001 version of the army's keystone doctrine, the numerical designation was changed from 100-5 to 3-0 to reflect the numerical designation of *joint* military doctrine. Kretchik, *U.S. Army Doctrine*, 247–48.

4. Betts pointed out the tendency in this direction with the transition to the all-volunteer force. Betts, *Soldiers, Statesmen, and Cold War Crises*, 185.

5. Jackson, "From Conservatism to Revolutionary Intoxication," 45.

6. Serena, *Revolution in Military Adaptation*, 46.

7. Serena, *Revolution in Military Adaptation*, 46.

8. Daniel Bolger warns this obsession with World War II–type operations would undermine the army's ability to prepare to fight the guerrillas of the post–Cold War. Bolger, "The Ghosts of Omdurman," 37–39.

9. Farrell, Rynning, and Terriff, *Transforming Military Power*, 19–20.

10. J. Q. Wilson, *Bureaucracy*, 224.

11. Harvey M. Sapolsky, Brendan Rittenhouse Green, and Benjamin H. Friedman, "The Missing Transformation," 7.

12. Farrell, Rynning, and Terriff, *Transforming Military Power*, 36–37; Serena, *Revolution in Military Adaptation*, 36.

13. Serena, *Revolution in Military Adaptation*, 45.

14. Deborah D. Avant and James H. Lebovic, "U.S. Military Responses to Post–Cold War Missions," 139.

15. Rumsfeld, *Known and Unknown*, 651–53.

16. Fitzgerald, *Learning to Forget*, 93.

17. Cassidy, *Counterinsurgency*, 121.

18. Cassidy, *Counterinsurgency*, 101, 103, 114, 115, 117–18; Farrell, Rynning, and Terriff, *Transforming Military Power*, 15; Fitzgerald, *Learning to Forget*, 86; Serena, *Revolution in Military Adaptation*, 111; Long, *Soul of Armies*, 172.

19. Fitzgerald, *Learning to Forget*, 86; Serena, *Revolution in Military Adaptation*, 36, 45.

20. Serena, *Revolution in Military Adaptation*, 36, 39.

21. General Starry pointed out that the weapons the Soviets were providing to these countries were not subpar but were highly advanced because Soviet modernization had produced so many new weapons systems. Starry, *Press On!*, 1155–57.

22. Gordon R. Sullivan and James M. Dubik, *Envisioning Future Warfare*, 4; Kretchik, *U.S. Army Doctrine*, 221; Farrell, Rynning, and Terriff, *Transforming Military Power*, 17.

23. 1992 Defense Planning Guidance quoted in Cheney, *In My Time*, 235.

24. Eric S. Edelman, "The Strange Career of the 1992 Defense Planning Guidance."

25. Jensen, *Forging the Sword*, 92.

26. Jensen, *Forging the Sword*, 93.

27. Aspin quoted in Jensen, *Forging the Sword*, 98.

28. Serena, *Revolution in Military Adaptation*, 32.

29. Edelman, "Strange Career," 73. See also Christopher Layne, "From Preponderance to Offshore Balancing: America's Future Grand Strategy"; and William C. Wohlforth, "The Stability of a Unipolar World."

30. Jackson, "From Conservatism to Revolutionary Intoxication," 44; Serena, *Revolution in Military Adaptation*, 32.

31. The failed operations in Somalia did sour the Clinton administration on the concept of peacekeeping in general, though. After the withdrawal of U.S. troops from Somalia, Presidential Decision Directive 25 stated that the United States would send forces into similar conflict zones only after a peace treaty had been signed and would do so with sufficient forces and an exit strategy. In short, Clinton applied the

Powell-Weinberger Doctrine to peacekeeping operations. Ucko, *New Counterinsurgency Era*, 49.

32. Sullivan and Dubik, *Envisioning Future Warfare*, 1.

33. *Operations 1993*, 2-1; Serena, *Revolution in Military Adaptation*, 32.

34. "The Army participates in force projection in both war and operations other than war." *Operations 1993*, 3-1.

35. Sullivan and Dubik, *Envisioning Future Warfare*, 5.

36. Kretchik, *U.S. Army Doctrine*, 217. In the 1990s, the Russian government stripped the military of much of its funding. In some cases, soldiers literally starved to death. Jennifer R. Mathers, "Reform and the Russian Military," 172–76.

37. NATO study quoted in Terry Terriff, "U.S. Ideas and Military Change in NATO, 1989–1994," 99.

38. Jensen, *Forging the Sword*, 96.

39. Army chief of staff, June 1987 to June 1991.

40. Jensen, *Forging the Sword*, 105.

41. Romjue, *American Army Doctrine*, 38.

42. Kretchik argues that "*some* senior officers" rejected the emphasis on LIC. Kretchik, *U.S. Army Doctrine*, 218 (emphasis added). While this is true, only a few years later the *majority* of senior army leaders were in favor of making "operations other than war" a key part of the new *Operations* manual. Romjue, *American Army Doctrine*, 97.

43. Romjue, *American Army Doctrine*, 28.

44. Romjue, *American Army Doctrine*, 53.

45. Romjue, *American Army Doctrine*, 53–54.

46. Army chief of staff, June 21, 1991, to June 20, 1995.

47. Sullivan quoted in Jensen, *Forging the Sword*, 96.

48. James R. McDonough served in Vietnam and wrote a famous combat journal, *Platoon Leader: A Memoir of Command in Combat*. See also Romjue, *American Army Doctrine*, 109; and Kretchik, *U.S. Army Doctrine*, 223.

49. Romjue, *American Army Doctrine*, 37–38.

50. Romjue, *American Army Doctrine*, 36, 97; Kretchik, *U.S. Army Doctrine*, 221; Farrell, Rynning, and Terriff, *Transforming Military Power*, 30.

51. Farrell, Rynning, and Terriff, *Transforming Military Power*, 24–27.

52. Romjue, *American Army Doctrine*, 42–44; Kretchik, *U.S. Army Doctrine*, 223.

53. Farrell, Rynning, and Terriff, *Transforming Military Power*, 21, 109.

54. *Operations 1993*, 1-1; Kretchik, *U.S. Army Doctrine*, 221–22.

55. Michael C. Desch, "The Keys That Lock Up the World: Identifying American Interests in the Periphery"; Barry R. Posen, "Command of the Commons: The Military Foundation of U.S. Hegemony."

56. Vuono made this statement to the House Committee on Appropriations in 1991. Quoted in Jensen, *Forging the Sword*, 92.

57. Jensen, *Forging the Sword*, 87.

58. Jensen, *Forging the Sword*, 99.

59. *Operations 1993*, 1-2.

60. *Operations 1993*, 3-1.

61. Jackson, "From Conservatism to Revolutionary Intoxication," 45; Romjue, *American Army Doctrine*, 65–66; Farrell, Rynning, and Terriff, *Transforming Military Power*, 21.

62. *Operations 1993*, 3-1 to 3-12.

63. *Operations 1993*, 1-2, 3-1 to 3-7.

64. *Operations 1993*, 3-1 to 3-12; Kretchik, *U.S. Army Doctrine*, 228.

65. Sullivan and Dubik, *Envisioning Future Warfare*, 3.

66. Sullivan and Dubik, *Envisioning Future Warfare*, 7.

67. Jensen, *Forging the Sword*, 91; Romjue, *American Army Doctrine*, 47.

68. Serena, *Revolution in Military Adaptation*, 32; Sullivan and Dubik, *Envisioning Future Warfare*, 7.

69. Jackson, "From Conservatism to Revolutionary Intoxication," 66n6; Rumsfeld, *Known and Unknown*, 280.

70. Jensen, *Forging the Sword*, 90.

71. Farrell, Rynning, and Terriff, *Transforming Military Power*, 18–19.

72. *Operations 1993*, 1-3; Sullivan and Dubik, *Envisioning Future Warfare*, 6–7.

73. Romjue, *American Army Doctrine*, 89; Farrell, Rynning, and Terriff, *Transforming Military Power*, 30–31.

74. Romjue, *American Army Doctrine*, 105–6.

75. Senior Leader Warfighting Conference, Fort Leavenworth, November 3–4, 1992; Kretchik, *U.S. Army Doctrine*, 225–26; Romjue, *American Army Doctrine*, 48, 97.

76. *Operations 1993*, 4-1 to 4-6, 5-1 to 5-5; Kretchik, *U.S. Army Doctrine*, 217, 221–22; Romjue, *American Army Doctrine*, 86–87, 89.

77. Kretchik, *U.S. Army Doctrine*, 218–19, 225–26; Senior Leader Warfighting Conference, 1992.

78. *Operations 1993*, 6-1.

79. Romjue, *American Army Doctrine*, 46.

80. William A. Owens, "Creating a U.S. Military Revolution," 207.

81. Owens, "Creating a U.S. Military Revolution," 207.

82. Harlan K. Ullman and James P. Wade, *Shock and Awe: Achieving Rapid Dominance*.

83. Rumsfeld, *Known and Unknown*, 293–94, 649.

84. Romjue, *American Army Doctrine*, 36; *Operations 1993*, 2-6; Kretchik, *U.S. Army Doctrine*, 226.

85. *Operations 1993*, 1-1. Post–Cold War operations could require significant shifts in operations—for instance, the rapid shift from combat operations to taking care of refugees during the Gulf War. The four tenets of AirLand Battle did not cover this new strategic situation. Romjue, *American Army Doctrine*, 64.

86. Romjue, *American Army Doctrine*, 88.

87. Fitzgerald, *Learning to Forget*, 93.

88. *Operations 1993*, 1-1 to 1-2; Romjue, *American Army Doctrine*, 71.

89. Romjue, *American Army Doctrine*, 32, 47.

90. Jensen, *Forging the Sword*, 97.

91. Romjue, *American Army Doctrine*, 72; Sullivan and Dubik, *Envisioning Future Warfare*, 22.

92. "Desert Storm One-Year Later Conference," March 2–3, 1992, in *American Army Doctrine*, by Romjue, 65–66.

93. The Soviets saw the new U.S. capabilities demonstrated by AirLand Battle and Follow on Forces Attack and came up with the term "military technical revolution (MTR)." In 1993 Andrew Marshall at the Office of Net Assessment ordered studies done on the concept of military revolutions and came to the conclusion that they were not caused by technology alone but by new "tactics, doctrine, and organization." Therefore, the MTR became the broader revolution in military affairs. Owens, "Creating a U.S. Military Revolution," 208. The key report was Andrew W. Marshall, "Some Thoughts on Military Revolutions," Memorandum for the Record, Office of the Secretary of Defense (OSD), Office of Net Assessment, July 27, 1993.

94. Jensen, *Forging the Sword*, 102–104.

95. *Operations 1993*, 2-3. Franks began to establish Battle Laboratories in April 1992 to flesh out these concepts with actual forces and simulations. Romjue, *American Army Doctrine*, 74–77; Sullivan and Dubik, *Envisioning Future Warfare*, 17–18.

96. Sullivan and Dubik, *Envisioning Future Warfare*, 19–20.

97. Sullivan and Dubik, *Envisioning Future Warfare*, 20.

98. This logic was nicely set out in 1993 in Sullivan and Dubik, *Envisioning Future Warfare*.

99. *Operations 1993*, 2-4.

100. *Operations 1993*, 2-5.

101. Romjue, *American Army Doctrine*, 80.

102. Williamson Murray points out the limits of technology when he notes that German successes in 1940 had nothing to do with technology; they actually had inferior tanks to the French. The Germans had their most advanced weapons in 1944–45, and they "went down to catastrophic defeat." Murray, *War, Strategy, and Military Effectiveness*, 80.

103. Murray, "Thinking about Revolutions," 76.

104. Thomas G. Mahnken and Barry D. Watts, "What the Gulf War Can (and Cannot) Tell Us about the Future of Warfare," 157.

105. Sullivan and Dubik, *Envisioning Future Warfare*, 15.

106. Sullivan quoted in Fitzgerald, *Learning to Forget*, 117.

107. *Operations 1993*, 2-6.

108. Farrell, Rynning, and Terriff, *Transforming Military Power*, 33.

109. Romjue, *American Army Doctrine*, 137; Farrell, Rynning, and Terriff, *Transforming Military Power*, 29.

110. Romjue, *American Army Doctrine*, 137; Jensen, *Forging the Sword*, 102–3, 118–19; Farrell, Rynning, and Terriff, *Transforming Military Power*, 33.

111. Farrell, Rynning, and Terriff, *Transforming Military Power*, 34–36.

112. Farrell, Rynning, and Terriff, *Transforming Military Power*, 36–37.

113. Chris C. Demchak, "Complexity and Theory of Networked Militaries," 233.

114. *Operations 1993*, 1-2.

115. Farrell, Rynning, and Terriff, *Transforming Military Power*, 37.

116. Jackson, "From Conservatism to Revolutionary Intoxication," 45; Kretchik, *U.S. Army Doctrine*, 216–17.

117. Romjue, *American Army Doctrine*, 98–99.

118. "Still another lesson was evident by its absence. Preparation for the Gulf War had had the luxury of uncontested buildup. Most future operations would not. The art of early entry with force was the lesson/non-lesson." Romjue, *American Army Doctrine*, 66–67.

119. Romjue, *American Army Doctrine*, 112.

120. The George H. W. Bush administration removed these weapons from the army in Europe at the end of the Cold War. Cheney, *In My Time*, 233–34; *Operations 1993*, 6-11.

121. *Operations 1993*, 6-11.

122. *Operations 1993*, 6-11.

123. *Operations 1993*, 2-14, 3-8, 5-3.

124. *Operations 1993*, 6-11.

125. There was one exception where the manual noted, "Maneuver may also exploit the effects of nuclear weapons." *Operations 1993*, 2-10. However, this is the only mention of this use of conventional-nuclear operations in the whole manual.

126. *Operations 1993*, 2-4.

127. *Operations 1993*, 2-4.

128. *Operations 1993*, 7-0.

129. *Operations 1993*, 2-4.

130. *Operations 1993*, 2-4.

131. *Operations 1993*, 6-16 to 6-18, 6-20 to 6-22.

132. *Operations 1993*, 9-0.

133. *Operations 1993*, 6-16.

134. *Operations 1993*, 6-19, 9-1.

135. "The defender disrupts the attacker's synchronization, degrades his strength and ability to concentrate, and defeats his force with effective use of combined arms. The defender simultaneously attacks the enemy throughout the full depth of his formations." *Operations 1993*, 6-20, 9-4.

136. *Operations 1993*, 7-0.

137. *Operations 1993*, 7-0.

138. *Operations 1993*, 6-16, 8-1 to 8-3.

139. *Operations 1993*, 2-6, 6-22.

140. "While advances in ground and airmobility enable the attacker to concentrate more rapidly, they also enable the defender to react more quickly. Moreover, the lethality of modern weaponry significantly increases the threat to concentrated formations." *Operations 1993*, 7-2.

141. *Operations 1993*, 2-6.

142. *Operations 1993*, 6-20, 9-5.

143. *Operations 1993*, 7-8. See also 2-4.

144. "Forced entry is clearly offensive, but it often leads directly to the defense of the newly gained lodgment area. On the other hand, the tempo of force-projection operations may move from the initial offensive objective to a defensive pause and then to a subsequent limited objective to seize key terrain essential to the defense." *Operations 1993*, 7-1, 7-4, 9-0.

145. *Operations 1993*, 6-8.

146. *Operations 1993*, 7-9.

147. *Operations 1993*, 2-3 to 2-4; Romjue, *American Army Doctrine*, 103.

148. *Operations 1993*, 2-2.

149. Kretchik, *U.S. Army Doctrine*, 240-41.

150. *Operations 1993*, 2-0 to 2-1, 13-0 to 13-8; Sullivan and Dubik, *Envisioning Future Warfare*, 5–6, 21.

151. Sullivan and Dubik, *Envisioning Future Warfare*, 6.

152. Ucko, *New Counterinsurgency Era*, 48–49.

153. Fitzgerald, *Learning to Forget*, 78–79.

154. "Operations other than war was a third major emphasis, the plethora of non-war activities that the passing of the Cold War had in great part opened up." Romjue, *American Army Doctrine*, 88.

155. *Operations 1993*, 1-1; Sullivan and Dubik, *Envisioning Future Warfare*, 9, 23.

156. "Senior Leader Warfighting Conference," Fort Leavenworth, November 3–4, 1992; Kretchik, *U.S. Army Doctrine*, 225–26.

157. Romjue, *American Army Doctrine*, 91–92.

158. *Operations 1993*, 1-1.

159. Kretchik, *U.S. Army Doctrine*, 230; Fitzgerald, *Learning to Forget*, 94; Nagl, *Soup with a Knife*.

160. Fitzgerald, *Learning to Forget*, 96.

161. *Operations 1993*, 13-1.

162. *Operations 1993*, 13-0 to 13-8. Serena cites *Field Manual 7-98, Operations in a Low-Intensity Environment* (1992) and *Field Manual 100-23, Peace Operations* (1994) as both emphasizing the import of training for combat operations as part of OOTW. Serena, *Revolution in Military Adaptation*, 38. See also Avant and Lebovic, "U.S. Military Responses to Post–Cold War Missions," 139. As Sullivan implied in his 1993 piece, combat operations in OOTW, which were "often indistinguishable from traditional war," would require combat skills and might require many of the precision and deep-strike elements of AirLand Battle doctrine. Sullivan and Dubik, *Envisioning Future Warfare*, 9.

163. Romjue, *American Army Doctrine*, 85n19.

164. *Operations 1993*, 14-1 to 14-5.

165. *Operations 1993*, 13-0 to 13-1 (emphasis added).

166. Galula, *Counterinsurgency Warfare*, 66.

167. Sullivan and Dubik, *Envisioning Future Warfare*, 22.

168. Ucko, *New Counterinsurgency Era*, 49.

169. *Operations 1993*, 3-12.

170. Kretchik, *U.S. Army Doctrine*, 223–24, 227.

171. After the debacle in Somalia, however, Clinton became less of an advocate of peacekeeping operations. Ucko, *New Counterinsurgency Era*, 49–50.

172. Serena, *Revolution in Military Adaptation*, 32.

173. Romjue, *American Army Doctrine*, 28, 85; "Senior Leader Warfighting Conference," Fort Leavenworth, KS, November 3–4, 1992; Kretchik, *U.S. Army Doctrine*, 225–26.

174. Kretchik, *U.S. Army Doctrine*, 244–46.

175. Ucko, *New Counterinsurgency Era*, 49.

176. Army chief of staff from June 1995 to June 1999.

177. Army chief of staff from June 1999 to June 2003.

178. Kretchik, *U.S. Army Doctrine*, 240.

179. "[The term] OOTW should not appear in this update of 100-5" because war and OOTW were not to be treated as "separate and special subsets." Hartzog to Holder, October 27, 1995, Combined Arms Research Library, quoted in Kretchik, *U.S. Army Doctrine*, 240.

180. Kretchik, *U.S. Army Doctrine*, 243–45.

181. Kretchik, *U.S. Army Doctrine*, 240.

182. Kretchik, *U.S. Army Doctrine*, 248.

183. Jensen, *Forging the Sword*, 97–98; Kretchik, *U.S. Army Doctrine*, 244–45.

184. Kretchik, *U.S. Army Doctrine*, 246.

185. Kretchik, *U.S. Army Doctrine*, 247–48.

186. Kretchik, *U.S. Army Doctrine*, 246.

187. Kretchik, *U.S. Army Doctrine*, 340n73.

188. *Operations 2001*, 3-12.

189. Kretchik, *U.S. Army Doctrine*, 247–48.

190. Kretchik, *U.S. Army Doctrine*, 248.

191. Farrell, Rynning, and Terriff, *Transforming Military Power*, 41.

192. Farrell, Rynning, and Terriff, *Transforming Military Power*, 39–40.

193. Farrell, Rynning, and Terriff, *Transforming Military Power*, 50–51.

194. Farrell, Rynning, and Terriff, *Transforming Military Power*, 51.

195. Farrell, Rynning, and Terriff, *Transforming Military Power*, 55–58.

196. Kretchik, *U.S. Army Doctrine*, 248.

197. Farrell, Rynning, and Terriff, *Transforming Military Power*, 42–43.

198. Farrell, Rynning, and Terriff, *Transforming Military Power,* 54.

199. Farrell, Rynning, and Terriff, *Transforming Military Power*, 53–55.

200. Farrell, Rynning, and Terriff, *Transforming Military Power*, 58–59.

201. Farrell, Rynning, and Terriff, *Transforming Military Power*, 58.

202. Kretchik, *U.S. Army Doctrine*, 248.

203. Farrell, Rynning, and Terriff, *Transforming Military Power*, 43.

204. Scales quoted in Farrell, Rynning, and Terriff, *Transforming Military Power*, 46.

205. *Operations 2001*, 3-12.

206. Serena, *Revolution in Military Adaptation*, 47.

207. Shinseki quoted in Serena, *Revolution in Military Adaptation*, 48.

208. Farrell, Rynning, and Terriff, *Transforming Military Power*, 47; Serena, *Revolution in Military Adaptation*, 45, 48.

209. *Operations 2001*, 4-13.

210. *Operations 2001*, 1-7, 4-8 to 4-9, 6-17.

211. *Operations 2001*, 4-1; Kretchik, *U.S. Army Doctrine*, 251.

212. *Operations 2001*, 4-13, 7-2.

213. Burke quoted in Fitzgerald, *Learning to Forget*, 118.

214. *Operations 2001*, 1-15.

215. *Operations 2001*, chap. 7.

216. *Operations 1993*, 9-0.

217. *Operations 2001*, 4-12.

218. *Operations 2001*, 4-12.

219. *Operations 2001*, 4-16.

220. *Operations 1993*, 9-1 to 9-6.

221. *Operations 2001*, 8-9 to 8-10 (emphasis added).

222. Kretchik, *U.S. Army Doctrine*, 244.

223. *Operations 2001*, 9-1 to 9-14.

224. *Operations 2001*, 1-15.

225. Lieutenant General Robert L. Caslen Jr., "Change 1 to Field Manual 3-0: The Way the Army Fights Today," 84–85.

226. *Operations 2001*, 9-1 to 9-14.

227. Kretchik, *U.S. Army Doctrine*, 249.

228. *Operations 2001*, 6-89.

229. Kretchik, *U.S. Army Doctrine*, 248.

230. Fitzgerald, *Learning to Forget*, 118–19.

231. Kretchik places too little emphasis on the important role that OOTW had in *Operations 1993*. Kretchik, *U.S. Army Doctrine*, 251, 255.

232. Kretchik, *U.S. Army Doctrine*, 248.

233. *Operations 2001*, 1-3.

234. *Operations 2001*, vi.

235. *Operations 2001*, 4-12.

236. Ucko, *New Counterinsurgency Era*, 50; Rumsfeld, *Known and Unknown*, 482.

237. *Operations 2001*, 4-16.

238. Ucko, *New Counterinsurgency Era*, 50–53.

239. Jensen, *Forging the Sword*, 106, 104.

240. Jensen, *Forging the Sword*, 106.

241. Romjue, *American Army Doctrine*, 98–99.

242. Ucko, *New Counterinsurgency Era*, 50–51.

243. Serena, *Revolution in Military Adaptation*, 38, 40, 47.

244. Serena, *Revolution in Military Adaptation*, 32.

245. "The larger effect of these [peacekeeping] campaigns was to entrench the historically consistent tendency of the U.S. military to dismiss the entire 'lower end' of the conflict spectrum as a distraction." Ucko, *New Counterinsurgency Era*, 50–51.

246. Serena, *Revolution in Military Adaptation*, 45.

247. Jensen, *Forging the Sword*, 123–24.

248. Farrell, Rynning, and Terriff acknowledge the way in which senior army leaders after the Cold War established ways of working around the army bureaucracy to develop the concepts central to transformation. Farrell, Rynning, and Terriff, *Transforming Military Power*, 112.

6. Transforming under Fire: The Global War on Terror, Counterinsurgency, Iraq, and *Operations 2008*

1. The actual degree of difference between the later Clinton view, which downplayed peacekeeping, in part because of the Somalia debacle, was probably not that great. Like Kennedy's new flexible-response strategy in relation to massive retaliation, Bush's "new" view was made to look new in order to present voters with an alternative to the Clinton era. Layne, "From Preponderance to Offshore Balancing."

2. Condoleezza Rice quoted in Ucko, *New Counterinsurgency Era*, 50.

3. Condoleezza Rice, "Campaign 2000: Promoting the National Interest." See also Fitzgerald, *Learning to Forget*, 121.

4. It should be noted, however, that the selection committee was made up of Rumsfeld, the chairman and vice chairman of the Joint Chiefs of Staff, and another civilian official. Rumsfeld, *Known and Unknown*, 299–300.

5. Kretchik, *U.S. Army Doctrine*, 256–57; Rumsfeld, *Known and Unknown*, 405.

6. Rumsfeld says that he originally wanted to give the job to Jack Keane but that Keane declined for family reasons. This is ironic, considering the central role that Keane would play in the debate surrounding strategy in Iraq.

7. Rumsfeld, *Known and Unknown*, 653.

8. Fred Kaplan, *The Insurgents: David Petraeus and the Plot to Change the American Way of War*, 94.

9. Rumsfeld, *Known and Unknown*, 653.

10. Rumsfeld, *Known and Unknown*, 654–55.

11. Robert D. Kaplan, "What Rumsfeld Got Right."

12. Feaver, "Right to Be Right."

13. Rumsfeld's neglect of postconflict operations in Iraq was actually consistent with the military policy of the Bush administration, which was to hand over the postconflict portion of operations to civilians and international agencies as soon as possible so that the military would not get embroiled in extended commitments.

14. Jackson, "From Conservatism to Revolutionary Intoxication," 43–44.

15. Ricks, *Fiasco*, 194.

16. Ricks, *Fiasco*, 195.

17. Long, *Soul of Armies*, 172.

18. Long, *The Soul of Armies*, 180–84.

19. See especially Rumsfeld, *Known and Unknown*.

20. Farrell, Rynning, and Terriff, *Transforming Military Power*, 60–61.

21. Fitzgerald, *Learning to Forget*, 114–15; Ucko, *New Counterinsurgency Era*, 47, 51. "Power is increasingly defined, not by mass or size, but by mobility and swiftness.

Influence is measured in information, safety is gained by stealth, and force is projected on the long arc of precision-guided weapons. . . . Our forces in the next century must be agile, lethal, readily deployable, and require a minimum of logistical support." President Bush quoted in Ucko, *New Counterinsurgency Era*, 52.

22. Quoted in Ucko, *New Counterinsurgency Era*, 50; Rumsfeld, *Known and Unknown*, 482. Rice was running the early meetings of Bush's foreign policy team. Cheney, *In My Time*, 252; Romjue, *American Army Doctrine*, 100.

23. Rumsfeld was secretary of defense from January 20, 2001, to December 18, 2006.

24. Ucko, *New Counterinsurgency Era*, 53.

25. Ucko, *New Counterinsurgency Era*, 51–52.

26. Thus, Rumsfeld agreed with some of the tenets of the Weinberger/Powell doctrine. Rumsfeld, *Known and Unknown*, 272.

27. "The Bush Doctrine called for a shift from the old 'shape, respond, prepare' posture to a new 'assure, dissuade, deter forward, and decisively defeat' paradigm. This required an expeditionary force capable of rapidly imposing America's will and maintaining a lasting presence overseas. The Army was the central player in both of these tasks. It provided the bulk of the land forces necessary to impose America's will and in the course of operations would be responsible for maintaining a lasting presence." Serena, *Revolution in Military Adaptation*, 49.

28. Serena, *Revolution in Military Adaptation*, 49.

29. Rumsfeld, *Known and Unknown*, 294.

30. Rumsfeld, *Known and Unknown*, 280, 649.

31. Donald Rumsfeld, "DOD Acquisitions and Logistics Excellence Week Kick-Off—Bureaucracy to Battlefield," remarks as delivered by Secretary of Defense Donald H. Rumsfeld, Pentagon, September 10, 2001, http://www.defenselink.mil/speeches/speech.aspx?speechid=430.

32. Rumsfeld, *Known and Unknown*, 649.

33. Farrell, Rynning, and Terriff, *Transforming Military Power*, 61.

34. Rumsfeld, *Known and Unknown*, 651.

35. Fitzgerald, *Learning to Forget*, 114; Rumsfeld, *Known and Unknown*, 293. Andrew Marshall was influential, and his report on the RMA, which found RMAs were more due to "tactics, doctrine, and organization" than technology, was important. Owens, "Creating a U.S. Military Revolution," 208.

36. Rumsfeld, *Known and Unknown*, 653; Ricks, *Fiasco*, 68.

37. Serena, *Revolution in Military Adaptation*, 50–51.

38. Rumsfeld, *Known and Unknown*, 649. Admiral Bill Owens's 2000 book, *Lifting the Fog of War*, argued that the biggest obstacle to the transformation of the U.S. military would be service parochialism and "traditions." These bureaucratic interests got in the way of the U.S. military developing a true system of systems across the services (151–53).

39. Farrell, Rynning, and Terriff agree, pointing out that "Rumsfeld seemingly harbored a distinct antipathy toward the Army, believing that the Army's leadership was too conservative in its mindset and too wedded to its Cold War ways of war." Farrell, Rynning, and Terriff, *Transforming Military Power*, 62.

40. "Transformation," Rumsfeld wrote, "began before I arrived at the Pentagon, and I knew it would need to continue after I left." Rumsfeld, *Known and Unknown*, 293–94.

41. Farrell, Rynning, and Terriff, *Transforming Military Power*, 114.

42. Rumsfeld, *Known and Unknown*, 293–94.

43. "We must be able to project our power over long distances, in days or weeks rather than months . . . must be able to identify targets by a variety of means . . . then be able to destroy those targets almost instantly with an array of weapons . . . must be organized in smaller more agile formations rather than cumbersome divisions." George W. Bush remarks, "A Period of Consequences," the Citadel, SC, September 23, 1999, quoted in Rumsfeld, *Known and Unknown*, 294.

44. Rumsfeld, *Known and Unknown*, 649. "Force projection replaces forward defense as a more likely employment of Army elements." *Operations 1993*, 1-2. See also Kretchik, *U.S. Army Doctrine*, 217, 221–22.

45. Farrell, Rynning, and Terriff, *Transforming Military Power*, 67.

46. William M. Donnelly, *Transforming an Army at War: Designing the Modular Force, 1991–2005*, 3; Rumsfeld, *Known and Unknown*, 654–55.

47. Farrell, Rynning, and Terriff, *Transforming Military Power*, 67–68.

48. Farrell, Rynning, and Terriff, *Transforming Military Power*, 67–68.

49. Cassidy, *Counterinsurgency*, 123–24.

50. Farrell, Rynning, and Terriff, *Transforming Military Power*, 77–78.

51. W. Donnelly, *Transforming an Army at War*, iii.

52. Farrell, Rynning, and Terriff, *Transforming Military Power*, 69.

53. Fitzgerald argues that Shinseki "began the process of restructuring the Army around modular brigades." Fitzgerald, *Learning to Forget*, 116.

54. W. Donnelly, *Transforming an Army at War*, 11.

55. Donnelly, *Transforming an Army at War*, 11–12.

56. Farrell, Rynning, and Terriff, *Transforming Military Power*, 71.

57. Donnelly, *Transforming an Army at War*, 14.

58. Serena, *Revolution in Military Adaptation*, 50–51. "The operational orientation of the SBCT(s) and the rest of the force became even more conventional and combat oriented following the attacks of 9/11 as the Bush administration, through the so-called Bush Doctrine, demanded a highly focused, conventional force capable of achieving a rapid and decisive defeat of America's enemies" (49).

59. Chad Serena makes this abundantly clear in his analysis of the development of the RMA within the army and its relation to the rise of Rumsfeld. Serena, *Revolution in Military Adaptation*, 49–51.

60. Kretchik, *U.S. Army Doctrine*, 261.

61. Kretchik, *U.S. Army Doctrine*, 262; Ricks, *Fiasco*, 194–95.

62. Long, *Soul of Armies*, 180–84.

63. Ricks, *Fiasco*, 208-9.

64. Ricks, *Fiasco*, 209.

65. F. Kaplan, *Insurgents*, 128.

66. Kretchik, *U.S. Army Doctrine*, 262.

67. Rumsfeld noticed his success in Mosul and chose him to lead the training of Iraqi security forces. Rumsfeld, *Known and Unknown*, 673.

68. Rumsfeld, *Known and Unknown*, 521–22.

69. Dana Milbank, "Rumsfeld's War on 'Insurgents,'" *Washington Post*, November 30, 2005, http://www.washingtonpost.com/wpdyn/content/article/2005/11/29/AR200 5112901405.html.

70. David S. Cloud and Greg Jaffe, *The Fourth Star: Four Generals and the Epic Struggle for the Future of the United States Army*, 207–208.

71. McMaster quoted in F. Kaplan, *Insurgents*, 171.

72. McMaster quoted in Kaplan, *Insurgents*, 171.

73. Cloud and Jaffe, *Fourth Star*, 199–201. In addition, although both examples here are from army units in Iraq, a number of U.S. Marine Corps units also engaged in COIN best practices and moved their forces out into the population rather than emphasizing force protection and remaining in large bases. Mansoor, *Surge*, 23.

74. Mansoor, *Surge*, 23–24.

75. Mansoor, *Surge*, 24.

76. Cloud and Jaffe, *Fourth Star*, 206–7.

77. Cloud and Jaffe, *Fourth Star*, 206–7.

78. Mansoor, *Surge*, 24.

79. F. Kaplan, *Insurgents*, 94.

80. F. Kaplan, *Insurgents*, 95–96.

81. F. Kaplan, *Insurgents*, 96.

82. Hix "acted almost as a tutor, schooling Casey in a form of warfare he didn't really understand. As Casey grew more comfortable, Hix evolved into a trusted advisor." Cloud and Jaffe, *Fourth Star*, 201. See also F. Kaplan, *Insurgents*, 97.

83. Mansoor, *Surge*, 18.

84. Kalev I. Sepp, "Best Practices in Counterinsurgency"; Jensen, *Forging the Sword*, 129. Best practices entailed the following: "Successful armies isolated the civilian population from the enemy by providing security, stable government, a strong police force, and decent jobs. They built sophisticated intelligence networks, used the minimum amount of force necessary in raids, and offered amnesty and rehabilitation to former insurgents." Cloud and Jaffe, *Fourth Star*, 202; Ricks, *Gamble*, 24–25.

85. Cloud and Jaffe, *Fourth Star*, 202; Ricks, *Gamble*, 24–25.

86. Cloud and Jaffe, *Fourth Star*, 202–4.

87. F. Kaplan, *Insurgents*, 97; Rumsfeld, *Known and Unknown*, 666–67.

88. Cloud and Jaffe, *Fourth Star*, 206.

89. Rumsfeld, *Known and Unknown*, 661–62, 665.

90. Mansoor, *Surge*, 20.

91. Noted COIN expert Thomas Marks calls a COIN campaign "a battle for legitimacy." F. Kaplan, *Insurgents*, 156.

92. Stanley McChrystal, *My Share of the Task: A Memoir*, 176.

93. F. Kaplan, *Insurgents*, 98.

94. Rumsfeld, *Known and Unknown*, 666–67.

95. Rumsfeld, *Known and Unknown*, 717.

96. Rumsfeld, *Known and Unknown*, 724.

97. Ricks, *Fiasco* and *Gamble*. Gian Gentile also argues that this narrative about Casey and COIN in Iraq is overwrought. Gentile, *Wrong Turn*, 101–3. However, David H. Ucko is correct to argue that Gentile takes his criticisms of COIN in Iraq too far. Ucko, "Critics Gone Wild: Counterinsurgency as the Root of All Evil."

98. McChrystal, *My Share of the Task*, 243.

99. Mansoor, *Surge*, 19.

100. Thomas E. Ricks, "U.S. Counterinsurgency Academy Giving Officers a New Mind-Set," *Washington Post*, February 21, 2006.

101. Jensen, *Forging the Sword*, 130.

102. Cloud and Jaffe, *Fourth Star*, 205.

103. Nagl had discovered that Schoomaker had a stack of the hardcover edition of the book in his office and was handing them "to every four-star who dropped by." When Nagl later moved to the Pentagon, he asked Schoomaker to write the foreword, and the army chief of staff agreed. F. Kaplan, *Insurgents*, 117–18.

104. General Peter J. Schoomaker, foreword to *Soup with a Knife*, by Nagl (emphasis added).

105. Schoomaker, foreword to *Soup with a Knife*, by Nagl (emphasis added).

106. Schoomaker, foreword to *Soup with a Knife*, by Nagl.

107. Rumsfeld, *Known and Unknown*, 654.

108. F. Kaplan, *Insurgents*, 95 (emphasis added).

109. "Between late February and early May [2006], 3,034 bodies were found in Baghdad." Cloud and Jaffe, *Fourth Star*, 223.

110. President George W. Bush, remarks to the City Club of Cleveland, March 20, 2006, http://www.youtube.com/watch?v=2FbKLrmp7YQ. This strategy ignored the role of the Shia-dominated security forces in the sectarian violence. On November 13, 2005, a raid by U.S. forces discovered a group of 169 prisoners in a secret prison, the Jadriya Bunker, likely run by the Iraqi government. Many of the prisoners bore signs of torture. Mansoor, *Surge*, 25–27. Rumsfeld wrote that in a National Security Council meeting in July 2006, it was said that Iraqi prime minister Nouri al-Maliki was likely supporting Shia death squads and that he was trying to infiltrate rogue militias into the Iraqi security forces. Rumsfeld, *Known and Unknown*, 697.

111. Mansoor, *Surge*, 31.

112. F. Kaplan, *Insurgents*, 202.

113. Cheney, *In My Time*, 448–49; Rumsfeld, *Known and Unknown*, 715.

114. Cheney cites Rice as saying that U.S. troops should pull back and engage only if they are "witnessing a massacre." Cheney, *In My Time*, 448–49; Rumsfeld, *Known and Unknown*, 695.

115. George W. Bush, *Decision Points*, 362–63.

116. Bush begins to really question the strategy in Iraq in June 2006. Rumsfeld, *Known and Unknown*, 694.

117. Retired army general Jack Keane and national security scholar Frederick Kagan briefed President Bush and later the same day, December 11, 2006, Vice President Cheney, on a COIN strategy for Iraq based on securing the population and requiring

additional U.S. troops. The new strategy had to have more troops, but more troops without the strategy would fail. The extra forces would be used to hold cleared areas with the Iraqis until the Iraqis were prepared to hold them themselves. The additional troops would also allow the United States to speed up the improvement of Iraqi forces. "Keane and Kagan had the full package. A new strategy and the way to implement it." The next day, December 12, 2006, Cheney described this to Bush. Cheney, *In My Time*, 450–51. Cheney called Keane "a real anchor and a source of wisdom." "His view that it was absolutely possible to do what needed to be done without breaking the force went a long way toward giving me and other policy makers a sense that a surge was doable." Keane explained to Cheney and Bush why the United States should surge despite the stress on the force that the JCS were worried about. Cheney, *In My Time*, 454.

118. Jensen, *Forging the Sword*, 128.

119. Jensen, *Forging the Sword*, 128.

120. Jensen, *Forging the Sword*, 129.

121. F. Kaplan, *Insurgents*, 135.

122. U.S. Department of the Army, *Field Manual-Interim 3-07.22, Counterinsurgency Operations*, October 2004, 1–3.

123. F. Kaplan, *Insurgents*, 135–36.

124. Kretchik, *U.S. Army Doctrine*, 266.

125. F. Kaplan, *Insurgents*, 136.

126. F. Kaplan, *Insurgents*, 129; Ricks, *Gamble*, 23. Some have interpreted Petraeus's assignment as an exile. Linda Robinson, *Tell Me How This Ends: General David Petraeus and the Search for a Way Out of Iraq*, 76. But Leavenworth has always been one of the most important commands in the army, held by those who would go on to be army chief of staff in the cases of Harold K. Johnson and Carl E. Vuono. Schoomaker assured Petraeus it was a preliminary assignment before he would be tapped to command in Iraq. F. Kaplan, *Insurgents*, 129.

127. Jensen, *Forging the Sword*, 129.

128. Kretchik, *U.S. Army Doctrine*, 264.

129. Cloud and Jaffe, *Fourth Star*, 218.

130. The entire October 2006 issue was dedicated to COIN. *Military Review* published one of the most critical articles on the conduct of U.S. operations in Iraq. Nigel Aylwin-Foster, "Changing the Army for Counterinsurgency Operations." See also Ricks, *Gamble*, 25.

131. Mansoor, *Surge*, 36–37.

132. Kretchik, *U.S. Army Doctrine*, 264.

133. Based on an interview with Dr. Conrad Crane by the author. U.S. Army Military History Institute, Carlisle, PA, November 19, 2012.

134. Kretchik, *U.S. Army Doctrine*, 264.

135. Jensen, *Forging the Sword*, 127, 130.

136. David Kilcullen, "Twenty-Eight Articles: Fundamentals of Company-Level Counterinsurgency," reprinted in *Military Review* in October 2006; Ricks, *Gamble*, 27–28.

137. Ricks, *Gamble*, 28.

138. Article 26 in Kilcullen, "Twenty-Eight Articles," 138–39.

139. Cavoli quoted in David Kilcullen, *The Accidental Guerrilla: Fighting Small Wars in the Midst of a Big One*, 96–97.

140. Article 28 in Kilcullen, "Twenty-Eight Articles," 139.

141. David Galula, "Galula on Adapting ROE [Rules of Engagement] to an Insurgency"; quote from Galula, *Counterinsurgency Warfare*, 66.

142. Galula, "Galula on Adapting ROE," 198.

143. Cloud and Jaffe, *Fourth Star*, 218–19.

144. Ricks, *Gamble*, 24–25.

145. Ricks, *Gamble*, 33–34.

146. Ricks, *Gamble*, 26.

147. F. Kaplan, *Insurgents*, 165.

148. Ricks, *Gamble*, 26.

149. F. Kaplan, *Insurgents*, 215–16.

150. Regarding the process, Conrad Crane said, "There has never been an Army manual created the way this one was. It was truly a unique process." Quoted in Ricks, *Gamble*, 25. Civilian intellectuals did make some important contributions. For instance, a passage that was ambiguous about the use of torture was stricken from the manual. But in general, Ricks overstates their role in the process. Ricks, *Gamble*, 25–26.

151. Long, *Soul of Armies*, 193.

152. Long, *Soul of Armies*, 193–94.

153. Ricks, *Gamble*.

154. Petraeus, "Light Infantry in Europe."

155. "I can't think of a precedent," General Jack Keane said, "for a commanding general to be so involved in writing doctrine. It is usually driven by bright young majors." Quoted in Ricks, *Gamble*, 29.

156. Ricks, *Gamble*, 24.

157. Farrell, Rynning, and Terriff, *Transforming Military Power*, 103.

158. Department of the Army United States, Headquarters, *Field Manual 3-24, Counterinsurgency*, 1-1, 1-23.

159. Department of the Army United States, Headquarters, *Field Manual 3-24*, chap. 1; Kretchik, *U.S. Army Doctrine*, 264–65.

160. Department of the Army United States, Headquarters, *Field Manual 3-24*, chap. 2.

161. Department of the Army United States, Headquarters, *Field Manual 3-24*, chaps. 4–5.

162. Mansoor, *Surge*, 38–39.

163. Mansoor, *Surge*, 38–39.

164. Department of the Army United States, Headquarters, *Field Manual 3-24*; Ricks, *Gamble*, 29.

165. Department of the Army United States, Headquarters, *Field Manual 3-24*, chap. 7.

166. Department of the Army United States, Headquarters, *Field Manual 3-24*, chap. 3.

167. Department of the Army United States, Headquarters, *Field Manual 3-24*, chap. 6.

168. Department of the Army United States, Headquarters, *Field Manual 3-24*, chap. 6.

169. Bob Woodward, *The War Within: A Secret White House History, 2006–2008*, 243, 248–50.

170. Michael Vickers, "Transitioning to an Indirect Approach in Iraq," memorandum for the president, June 12, 2006, Rumsfeld Papers, http://library.rumsfeld.com/doclib/sp/466/2006-06-12%20Vickers%20to%20Bush%20re%20Transitioning%20to%20an%20Indirect%20Approach%20in%20Iraq.pdf; Rumsfeld, *Known and Unknown*, 696.

171. Vickers, "Transitioning to an Indirect Approach," 2, 4.

172. Woodward, *War Within*, 288.

173. Woodward, *War Within*, 243.

174. Woodward, *War Within*, 249.

175. Woodward, *War Within*, 288.

176. Woodward, *War Within*, 289.

177. Cheney, *In My Time*, 451–53.

178. Cheney, *In My Time*, 452.

179. Gates, *Duty*, 197–238.

180. Feaver, "Right to Be Right"; Betts, Desch, and Feaver, "Correspondence"; Stephen D. Biddle, Jeffrey Friedman, and Jacob Shapiro, "Testing the Surge: Why Did Violence Decline in Iraq in 2007?"

181. Peter Mansoor argues that the new COIN doctrine prepared the army intellectually to effectively use the surge troops in Iraq. Mansoor, *Surge*, 267–68.

182. Kretchik, *U.S. Army Doctrine*, 268.

183. Cassidy, *Counterinsurgency*, 121–22.

184. Kretchik, *U.S. Army Doctrine*, 269.

185. Kretchik, *U.S. Army Doctrine*, 270.

186. *Operations 2008*, foreword.

187. Kretchik, *U.S. Army Doctrine*, 270.

188. *Operations 2008*, 1-3, 1-4, 4-5 to 4-6.

189. *Operations 2008*, 1-16.

190. *Operations 2008*, 1-16.

191. *Operations 2008*, 1-16.

192. *Operations 2008*, 3-2.

193. *Operations 2008*, viii.

194. *Operations 1993*, 3-12.

195. *Operations 2008*, 3-1.

196. *Operations 2008*, 3-8 (emphasis added); *Operations 2008,* A-2.

197. *Operations 2008*, 3-1, 3-5, 3-8.

198. *Operations 2008*, 6-16.

199. *Operations 2008*, C-1 to C-13.

200. Mansoor, *Surge*, 268–69.

201. Mansoor, *Surge*, 243.

202. Farrell, Rynning, and Terriff, *Transforming Military Power*, 93.

203. Farrell, Rynning, and Terriff, *Transforming Military Power*, 78–99.

204. Farrell, Rynning, and Terriff, *Transforming Military Power*, 97–98.

205. John Gordon IV and Bruce Pirnie quoted in Farrell, Rynning, and Terriff, *Transforming Military Power*, 94.

206. *Operations 2008*, v.

207. *Operations 2008*, A-3 to A-4.

208. *Operations 2008*, chaps. 2–3.

209. *Operations 2008*, 3-8, 3-9 to 3-10.

210. *Operations 2008*, 3-3.

211. *Operations 2008*, 3-9 to 3-10.

212. *Operations 2008*, 3-10.

213. *Operations 2008*, 3-8.

214. *Operations 2008*, 3-10.

215. Mansoor, *Surge*.

216. Mansoor, *Surge*, 38–39.

217. *Operations 2008*, 3-2.

218. *Operations 2008*, 3-8.

219. *Operations 2008*, 2-1; Kretchik, *U.S. Army Doctrine*, 272.

220. *Operations 2008*, 3-1 to 3-22; Kretchik, *U.S. Army Doctrine*, 273.

221. "Stability and civil support operations cannot be something that the Army conducts in 'other than war' operations. Army forces must address the civil situation directly and continuously, combining tactical tasks directed at noncombatants with tactical tasks directed against the enemy." *Operations 2008*, viii, 3-2.

222. *Operations 2008*, 3-4.

223. *Operations 2008*, 3-16.

224. *Operations 2008*, 1-1 to 1-21; Kretchik, *U.S. Army Doctrine*, 272.

225. *Operations 2008*, 3-12.

226. *Operations 2008*, 3-3.

227. Kilcullen, *Accidental Guerrilla*, 96–97; Kilcullen, "Twenty-Eight Articles," 139; Petraeus, "Multinational Force—Iraq Commander's Counterinsurgency Guidance," Baghdad, July 15, 2008, in *Surge*, by Mansoor, appx. 2, 287–90.

228. *Operations 2008*, 3-16.

229. *Operations 1993*, 3-12.

230. *Operations 2008*, vii–viii; Kretchik, *U.S. Army Doctrine*, 273.

231. *Operations 2008*, 3-2 to 3-3.

232. Rosen, *Winning the Next War*, 18.

233. Fitzgerald, *Learning to Forget*, 132.

234. The actual difference between the Bush and later Clinton grand strategies was likely overstated by the Bush campaign to make candidate Bush distinct from Gore, Clinton's vice president and Bush's opponent in the election. Layne, "From Preponderance to Offshore Balancing."

235. Kretchik, *U.S. Army Doctrine*, 256–57; Rumsfeld, *Known and Unknown*, 405.

236. Farrell, Rynning, and Terriff acknowledge that the army was a learning organization in this period, in Iraq especially. Farrell, Rynning, and Terriff, *Transforming Military Power*, 111–13.

237. Farrell, Rynning, and Terriff, *Transforming Military Power*, 114.

Conclusion

1. For a discussion of this distinction, see Levy and Thompson, *Causes of War*, 30–31.

2. Colonel Clinton J. Ancker III and Lieutenant Colonel Michael A. Scully, "Army Doctrine Publication 3-0: An Opportunity to Meet the Challenges of the Future," 39.

3. Major Cornelius Granai, *A Complex and Volatile Environment: The Doctrinal Evolution from Full Spectrum Operations to Unified Land Operations*, 31.

4. Ancker and Scully, "Army Doctrine Publication 3-0," 38.

5. Ancker and Scully, "Army Doctrine Publication 3-0," 41.

6. Ancker and Scully, "Army Doctrine Publication 3-0," 42n20.

7. Ancker and Scully, "Army Doctrine Publication 3-0," 41.

8. Granai, *Complex and Volatile Environment*, 32.

9. It is clear from the preface of ADP 3-0 that it is meant to replace *Field Manual 3-0, Operations*.

10. Ancker and Scully, "Army Doctrine Publication 3-0," 42n8.

11. Ancker and Scully, "Army Doctrine Publication 3-0," 42n8.

12. Ancker and Scully, "Army Doctrine Publication 3-0," 41, 42n2; Granai, *Complex and Volatile Environment*, 32.

13. Raymond T. Odierno, "The U.S. Army in a Time of Transition: Building a Flexible Force," 10.

14. Granai, *Complex and Volatile Environment*, 2.

15. ADP 3-0, 4.

16. Odierno, "U.S. Army in a Time of Transition," 10.

17. Odierno, "U.S. Army in a Time of Transition," 7, 9, 10.

18. ADRP 3-0, 1–12.

19. Lieutenant General Mike Lundy and Colonel Rich Creed, "The Return of U.S. Army Field Manual 3-0, Operations," 14.

20. Lundy and Creed, "Return of U.S. Army Field Manual 3-0," 14.

21. General David G. Perkins, "Multi-Domain Battle: Driving Change to Win in the Future," 9.

22. General David G. Perkins, "Preparing for the Fight Tonight: Multi-Domain Battle and Field Manual 3-0," 8.

23. Lundy and Creed, "Return of U.S. Army Field Manual 3-0," 15.

24. Lundy and Creed, "Return of U.S. Army Field Manual 3-0," 15.

25. Perkins, "Preparing for the Fight Tonight," 10.

26. Michael E. O'Hanlon, *The Future of Land Warfare*, 42–43.

27. Lundy and Creed, "Return of U.S. Army Field Manual 3-0," 14.

28. Perkins, "Multi-Domain Battle," 6.

29. Department of Defense, *Sustaining U.S. Global Leadership: Priorities for 21st Century Defense.*

30. President Obama quoted in O'Hanlon, *Future of Land Warfare*, 139.

31. Gates, "A House Divided," chap. 10 in *Duty.*

32. Quoted in Ucko, *New Counterinsurgency Era*, 50; Rumsfeld, *Known and Unknown*, 482. Rice was running the early meetings of Bush's foreign policy team. Cheney, *In My Time*, 252; Romjue, *American Army Doctrine*, 100.

33. Perkins, "Preparing for the Fight Tonight," 10.

34. Perkins, "Preparing for the Fight Tonight," 11.

35. Lundy and Creed, "Return of U.S. Army Field Manual 3-0," 16.

36. Perkins, "Preparing for the Fight Tonight," 11.

37. *ADP 3-0, Operations*, foreword and figure 1, iv and 3.

38. Preface to *Operations 2017.*

39. *Operations 2017*, xi.

40. *Operations 2017*, xi.

41. ADRP 3-0, 5-7; *Operations 2017*, 1-4, 2-51; *Operations 2017*, 1-4.

42. David S. Cloud, "Trump Strategy Review Calls for Building Smaller Nuclear Weapons and Adding Scenarios for Their Use," *Los Angeles Times*, February 2, 2018, http://www.latimes.com/nation/la-na-pol-nuclear-trump-20180202-story.html.

43. Caslen, "Change 1 to Field Manual 3-0," 87; *Operations 2008 Change 1*, 2-4.

44. "Doctrine 2015 Briefing," February 29, 2012, U.S. Army Combined Arms Center, https://usacac.army.mil/cac2/adp/Repository/Doctrine%202015%20Briefing%2029%20FEB%202012.pdf.

45. Department of the Army, Headquarters, *Field Manual 3-24/Marine Corps Warfighting Publication 3-33.5, Insurgencies and Countering Insurgencies.*

46. FM 3-24, 2014, 1-19 and chap. 3.

47. FM 3-24, 2014, 1-19.

48. Seth Robson, "Military to Unveil New Counterinsurgency Field Manual," *Stars and Stripes*, January 28, 2013, https://www.stripes.com/news/military-to-unveil-new-counterinsurgency-field-manual-1.205579.

49. FM 3-24, 2014, chap. 10.

50. FM 3-24, 2014, 1-19.

51. *Operations 2008 Change 1*, 2-9.

52. ADRP 3-0, 2016, 1-6.

53. ADRP 3-0, 2016, 1-6.

54. Granai, *Complex and Volatile Environment*, 26–27.

55. ADP 3-0, iii. "Decisive action is the continuous, simultaneous combinations of offensive, defensive, and stability or defense support of civil authorities tasks." ADRP 3-0, 3-1.

56. "Doctrine 2015 Briefing," February 29, 2012, U.S. Army Combined Arms Center, https://usacac.army.mil/cac2/adp/Repository/Doctrine%202015%20Briefing%2029%20FEB%202012.pdf.

57. ADP 3-0, Operations 2017, figure 1, iv, 7.

58. *ADP 3-0, Operations 2017*, 6 (emphasis added).

59. *ADP 3-0, Operations 2017*, 6 (emphasis added).

60. *ADP 3-0, Operations 2017*, 6.

61. *ADP 3-0, Operations 2017*, 1, 6.

62. Operations 2017, x.

63. Mansoor, *Surge*, 38–39; *Operations 2008*, 3-8; *Operations 2008 Change 1*, 2011, 3-7, 3-10 to 3-15.

64. *ADP 3-0, Operations 2017*, 2.

65. Lundy and Creed, "Return of U.S. Army Field Manual 3-0," 19.

66. Lundy and Creed, "Return of U.S. Army Field Manual 3-0," 19.

67. *ADP 3-0, Operations 2017*, 3.

68. *ADP 3-0, Operations 2017*, 7.

69. *ADP 3-0, Operations 2017*, 2.

70. ADRP 3-0, 3-3.

71. *ADP 3-0, Operations 2017*, 5.

72. *Operations 2008*, 3-2 to 3-3.

73. See section titled "Consolidate Gains." ADRP 3-0, 3-7 to 3-8.

74. *Operations 2008*, A-3 to A-4.

75. Joint Operations, 1-2.

76. ADRP 3-0, 2-2.

77. ADRP 3-0, 2-2.

78. ADP 3-90, 5-6.

79. ADP 3-90, 5-6.

80. *ADP 3-0, Operations 2017*, 6.

81. *Operations 2017*, x.

82. *ADP 3-0, Operations 2017*, 2-2.

83. *ADP 3-0, Operations 2017*, 2-9.

84. *ADP 3-0, Operations 2017*, 3-6, 3-14.

85. *Operations 2008*, 3-3 (emphasis added).

86. Granai, *Complex and Volatile Environment*, 6.

87. *Mission command* entered the doctrinal lexicon in 2003 with *Field Manual 6-0, Mission Command and Control of Army Forces* (Washington, DC: U.S. Government Printing Office, 2003). See also subsequent update *ADP 6-0, Mission Command*.

88. Caslen, "Change 1 to Field Manual 3-0," 86.

89. *Operations 2017*, 1-19.

90. *Operations 2017*, ix.

91. ADRP 3-0, 1-5, 1-9, 1-11, 5-3 (emphasis added).

92. Lundy and Creed, "Return of U.S. Army Field Manual 3-0," 19.

93. *ADP 3-0, 2017*, 8.

94. *ADP 3-0, 2017*, 7.

95. *ADP 3-90, Offense and Defense*, 2.

96. *ADP 3-90, Offense and Defense*, 10–11.

97. *Operations 2017*, 6-1.

98. ADRP 3-0, 1-2, Glossary-7.

99. Granai, *Complex and Volatile Environment*, 2, 18–19.

100. Caslen, "Change 1 to Field Manual 3-0," 85.

101. *ADP 3-0, Operations 2017*, 1.

102. *ADP 3-0, Operations 2017*, 3.

103. ADRP 3-0 retains this definition. ADRP 3-0, vi.

104. *ADP 3-0, Operations 2017*, 8.

105. *ADP 3-0, Operations 2017*, 14 (emphasis added).

106. *ADP 3-0, Operations 2017*, 14.

107. U.S. Army, *Army Doctrine Publication 3-0, Unified Land Operations*, foreword.

108. *Operations 2008*, 1-1 to 1-21; Kretchik, *U.S. Army Doctrine*, 272.

109. *ADP 3-0, Operations 2017*, 3.

110. Granai, *Complex and Volatile Environment*, 10–11 (emphasis added).

111. Granai, *Complex and Volatile Environment*, 10–11.

112. ADP 3-90, 5.

113. ADRP 3-0, 3-1.

114. *Operations 2017*, ix; Lundy and Creed, "Return of U.S. Army Field Manual 3-0," 17.

115. *ADP 3-0, Operations 2017*, 4.

116. Perkins, "Multi-Domain Battle," 10, 13.

117. Ancker and Scully, "Army Doctrine Publication 3-0", 39.

118. Odierno, "U.S. Army in a Time of Transition," 7.

119. *Operations 2008*, 3-1; Granai, *Complex and Volatile Environment*, 12."

120. Lundy and Creed, "Return of U.S. Army Field Manual 3-0," 17.

121. Lundy and Creed, "Return of U.S. Army Field Manual 3-0," 17.

122. Odierno, "U.S. Army in a Time of Transition," 10.

123. *ADP 3-0, Operations 2017*, 1.

124. *ADP 3-0, Operations 2017*, foreword.

125. Betts, *Soldiers, Statesmen, and Cold War Crises*.

126. Petraeus, "Lessons of Vietnam."

127. O'Hanlon, *Future of Land Warfare*, 138–39.

128. *National Security Strategy of the United States of America*.

129. Peter Campbell, "Generals in Cyberspace: Military Insights for Defending Cyberspace."

130. *Operations 1962*, 74.

131. Donald Trump, "2018 State of the Union Address," https://www.whitehouse .gov/sotu/. See also Department of Defense, "Summary of the 2018 National Defense Strategy of the United States: Sharpening the American Military's Competitive Edge," 5, https://www.defense.gov/Portals/1/Documents/pubs/2018-National-Defense -Strategy-Summary.pdf.

132. Gates, *Duty*, 335–86.

BIBLIOGRAPHY

Adamsky, Dima. *The Culture of Military Innovation: The Impact of Cultural Factors on the Revolution in Military Affairs in Russia, the US and Israel.* Stanford, CA: Stanford University Press, 2010.

Alanbrooke, Field Marshal Lord (Alan Francis Brooke). *War Diaries, 1939–1945.* Edited by Alex Danchev and Daniel Todman. Berkeley: University of California Press, 2001.

Alger, John I. *The Quest for Victory: The History of the Principles of War.* Westport, CT: Greenwood, 1982.

Allison, Graham, and Philip Zelikow. *Essence of Decision: Explaining the Cuban Missile Crisis.* 2nd ed. New York: Addison Wesley Longman, 1999.

Ancker, Colonel Clinton J., III, and Lieutenant Colonel Michael A. Scully. "Army Doctrine Publication 3-0: An Opportunity to Meet the Challenges of the Future." *Military Review* 93, no. 1 (2013): 38–42.

Andrade, Dale. "Westmoreland Was Right: Learning the Wrong Lesson from the Vietnam War." *Small Wars and Insurgencies* 19, no. 2 (2008): 145–81.

Aron, Raymond. *On War.* New York: Doubleday Anchor, 1958.

Art, Robert J. "Bureaucratic Politics and American Foreign Policy: A Critique." *Policy Sciences* 4 (December 1973).

Avant, Deborah D. *Political Institutions and Military Change: Lessons from Peripheral Wars.* Ithaca, NY: Cornell University Press, 1994.

Avant, Deborah D., and James H. Lebovic. "U.S. Military Responses to Post–Cold War Missions." In *The Sources of Military Change: Culture, Politics, Technology,* edited by Theo Farrell and Terry Terriff, 139–60. Boulder, CO: Lynne Rienner, 2002.

Aylwin-Foster, Nigel. "Changing the Army for Counterinsurgency Operations." *Military Review* 85, no. 6 (2005): 2–25.

Bacevich, A. J. *The Pentomic Era: The U.S. Army between Korea and Vietnam.* Washington, DC: National Defense University Press, 1986.

Beevor, Anthony. *The Second World War.* New York: Little, Brown, 2012.

Bennett, W. S., R. R. Sandoval, R. G. Shreffler, and Alain C. Enthoven. "Correspondence." *Foreign Affairs* 53, no. 4 (1975): 773–76.

Berger, Thomas U. "From Sword to Chrysanthemum: Japan's Culture of Anti-militarism." *International Security* 17, no. 4 (1993): 119–50.

Bibliography

Beschloss, Michael R., ed. *Taking Charge: The Johnson White House Tapes, 1963–1964.* New York: Simon & Schuster, 1997.

Betts, Richard K. *Soldiers, Statesmen and Cold War Crises.* Cambridge, MA: Harvard University Press, 1977.

Betts, Richard K., Michael C. Desch, and Peter D. Feaver. "Correspondence: Civilians, Soldiers, and the Iraq Surge Decision." *International Security* 36, no. 3 (2011–12): 179–99.

Bianco, William T., and Jamie Markham. "Vanishing Veterans: The Decline of Military Experience in Congress." In *Soldiers and Civilians: The Civil-Military Gap and American National Security*, edited by Peter D. Feaver and Richard H. Kohn, 275–88. Cambridge, MA: MIT Press, 2001.

Biddle, Stephen D. "Afghanistan and the Future of Warfare." *Foreign Affairs* 82, no. 2 (2003): 31–46.

———. *Military Power: Explaining Victory and Defeat in Modern Battle.* Princeton, NJ: Princeton University Press, 2004.

———. "Rebuilding the Foundations of Offense-Defense Theory." *Journal of Politics* 63, no. 3 (2001): 741–74.

———. *The 2006 Lebanon Campaign and the Future of Warfare: Implications for Army and Defense Policy.* Carlisle, PA: Strategic Studies Institute, 2008.

Biddle, Stephen D., Jeffrey Friedman, and Jacob Shapiro. "Testing the Surge: Why Did Violence Decline in Iraq in 2007?" *International Security* 37, no. 1 (2012): 7–40.

Birtle, Andrew J. *U.S. Army Counterinsurgency and Contingency Operations Doctrine, 1942–1976.* Washington, DC: Center of Military History, U.S. Army, 2006.

Blaufarb, Douglas S. *The Counterinsurgency Era: U.S. Doctrine and Performance, 1950 to the Present.* New York: Free Press, 1977.

Bolger, Daniel P. "The Ghosts of Omdurman." *Parameters* 21 (Autumn 1991): 28–39.

Boman, Lieutenant Colonel Truman R. "Current Soviet Tactics." *Military Review* 42, no. 3 (1962): 41–46.

Boot, Max. *The Savage Wars of Peace: Small Wars and the Rise of American Power.* New York: Basic Books, 2002.

Brodie, Bernard. *Strategy in the Missile Age.* Princeton, NJ: Princeton University Press, 1965.

Brooks, Stephen G., and William C. Wohlforth. *World Out of Balance: International Relations and the Challenge of American Primacy.* Princeton, NJ: Princeton University Press, 2008.

Builder, Carl H. *The Masks of War: American Military Style in Strategy and Analysis.* Baltimore: Johns Hopkins University Press, 1989.

Burr, William, ed. *The Kissinger Transcripts: The Top Secret Talks with Beijing and Moscow.* New York: New Press, 1999.

Bush, George W. *Decision Points.* New York: Crown, 2010.

Cameron, Craig M. "The US Military's 'Two-Front War,' 1963–1988." In *The Sources of Military Change: Culture, Politics, Technology*, edited by Theo Farrell and Terry Terriff, 119–38. Boulder, CO: Lynne Rienner, 2002.

Campbell, Peter. "Generals in Cyberspace: Military Insights for Defending Cyberspace." *Orbis* 62, no. 2 (2018): 262–77.

Caslen, Lieutenant General Robert L., Jr. "Change 1 to Field Manual 3-0: The Way the Army Fights Today." *Military Review* 91, no. 2 (2011): 84–88.

Cassidy, Robert M. *Counterinsurgency and the Global War on Terror: Military Culture and Irregular War*. Stanford, CA: Stanford University Press, 2008.

Chambers, John Whiteclay, II. *The Oxford Companion to American Military History*. New York: Oxford University Press, 1999.

Cheney, Dick. *In My Time: A Personal and Political Memoir*. With Liz Cheney. New York: Simon & Schuster, 2011.

Clausewitz, Carl von. *On War*. Translated by J. J. Graham. London: Routledge & Kegan Paul, 1949.

———. *On War*. Translated by Michael Howard and Peter Paret. Princeton, NJ: Princeton University Press, 1976.

Cloud, David S., and Greg Jaffe. *The Fourth Star: Four Generals and the Epic Struggle for the Future of the United States Army*. New York: Crown, 2009.

Cohen, Eliot A. *Supreme Command: Soldiers, Statesmen, and Leadership in Wartime*. New York: Free Press, 2002.

Committee on Appropriations, 86th Congress. *Department of Defense Appropriations for 1960*. Washington, DC: Government of the United States, 1958.

Crane, Conrad C. *Avoiding Vietnam: The U.S. Army's Response to Defeat in Southeast Asia*. Carlisle, PA: Strategic Studies Institute, 2002.

Daddis, Gregory A. *No Sure Victory: Measuring U.S. Army Effectiveness and Progress in the Vietnam War*. New York: Oxford University Press, 2011.

———. *Westmoreland's War: Reassessing American Strategy in Vietnam*. New York: Oxford University Press, 2014.

Dallek, Robert. *Camelot's Court: Inside the Kennedy White House*. New York: HarperCollins, 2013.

———. *Flawed Giant: Lyndon Johnson and His Times, 1961–1975*. New York: Oxford University Press, 1998.

———. *Nixon and Kissinger: Partners in Power*. New York: HarperCollins, 2007.

Dastrup, Boyd L. *The U.S. Army Command and General Staff College: A Centennial History*. Manhattan, KS: Sunflower University Press, 1982.

Decker, George H. "Doctrine: The Cement That Binds." *Army* 11, no. 7 (1961): 60–61.

———. *Oral History*. Carlisle, PA: U.S. Army Military History Institute, 1972.

Demchak, Chris C. "Complexity and Theory of Networked Militaries." In *The Sources of Military Change: Culture, Politics, Technology*, edited by Theo Farrell and Terry Terriff, 221–64. Boulder, CO: Lynne Rienner, 2002.

Department of Defense. *Sustaining U.S. Global Leadership: Priorities for 21st Century Defense*. January 2012. http://www.defense.gov/news/Defense_Strategic_Guidance.pdf.

Department of the Army, Headquarters. *Field Manual 3-24: Counterinsurgency*. Chicago: University of Chicago Press, 2007.

DePuy, William E. *Changing an Army: An Oral History of General William E. DePuy.* Carlisle Barracks, PA: Military History Institute / Washington, DC: Army Center of Military History, 1988.

———. "The Light Infantry: Indispensable Element of a Balanced Force." *Army* 35 (June 1985): 26–41.

———. *The Selected Papers of General William E. DePuy.* Leavenworth, KS: Combat Studies Institute, 1985.

Desch, Michael C. "America's Liberal Illiberalism: The Ideological Origins of Overreaction in U.S. Foreign Policy." *International Security* 32, no. 3 (2007–8): 7–43.

———. *Civilian Control of the Military: The Changing Security Environment.* Baltimore: Johns Hopkins University Press, 1999.

———. "Civil-Militarism: The Civilian Origins of the New American Militarism." *Orbis* 50, no. 3 (2006): 573–83.

———. "Explaining the Gap: Vietnam, the Republicanization of the South, and the End of the Mass Army." In *Soldiers and Civilians: The Civil-Military Gap and American National Security,* edited by Peter D. Feaver and Richard H. Kohn, 289–324. Cambridge: MIT Press, 2001.

———. "The Keys That Lock Up the World: Identifying American Interests in the Periphery." *International Security* 14, no. 1 (1989): 86–121.

Deutsche, Harold C. *Hitler and His Generals: The Hidden Crisis, January–June 1938.* Minneapolis: University of Minnesota Press, 1974.

Dixon, Paul. "'Hearts and Minds'? British Counterinsurgency from Malaya to Iraq." *Journal of Strategic Studies* 32, no. 3 (2009): 353–81.

Donnelly, Christopher N. "Soviet Tactics for Overcoming NATO Anti-tank Defenses." *International Defense Review* 12, no. 7 (1979): 1099–1106.

———. "Tactical Problems Facing the Soviet Army: Recent Debates in the Soviet Military Press." *International Defense Review* 11, no. 9 (1978): 1405–12.

Donnelly, William M. *Transforming an Army at War: Designing the Modular Force, 1991–2005.* Washington, DC: Center of Military History, U.S. Army, 2007.

Doughty, Major Robert A. *The Evolution of U.S. Army Tactical Doctrine, 1946–76.* Fort Leavenworth, KS: Combat Studies Institute, U.S. Army Command and General Staff College, August 1979.

Downs, Anthony. *Inside Bureaucracy.* Boston: Little, Brown, 1967.

Drummond, Raymond R. *Light Infantry: A Tactical Deep Battle Asset for Central Europe.* Fort Leavenworth, KS: School of Advanced Military Studies, 1985.

Duffield, John S., Theo Farrell, Richard Price, and Michael C. Desch. "Isms and Schisms: Culturalism versus Realism in Security Studies." *International Security* 24, no. 1 (1999): 156–80.

Eckstein, Harry. "A Culturalist Theory of Political Change." *American Political Science Review* 82, no. 3 (1988): 789–804.

Eddleman, Clive D. "The Concept of Warfare in 1967." Speech to the Canadian National Defense College, Kingston, Ontario, March 21, 1957.

Edelman, Eric S. "The Strange Career of the 1992 Defense Planning Guidance." In *In Uncertain Times: American Foreign Policy after the Berlin Wall and 9/11,* edited by Melvyn P. Leffler and Jeffrey W. Legro, 63–77. Ithaca, NY: Cornell University Press, 2011.

Enthoven, Alain C., and K. Wayne Smith. *How Much Is Enough? Shaping the Defense Program, 1961–1969*. Santa Monica, CA: RAND, 2005.

Farrell, Theo. "World Culture and the Irish Army, 1922–1942." In *The Sources of Military Change: Culture, Politics, Technology*, edited by Theo Farrell and Terry Terriff, 69–90. Boulder, CO: Lynne Rienner, 2002.

Farrell, Theo, Sten Rynning, and Terry Terriff. *Transforming Military Power since the Cold War: Britain, France, and the United States, 1991–2012*. New York: Cambridge University Press, 2013.

Farrell, Theo, and Terry Terriff, eds. *The Sources of Military Change: Culture, Politics, Technology*. Boulder, CO: Lynne Rienner, 2002.

Feaver, Peter D. *Guarding the Guardians: Civilian Control of Nuclear Weapons in the United States*. Ithaca, NY: Cornell University Press, 1992.

———. "The Right to Be Right: Civil-Military Relations and the Iraq Surge Decision." *International Security* 35, no. 4 (2011): 87–125.

Feaver, Peter D., and Richard H. Kohn, eds. *Soldiers and Civilians: The Civil-Military Gap and American National Security*. Cambridge, MA: MIT Press, 2001.

Fitzgerald, David. *Learning to Forget: U.S. Army Counterinsurgency Doctrine and Practice from Vietnam to Iraq*. Stanford, CA: Stanford University Press, 2013.

Friedman, B. A. *On Tactics: A Theory of Victory in Battle*. Annapolis, MD: Naval Institute Press, 2017.

Frost, Peter J., Larry F. Morre, Meryl Reis Louis, Craig C. Lundberg, and Joanne Martin, eds. *Organizational Culture*. Beverly Hills: Sage, 1985.

Gaddis, John Lewis. "Grand Strategy in the Second Term." *Foreign Affairs* 84, no. 1 (2005): 2–15.

———. *Strategies of Containment: A Critical Appraisal of American National Security Policy during the Cold War*. New York: Oxford University Press, 2005.

Galula, David. *Counterinsurgency Warfare: Theory and Practice*. Westport, CT: Praeger, 1964.

———. "Galula on Adapting ROE [Rules of Engagement] to an Insurgency." *Military Review* 86, no. 5 (2006): 198.

Garthoff, Raymond L. "Soviet Doctrine on the Decisive Factors in Modern War." *Military Review* 39, no. 4 (1959): 3–22.

Gartner, Scott Sigmund, and Marissa Edson Myers. "Body Counts and 'Success' in the Vietnam and Korean Wars." *Journal of Interdisciplinary History* 25, no. 3 (1995): 377–95.

Gates, Robert M. *Duty: Memoirs of a Secretary at War*. New York: Alfred A. Knopf, 2014.

———. *From the Shadows: The Ultimate Insider's Story of Five Presidents and How They Won the Cold War*. New York: Simon & Schuster, 1996.

Gavin, Francis J. "Myths of Flexible Response: United States Strategy in Europe during the 1960s." *International History Review* 23, no. 4 (2001): 847–75.

————. *Nuclear Statecraft: History and Strategy in America's Atomic Age*. Ithaca, NY: Cornell University Press, 2012.

Gelb, Leslie H., and Richard K. Betts. *The Irony of Vietnam: The System Worked*. Washington, DC: Brookings Institution, 1979.

Gentile, Gian. *Wrong Turn: America's Deadly Embrace of Counterinsurgency*. New York: New Press, 2013.

George, Alexander L., and Andrew Bennett. *Case Studies and Theory Development in the Social Sciences*. Cambridge, MA: MIT Press, 2005.

Gerring, John. *Case Study Research: Principles and Practices*. New York: Cambridge University Press, 2007.

Glaser, Charles L. "The Security Dilemma Revisited." *World Politics* 50, no. 1 (1997): 171–201.

Goldenthal, Lieutenant Colonel Mitchel (Corps of Engineers Faculty, USA CGSC). "Corps in the Mobile Defense." *Military Review*, 37, no. 6 (1957): 14–24.

Goldstein, Judith, and Robert Keohane, eds. *Ideas and Foreign Policy: Beliefs, Institutions, and Political Change*. Ithaca, NY: Cornell University Press, 1993.

Granai, Major Cornelius. *A Complex and Volatile Environment: The Doctrinal Evolution from Full Spectrum Operations to Unified Land Operations*. Fort Leavenworth, KS: School of Advanced Military Studies, 2015.

Gray, Colin S. "National Style in Strategy: The American Example." *International Security* 6, no. 2 (1981): 21–47.

Griffin, Stuart. "Military Innovation Studies: Multidisciplinary or Lacking Discipline?" *Journal of Strategic Studies* 40, nos. 1–2 (2017): 196–224.

Grissom, Adam. "The Future of Military Innovation Studies." *Journal of Strategic Studies* 29, no. 5 (2006): 905–34.

Halberstam, David. *The Best and the Brightest*. New York: Random House, 1972.

Halder, Franz. *The Halder War Diary, 1939–1942*. Novato, CA: Presidio, 1988.

Halperin, Morton H., and Priscilla A. Clapp. *Bureaucratic Politics and Foreign Policy*. 2nd ed. Washington, DC: Brookings Institution, 2006.

Hasegawa, Tsuyoshi. *Racing the Enemy: Stalin, Truman, and the Surrender of Japan*. Cambridge, MA: Belknap Press of Harvard University Press, 2005.

Hay, John H. *Vietnam Studies: Tactical and Material Innovations*. Washington, DC: Department of the Army, 1989.

Herbert, Paul H. *Deciding What Has to Be Done: General William E. DePuy and the 1976 Edition of "FM 100-5 Operations."* Fort Leavenworth, KS: Combat Studies Institute, U.S. Army Command and General Staff College, 1988.

Hobson, Colonel Victor W., Jr., and Colonel Oliver G. Kinney. "Keeping Pace with the Future: Development of Doctrine at USA CGSC." *Military Review* 37, no. 8 (1957): 10–22.

Hoiback, Harald. "What Is Doctrine?" *Journal of Strategic Studies* 34, no. 6 (2011): 879–900.

Holder, L. D. "Development of Army Doctrine, 1975 to 1985." *Military Review* 65, no. 5 (1985): 50–52.

Horne, Alistair. *A Savage War of Peace: Algeria, 1954–1962.* New York: New York Review of Books, 2006.

Howard, Michael. "Men against Fire: Expectations of War in 1914." *International Security* 9, no. 1 (1984): 48–53.

Howze, Hamilton H. *A Cavalryman's Story: Memoirs of a Twentieth-Century Army General.* Washington, DC: Smithsonian Institution Press, 1996.

Hull, Isabel V. *Absolute Destruction: Military Culture and the Practices of War in Imperial Germany.* Ithaca, NY: Cornell University Press, 2005.

Huntington, Samuel P. *The Soldier and the State: The Theory and Politics of Civil-Military Relations.* Cambridge, MA: Harvard University Press, 1957.

Inderfurth, Karl F., and Lock K. Johnson, eds. *Fateful Decisions: Inside the National Security Council.* New York: Oxford University Press, 2004.

Jackson, Colin. "From Conservatism to Revolutionary Intoxication: The U.S. Army and the Second Interwar Period." In *US Military Innovation since the Cold War: Creation without Destruction*, edited by Harvey M. Sapolsky, Benjamin H. Friedman, and Brendan Rittenhouse Green, 43–70. New York: Routledge, 2012.

Janowitz, Morris. *The Professional Soldier: A Social and Political Portrait.* Glencoe, IL: Free Press, 1960.

Jenkins, Brian M. *The Unchangeable War.* Santa Monica, CA: RAND, 1970.

Jensen, Benjamin M. *Forging the Sword: Doctrinal Change in the U.S. Army.* Stanford, CA: Stanford University Press, 2016.

Jervis, Robert. "Cooperation under the Security Dilemma." *World Politics* 30, no. 2 (1978): 167–214.

Johnson, Harold K. *Oral History.* Carlisle, PA: U.S. Army Military History Institute. 1972.

Johnston, Alastair Iain. "Thinking about Strategic Culture." *International Security* 19, no. 4 (1995): 32–64.

Kafkalas, Peter N. "The Light Infantry Divisions and Low-Intensity Conflict: Are They Losing Sight of Each Other?" *Military Review* 66 (January 1986): 18–27.

Kagan, Donald. *On the Origins of War and the Preservation of Peace.* New York: Anchor, 1995.

Kaplan, Fred. *The Insurgents: David Petraeus and the Plot to Change the American Way of War.* New York: Simon & Schuster, 2013.

Kaplan, Robert D. "What Rumsfeld Got Right." *Atlantic*, July 1, 2008. http://www.theatlantic.com/magazine/archive/2008/07/what-rumsfeld-got-right/306870/.

Katzenstein, Peter J., and Nobuo Okawara. "Japan's National Security: Structures, Norms, and Policies." *International Security* 17, no. 4 (1993): 84–118.

Kearns, Doris. *Lyndon Johnson and the American Dream.* New York: Harper & Row, 1976.

Kedzior, Richard W. *Evolution and Endurance: The U.S. Army Division in the Twentieth Century.* Santa Monica, CA: RAND, 2000.

Keegan, John. *The Face of Battle: A Study of Agincourt, Waterloo, and the Somme.* New York: Viking, 1976.

———. *A History of Warfare.* New York: Random House, 1993.

Bibliography

Kennedy, John F. *Public Papers of the Presidents of the United States: John F. Kennedy, 1961*. Washington, DC: U.S. Government Printing Office, 1962.

Kennedy, Robert F. *Robert Kennedy in His Own Words: The Unpublished Recollections of the Kennedy Years*. New York: Bantam, 1988.

Kier, Elizabeth. *Imagining War: French and British Military Doctrine between the Wars*. Princeton, NJ: Princeton University Press, 1997.

Kilcullen, David. *The Accidental Guerrilla: Fighting Small Wars in the Midst of a Big One*. New York: Oxford University Press, 2009.

———. "Twenty-Eight Articles: Fundamentals of Company-Level Counterinsurgency." *Military Review* 86, no. 3 (2006): 103–8.

Kissinger, Henry. *Nuclear Weapons and Foreign Policy*. New York: Harper, 1957.

———. *The White House Years*. New York: Simon & Schuster, 1979.

———. *Years of Upheaval*. New York: Simon & Schuster, 2011.

Kozlov, Colonel S. "Soviet Military Art and Science." Translated by Walter Darnell Jacobs. *Military Review* 39, no. 6 (1959): 93–100.

Krasner, Stephen D. "Are Bureaucracies Important? (or Allison Wonderland)." *Foreign Policy* 7 (Summer 1972): 159–79.

Krepinevich, Andrew F. *The Army and Vietnam*. Baltimore: Johns Hopkins University Press, 1986.

Kretchik, Walter E. *U.S. Army Doctrine: From the American Revolution to the War on Terror*. Lawrence: University Press of Kansas, 2011.

Kudelia, Serhiy. "Choosing Violence in Irregular Wars: The Case of Anti-Soviet Insurgency in Western Ukraine." *East European Politics & Societies* 27, no. 1 (2013): 149–81.

Kydd, Andrew. "Sheep in Sheep's Clothing: Why Security Seekers Do Not Fight One Another." *Security Studies* 7, no. 1 (1997): 114–54.

Lakatos, Imre. *The Methodology of Scientific Research Programmes*. Edited by John Worrall and Gregory Currie. New York: Cambridge University Press, 1978.

Layne, Christopher. "From Preponderance to Offshore Balancing: America's Future Grand Strategy." *International Security* 22, no. 1 (1997): 86–124.

Leffler, Melvyn P., and Jeffrey W. Legro, eds. *In Uncertain Times: American Foreign Policy after the Berlin Wall and 9/11*. Ithaca, NY: Cornell University Press, 2011.

Legro, Jeffrey W. *Cooperation under Fire: Anglo-German Restraint during World War II*. Ithaca, NY: Cornell University Press, 1995.

———. "Military Culture and Inadvertent Escalation in World War II." *International Security* 18, no. 4 (1994): 108–42.

———. *Rethinking the World: Great Power Strategies and International Order*. Ithaca, NY: Cornell University Press, 2005.

Lemnitzer, Lyman L. *Oral History*. Carlisle, PA: U.S. Army Military History Institute, 1972.

Levy, Jack S., and William R. Thompson. *Causes of War*. Malden, MA: Wiley-Blackwell, 2010.

Lewis, Adrian R. *The American Culture of War: The History of U.S. Military Force from World War II to Operation Iraqi Freedom*. New York: Routledge, 2007.

Liddell Hart, B. H. *Strategy*. New York: Praeger, 1954.

Lind, William S. "Some Doctrinal Questions for the United States Army." *Military Review* 57, no. 3 (1977): 54–65.

Linn, Brian McAllister. *The Echo of Battle: The Army's Way of War*. Cambridge, MA: Harvard University Press, 2007.

———. *Elvis' Army: Cold War GIs and the Atomic Battlefield*. Cambridge, MA: Harvard University Press, 2016.

Lock-Pullan, Richard. "Civilian Ideas and Military Innovation: Manoeuvre Warfare and Organisational Change in the U.S. Army." *War and Society* 20, no. 1 (2002): 125–47.

———. "'An Inward Looking Time': The United States Army, 1973–1976." *Journal of Military History* 67, no. 2 (2003): 483–511.

Long, Austin. *The Soul of Armies: Counterinsurgency Doctrine and Military Culture in the US and UK*. Ithaca, NY: Cornell University Press, 2016.

Lundy, Lieutenant General Mike, and Colonel Rich Creed. "The Return of U.S. Army Field Manual 3-0, Operations." *Military Review* 97, no. 6 (2017): 14–21.

Luttwak, Edward N. "The American Style of Warfare and the Military Balance." *Survival* 21, no. 2 (1979): 57–60.

———. "The Operational Level of War." *International Security* 5, no. 3 (1980–81): 61–79.

Lynn, John A. *Battle: A History of Combat and Culture*. New York: Basic Books, 2003.

MacMillan, Margaret. *Nixon and Mao: The Week That Changed the World*. New York: Random House, 2008.

———. *The War That Ended Peace: The Road to 1914*. New York: Random House, 2013.

Mahnken, Thomas G., and Barry D. Watts. "What the Gulf War Can (and Cannot) Tell Us about the Future of Warfare." *International Security* 22, no. 2 (1997): 151–62.

Mako, William P. *U.S. Ground Forces and the Defense of Central Europe*. Washington, DC: Brookings Institution, 1983.

Manhunt: The Inside Story of the Hunt for Bin Laden. DVD. Directed by Greg Barker. Home Box Office, 2013.

Mansoor, Peter R. *Surge: My Journey with General David Petraeus and the Remaking of the Iraq War*. New Haven, CT: Yale University Press, 2013.

Mao, Zedong. *On Guerrilla Warfare*. Translated by Samuel B. Griffith. New York: Praeger, 1961.

Mathers, Jennifer R. "Reform and the Russian Military." In *The Sources of Military Change: Culture, Politics, Technology*, edited by Theo Farrell and Terry Terriff, 161–84. Boulder, CO: Lynne Rienner, 2002.

Mazaar, Michael J. *Light Forces and the Future of U.S. Military Strategy*. New York: Brassey's, 1990.

McChrystal, Stanley. *My Share of the Task: A Memoir*. New York: Penguin, 2014.

McDonough, James R. *Platoon Leader: A Memoir of Command in Combat*. New York: Ballantine, 1985.

McMaster, H. R. *Dereliction of Duty: Johnson, McNamara, the Joint Chiefs of Staff, and the Lies That Led to Vietnam*. New York: HarperCollins, 1997.

McPherson, James M. *Battle Cry of Freedom: The Civil War Era*. New York: Oxford University Press, 1988.

Mearsheimer, John J. "Assessing the Conventional Balance: The 3:1 Rule and Its Critics." *International Security* 13, no. 4 (1989): 54–89.

———. *Conventional Deterrence*. Ithaca, NY: Cornell University Press, 1985.

———. "Maneuver, Mobile Defense, and the NATO Central Front." *International Security* 6, no. 3 (1981–82): 104–22.

Millet, Allan R. "Patterns of Military Innovation in the Interwar Period." In *Military Innovation in the Interwar Period*, edited by Williamson Murray and Allan R. Millet, 329–68. Cambridge: Cambridge University Press, 1996.

Moore, Harold G., and Joseph L. Galloway. *We Were Soldiers Once . . . and Young: Ia Drang, the Battle That Changed the War in Vietnam*. New York: Random House, 1992.

Murray, Williamson. *Military Adaptation in War: With Fear of Change*. New York: Cambridge University Press, 2011.

———. "Thinking about Revolutions in Military Affairs." *Joint Forces Quarterly* (Summer 1997): 69–76.

———. *War, Strategy, and Military Effectiveness*. New York: Cambridge University Press, 2011.

Murray, Williamson, MacGregor Knox, and Alvin Bernstein, eds. *The Making of Strategy: Rulers, States, and War*. New York: Cambridge University Press, 1994.

Murray, Williamson, and Allan R. Millett, eds. *Military Innovation in the Interwar Period*. Cambridge: Cambridge University Press, 1996.

Nagl, John A. *Learning to Eat Soup with a Knife: Counterinsurgency Lessons from Malaya and Vietnam*. Chicago: University of Chicago Press, 2002.

National Security Strategy of the United States of America. December 2017. https://www.whitehouse.gov/wp-content/uploads/2017/12/NSS-Final-12-18-2017-0905.pdf.

Nixon, Richard M. "A Redefining of the United States Role in the World." February 25, 1971, US Foreign Policy—1971. Washington, DC: U.S. Department of State, 1972.

Nolan, Janne E. *Guardians of the Arsenal: The Politics of Nuclear Strategy*. New York: Basic Books, 1989.

Odierno, Raymond T. "The U.S. Army in a Time of Transition: Building a Flexible Force." *Foreign Affairs* 91, no. 3 (2012): 7–11.

O'Hanlon, Michael E. *The Future of Land Warfare*. Washington, DC: Brookings Institution, 2015.

Owens, William A. "Creating a U.S. Military Revolution." In *The Sources of Military Change: Culture, Politics, Technology*, edited by Theo Farrell and Terry Terriff, 205–20. Boulder, CO: Lynne Rienner, 2002.

———. *Lifting the Fog of War*. With Ed Offley. New York: Farrar, Straus and Giroux, 2000.

Pach, Chester. "The Reagan Doctrine: Principle, Pragmatism, and Policy." *Presidential Studies Quarterly* 36, no. 1 (2006): 75–88.

Palmer, Bruce. *Oral History*. Carlisle, PA: U.S. Army Military History Institute, 1976.

———. *The 25-Year War: America's Military Role in Vietnam*. Lexington: University Press of Kentucky, 1984.

Parson, Major Nels A., Jr. (Artillery, Office of the Deputy Chief of Staff for Operations). "The Confederates Talk on Nuclear Warfare." *Military Review* 40, no. 4 (1960): 23–30.

Perkins, General David G. "Multi-Domain Battle: Driving Change to Win in the Future." *Military Review* 97, no. 4 (2017): 6–13.

———. "Preparing for the Fight Tonight: Multi-Domain Battle and Field Manual 3-0." *Military Review* 97, no. 5 (2017): 6–13.

Peterson, Michael E. *The Combined Action Platoons: The U.S. Marines' Other War in Vietnam*. New York: Praeger, 1989.

Petraeus, David H. "The American Military and the Lessons of Vietnam: A Study of Military Influence and the Use of Force in the Post-Vietnam Era." PhD diss., Princeton University, 1987.

———. "Light Infantry in Europe: Strategic Flexibility and Conventional Deterrence." *Military Review* 64, no. 12 (1984): 35–55.

Porch, Douglas. *Counterinsurgency: Exposing the Myths of the New Way of War*. New York: Cambridge University Press, 2013.

Porter, Patrick. "Good Anthropology, Bad History: The Cultural Turn in Studying War." *Parameters* (Summer 2007): 45–58.

———. *Military Orientalism: Eastern War through Western Eyes*. New York: Oxford University Press, 2014.

Posen, Barry R. "Command of the Commons: The Military Foundation of U.S. Hegemony." *International Security* 28, no. 1 (2003): 5–46.

———. *Inadvertent Escalation: Conventional War and Nuclear Risks*. Ithaca, NY: Cornell University Press, 1991.

———. "Nationalism, the Mass Army, and Military Power." *International Security* 18, no. 2 (1993): 80–124.

———. *The Sources of Military Doctrine: France, Britain, and Germany between the World Wars*. Ithaca, NY: Cornell University Press, 1984.

Posen, Barry R., and Stephen Van Evera. "Defense Policy and the Reagan Administration: Departure from Containment." *International Security* 8, no. 1 (1983): 3–45.

Powell, Colin L. *My American Journey*. With Joseph E. Persico. New York: Random House, 1995.

"Readiness for the Little War: Optimum Integrated Strategy." *Military Review* 37, no. 1 (1957): 14–26.

Resende-Santos, João. *Neorealism, States, and the Modern Mass Army*. New York: Cambridge University Press, 2007.

Rhodes, Edward. "Do Bureaucratic Politics Matter? Some Disconfirming Findings from the Case of the U.S. Navy." *World Politics* 47 (October 1994): 1–41.

Rice, Condoleezza. "Campaign 2000: Promoting the National Interest." *Foreign Affairs* 79, no. 1 (2000): 45–62.

Ricks, Thomas E. *Fiasco: The American Military Adventure in Iraq, 2003 to 2005*. New York: Penguin, 2006.

———. *The Gamble: General David Petraeus and the American Military Adventure in Iraq, 2006–2008*. New York: Penguin, 2009.

———. *The Generals: American Military Command from World War II to Today*. New York: Penguin, 2012.

Ritter, Gerhard. *The Schlieffen Plan*. New York: Praeger, 1958.

Robinson, Linda. *Tell Me How This Ends: General David Petraeus and the Search for a Way Out of Iraq*. New York: PublicAffairs, 2008.

Romjue, John L. *American Army Doctrine for the Post–Cold War*. Fort Monroe, VA: Military History Office, U.S. Army Training and Doctrine Command, 1996.

———. *From Active Defense to AirLand Battle: The Development of Army Doctrine, 1973–1982*. Fort Monroe, VA: Historical Office, U.S. Army Training and Doctrine Command, 1984.

Rosen, Stephen Peter. "Military Effectiveness: Why Society Matters." *International Security* 19, no. 4 (1995): 5–31.

———. *Winning the Next War: Innovation and the Modern Military*. Ithaca, NY: Cornell University Press, 1991.

Rostow, W. W. *The Stages of Economic Growth: A Non-communist Manifesto*. 3rd ed. New York: Cambridge University Press, 1991.

Rumsfeld, Donald. *Known and Unknown: A Memoir*. New York: Sentinel, 2011.

Rynning, Sten. *Changing Military Doctrine: Presidents and Military Power in Fifth Republic France, 1958–2000*. Westport, CT: Praeger, 2002.

Sapolsky, Harvey M. *Polaris System Development: Bureaucratic and Pragmatic Success in Government*. Cambridge, MA: Harvard University Press, 1972.

Sapolsky, Harvey M., Benjamin H. Friedman, and Brendan Rittenhouse Green, eds. *US Military Innovation since the Cold War: Creation without Destruction*. New York: Routledge, 2009.

Sapolsky, Harvey M., Brendan Rittenhouse Green, and Benjamin H. Friedman. "The Missing Transformation." In *US Military Innovation since the Cold War: Creation without Destruction*, edited by H. M. Sapolsky, B. H. Friedman, and B. R. Green, 1–13. New York: Routledge, 2009.

Sarkesian, Sam C., John Allen Williams, and Stephen J. Cimbala, eds. *US National Security: Policymakers, Processes and Politics*. 5th ed. Boulder, CO: Lynne Rienner, 2013.

Schelling, Thomas C. *Arms and Influence*. New Haven, CT: Yale University Press, 1966.

Schoomaker, General Peter J. Foreword to *Learning to Eat Soup with a Knife: Counterinsurgency Lessons from Malaya to Vietnam*, by John A. Nagl, ix–x. Chicago: University of Chicago Press, 2002.

Schwartz, Thomas Alan. *Johnson and Europe: In the Shadow of Vietnam*. Cambridge, MA: Harvard University Press, 2003.

Sepp, Kalev I. "Best Practices in Counterinsurgency." *Military Review* 85, no. 3 (2005): 8–12.

Serena, Chad C. *A Revolution in Military Adaptation: The U.S. Army in the Iraq War.* Washington, DC: Georgetown University Press, 2011.

Shafritz, Jay M., J. Steven Ott, and Yong Suk Jang, eds. *Classics of Organization Theory.* 7th ed. Boston: Wadsworth Cengage Learning, 2011.

Sheffield, Gary. *The Chief: Douglas Haig and the British Army.* London: Aurum, 2012.

Shultz, George P. *Turmoil and Triumph: My Years as Secretary of State.* New York: Scribner's, 1993.

Shy, John. "The American Military Experience: History and Learning." *Journal of Interdisciplinary History* 1, no. 2 (1971): 205–28.

Smith, Brigadier General Lynn D. (United States Army). "Gettysburg + 100." *Military Review* 42, no. 7 (1962): 13–24.

Snyder, Jack. "Civil-Military Relations and the Cult of the Offensive, 1914 and 1984." *International Security* 9, no. 1 (1984): 108–46.

———. *The Ideology of the Offensive: Military Decision Making and the Disasters of 1914.* Ithaca, NY: Cornell University Press, 1984.

Sorley, Lewis. *A Better War: The Unexamined Victories and Final Tragedy of America's Last Years in Vietnam.* New York: Harcourt Brace, 1999.

———. *Honorable Warrior: General Harold K. Johnson and the Ethics of Command.* Lawrence: University Press of Kansas, 1998.

———. *Westmoreland: The General Who Lost Vietnam.* New York: Houghton Mifflin Harcourt, 2011.

Stahr, Elvis J. *Oral History.* Boston: John F. Kennedy Library, 1964.

Starry, Donn A. "Modern Armor Battle II: The Defense." *Armor* 84 (January–February 1975): 39–44.

———. *Press On! Selected Works of General Donn A. Starry.* Edited by Lewis Sorley. Fort Leavenworth, KS: Combat Studies Institute Press, 2009.

Strachan, Hew. *Clausewitz's "On War": A Biography.* New York: Grove, 2007.

Stringer, Kevin D. "Light Infantry Divisions: Cold War Chimera." *Virginia Military Institute Adams Center Paper.* Lexington, VA: Virginia Military Institute, 2009. http://www.vmi.edu/uploadedFiles/Archives/Adams_Center/EssayContest/20082009/AdamsCenterEssay_StringerKD.pdf.

Sullivan, Gordon R., and James M. Dubik. *Envisioning Future Warfare.* Fort Leavenworth, KS: U.S. Army Command and General Staff College Press, 1995.

Summers, Harry G., Jr. *On Strategy: A Critical Analysis of the Vietnam War.* Novato, CA: Presidio, 1995.

Swidler, Ann. "Culture in Action: Symbols and Strategies." *American Sociological Review* 51, no. 2 (1986): 273–86.

Tamminen, David L. "How to Defend Outnumbered and Win." *Armor* 84 (November–December 1975): 39–44.

Taylor, John M. *General Maxwell Taylor: The Sword and the Pen.* New York: Bantam Doubleday Dell, 1989.

Taylor, Maxwell D. *Swords and Plowshares: A Memoir*. Cambridge, MA: Da Capo, 1990.

——. *The Uncertain Trumpet*. New York: Atlantic Books, 1960.

Terriff, Terry. *The Nixon Administration and the Making of US Nuclear Strategy*. Ithaca, NY: Cornell University Press, 1995.

——. "U.S. Ideas and Military Change in NATO, 1989–1994." In *The Sources of Military Change: Culture, Politics, Technology*, edited by Theo Farrell and Terry Terriff, 91–116. Boulder, CO: Lynne Rienner, 2002.

Thompson, James D. *Organizations in Action*. New York: McGraw-Hill, 1967.

Thucydides. *The Landmark Thucydides: A Comprehensive Guide to the Peloponnesian War*. Edited by Robert B. Strassler. Translated by Richard Crawley. New York: Simon & Schuster, 1996.

Trachtenberg, Marc. *A Constructed Peace: The Making of the European Settlement, 1945–1963*. Princeton, NJ: Princeton University Press, 1999.

——. "Strategic Thought in America, 1952–1966." *Political Science Quarterly* 104, no. 2 (1989): 301–34.

Trauschweizer, Ingo. *The Cold War U.S. Army: Building Deterrence for Limited War*. Lawrence: University Press of Kansas, 2008.

Turner, L. C. F. "The Significance of the Schlieffen Plan." In *The War Plans of the Great Powers, 1880–1914*, edited by Paul M. Kennedy, 199–221. Boston: George Allen & Unwin, 1979.

Ucko, David H. "Critics Gone Wild: Counterinsurgency as the Root of All Evil." *Small Wars and Insurgencies* 25, no. 1 (2014): 161–79.

——. *The New Counterinsurgency Era: Transforming the U.S. Military for Modern Wars*. Washington, DC: Georgetown University Press, 2009.

Ullman, Harlan K., and James P. Wade. *Shock and Awe: Achieving Rapid Dominance*. Washington, DC: National Defense University, 1996.

United States. *Field Manual 3-24/Marine Corps Warfighting Publication 3-33.5, Insurgencies and Countering Insurgencies*. Washington, DC: Headquarters, Department of the Army, 2014.

——. *Foreign Relations of the United States*. Washington, DC: U.S. Department of State.

——. *Operations: Field Manual 100-5*. Washington, DC: Headquarters, Department of the Army, 1941.

——. *Operations: Field Manual 100-5*. Washington, DC: Headquarters, Department of the Army, 1954.

——. *Operations: Field Manual 100-5*. Washington, DC: Headquarters, Department of the Army, 1962.

——. *Operations: Field Manual 100-5*. Washington, DC: Headquarters, Department of the Army, 1976.

——. *Operations: Field Manual 100-5*. Washington, DC: Headquarters, Department of the Army, 1982.

——. *Operations: Field Manual 100-5*. Washington, DC: Headquarters, Department of the Army, 1986.

———. *Operations: Field Manual 100-5*. Washington, DC: Headquarters, Department of the Army, 1993.

———. *Operations: Field Manual 3-0*. Washington, DC: Headquarters, Department of the Army, 2001.

———. *Operations: Field Manual 3-0*. Washington, DC: Headquarters, Department of the Army, 2008.

———. *Operations of Army Forces in the Field: Field Manual 100-5*. Washington, DC: Headquarters, Department of the Army, 1968.

Vacca, Alexander W. "Military Culture and Cyber Security." *Survival* 53, no. 6 (2011–12): 159–76.

van Creveld, Martin. *The Culture of War*. New York: Presidio Press/Ballantine Books, 2008.

Van Evera, Stephen. *Causes of War: Power and the Roots of Conflict*. Ithaca, NY: Cornell University Press, 1999.

Vardi, Gil-li. "The Enigma of German Operational Theory: The Evolution of Military Thought in Germany, 1919–1938." PhD diss., London School of Economics, 2008.

Waddell, Ricky Lynn. "The Army and Peacetime Low Intensity Conflict, 1961–1993: The Process of Peripheral and Fundamental Military Change." PhD diss., Columbia University, 1994.

Walt, Stephen M. "The Relationship between Theory and Policy in International Relations." *Annual Review of Political Science* 8, no. 1 (2005): 23–48.

Waltz, Kenneth. *Theory of International Politics*. New York: McGraw-Hill, 1979.

Wass de Czege, Huba. *NATO Interim Report: Employment Concepts for Light Infantry in Europe*. Fort Leavenworth, KS: School of Advanced Military Studies, 1988.

Watts, Barry, and Williamson Murray. "Military Innovation in Peacetime." In *Military Innovation in the Interwar Period*, edited by Williamson Murray and Allan R. Millet, 369–415. Cambridge: Cambridge University Press, 1996.

Weigley, Russell F. *The American Way of War: A History of United States Military Strategy and Policy*. Bloomington: Indiana University Press, 1977.

———. *History of the United States Army*. Bloomington: Indiana University Press, 1984.

Weinberger, Caspar W. *Annual Report to the Congress: Fiscal Year 1983*. Washington, DC: U.S. Government Printing Office, 1982.

———. *Fighting for Peace: Seven Critical Years in the Pentagon*. New York: Warner Books, 1990.

———. *In the Arena: A Memoir of the 20th Century*. With Gretchen Roberts. Washington, DC: Regnery, 2001.

West, Francis J. *The Strongest Tribe: War, Politics, and the Endgame in Iraq*. New York: Random House, 2008.

Westmoreland, William C. *A Soldier Reports*. Garden City, NY: Doubleday, 1976.

Wharry, Major D. F. (British Artillery). "Atomic Weapons and the Principles of War." *Military Review* 36, no. 8 (1956): 106–9.

Wilson, James Graham. "How Grand Was Reagan's Strategy, 1976–1984?" *Diplomacy & Statecraft* 18, no. 4 (2007): 773–803.

Wilson, James Q. *Bureaucracy: What Government Agencies Do and Why They Do It.* New York: Basic Books, 1989.

Wilson, John B. *Maneuver and Firepower: The Evolution of Divisions and Separate Brigades.* Washington, DC: U.S. Army Center for Military History, 1998.

Wohlforth, William C. "The Stability of a Unipolar World." *International Security* 24, no. 1 (1999): 5–41.

Woodward, Bob. *The War Within: A Secret White House History, 2006–2008.* New York: Simon & Schuster, 2008.

Wray, Timothy A. *The Army's Light Infantry Divisions: An Analysis of Advocacy and Opposition.* Fort McNair, Washington, DC: U.S. National War College, 2005.

Zisk, Kimberly Martin. *Engaging the Enemy: Organizational Theory and Soviet Military Innovation, 1955–1991.* Princeton, NJ: Princeton University Press, 1993.

INDEX

Page references with *n* indicate note numbers; those with *fig* indicate figures.